In Their Own Words

Volume 1
The New England Colonies

In Their

Own
Words

Volume 1
The New England Colonies

Today's God-less America ...
What Would Our Founding Fathers Think?

JUDGE MARK T. BOONSTRA
CONTRIBUTOR: MARTHA RABAUT BOONSTRA, ESQ.

LIBERT HILL PRESS ELITE

Liberty Hill Press
2301 Lucien Way #415
Maitland, FL 32751
407.339.4217
www.libertyhillpublishing.com

Paperback ISBN-13: 978-1-6628-2020-5
Dust Jacket ISBN-13: 978-1-6628-2187-5
Ebook ISBN-13: 978-1-6628-2022-9

*Dedicated to our
children and grandchildren,
and to Martha's grandfather,
Congressman Louis C. Rabaut,
author of the
"Under God"
amendment
to the
Pledge of Allegiance.*

In Three Volumes

VOLUME 1
THE NEW ENGLAND COLONIES
(Massachusetts, New Hampshire, Connecticut,
Rhode Island, New York)

VOLUME 2
THE MIDDLE COLONIES
(Pennsylvania, New Jersey, Delaware, Maryland)

VOLUME 3
THE SOUTHERN COLONIES
(Virginia, North Carolina, South Carolina, Georgia)

The Signers of the Declaration of Independence,
the Articles of Confederation, and
the United States Constitution

Volume 1

THE NEW ENGLAND COLONIES

(Massachusetts, New Hampshire, Connecticut,
Rhode Island, New York)

Table of Contents

Introduction

O ur country is in trouble.

We need to wake up — NOW. The secularists are transforming America before our very eyes. You see it in our schools, our government, our workplaces, and in our everyday life. In the land of the free, the world's bastion of liberty and home of freedom of speech and expression . . . our very words and thoughts are now under scrutiny and attack. We must conform.

Good vs. Evil. God's ongoing battle with Satan since the day he fell from Heaven. A battle perhaps never more evident than it is today. In America today, we can see it playing out before our very eyes — if only we would open them.

Our Founding Fathers[1] were men of God. They knew that our liberties came from God. They built our country on that fundamental premise. They gave America a moral compass that guided it for more than two centuries.

But we have been transformed. Our Founders would no longer recognize America as the country they established. We have erased God. And in doing so, we have launched America on a journey without a compass — without the moral compass our Founders deemed essential to its unique character, and to its very survival as a nation of liberty.

---

[1] This book will identify our "Founding Fathers" as those persons who signed one or more of our nation's three principal founding documents: the Declaration of Independence, the Articles of Confederation, and the United States Constitution. Surely, others who did not sign these documents are also deserving of the Founding Father title, but an examination of their views will be left to another day.

America is at a crossroads. Do we wish to be a nation of liberty—under God—as our Founding Fathers intended? Or do we wish to be forever transformed into a secular bastion of God-less conformity?

What follows is a synopsis of our Founders' views of God and His place in America.

Contrast it with real-life examples from modern-day American life.

What would our Founding Fathers think?

America, it's time to decide.

Prologue

A s the title of this book suggests, we should all be greatly concerned for the future of our country as it near its 250th birthday—and for the futures of our children and grandchildren. This book—beginning with this Volume 1 (The New England Colonies)—represents a modest effort to help wake America up to the dangers that threaten its very existence as anything resembling what our Founding Fathers intended it to be; to remind Americans of the foundational tenets upon which the Founders established what came to be an exceptional nation; and to instill in our fellow citizens a recognition that we must return to our founding principles to salvage for the generations to come the future that our Founders toiled and sacrificed to provide for them.

Throughout our history, Americans have truly been blessed. Never before (or since) has the world seen such a successful effort, of such long standing, to establish a government comprised of "We the People," one that afforded liberty to its citizenry unlike anything before in the history of the earth. The Founding Fathers masterfully developed a new system of governance, one that uniquely blended a limited, national government (designed primarily to defend the nation from external threats) with a federalist system that empowered the individual states (and their local constituent parts) with all governmental authority not specifically assigned to the national government. They created separate branches of government with distinct responsibilities, and a system of checks and balances that, by its very design, frustrated the ability of any particular branch to garner and exercise a degree of authority sufficient to threaten the freedoms that our Founders were determined to guarantee. Was it perfect? Of course not; nothing ever is. The inadequacies of the Articles of Confederation led to the adoption of the United States Constitution. The Bill of Rights followed. So did other constitutional amendments. The abomination that was the institution of slavery, which through compromise was allowed to continue in this country upon its founding (just as it had existed—and even today exists—elsewhere), was abolished only with the passage of time and through the mechanism of a civil war. Women were afforded the right to vote. Civil rights were guaranteed.

But our Founding Fathers crafted a country whose foundational principles were immutable and lasting, and that would remain fundamental to our society through the generations to come. As a result, and due to the wisdom and commitment of its Founders, the United States of America—for now nearly two and one-half centuries—has been the envy of the world. It has flourished economically. It has sparked unimaginable technological innovations. It has not only secured freedom for its own people, but has fought for and secured the liberty of other peoples around the world when threatened. It has welcomed immigrants from every corner of the globe who have come seeking the same freedoms that we have been so fortunate to enjoy. It afforded its citizens the opportunity, in freedom, to live the "American Dream," and it has invited others around the world to share in that dream. It has served as a model and a guiding light for other societies whose peoples similarly have yearned for liberty. In the words of President Ronald Reagan, the United States of America has stood, for all the world to see, as that "shining city on a hill." This is what the term, "American exceptionalism," means.

Sadly, it is ironically inherent in the very long-standing nature of the freedoms that Americans have enjoyed that it has become all too easy for us to forget—or to fail to fully appreciate—just what it means to possess those freedoms, and just what is at stake when we are threatened with their loss. After all, none of us who is alive today was here when our country was founded. None is so privileged as to have met George Washington, James Madison, Alexander Hamilton, or others of our Founding Fathers. We were not privy to their founding deliberations, and we cannot hear from them directly about the fundamental principles on which they founded our nation. Similarly, few of us have lived under tyranny. We don't know what it is like to live under a government with the ability and the authority to direct our lives in any respect it wishes—to tell us, for example, what we may say and do; whether and how we and our children may be educated; how we may make our livelihood; whether we may fulfill our hopes and dreams; the extent to which we may provide for our families; whether we are allowed to worship the God of our choosing. In many ways, the American people of today are victims of the very success that our country has enjoyed. We grew up with—and know nothing other than—the nation of liberty that our Founders bequeathed to us, and a degree of complacency inevitably results. We are so much the beneficiaries of the freedoms that our Founding Fathers secured for us that our individual life experiences afford us no basis on which to fully comprehend the dangers that we face and that threaten our very freedoms.

This book will not endeavor to catalogue those dangers or the myriad ways in which our country has strayed from the course set by our Founders. Volumes surely could be written. There's the ever-expanding federal government; the explosion of bureaucratic power and authority; the increasing governmental regulation of more and more facets of our lives; the concentration of authority in the executive branch; the "deep state"; rising totalitarianism and "Orwellianism"; a judicial branch that often no longer adheres to the Constitution as written and intended by our Founders; American impotence in the face of internal and external threats to our security—all facilitated by a media that has lost its way and "big tech" censorship and information manipulation. And that is just the beginning.

Rather, this book will focus on something more fundamental—the decaying moral fabric of our nation—which underlies all else. And fundamental to the decaying moral fabric of our nation is the fact that it has strayed from certain of our Founding Fathers' core principles and beliefs, tenets that laid the foundation for the very thinking that gave rise to the birth of our nation and the freedoms that it guaranteed to us. It is our nation's straying from those core precepts that—at its essence—threatens our continued freedoms.

What were the core precepts of our Founding Fathers that modern-day society has lost? In a word . . . God. A fundamental and overriding belief in a Supreme Being, Who created and guides the universe, and from Whom all of our natural rights flow. A conviction that we derive our rights and liberties not from government, but from One greater than ourselves, and that our freedoms transcend government because they come from a Source higher than any government.

One needn't look far for confirmation of the fundamental nature of our Founders' religious beliefs. The text of our founding documents (and those of our states). The inscriptions on our monuments and historic buildings. Our national motto ("In God We Trust") and its placement upon our coins. Our Pledge of Allegiance ("One Nation, Under God"). Our long tradition of opening legislative and judicial sessions with prayer or acknowledgements of God. Supreme Court decisions acknowledging that America is "a Christian nation" and "We are a Christian people." While some of those developments came at later points in the history of our country, they were made in confirmation, not contradiction, of the core principles of the Founding Fathers that laid the very groundwork for our country.

But we needn't rely on those expressions, as convincing as they are, of the religious underpinnings of our nation. For they simply confirm what the Founders themselves told us. And that is where this book will focus the reader—on the very words of the Founders (as well as the words of those who knew them), because they provide a first-hand account of the religious convictions of the Founders and the importance of those convictions in establishing the framework of our nation.

A dispassionate reader—anyone with an open mind—will no doubt agree that the words of the Founding Fathers themselves demonstrate that they were men of faith, men of God, and that it was their religious principles that formed the foundation on which our great nation — and the freedoms our Founders sought to secure — were erected. So, this book will endeavor to provide a sense of the religious component of the Founders' lives and how it impacted their thinking and their role in the foundation of America. Where possible, it will set forth the actual words of the Founding Fathers that reflect their views regarding religion, and where their actual words may not be available, it will supplement with the words of others who were in a position to describe their views.

Certainly, the forces of evil in America today will argue otherwise. There has long been an effort in America to rewrite the history of its founding; to propagate the myth that our Founders were not men of faith and religion; to convert our Founders' First Amendment declaration that "Congress shall make no law respecting an establishment of religion, or prohibiting the free exercise thereof" into an unintended bright-line separation of church and state; to eliminate prayer from our schools; to marginalize and denigrate persons of faith (and their "clinging to religion"); and to create an environment that teaches our youth that all behaviors are "moral equivalents."

Our Founding Fathers must be rolling over in their graves. In truth, nothing can negate the religious underpinnings of our founding. While America may no longer be "a Christian nation" in the sense that it was at one time, our Founders' fundamental and core belief in an Almighty Being from Whom we derive our freedoms endures. Yet, an America that rejects their core belief is the America in which our children and grandchildren are destined to grow up and raise their own families unless we act — and act quickly.

So, who is to blame for the mess we're now in? Certainly, no single source. After all, God has been battling Satan at least since the days of Adam and Eve. And Satan no doubt today employs minions far outnumbering the single serpent of the Garden of Eden.

The point is not to cast blame anywhere, but rather to focus on the problem, to wake America up to its existence, and to implore all who share the Founding Fathers' reverence in God to join together; to speak with a loud and unified voice; to insist upon a return to virtue and good moral order; to declare their fervent belief and faith in God Almighty; to stand up to the forces—including our own government when necessary—that threaten the foundational premise of our Founders that our rights come from God—not government—and that our government's authority over us must therefore be sufficiently limited that our freedoms will remain protected.

This book is not intended to be "political" or "partisan" in nature. Indeed, neither major political party has stanched America's decline from the moral underpinnings that our Founding Fathers established for it. The once-great party of Martha's grandfather, Congressman Louis Rabaut (D-MI), author of the 1954 "Under God" amendment to the Pledge of Allegiance, would seem no longer to welcome him. And it should not be assumed that the opposing political party would embrace him either.

It is the hope of this book that the American people will rise above partisan politics to demand of all political parties, governmental and societal institutions of all sorts, and of themselves, a return to the foundational principles of our Founding Fathers—including, most especially, a humble recognition of the Supremacy of an Almighty God from whom our rights as human beings, and as citizens of the United States of America, flow. Only by doing so can we restore the moral fabric of our nation, return government to the limited role that our Founders intended, and secure for our children and grandchildren the liberties for which America was built.

Tribute to Congressman Louis C. Rabaut

Author Of The
"Under God" Amendment
To The Pledge Of Allegiance

Congressman Louis C. Rabaut

On April 20, 1953, Congressman Louis C. Rabaut (D-MI) introduced a bill to add the words "Under God" to the Pledge of Allegiance to the United States of America. President Dwight D. Eisenhower signed the amendment into law on June 14 (Flag Day), 1954.

As this book demonstrates, the addition of "Under God" to the Pledge of Allegiance flowed from our Founding Fathers' fervent belief, as reflected in their own words, that our rights and liberties come from God, and that the bastion of liberty that is America fundamentally derives its legitimacy from the guiding, moral precepts of One higher than ourselves.

In His Own Words:

"You may argue from dawn to dusk about differing political, economic, and social systems, but the fundamental issue which is the unbridgeable gap between America and Communist Russia is a belief in Almighty God. From the root of atheism stems the evil weed of communism and its branches of materialism and political dictatorship. Unless we are willing to affirm our belief in the existence of God and His creator-creature relation to man, we drop man himself to the significance of a grain of sand and open the floodgates to tyranny and oppression."

Congressman Louis C. Rabaut

What follows is a
summary of an article
from contemporary American life . . .

Nearly 70 years after
Congressman Louis C. Rabaut authored

the "Under God" amendment to
the Pledge of Allegiance.

What Would Congressman Louis C. Rabaut Think?

DNC delegates drop 'under God' from Pledge of Allegiance

By Victor Morton - *The Washington Times - Wednesday, August 19, 2020*

Democrats at the 2020 Democratic National Convention omitted the words "Under God" in their recitation of the Pledge of Allegiance at least twice . . . at the DNC LBGTQ Caucus Meeting and at the DNC Caucus and Council Meeting: Muslim Delegates and Allies Assembly. They didn't explain why.

Just as the words, "the Flag of the United States of America" were added to the original Pledge in 1923, the words, "Under God" were added during the administration of President Dwight D. Eisenhower in 1954, in response to the threat of communism.

https://www.washingtontimes.com/news/2020/aug/19/ dnc-delegates-drop-under-god-pledge-allegiance/.

Chapter One:

Our Founding Documents

THE DECLARATION OF INDEPENDENCE

THE ARTICLES OF CONFEDERATION OF PERPETUAL UNION

THE CONSTITUTION OF THE UNITED STATES

Introduction
to Our Founding Documents

J uly 4, 1776. The birth of a new nation. A nation of individual liberty. Of unalienable rights. Of rights that come from God. So declared our Founding Fathers, risking life and limb, yet boldly asserting those rights and proclaiming them the foundation of a new United States of America. Invoking the right of a free people "to assume among the powers of the earth, separate and equal station to which the Laws of Nature and of Nature's God entitle them," and "appealing to the Supreme Judge of the world for the rectitude of our intentions," the Founders thus declared:

> **We hold these truths to be self-evident, that all men are created equal, that they are endowed by their Creator with certain unalienable Rights, that among these are Life, Liberty and the pursuit of Happiness.**

And as they set out to establish a new form of government based upon the rights bestowed upon them by God, they pledged:

> **And for the support of this Declaration, with a firm reliance on the protection of divine Providence, we mutually pledge to each other our Lives, our Fortunes and our sacred Honor.**

The first governing constitution of the fledgling new nation was crafted as the war for independence raged with the former motherland. That effort gave birth to the Articles of Confederation of Perpetual Union in 1777, ratified by the last of the thirteen states in 1781. Under the Articles of Confederation, the national government lacked an executive branch, governed instead by a national Congress of the Confederation, over which presided a president of the Congress. In affixing their signatures to the Articles of Confederation, the delegates to the Continental

Congress reaffirmed that the authority by which they did so came from God:

> **Whereas it hath pleased the Great Governor of the World to incline the hearts of the legislatures we respectively represent in congress, to approve of, and to authorize us to ratify the said articles of confederation and perpetual union,** Know Ye, that we, the undersigned delegates, by virtue of the power and authority to us given for that purpose, do, by these presents, in the name and in behalf of our respective constituents, fully and entirely ratify and confirm each and every of the said articles of confederation and perpetual union, and all and singular the matters and things therein contained.

In 1787, the Articles of Confederation gave way to the United States Constitution, which established a more durable form of government comprised of a bicameral legislature, an executive branch, and a judicial branch. The Constitution was drafted at the Constitutional Convention in 1787, was first ratified by the state of Delaware in December of that year, became effective upon ratification by the state of New Hampshire in 1788 (ratification by nine states being required), and saw ratification become unanimous among the original thirteen states in 1790, upon the assent of the state of Rhode Island.

The United States Constitution, like the Articles of Confederation before it, set forth a governmental structure, and outlined the responsibilities and authorities of its component parts. Yet, like the Articles, the Constitution described the liberties it assured as "Blessings" from One greater than ourselves:

> We the People of the United States, in Order to form a more perfect Union, establish Justice, insure domestic Tranquility, provide for the common defence, promote the general Welfare, and **secure the Blessings of Liberty** to ourselves and our

Posterity, do ordain and establish this Constitution for the United States of America.

Proclaiming that our individual liberties and unalienable rights are "blessings" from "God," "endowed to us by our Creator," our Founding Fathers appealed to the "Supreme Judge of the World," invoked the authority of the "Great Governor of the World," and with "a firm reliance on the protection of divine Providence" gave birth to a new nation unlike any that had gone before it, the United States of America.

As you read this book, as you familiarize yourself with our founding documents, as you learn about our Founding Fathers, and as you assess what is happening in our country today, ask yourself:

What Would Our Founding Fathers Think?

The Declaration of Independence

IN CONGRESS, July 4, 1776.
The unanimous Declaration of
the thirteen united States of America,

When in the Course of human events, it becomes necessary for one people to dissolve the political bands which have connected them with another, and to assume among the powers of the earth, the separate and equal station **to which the Laws of Nature and of Nature's God entitle them**, a decent respect to the opinions of mankind requires that they should declare the causes which impel them to the separation. **We hold these truths to be self-evident, that all men are created equal, that they are endowed by their Creator with certain unalienable Rights, that among these are Life, Liberty and the pursuit of Happiness.** — That to secure these rights, Governments are instituted among Men, deriving their just powers from the consent of the governed, — That whenever any Form of Government becomes destructive of these ends, it is the Right of the People to alter or to abolish it, and to institute new Government, laying its foundation on such principles and organizing its powers in such form, as to them shall seem most likely to effect their Safety and Happiness. Prudence, indeed, will dictate that Governments long established should not be changed for light and transient causes; and accordingly all experience hath shewn, that mankind are more disposed to suffer, while evils are sufferable, than to right themselves by abolishing the forms to which they are accustomed. But when a long train of abuses and usurpations, pursuing invariably the same Object evinces a design to reduce them under absolute Despotism, it is their right, it is their duty, to throw off such Government, and to provide new Guards for their future security. — Such has been the patient sufferance of these Colonies; and such is now the necessity which constrains them to alter their former Systems of Government. The history of the present King of Great Britain is a history of repeated injuries and usurpations, all having in direct object the establishment of an absolute Tyranny over these States. To prove this, let Facts be submitted to a candid world. — He has refused his Assent to Laws, the most wholesome and necessary for the public good. — He has forbidden his Governors to pass Laws of immediate and pressing importance, unless suspended in their operation till his Assent should be obtained; and when so suspended, he has utterly neglected to attend to them. — He has refused to pass other Laws for the accommodation of large districts of people, unless those people would relinquish the right of Representation in the Legislature, a right inestimable to them and formidable to tyrants only. — He has called together legislative bodies at places unusual, uncomfortable, and distant from the depository of their public Records, for the sole purpose of fatiguing them into compliance with his measures. — He has dissolved Representative Houses repeatedly, for opposing with manly firmness his invasions on the rights of the people. — He has refused for a long time, after such dissolutions, to cause others to be elected; whereby the Legislative powers, incapable of Annihilation, have returned to the People at large for their exercise; the State remaining in the mean time exposed to all the dangers of invasion from without, and convulsions within. — He has endeavoured to prevent the population of these States; for that purpose obstructing the Laws for Naturalization of Foreigners; refusing to pass others to encourage their migrations hither, and raising the conditions of new Appropriations of Lands. — He has obstructed the Administration of Justice, by refusing his Assent to Laws for establishing Judiciary powers. — He has made Judges dependent on his Will alone, for the tenure of their offices, and the amount and payment of their salaries. — He has erected a multitude of New Offices, and sent hither swarms of Officers to harrass our people, and eat out their substance. — He has kept among us, in times of peace, Standing Armies without the Consent of our legislatures. — He has affected to render the Military independent of and superior to the Civil power. — He has combined with others to subject us to a jurisdiction foreign to our constitution, and unacknowledged by our laws; giving his Assent to their Acts of pretended Legislation: — For Quartering large bodies of armed troops among us:—For protecting them, by a mock Trial, from punishment for any Murders which they should commit on the Inhabitants of these States:—For cutting off our Trade with all parts of the world:—For imposing Taxes on us without our Consent:—For depriving us in many cases, of the benefits of Trial by Jury:—For transporting us beyond Seas to be tried for pretended offences:—For abolishing the free System of English Laws in a neighbouring Province, establishing therein an Arbitrary government, and enlarging its Boundaries so as to render it at once an example and fit instrument for introducing the same absolute rule into these Colonies:—For taking away our Charters, abolishing our most valuable Laws, and altering fundamentally the Forms of our Governments:—For suspending our own Legislatures, and declaring themselves invested with power to legislate for us in all cases whatsoever.—He has abdicated Government here, by declaring us out of his Protection and waging War against us.—He has plundered our seas, ravaged our Coasts, burnt our towns, and destroyed the lives of our people.—He is at this time transporting large Armies of foreign Mercenaries to compleat the works of death, desolation and tyranny, already begun with circumstances of Cruelty & perfidy scarcely paralleled in the most barbarous ages, and totally unworthy the Head of a civilized nation.—He has constrained our fellow Citizens taken Captive on the high Seas to bear Arms against their Country, to become the executioners of their friends and Brethren, or to fall themselves by their Hands. He has excited domestic insurrections amongst us, and has endeavoured to bring on the inhabitants of our frontiers, the merciless Indian Savages, whose known rule of warfare, is an undistinguished destruction of all ages, sexes and conditions. In every stage of these Oppressions We have Petitioned for Redress in the most humble terms: Our repeated Petitions have been answered only by repeated injury. A Prince whose character is thus marked by every act which may define a Tyrant, is unfit to be the ruler of a free people. Nor have We been wanting in attentions to our Brittish brethren. We have warned them from time to time of attempts by their legislature to extend an unwarrantable jurisdiction over us. We have reminded them of the circumstances of our emigration and settlement here. We have appealed to their native justice and magnanimity, and we have conjured them by the ties of our common kindred to disavow these usurpations, which, would inevitably interrupt our connections and correspondence. They too have been deaf to the voice of justice and of consanguinity. We must, therefore, acquiesce in the necessity, which denounces our Separation, and hold them, as we hold the rest of mankind, Enemies in War, in Peace Friends.

We, therefore, the Representatives of the united States of America, in General Congress, Assembled, **appealing to the Supreme Judge of the world for the rectitude of our intentions**, do, in the Name, and by Authority of the good People of these Colonies, solemnly publish and declare, That these United Colonies are, and of Right ought to be Free and Independent States; that they are Absolved from all Allegiance to the British Crown, and that all political connection between them and the State of Great Britain, is and ought to be totally dissolved; and that as Free and Independent States, they have full Power to levy War, conclude Peace, contract Alliances, establish Commerce, and to do all other Acts and Things which Independent States may of right do. And for the support of this Declaration, **with a firm reliance on the protection of divine Providence**, we mutually pledge to each other our Lives, our Fortunes and our sacred Honor.

The 56 signers of the Declaration of Independence were:

Connecticut:
Samuel Huntington
Roger Sherman
William Williams
Oliver Wolcott

Delaware:
Thomas McKean
George Read
Caesar Rodney

Georgia:
Button Gwinnett
Lyman Hall
George Walton

Maryland:
Charles Carroll of
Carrollton
Samuel Chase
William Paca
Thomas Stone

Massachusetts:
John Adams
Samuel Adams
Elbridge Gerry
John Hancock
Robert Treat Paine

New Hampshire:
Josiah Bartlett
Matthew Thornton
William Whipple

New Jersey:
Abraham Clark
John Hart
Francis Hopkinson
Richard Stockton
John Witherspoon

New York:
William Floyd
Francis Lewis
Philip Livingston
Lewis Morris

North Carolina:
Joseph Hewes
William Hooper
John Penn

Pennsylvania:
George Clymer
Benjamin Franklin
Robert Morris
John Morton
George Ross
Benjamin Rush
James Smith
George Taylor
James Wilson

Rhode Island:
William Ellery
Stephen Hopkins

South Carolina:
Thomas Heyward Jr.
Thomas Lynch Jr.
Arthur Middleton
Edward Rutledge

Virginia:
Carter Braxton
Benjamin Harrison
Thomas Jefferson
Francis Lightfoot Lee
Richard Henry Lee
Thomas Nelson Jr.
George Wythe

The Declaration of Independence

The Signing of the Declaration of Independence

Painting by Charles Édouard Armand-Dumaresq

The Articles of Confederation of Perpetual Union

To all to whom

these Presents shall come, we, the undersigned Delegates of the States affixed to our Names send greeting. Whereas the Delegates of the United States of America in Congress assembled did on the fifteenth day of November in the year of our Lord One Thousand Seven Hundred and Seventy seven, and in the Second Year of the Independence of America agree to certain articles of Confederation and perpetual Union between the States of Newhampshire, Massachusetts-bay, Rhodeisland and Providence Plantations, Connecticut, New York, New Jersey, Pennsylvania, Delaware, Maryland, Virginia, North Carolina, South Carolina, and Georgia in the Words following, viz. Articles of Confederation and perpetual Union between the States of Newhampshire, Massachusetts-bay, Rhodeisland and Providence Plantations, Connecticut, New York, New Jersey, Pennsylvania, Delaware, Maryland, Virginia, North Carolina, South Carolina, and Georgia.

Article I. The Stile of this confederacy shall be, "The United States of America."

Article II. Each state retains its sovereignty, freedom and independence, and every Power, Jurisdiction and right, which is not by this confederation expressly delegated to the United States, in Congress assembled.

Article III. The said states hereby severally enter into a firm league of friendship with each other, for their common defence, the security of their Liberties, and their mutual and general welfare, binding themselves to assist each other, against all force offered to, or attacks made upon them, or any of them, on account of religion, sovereignty, trade, or any other pretence whatever.

Article IV. The better to secure and perpetuate mutual friendship and intercourse among the people of the different states in this union, the free inhabitants of each of these states, paupers, vagabonds and fugitives from Justice excepted, shall be entitled to all privileges and immunities of free citizens in the several states; and the people of each state shall have free ingress and regress to and from any other state, and shall enjoy therein all the privileges of trade and commerce, subject to the same duties, impositions and restrictions as the inhabitants thereof respectively, provided that such restrictions shall not extend so far as to prevent the removal of property imported into any state, to any other State of which the Owner is an inhabitant; provided also that no imposition, duties or restriction shall be laid by any state, on the property of the united states, or either of them.

If any Person guilty of, or charged with, treason, felony, or other high misdemeanor in any state, shall flee from Justice, and be found in any of the united states, he shall upon demand of the Governor or executive power of the state from which he fled, be delivered up, and removed to the state having jurisdiction of his offence.

Full faith and credit shall be given in each of these states to the records, acts and judicial proceedings of the courts and magistrates of every other state.

Article V. For the more convenient management of the general interests of the united states, delegates shall be annually appointed in such manner as the legislature of each state shall direct, to meet in Congress on the first Monday in November, in every year, with a power reserved to each state to recall its delegates, or any of them, at any time within the year, and to send others in their stead, for the remainder of the Year.

No State shall be represented in Congress by less than two, nor by more than seven Members; and no person shall be capable of being delegate for more than three years, in any term of six years; nor shall any person, being a delegate, be capable of holding any office under the united states, for which he, or another for his benefit receives any salary, fees or emolument of any kind.

Each State shall maintain its own delegates in a meeting of the states, and while they act as members of the committee of the states.

In determining questions in the united states, in Congress assembled, each state shall have one vote.

Freedom of speech and debate in Congress shall not be impeached or questioned in any Court, or place out of Congress, and the members of congress shall be protected in their persons from arrests and imprisonments, during the time of their going to and from, and attendance on congress, except for treason, felony, or breach of the peace.

Article VI. No State, without the Consent of the united States, in congress assembled, shall send any embassy to, or receive any embassy from, or enter into any conferrence, agreement, alliance, or treaty, with any King prince or state; nor shall any person holding any office of profit or trust under the united states, or any of them, accept of any present, emolument, office, or title of any kind whatever, from any king, prince, or foreign state; nor shall the united states, in congress assembled, or any of them, grant any title of nobility.

No two or more states shall enter into any treaty, confederation, or alliance whatever between them, without the consent of the united states, in congress assembled, specifying accurately the purposes for which the same is to be entered into, and how long it shall continue.

No State shall lay any imposts or duties, which may interfere with any stipulations in treaties, entered into by the united States in congress assembled, with any king, prince, or State, in pursuance of any treaties already proposed by congress, to the courts of France and Spain.

No vessels of war shall be kept up in time of peace, by any state, except such number only, as shall be deemed necessary by the united states, in congress assembled, for the defence of such state, or its trade; nor shall any body of forces be kept up, by any state, in time of peace, except such number only as, in the judgment of the united states, in congress assembled, shall be deemed requisite to garrison the forts necessary for the defence of such state; but every state shall always keep up a well regulated and disciplined militia, sufficiently armed and accounted, and shall provide and constantly have ready for use, in public stores, a due number of field pieces and tents, and a proper quantity of arms, ammunition, and camp equipage.

No State shall engage in any war without the consent of the united States in congress assembled, unless such State be actually invaded by enemies, or shall have received certain advice of a resolution being formed by some nation of Indians to invade such State, and the danger is so imminent as not to admit of a delay till the united states in congress assembled, can be consulted: nor shall any state grant commissions to any ships or vessels of war, nor letters of marque or reprisal, except it be after a declaration of war by the united states in congress assembled, and then only against the kingdom or State, and the subjects thereof, against which war has been so declared, and under such regulations as shall be established by the united states in congress assembled, unless such state be infested by pirates, in which case vessels of war may be fitted out for that occasion, and kept so long as the danger shall continue, or until the united states in congress assembled shall determine otherwise.

Article VII. When land forces are raised by any state, for the common defence, all officers of or under the rank of colonel, shall be appointed by the legislature of each state respectively by whom such forces shall be raised, or in such manner as such state shall direct, and all vacancies shall be filled up by the state which first made appointment.

Article VIII. All charges of war, and all other expenses that shall be incurred for the common defence or general welfare, and allowed by the united states in congress assembled, shall be defrayed out of a common treasury, which shall be supplied by the several states, in proportion to the value of all land within each state, granted to or surveyed for any Person, as such land and the buildings and improvements thereon shall be estimated, according to such mode as the united states, in congress assembled, shall, from time to time, direct and appoint. The taxes for paying that proportion shall be laid and levied by the authority and direction of the legislatures of the several states within the time agreed upon by the united states in congress assembled.

Article IX. The united states, in congress assembled, shall have the sole and exclusive right and power of determining on peace and war, except in the cases mentioned in the sixth article—of sending and receiving ambassadors—entering into treaties and alliances, provided that no treaty of commerce shall be made, whereby the legislative power of the respective states shall be restrained from imposing such imposts and duties on foreigners, as their own people are subjected to, or from prohibiting the exportation or importation of any species of goods or commodities whatsoever—of establishing rules for deciding, in all cases, what captures on land or water shall be legal, and in what manner prizes taken by land or naval forces in the service of the united States, shall be divided or appropriated—of granting letters of marque and reprisal in times of peace—appointing courts for the trial of piracies and felonies committed on the high seas; and establishing courts; for receiving and determining finally appeals in all cases of captures; provided that no member of congress shall be appointed a judge of any of the said courts.

The united states, in congress assembled, shall also be the last resort on appeal, in all disputes and differences now subsisting, or that hereafter may arise between two or more states concerning boundary, jurisdiction, or any other cause whatever; which authority shall always be exercised in the manner following. Whenever the legislative or executive authority, or lawful agent of any state in controversy with another, shall present a petition to congress, stating the matter in question, and praying for a hearing, notice thereof shall be given, by order of congress, to the legislative or executive authority of the other state in controversy, and a day assigned for the appearance of the parties by their lawful agents, who shall then be directed to appoint, by joint consent, commissioners or judges to constitute a court for hearing and determining the matter in question: but if they cannot agree, congress shall name three persons out of each of the united states, and from the list of such persons each party shall alternately strike out one, the petitioners beginning, until the number shall be reduced to thirteen; and from that number not less than seven, nor more than nine names, as congress shall direct, shall, in the presence of congress, be drawn out by lot, and the persons whose names shall be so drawn, or any five of them, shall be commissioners or judges, to hear and finally determine the controversy, so always as a major part of the judges, who shall hear the cause, shall agree in the determination: and if either party shall neglect to attend at the day appointed, without showing reasons which congress shall judge sufficient, or being present, shall refuse to strike, the congress shall proceed to nominate three persons out of each State, and the secretary of congress shall strike in behalf of such party absent or refusing; and the judgment and sentence of the court, to be appointed in the manner before prescribed, shall be final and conclusive; and if any of the parties shall refuse to submit to the authority of such court, or to appear or defend their claim or cause, the court shall nevertheless proceed to pronounce sentence, or judgment, which shall in like manner be final and decisive; the judgment or sentence and other proceedings being in either case transmitted to congress, and lodged among the acts of congress, for the security of the parties concerned: provided that every commissioner, before he sits in judgment, shall take an oath to be administered by one of the judges of the supreme or superior court of the State where the cause shall be tried, "well and truly to hear and determine the matter in question, according to the best of his judgment, without favour, affection, or hope of reward: "provided, also, that no State shall be deprived of territory for the benefit of the united states.

All controversies concerning the private right of soil claimed under different grants of two or more states, whose jurisdictions as they may respect such lands, and the states which passed such grants are adjusted, the said grants or either of them being at the same time claimed to have originated antecedent to such settlement of jurisdiction, shall, on the petition of either party to the congress of the united states, be finally determined, as near as may be, in the same manner as is before prescribed for deciding disputes respecting territorial jurisdiction between different states.

The united states, in congress assembled, shall also have the sole and exclusive right and power of regulating the alloy and value of coin struck by their own authority, or by that of the respective states—fixing the standard of weights and measures throughout the united states—regulating the trade and managing all affairs with the Indians, not members of any of the states; provided that the legislative right of any state, within its own limits, be not infringed or violated—establishing and regulating post-offices from one state to another, throughout all the united states, and exacting such postage on the papers passing through the same, as may be requisite to defray the expenses of the said office—appointing all officers of the land forces in the service of the united States, excepting regimental officers—appointing all the officers of the naval forces, and commissioning all officers whatever in the service of the united states; making rules for the government and regulation of the said land and naval forces, and directing their operations.

The united States, in congress assembled, shall have authority to appoint a committee, to sit in the recess of congress, to be denominated, "A Committee of the States," and to consist of one delegate from each State; and to appoint such other committees and civil officers as may be necessary for managing the general affairs of the united states under their direction—to appoint one of their number to preside; provided that no person be allowed to serve in the office of president more than one year in any term of three years; to ascertain the necessary sums of money to be raised for the service of the united states, and to appropriate and apply the same for defraying the public expenses; to borrow money or emit bills on the credit of the united states, transmitting every half year to the respective states an account of the sums of money so borrowed or emitted, —to build and equip a navy—to agree upon the number of land forces, and to make requisitions from each state for its quota, in proportion to the number of white inhabitants in such state, which requisition shall be binding; and thereupon the legislature of each state shall appoint the regimental officers, raise the men, and clothe, arm, and equip them, in a soldier-like manner, at the expense of the united states; and the officers and men so clothed, armed, and equipped, shall march to the place appointed, and within the time agreed on by the united states, in congress assembled; but if the united states, in congress assembled, shall, on consideration of circumstances, judge proper that any state should not raise men, or should raise a smaller number than its quota, and that any other state should raise a greater number of men than the quota thereof, such extra number shall be raised, officered, clothed, armed, and equipped in the same manner as the quota of such state, unless the legislature of such state shall judge that such extra number cannot be safely spared out of the same, in which case they shall raise, officer, clothe, arm, and equip, as many of such extra number as they judge can be safely spared. And the officers and men so clothed, armed, and equipped, shall march to the place appointed, and within the time agreed on by the united states in congress assembled.

The united states, in congress assembled, shall never engage in a war, nor grant letters of marque and reprisal in time of peace, nor enter into any treaties or alliances, nor coin money, nor regulate the value thereof nor ascertain the sums and expenses necessary for the defence and welfare of the united states, or any of them, nor emit bills, nor borrow money on the credit of the united states, nor appropriate money, nor agree upon the number of vessels of war to be built or purchased, or the number of land or sea forces to be raised, nor appoint a commander in chief of the army or navy, unless nine states assent to the same, nor shall a question on any other point, except for adjourning from day to day, be determined, unless by the votes of a majority of the united states in congress assembled.

The congress of the united states shall have power to adjourn to any time within the year, and to any place within the united states, so that no period of adjournment be for a longer duration than the space of six Months, and shall publish the Journal of their proceedings monthly, except such parts thereof relating to treaties, alliances, or military operations, as in their judgment require secrecy; and the yeas and nays of the delegates of each State, on any question, shall be entered on the Journal, when it is desired by any delegate; and the delegates of a State, or any of them, at his or their request, shall be furnished with a transcript of the said Journal, except such parts as are above excepted, to lay before the legislatures of the several states.

Article X. The committee of the states, or any nine of them, shall be authorized to execute, in the recess of congress, such of the powers of congress as the united states, in congress assembled, by the consent of nine states, shall, from time to time, think expedient to vest them with; provided that no power be delegated to the said committee, for the exercise of which, by the articles of confederation, the voice of nine states, in the congress of the united states assembled, is requisite.

Article XI. Canada acceding to this confederation, and joining in the measures of the united states, shall be admitted into, and entitled to all the advantages of this union: but no other colony shall be admitted into the same, unless such admission be agreed to by nine states.

Article XII. All bills of credit emitted, monies borrowed, and debts contracted by or under the authority of congress, before the assembling of the united states, in pursuance of the present confederation, shall be deemed and considered as a charge against the united States, for payment and satisfaction whereof the said united states and the public faith are hereby solemnly pledged.

Article XIII. Every State shall abide by the determinations of the united states, in congress assembled, on all questions which by this confederation are submitted to them. And the Articles of this confederation shall be inviolably observed by every state, and the union shall be perpetual; nor shall any alteration at any time hereafter be made in any of them, unless such alteration be agreed to in a congress of the united states, and be afterwards con-firmed by the legislatures of every state.

And **Whereas it hath pleased the Great Governor of the World to incline the hearts of the legislatures we respectively represent in congress, to approve of, and to authorize us to ratify the said articles of confederation and perpetual union,** Know Ye, that we, the undersigned delegates, by virtue of the power and authority to us given for that purpose, do, by these presents, in the name and in behalf of our respective constit-uents, fully and entirely ratify and confirm each and every of the said articles of confederation and perpetual union, and all and singular the matters and things therein contained. And we do further solemnly plight and engage the faith of our respec-tive constituents, that they shall abide by the determinations of the united states in congress assembled, on all questions, which by the said confederation are submitted to them. And that the articles thereof shall be inviolably observed by the states we respectively represent, and that the union shall be perpetual. In Witness whereof, we have hereunto set our hands, in Congress. Done at Philadelphia, in the State of Pennsylvania, the ninth Day of July, in the Year of our Lord one Thousand seven Hundred and Seventy eight, and in the third year of the Independence of America.

The 48 signers of the Articles of Confederation were:

Connecticut
Andrew Adams
Titus Hosmer
Samuel Huntington
Roger Sherman
Oliver Wolcott
Delaware
John Dickinson
Thomas McKean
Nicholas Van Dyke
Georgia
Edward Langworthy
Edward Telfair
John Walton
Maryland
Daniel Carroll
John Hanson
Massachusetts Bay
Samuel Adams
Francis Dana
Elbridge Gerry
John Hancock
Samuel Holten
James Lovell
New Hampshire
Josiah Bartlett
John Wentworth Jr.
New Jersey
Nathaniel Scudder
John Witherspoon

New York
James Duane
William Duer
Francis Lewis
Gouverneur Morris
North Carolina
Cornelius Harnett
John Penn
John Williams
Pennsylvania
William Clingan
Robert Morris
Joseph Reed
Daniel Roberdeau
Jonathan Bayard Smith
Rhode Island and Providence Plantations
John Collins
William Ellery
Henry Marchant
South Carolina
William Henry Drayton
Thomas Heyward Jr.
Richard Hutson
Henry Laurens
John Mathews
Virginia
Thomas Adams
John Banister
John Harvie
Francis Lightfoot Lee
Richard Henry Lee

The Articles of Confederation of Perpetual Union

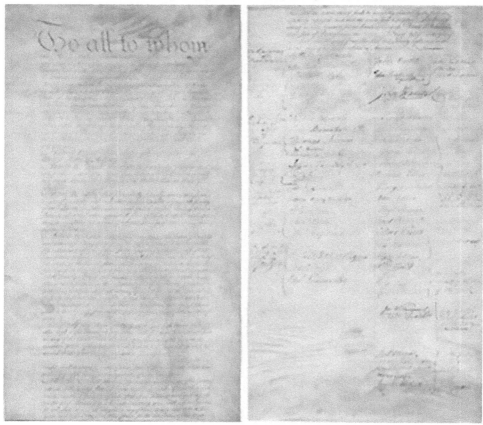

The original document featured here is actually a scroll consisting of
6 sheets of parchment that were sewn together.

The Constitution of the United States

We the People of the United States, in Order to form a more perfect Union, establish Justice, insure domestic Tranquility, provide for the common defence, promote the general Welfare, and **secure the Blessings of Liberty** to ourselves and our Posterity, do ordain and establish this Constitution for the United States of America.

Article. I.

Section. 1. All legislative Powers herein granted shall be vested in a Congress of the United States, which shall consist of a Senate and House of Representatives.

Section. 2. The House of Representatives shall be composed of Members chosen every second Year by the People of the several States, and the Electors in each State shall have the Qualifications requisite for Electors of the most numerous Branch of the State Legislature.

No Person shall be a Representative who shall not have attained to the Age of twenty five Years, and been seven Years a Citizen of the United States, and who shall not, when elected, be an Inhabitant of that State in which he shall be chosen.

Representatives and direct Taxes shall be apportioned among the several States which may be included within this Union, according to their respective Numbers, which shall be determined by adding to the whole Number of free Persons, including those bound to Service for a Term of Years, and excluding Indians not taxed, three fifths of all other Persons. The actual Enumeration shall be made within three Years after the first Meeting of the Congress of the United States, and within every subsequent Term of ten Years, in such Manner as they shall by Law direct. The Number of Representatives shall not exceed one for every thirty Thousand, but each State shall have at Least one Representative; and until such enumeration shall be made, the State of New Hampshire shall be entitled to chuse three, Massachusetts eight, Rhode-Island and Providence Plantations one, Connecticut five, New-York six, New Jersey four, Pennsylvania eight, Delaware one, Maryland six, Virginia ten, North Carolina five, South Carolina five, and Georgia three.

When vacancies happen in the Representation from any State, the Executive Authority thereof shall issue Writs of Election to fill such Vacancies.

The House of Representatives shall chuse their Speaker and other Officers; and shall have the sole Power of Impeachment.

Section. 3. The Senate of the United States shall be composed of two Senators from each State, chosen by the Legislature thereof, for six Years; and each Senator shall have one Vote.

Immediately after they shall be assembled in Consequence of the first Election, they shall be divided as equally as may be into three Classes. The Seats of the Senators of the first Class shall be vacated at the Expiration of the second Year, of the second Class at the Expiration of the fourth Year, and of the third Class at the Expiration of the sixth Year, so that one third may be chosen every second Year; and if Vacancies happen by Resignation, or otherwise, during the Recess of the Legislature of any State, the Executive thereof may make temporary Appointments until the next Meeting of the Legislature, which shall then fill such Vacancies.

No Person shall be a Senator who shall not have attained to the Age of thirty Years, and been nine Years a Citizen of the United States, and who shall not, when elected, be an Inhabitant of that State for which he shall be chosen.

The Vice President of the United States shall be President of the Senate, but shall have no Vote, unless they be equally divided.

The Senate shall chuse their other Officers, and also a President pro tempore, in the Absence of the Vice President, or when he shall exercise the Office of President of the United States.

The Senate shall have the sole Power to try all Impeachments. When sitting for that Purpose, they shall be on Oath or Affirmation. When the President of the United States is tried, the Chief Justice shall preside: And no Person shall be convicted without the Concurrence of two thirds of the Members present.

Judgment in Cases of Impeachment shall not extend further than to removal from Office, and disqualification to hold and enjoy any Office of honor, Trust or Profit under the United States: but the Party convicted shall nevertheless be liable and subject to Indictment, Trial, Judgment and Punishment, according to Law.

Section. 4. The Times, Places and Manner of holding Elections for Senators and Representatives, shall be prescribed in each State by the Legislature thereof; but the Congress may at any time by Law make or alter such Regulations, except as to the Places of chusing Senators.

The Congress shall assemble at least once in every Year, and such Meeting shall be on the first Monday in December, unless they shall by Law appoint a different Day.

Section. 5. Each House shall be the Judge of the Elections, Returns and Qualifications of its own Members, and a Majority of each shall constitute a Quorum to do Business; but a smaller Number may adjourn from day to day, and may be authorized to compel the Attendance of absent Members, in such Manner, and under such Penalties as each House may provide.

Each House may determine the Rules of its Proceedings, punish its Members for disorderly Behaviour, and, with the Concurrence of two thirds, expel a Member.

Each House shall keep a Journal of its Proceedings, and from time to time publish the same, excepting such Parts as may in their Judgment require Secrecy; and the Yeas and Nays of the Members of either House on any question shall, at the Desire of one fifth of those Present, be entered on the Journal.

Neither House, during the Session of Congress, shall, without the Consent of the other, adjourn for more than three days, nor to any other Place than that in which the two Houses shall be sitting.

Section. 6. The Senators and Representatives shall receive a Compensation for their Services, to be ascertained by Law, and paid out of the Treasury of the United States. They shall in all Cases, except Treason, Felony and Breach of the Peace, be privileged from Arrest during their Attendance at the Session of their respective Houses, and in going to and returning from the same; and for any Speech or Debate in either House, they shall not be questioned in any other Place.

No Senator or Representative shall, during the Time for which he was elected, be appointed to any civil Office under the Authority of the United States, which shall have been created, or the Emoluments whereof shall have been encreased during such time; and no Person holding any Office under the United States, shall be a Member of either House during his Continuance in Office.

Section. 7. All Bills for raising Revenue shall originate in the House of Representatives; but the Senate may propose or concur with Amendments as on other Bills.

Every Bill which shall have passed the House of Representatives and the Senate, shall, before it become a Law, be presented to the President of the United States; If he approve he shall sign it, but if not he shall return it, with his Objections to that House in which it shall have originated, who shall enter the Objections at large on their Journal, and proceed to reconsider it. If after such Reconsideration two thirds of that House shall agree to pass the Bill, it shall be sent, together with the Objections, to the other House, by which it shall likewise be reconsidered, and if approved by two thirds of that House, it shall become a Law. But in all such Cases the Votes of both Houses shall be determined by yeas and Nays, and the Names of the Persons voting for and against the Bill shall be entered on the Journal of each House respectively. If any Bill shall not be returned by the President within ten Days (Sundays excepted) after it shall have been presented to him, the Same shall be a Law, in like Manner as if he had signed it, unless the Congress by their Adjournment prevent its Return, in which Case it shall not be a Law.

Every Order, Resolution, or Vote to which the Concurrence of the Senate and House of Representatives may be necessary (except on a question of Adjournment) shall be presented to the President of the United States; and before the Same shall take Effect, shall be approved by him, or being disapproved by him, shall be repassed by two thirds of the Senate and House of Representatives, according to the Rules and Limitations prescribed in the Case of a Bill.

Section. 8. The Congress shall have Power To lay and collect Taxes, Duties, Imposts and Excises, to pay the Debts and provide for the common Defence and general Welfare of the United States; but all Duties, Imposts and Excises shall be uniform throughout the United States;

To borrow Money on the credit of the United States;

To regulate Commerce with foreign Nations, and among the several States, and with the Indian Tribes;

To establish an uniform Rule of Naturalization, and uniform Laws on the subject of Bankruptcies throughout the United States;

To coin Money, regulate the Value thereof, and of foreign Coin, and fix the Standard of Weights and Measures;

To provide for the Punishment of counterfeiting the Securities and current Coin of the United States;

To establish Post Offices and post Roads;

To promote the Progress of Science and useful Arts, by securing for limited Times to Authors and Inventors the exclusive Right to their respective Writings and Discoveries;

To constitute Tribunals inferior to the supreme Court;

To define and punish Piracies and Felonies committed on the high Seas, and Offences against the Law of Nations;

To declare War, grant Letters of Marque and Reprisal, and make Rules concerning Captures on Land and Water;

To raise and support Armies, but no Appropriation of Money to that Use shall be for a longer Term than two Years;

To provide and maintain a Navy;

To make Rules for the Government and Regulation of the land and naval Forces;

To provide for calling forth the Militia to execute the Laws of the Union, suppress Insurrections and repel Invasions;

To provide for organizing, arming, and disciplining, the Militia, and for governing such Part of them as may be employed in the Service of the United States, reserving to the States respectively, the Appointment of the Officers, and the Authority of training the Militia according to the discipline prescribed by Congress;

To exercise exclusive Legislation in all Cases whatsoever, over such District (not exceeding ten Miles square) as may, by Cession of particular States, and the Acceptance of Congress, become the Seat of the Government of the United States, and to exercise like Authority over all Places purchased by the Consent of the Legislature of the State in which the Same shall be, for the Erection of Forts, Magazines, Arsenals, dock-Yards, and other needful Buildings; — And

To make all Laws which shall be necessary and proper for carrying into Execution the foregoing Powers, and all other Powers vested by this Constitution in the Government of the United States, or in any Department or Officer thereof.

Section. 9. The Migration or Importation of such Persons as any of the States now existing shall think proper to admit, shall not be prohibited by the Congress prior to the Year one thousand eight hundred and eight, but a Tax or duty may be imposed on such Importation, not exceeding ten dollars for each Person.

The Privilege of the Writ of Habeas Corpus shall not be suspended, unless when in Cases of Rebellion or Invasion the public Safety may require it.

No Bill of Attainder or ex post facto Law shall be passed.

No Capitation, or other direct, Tax shall be laid, unless in Proportion to the Census or enumeration herein before directed to be taken.

No Tax or Duty shall be laid on Articles exported from any State.

No Preference shall be given by any Regulation of Commerce or Revenue to the Ports of one State over those of another: nor shall Vessels bound to, or from, one State, be obliged to enter, clear, or pay Duties in another.

No Money shall be drawn from the Treasury, but in Consequence of Appropriations made by Law; and a regular Statement and Account of the Receipts and Expenditures of all public Money shall be published from time to time.

No Title of Nobility shall be granted by the United States: And no Person holding any Office of Profit or Trust under them, shall, without the Consent of the Congress, accept of any present, Emolument, Office, or Title, of any kind whatever, from any King, Prince, or foreign State.

Section. 10. No State shall enter into any Treaty, Alliance, or Confederation; grant Letters of Marque and Reprisal; coin Money; emit Bills of Credit; make any Thing but gold and silver Coin a Tender in Payment of Debts; pass any Bill of Attainder, ex post facto Law, or Law impairing the Obligation of Contracts, or grant any Title of Nobility.

No State shall, without the Consent of the Congress, lay any Imposts or Duties on Imports or Exports, except what may be absolutely necessary for executing its inspection Laws: and the net Produce of all Duties and Imposts, laid by any State on Imports or Exports, shall be for the Use of the Treasury of the United States; and all such Laws shall be subject to the Revision and Controul of the Congress.

No State shall, without the Consent of Congress, lay any Duty of Tonnage, keep Troops, or Ships of War in time of Peace, enter into any Agreement or Compact with another State, or with a foreign Power, or engage in War, unless actually invaded, or in such imminent Danger as will not admit of delay.

Article. II.

Section. 1. The executive Power shall be vested in a President of the United States of America. He shall hold his Office during the Term of four Years, and, together with the Vice President, chosen for the same Term, be elected, as follows

Each State shall appoint, in such Manner as the Legislature thereof may direct, a Number of Electors, equal to the whole Number of Senators and Representatives to which the State may be entitled in the Congress: but no Senator or Representative, or Person holding an Office of Trust or Profit under the United States, shall be appointed an Elector.

The Electors shall meet in their respective States, and vote by Ballot for two Persons, of whom one at least shall not be an Inhabitant of the same State with themselves. And they shall make a List of all the Persons voted for, and of the Number of Votes for each; which List they shall sign and certify, and transmit sealed to the Seat of the Government of the United States, directed to the President of the Senate. The President of the Senate shall, in the Presence of the Senate and House of Representatives, open all the Certificates, and the Votes shall then be counted. The Person having the greatest Number of Votes shall be the President, if such Number be a Majority of the whole Number of Electors appointed; and if there be more than one who have such Majority, and have an equal Number of Votes, then the House of Representatives shall immediately chuse by Ballot one of them for President; and if no Person have a Majority, then from the five highest on the List the said House shall in like Manner chuse the President. But in chusing the President, the Votes shall be taken by States, the Representation from each State having one Vote; A quorum for this Purpose shall consist of a Member or Members from two thirds of the States, and a Majority of all the States shall be necessary to a Choice. In every Case, after the Choice of the President, the Person having the greatest Number of Votes of the Electors shall be the Vice President. But if there should remain two or more who have equal Votes, the Senate shall chuse from them by Ballot the Vice President.

The Congress may determine the Time of chusing the Electors, and the Day on which they shall give their Votes; which Day shall be the same throughout the United States.

No Person except a natural born Citizen, or a Citizen of the United States, at the time of the Adoption of this Constitution, shall be eligible to the Office of President; neither shall any Person be eligible to that Office who shall not have attained to the Age of thirty five Years, and been fourteen Years a Resident within the United States.

In Case of the Removal of the President from Office, or of his Death, Resignation, or Inability to discharge the Powers and Duties of the said Office, the Same shall devolve on the Vice President, and the Congress may by Law provide for the Case of Removal, Death, Resignation or Inability, both of the President and Vice President, declaring what Officer shall then act as President, and such Officer shall act accordingly, until the Disability be removed, or a President shall be elected.

The President shall, at stated Times, receive for his Services, a Compensation, which shall neither be encreased nor diminished during the Period for which he shall have been elected, and he shall not receive within that Period any other Emolument from the United States, or any of them.

Before he enter on the Execution of his Office, he shall take the following Oath or Affirmation: — "I do solemnly swear (or affirm) that I will faithfully execute the Office of President of the United States, and will to the best of my Ability, preserve, protect and defend the Constitution of the United States."

Section. 2. The President shall be Commander in Chief of the Army and Navy of the United States, and of the Militia of the several States, when called into the actual Service of the United States; he may require the Opinion, in writing, of the principal Officer in each of the executive Departments, upon any Subject relating to the Duties of their respective Offices, and he shall have Power to grant Reprieves and Pardons for Offences against the United States, except in Cases of Impeachment.

He shall have Power, by and with the Advice and Consent of the Senate, to make Treaties, provided two thirds of the Senators present concur; and he shall nominate, and by and with the Advice and Consent of the Senate, shall appoint Ambassadors, other public Ministers and Consuls, Judges of the supreme Court, and all other Officers of the United States, whose Appointments are not herein otherwise provided for, and which shall be established by Law: but the Congress may by Law vest the Appointment of such inferior Officers, as they think proper, in the President alone, in the Courts of Law, or in the Heads of Departments.

The President shall have Power to fill up all Vacancies that may happen during the Recess of the Senate, by granting Commissions which shall expire at the End of their next Session.

Section. 3. He shall from time to time give to the Congress Information of the State of the Union, and recommend to their Consideration such Measures as he shall judge necessary and expedient; he may, on extraordinary Occasions, convene both Houses, or either of them, and in Case of Disagreement between them, with Respect to the Time of Adjournment, he may adjourn them to such Time as he shall think proper; he shall receive Ambassadors and other public Ministers; he shall take Care that the Laws be faithfully executed, and shall Commission all the Officers of the United States.

Section. 4. The President, Vice President and all civil Officers of the United States, shall be removed from Office on Impeachment for, and Conviction of, Treason, Bribery, or other high Crimes and Misdemeanors.

Article III.

Section. 1. The judicial Power of the United States, shall be vested in one supreme Court, and in such inferior Courts as the Congress may from time to time ordain and establish. The Judges, both of the supreme and inferior Courts, shall hold their Offices during good Behaviour, and shall, at stated Times, receive for their Services, a Compensation, which shall not be diminished during their Continuance in Office.

Section. 2. The judicial Power shall extend to all Cases, in Law and Equity, arising under this Constitution, the Laws of the United States, and Treaties made, or which shall be made, under their Authority;—to all Cases affecting Ambassadors, other public Ministers and Consuls;—to all Cases of admiralty and maritime Jurisdiction;—to Controversies to which the United States shall be a Party;—to Controversies between two or more States;— between a State and Citizens of another State, —between Citizens of different States, —between Citizens of the same State claiming Lands under Grants of different States, and between a State, or the Citizens thereof, and foreign States, Citizens or Subjects.

In all Cases affecting Ambassadors, other public Ministers and Consuls, and those in which a State shall be Party, the supreme Court shall have original Jurisdiction. In all the other Cases before mentioned, the supreme Court shall have appellate Jurisdiction, both as to Law and Fact, with such Exceptions, and under such Regulations as the Congress shall make.

The Trial of all Crimes, except in Cases of Impeachment, shall be by Jury; and such Trial shall be held in the State where the said Crimes shall have been committed; but when not committed within any State, the Trial shall be at such Place or Places as the Congress may by Law have directed.

Section. 3. Treason against the United States, shall consist only in levying War against them, or in adhering to their Enemies, giving them Aid and Comfort. No Person shall be convicted of Treason unless on the Testimony of two Witnesses to the same overt Act, or on Confession in open Court.

The Congress shall have Power to declare the Punishment of Treason, but no Attainder of Treason shall work Corruption of Blood, or Forfeiture except during the Life of the Person attainted.

Article. IV.

Section. 1. Full Faith and Credit shall be given in each State to the public Acts, Records, and judicial Proceedings of every other State. And the Congress may by general Laws prescribe the Manner in which such Acts, Records and Proceedings shall be proved, and the Effect thereof.

Section. 2. The Citizens of each State shall be entitled to all Privileges and Immunities of Citizens in the several States.

A Person charged in any State with Treason, Felony, or other Crime, who shall flee from Justice, and be found in another State, shall on Demand of the executive Authority of the State from which he fled, be delivered up, to be removed to the State having Jurisdiction of the Crime.

No Person held to Service or Labour in one State, under the Laws thereof, escaping into another, shall, in Consequence of any Law or Regulation therein, be discharged from such Service or Labour, but shall be delivered up on Claim of the Party to whom such Service or Labour may be due.

Section. 3. New States may be admitted by the Congress into this Union; but no new State shall be formed or erected within the Jurisdiction of any other State; nor any State be formed by the Junction of two or more States, or Parts of States, without the Consent of the Legislatures of the States concerned as well as of the Congress.

The Congress shall have Power to dispose of and make all needful Rules and Regulations respecting the Territory or other Property belonging to the United States; and nothing in this Constitution shall be so construed as to Prejudice any Claims of the United States, or of any particular State.

Section. 4. The United States shall guarantee to every State in this Union a Republican Form of Government, and shall protect each of them against Invasion; and on Application of the Legislature, or of the Executive (when the Legislature cannot be convened), against domestic Violence.

Article. V.

The Congress, whenever two thirds of both Houses shall deem it necessary, shall propose Amendments to this Constitution, or, on the Application of the Legislatures of two thirds of the several States, shall call a Convention for proposing Amendments, which, in either Case, shall be valid to all Intents and Purposes, as Part of this Constitution, when ratified by the Legislatures of three fourths of the several States, or by Conventions in three fourths thereof, as the one or the other Mode of Ratification may be proposed by the Congress; Provided that no Amendment which may be made prior to the Year One thousand eight hundred and eight shall in any Manner affect the first and fourth Clauses in the Ninth Section of the first Article; and that no State, without its Consent, shall be deprived of its equal Suffrage in the Senate.

Article. VI.

All Debts contracted and Engagements entered into, before the Adoption of this Constitution, shall be as valid against the United States under this Constitution, as under the Confederation.

This Constitution, and the Laws of the United States which shall be made in Pursuance thereof; and all Treaties made, or which shall be made, under the Authority of the United States, shall be the supreme Law of the Land; and the Judges in every State shall be bound thereby, any Thing in the Constitution or Laws of any State to the Contrary notwithstanding.

The Senators and Representatives before mentioned, and the Members of the several State Legislatures, and all executive and judicial Officers, both of the United States and of the several States, shall be bound by Oath or Affirmation, to support this Constitution; but no religious Test shall ever be required as a Qualification to any Office or public Trust under the United States.

Article. VII.

The Ratification of the Conventions of nine States, shall be sufficient for the Establishment of this Constitution between the States so ratifying the Same.

The Word, "the," being interlined between the seventh and eighth Lines of the first Page, The Word "Thirty" being partly written on an Erazure in the fifteenth Line of the first Page, The Words "is tried" being interlined between the thirty second and thirty third Lines of the first Page and the Word "the" being interlined between the forty third and forty fourth Lines of the second Page.

Attest William Jackson Secretary

done in Convention by the Unanimous Consent of the States present the Seventeenth Day of September in the Year of our Lord one thousand seven hundred and Eighty seven and of the Independance of the United States of America the Twelfth In witness whereof We have hereunto subscribed our Names,

The 39 signers[2] of the United States Constitution were:

Connecticut
William Samuel Johnson
Roger Sherman
Delaware
Richard Bassett
Gunning Bedford Jr.
Jacob Broom
John Dickinson
George Read
Georgia
Abraham Baldwin
William Few
Maryland
Daniel Carroll
Daniel of St. Thomas
Jenifer
James McHenry
Massachusetts
Nathaniel Gorham
Rufus King
New Hampshire
Nicholas Gilman
John Langdon
New Jersey
David Brearley
Jonathan Dayton
William Livingston
William Paterson

New York
Alexander Hamilton
North Carolina
William Blount
Richard Dobbs Spaight
Hugh Williamson
Pennsylvania
George Clymer
Thomas FitzSimons
Benjamin Franklin
Jared Ingersoll
Thomas Mifflin
Gouverneur Morris
Robert Morris
James Wilson
South Carolina
Pierce Butler
Charles Pinckney
Charles Cotesworth
Pinckney
John Rutledge
Virginia
John Blair
James Madison Jr.
George Washington

---

[2] A 40th "signer," William Jackson, "attested" to the document as secretary to the constitutional convention, but he was not a delegate entitled to debate or vote. No signers represented the state of Rhode Island.

The Constitution of the United States

The Signing of the Constitution of the United States

George Washington presiding at the
1787 Constitutional Convention in Philadelphia
Painting by Howard Chandler Christy

Chapter Two:

Massachusetts Signers

John Adams
(1735-1826)

Signer of the Declaration of Independence

John Adams

Highest Office Attained:
President of the United States

Religious Affiliation:
Congregationalist; Unitarian

Considered one of our greatest Founding Fathers, John Adams was born in 1735 in Braintree (now, Quincy), Massachusetts. He was a fourth-generation descendent of Henry Adams, a Puritan from Barton St. David in Somersetshire, England; Henry emigrated to Massachusetts in 1638 with his wife, Edith Squire, and nine children. They came as part of the great puritan migration, in which dissenters from the Church of England sought to escape religious persecution and establish a new city of God.

Adams's mother, Susanna Boyleston Adams, came from a prominent family of scientists and doctors whose numbers included John Alden, a passenger on the *Mayflower*. Adams's father, John Adams Sr., attended Harvard College, but spent most of his life as a farmer and shoemaker; he was also a selectman (town councilman) in Braintree. Perhaps most importantly, however, John Sr. was a deacon in the First (Congregational) Church of Braintree, a position held by his maternal great-grandfather, Deacon Samuel Bass, for fifty years commencing with the first organization of the church. Deacon John similarly instilled in his own son, Adams, who was baptized in that same church, the religious precepts that guided him not only in his own life but in the founding of America.

As a youngster, Adams was schooled by Joseph Marsh in the home of Rev. John Hancock—the father of the Founding Father of the same name. Marsh was the son of Rev. Joseph Marsh, who had preceded Rev. Hancock as pastor of First Church, and whose own predecessor in that pulpit was his father-in-law, Rev. Moses Fiske. At the age of sixteen, Adams enrolled at Harvard. His father encouraged him to pursue the ministry, and thus to follow in the footsteps of Deacon John's elder brother, Rev. Joseph Adams; after attending Harvard,

Rev. Adams had pastored for sixty-eight years at the Newington Town (Congregational) Church in New Hampshire. But Adams found himself otherwise inclined. After completing his studies at Harvard, he taught for a time in Worcester, and then studied law under James Putnam, a prominent lawyer in town.

In 1758, Adams returned to Braintree to open his own law practice. There he reunited with Rev. Anthony Wibird. While Adams was in Worcester, Rev. Wibird had assumed the pulpit at First Church; he and Adams would remain friends throughout Rev. Wibird's forty-five-year pastorate there. By then, First Church had revised its creed from traditional Congregationalism to what was developing as Unitarianism, although Adams's religious beliefs continued to be firmly rooted in the teachings of Jesus Christ. Adams also soon met a shy, frail, fifteen-year-old Abigail Smith of nearby Weymouth. Abigail was the daughter of Rev. William Smith, pastor of North Parish Congregational Church of Weymouth, and Elizabeth Quincy Smith. The Smiths, like the Adamses, were devoutly puritan in their religious beliefs. Yet, as products of prominent New England families of merchants, statesmen, and ministers, they were of a decidedly higher social status. Adams's pairing with his beloved partner, Abigail—the future First Lady and the future mother of the sixth President of the United States, John Quincy Adams—was consummated in marriage in 1764; Rev. Smith performed the ceremony at the Weymouth church parsonage.

Adams became active in local affairs and quickly rose to prominence in his hometown. In 1765, Adams, then the surveyor of highways in Braintree (and soon to be, like his father, a selectman), authored *A Dissertation on the Canon and the Feudal Law*, a patriotic political essay in which Adams declared liberty to be a right "derived from our Maker." Also that year, Great Britain passed the Stamp Act, and Adams petitioned the selectmen of the town to oppose it. He drafted what became known as the *Braintree Instructions*, and delivered them from the pulpit of First Church. They instructed Braintree's legislative representatives in the defense of colonial rights and liberties, and served as a model for other towns as well. Delivering a speech before the governor and Provincial Council of Massachusetts, Adams declared the Stamp Act invalid because the people of Massachusetts had not assented to it. In 1768, Adams moved to Boston and built a prominent law practice. While declining appointment as advocate general in the Court of Admiralty, he successfully defended both colonial sailors charged with killing a British naval officer and, believing everyone entitled to the right to counsel and a fair trial, British soldiers charged with killing innocent civilians in the Boston Massacre. Once in Boston, Adams attended the Brattle Street (Congregational) Church, then pastored by Rev. Samuel Cooper. He also was a close confidant of Rev. Jonathan Mayhew of the Old West (Congregational) Church, another early forerunner of Unitarianism whose sermonic reference to the levying of "taxes upon the people without consent" presaged the revolutionary phrase, often attributed to Adams, "no taxation without representation."

In 1770, Adams was elected to the Massachusetts legislature, and, in 1774, he was chosen by the legislature to be one of five Massachusetts delegates to the Continental Congress. Thus uprooted to Philadelphia, but ever mindful of his faith amidst the hullabaloo of activity surrounding him, Adams sought refuge on Sundays in the local houses of worship. His Congregationalism/Unitarianism was ne'er to be found, however, so he sampled those that were available, often attending two or three services on a Sunday — Anglican, Baptist, Presbyterian, Methodist, Quaker, German Moravian, and even Roman Catholic — sometimes more critically than others. In 1775, Adams nominated George Washington, for whom he would later serve as vice president, as commander-in-chief of the army.

By early 1776, Adams was more convinced than ever that the only pathway forward was that of independence, penning in his diary of a "Declaration of Independency." There became no more forceful or persuasive an advocate for independence in the Congress than Adams. His pamphlet, *Thoughts on Government*, sought to describe what a post-independence government should look like, and it was enormously influential not only in the Congress, but in the future framing of many state constitutions. In May, Adams and Richard Henry Lee put forth a resolution, for which Adams drafted a preamble, recommending that individual colonies assume all powers of government. It was almost — but not quite — a declaration of independence, and it set the stage for what was to come. On June 7, 1776, Lee offered a motion to formally declare independence from Great Britain, and Adams quickly seconded it. Debate ensued, a draft declaration was crafted by Thomas Jefferson, and it fell to Adams, more than anyone, to persuade those who were reluctant to so declare their God-given rights and liberties. The vote for independence followed on July 2, and "by the solemn acts of devotion to God Almighty," Adams wrote to Abigail, America had been born.

In the ensuing years, Adams embarked on diplomatic missions to France and The Netherlands, and later as Minister to the Court of St. James in London. Between missions, Adams found himself back in Braintree in 1779, and he was chosen as a delegate to the Massachusetts state convention. There, he became the principal author of the constitution of the commonwealth. Among its provisions was one that declared the worship of God to be both a right and a duty. It was during his time abroad that America secured its independence from Great Britain militarily, operated for a time under the Articles of Confederation, and, in 1787, adopted its new United States Constitution.

In 1788, Adams returned to America and once again found himself at home in Braintree. His stay there was brief, however, as he was soon chosen as the first Vice President of the United States, under President George Washington. In 1796, Adams was elected to succeed Washington as president, narrowly defeating his long-time rival and friend, Thomas Jefferson. After Jefferson returned the favor in the election of 1800, Adams returned home to Braintree. Their political battles left them wounded, but eventually Adams and Jefferson would rekindle a relationship of mutual love and respect, as reflected in a long series of correspondence in their later years. In 1818, as Adams mourned the passing of his dear Abigail, he and Jefferson found comfort in their belief in God.

In 1820, Adams was elected, at the age of eighty-five, as a delegate to a state convention charged with revising the Massachusetts constitution that he had drafted some forty years before. While unsuccessful, he proposed an amendment that would have guaranteed complete religious freedom within the commonwealth, specifically including those of the Jewish faith. Adams lived to see his son, John Quincy Adams, sworn in as President of the United States in 1825, the oath of office administered by Chief Justice John Marshall, whom Adams had appointed to that position years earlier.

On July 4, 1826, the fiftieth anniversary of the Declaration of Independence, John Adams died at the age of ninety. Before passing, he whispered, "Thomas Jefferson survives," knowing not that Jefferson had himself passed earlier that same day. Four thousand people gathered for his funeral at the First Church, where Deacon John and Deacon Bass had served for so many years, and there Adams was laid to rest, in death as in life a fervent Christian.

In His Own Words:

Diary Entry by John Adams
February 22, 1756[1]

> **Suppose a nation in some distant region should take the Bible for their only law book and every member should regulate his conduct by the precepts there exhibited. . . . What a Eutopia— what a Paradise would this region be!**

***Dissertation on the Canon and Feudal Law*, by John Adams**
1765[2]

> The poor people, it is true, have been much less successful than the great. They have seldom found either leisure or opportunity to form a union and exert their strength; ignorant as they were of arts

and letters, they have seldom been able to frame and support a regular opposition. This, however, has been known by the great to be the temper of mankind; and they have accordingly labored, in all ages, to wrest from the populace, as they are contemptuously called, the knowledge of their rights and wrongs, and the power to assert the former or redress the latter. I say **RIGHTS, for such they have, undoubtedly, antecedent to all earthly government,** *—Rights,* **that cannot be repealed or restrained by human laws** *—Rights* **derived from the great Legislator of the universe.** . . .

Be it remembered, however, that **liberty must at all hazards be supported. We have a right to it, derived from our Maker.** But if we had not, our fathers have earned and bought it for us, at the expense of their ease their estates their pleasure and their blood. **And liberty cannot be preserved without a general knowledge among the people, who have a right, from the frame of their nature, to knowledge, as their great Creator who does nothing in vain, has given them understandings, and a desire to know;** but besides this, **they have a right, an indisputable, unalienable, indefeasible, divine right to that most dreaded and envied kind of knowledge, I mean, of the characters and conduct of their rulers.** Rulers are no more than attorneys, agents, and trustees, for the people; and if the cause, the interest and trust, is insidiously betrayed or wantonly trifled away, the people have a right to revoke the authority that they themselves have deputed, and to constitute abler and better agents, attorneys, and trustees.

Letter from John Adams to His Wife, Abigail Adams (regarding their children)
April 15, 1776[3]

> Let them revere nothing but religion, morality and liberty.

Letter from John Adams to Mercy Otis Warren
April 16, 1776[4]

> The Form of Government, which you admire, when its Principles are pure, is admirable indeed. It is productive of every Thing, which is great and excellent among Men. But its Principles are as easily destroyed, as human Nature is corrupted. Such a Government is only to be supported by pure Religion, or Austere Morals. Public Virtue cannot exist in a Nation without private, and public Virtue is the only Foundation of Republics.

Letter from John Adams to Zabdiel Adams
June 21, 1776[5]

> Statesmen my dear Sir, may plan and speculate for Liberty, but it is Religion and Morality alone, which can establish the Principles upon which Freedom can securely stand. . . . The only foundation of a free Constitution, is pure Virtue, and if this cannot be inspired into our People, in a greater Measure, than they have it now, They may change their Rulers, and the forms of Government, but they will not obtain a lasting Liberty. — They will only exchange Tyrants and Tyrannies.

Speech by John Adams to the Continental Congress July 1, 1776[6]

Sir, before God, I believe the hour has come. My judgment approves this measure, and my whole heart is in it. All that I have, and all that I am, and all that I hope, in this life, I am now ready here to stake upon it; and I leave off as I began, that live or die, survive or perish, I am for the declaration. **It is my living sentiment; by the blessing of God it shall be my dying sentiment. Independence *now*, and independence *forever*!**

Letter from John Adams to His Wife, Abigail Adams July 3, 1776[7]

It ought to be commemorated, as the Day of Deliverance by solemn Acts of Devotion to God Almighty. It ought to be solemnized with Pomp and Parade, with Shews, Games, Sports, Guns, Bells, Bonfires and Illuminations from one End of this Continent to the other from this Time forward forever more.

You will think me transported with Enthusiasm but I am not. — I am well aware of the Toil and Blood and Treasure, that it will cost Us to maintain this Declaration, and support and defend these States. — Yet through all the Gloom I can see the Rays of ravishing Light and Glory. I can see that the End is more than worth all the Means. And that Posterity will tryumph in that Days Transaction, even altho We should rue it, which **I trust in God We shall not.**

Response from John Adams to Benjamin Rush (regarding whether America would succeed in its struggle) October 1776[8]

Yes, if we fear God and repent our sins.

Massachusetts Constitution of 1780, Drafted by John Adams[9]

We, therefore, the people of Massachusetts, acknowledging, with grateful hearts, the goodness of the great Legislator of the universe, in affording us, in the course of His providence, an opportunity, deliberately and peaceably, without fraud, violence, or surprise, of entering into an original, explicit, and solemn compact with each other, and of forming a new constitution of civil government for ourselves and posterity; and devoutly imploring His direction in so interesting a design, do agree upon, ordain, and establish the following declaration of rights and frame of government as the constitution of the commonwealth of Massachusetts. . . .

A Declaration of the Rights of the Inhabitants of the Commonwealth of Massachusetts

Article I. All men are born free and equal, and have certain natural, essential, and unalienable rights . . .

Art. II. It is the right as well as the duty of all men in society, publicly and at stated seasons, to worship the Supreme Being, the great Creator and Preserver of the universe. And no subject shall be hurt, molested, or restrained, in his person, liberty, or estate, for worshipping God in the manner and season most agreeable to the dictates of his own conscience, or for his religious profession or

sentiments, provided he doth not disturb the public peace or obstruct others in their religious worship.

Art. III. As the happiness of a people and the good order and preservation of civil government essentially depend upon piety, religion, and morality, and as these cannot be generally discussed through a community but by the institution of the public worship of God and of the public instructions in piety, religion, and morality: Therefore, To promote their happiness and to secure the good order and preservation of their government, the people of this commonwealth have a right to invest their legislature with power to authorize and require, and the legislature shall, from time to time, authorize and require, the several towns, parishes, precincts, and other bodies-politic or religious societies to make suitable provision, at their own expense, for the institution of the public worship of God and for the support and maintenance of public Protestant teachers of piety, religion, and morality in all cases where such provision shall not be made voluntarily. . . .

And all moneys paid by the subject to the support of public worship and of public teachers aforesaid shall, if he require it, be uniformly applied to the support of the public teacher or teachers of his own religious sect or denomination, provided there be any on whose instructions he attends; otherwise it may be paid toward the support of the teacher or teachers of the parish or precinct in which the said moneys are raised.

And every denomination of Christians, demeaning themselves peaceably and as good subjects of the commonwealth, shall be equally under the protection of the law; and no subordination of any sect or denomination to another shall ever be established by law.

Diary Entry by John Adams
July 26, 1796[10]

The Christian religion is, above all the religions that ever prevailed or existed in ancient or modern times, the religion of wisdom, virtue, equity and humanity.

Letter from President John Adams to the First Brigade of the Third Division of the Massachusetts Militia
October 11, 1798[11]

We have no Government armed with Power capable of contending with human Passions unbridled by morality and Religion. Avarice, Ambition, Revenge or Galantry, would break the strongest Cords of our Constitution as a Whale goes through a Net. Our Constitution was made only for a moral and religious People. It is wholly inadequate to the government of any other.

Proclamation for a National Fast, **by President John Adams**
March 6, 1799[12]

PROCLAMATION
FOR A NATIONAL FAST
6 MARCH, 1799

As no truth is more clearly taught in the volume of inspiration, nor any more fully demonstrated by the experience of all ages, than that a deep sense and a due acknowledgment of the governing providence of a Supreme Being, and of the accountableness of men to Him as the searcher of hearts and righteous distributor of rewards and punishments, are conducive equally to the happiness and rectitude of individuals, and to the well being of communities; as it is, also, most reasonable in itself, that men who are made capable of social acts and relations, who owe their improvements to the social state, and who derive their enjoyments from it should as a society, make their acknowledgments of dependence and obligation to Him, who hath endowed them with these capacities, and elevated them in the scale of existence by these distinctions; as it is, likewise, a plain dictate of duty, and a strong sentiment of nature, that in circumstances of great urgency and seasons of imminent danger, earnest and particular supplications should be made to Him who is able to defend or to destroy; as, moreover, the most precious interests of the people of the United States are still held in jeopardy by the hostile designs and insidious acts of a foreign nation, as well as by the dissemination among them of those principles, subversive of the foundations of all religious, moral, and social obligations, that have produced incalculable mischief and misery in other countries; and as, in fine, the observance of special seasons for public religious solemnities, is happily calculated to avert the evils which we ought to deprecate, and to excite to the performance of the duties which we ought to discharge, by calling and fixing the attention of the people at large to the momentous truths already recited, by affording opportunity to teach and inculcate them, by animating devotion, and giving to it the character of a national act:

For these reasons I have thought proper to recommend, and I do hereby recommend

accordingly, that Thursday, the twenty-fifth day
of April next, be observed, throughout the United
States of America, as a day of solemn humiliation,
fasting, and prayer; that the citizens, on that
day, abstain as far as may be from their secular
occupations, devote the time to the sacred duties
of religion in public and in private; that they
call to mind our numerous offences against the
most high God, confess them before him with the
sincerest penitence, implore his pardoning mercy,
through the Great Mediator and Redeemer, for
our past transgressions, and that, through the
grace of his Holy Spirit, we may be disposed
and enabled to yield a more suitable obedience
to his righteous requisitions in time to come;
that he would interpose to arrest the progress of
that impiety and licentiousness in principle and
practice, so offensive to himself and so ruinous to
mankind; that he would make us deeply sensible,
that "righteousness exalteth a nation, but that
sin is the reproach of any people"; that he would
turn us from our transgressions, and turn his
displeasure from us; that he would withhold us
from unreasonable discontent, from disunion,
faction, sedition, and insurrection; that he would
preserve our country from the desolating sword;
that he would save our cities and towns from a
repetition of those awful pestilential visitations
under which they have lately suffered so severely,
and that the health of our inhabitants, generally,
may be precious in his sight; that he would favor
us with fruitful seasons, and so bless the labors
of the husbandman as that there may be food
in abundance for man and beast; that he would
prosper our commerce, manufactures, and fisheries,
and give success to the people in all their lawful
industry and enterprise; that he would smile on

our colleges, academies, schools, and seminaries of learning, and make them nurseries of sound science, morals, and religion; that he would bless all magistrates from the highest to the lowest, give them the true spirit of their station, make them a terror to evil-doers, and a praise to them that do well; that he would preside over the councils of the nation at this critical period, enlighten them to a just discernment of the public interest, and save them from mistake, division, and discord; that he would make succeed our preparations for defence, and bless our armaments by land and by sea; that he would put an end to the effusion of human blood and the accumulation of human misery among the contending nations of the earth, by disposing them to justice, to equity, to benevolence, and to peace; and that he would extend the blessings of knowledge, of true liberty, and of pure and undefiled religion, throughout the world.

And I do, also, recommend that, with these acts of humiliation, penitence, and prayer, fervent thanksgiving to the author of all good be united, for the countless favors which he is still continuing to the people of the United States, and which render their condition as a nation eminently happy, when compared with the lot of others.

Given, &c.

JOHN ADAMS

Letter from John Adams to Benjamin Rush
August 28, 1811[13]

I agree with you in Sentiment that Religion and Virtue are the only Foundations; not only of Republicanism and of all free Government: but of

Social Felicity under all Governments and in all the Combinations of human Society.

Letter from John Adams to Thomas Jefferson June 28, 1813[14]

The general principles on which the fathers achieved independence were the general principles of Christianity. I will avow that I then believed, and now believe, that those general principles of Christianity are as eternal and immutable as the existence and attributes of God.

Letter from John Adams to Thomas Jefferson September 14, 1813[15]

Now, my Friend, can Prophecies, or miracles convince You, or me, that infinite Benevolence, Wisdom and Power, created and preserves, for a time, innumerable millions to make them miserable, forever, for his own Glory? Wretch! What is his Glory? Is he ambitious? does he want promotion? Is he vain? tickled with Adulation? Exulting and tryumphing in his Power and the Sweetness of his Vengeance? Pardon me, my Maker, for these Aweful Questions. **My Answer to them is always ready: I believe no such Things. My Adoration of the Author of the Universe is too profound and too Sincere. The Love of God and his Creation; delight, Joy, tryumph, Exultation in my own existence, 'tho but an Atom, a Molecule organique, in the Universe; are my religion. Howl, Snarl, bite, Ye Calvinistick! Ye Athanasian Divines, if You will. Ye will Say, I am no Christian: I Say Ye are no Christians: and there the Account is ballanced. Yet I believe all the honest men among you, are Christians in my Sense of the Word. . . .**

Now, my Friend Jefferson, Suppose an eternal Self existent Being existing from Eternity, possessed of infinite Wisdom, Goodness and Power, in absolute total Solitude, Six thousand Years ago, conceiving the benevolent project of creating a Universe! I have no more to Say, at present.

It has been long, very long, a Settled opinion in my Mind that there is now, never will be, and never was but one being who can Understand the Universe. And that it is not only vain but wicked for insects to pretend to comprehend it.

Letter from John Adams to Thomas Jefferson
December 25, 1813[16]

I have examined all religions, and the result is that the Bible is the best book in the world.

Letter from John Adams to Thomas Jefferson
April 19, 1817[17]

Without religion, this world would be something not fit to be mentioned in polite company: I mean hell.

Letter from John Adams to Thomas Jefferson
(upon the death of Abigail Adams)
December 8, 1818[18]

I believe in God and in his Wisdom and Benevolence: and I cannot conceive that Such a Being could make Such a Species as the human merely to live and die on this Earth. If I did not believe a future State I Should believe in no God. This Unverse; this all; this To Παν [totality]; would appear with all its Swelling Pomp, a boyish Fire Work.

What follows is a
summary of an article
from contemporary American life . . .

nearly 250 years after
John Adams
signed

the Declaration of Independence.

What Would John Adams Think?

TODD STARNES · Published June 3, 2016

School sends sheriff to order child to stop sharing Bible verses

OPINION By Todd Starnes, | Fox News

Christina Zavala lovingly packed a lunch for her son before he would begin his first-grade school day at Desert Rose Elementary School in Palmdale, California. When he opened his lunch bag, he would find that his mom had included not only nourishment for his body, but nourishment for his soul in the form of a Bible verse and an encouraging note that explained it. The youngster would tell his friends about the notes and read them aloud. And they liked them so much that they began to ask for copies.

When the boy's teacher learned of this, she called Christina and informed her that her son was "not allowed to share such things while at school," that he "could no longer read or share Bible verses or stories at lunch," and that because of the "separation of church and state," he could only share the notes after school and could only do so outside the school gate. Although the Zavalas complied with the teacher's demands, the school's principal went further, ordering a complete ban on Bible verse sharing because "it was against school policy." Again, the Zavalas complied.

But, apparently, the Zavalas's compliance was not enough to satisfy the school, which then sent the sheriff to pay the Zavalas a visit at their home. In what appeared to be a friendly warning, the sheriff advised the Zavalas that the school feared that someone might be offended by the Bible verses. As the superintendent of the school district explained, "The District remains committed to ensuring an environment where all students, regardless of religious affiliation or belief, are free to learn and reach their full potential." The Zevalas, through their legal counsel, saw it differently, noting that "Apparently all the real criminals have been dealt with in Palmdale—and now they're going after kids who share Bible verses during lunch time."

https://www.foxnews.com/opinion/school-sends-sheriff-to-order-child-to-stop-sharing-bible-verses.

Samuel Adams
(1722-1803)

**Signer of the Declaration of Independence and
the Articles of Confederation**

Highest Office Attained:
Representative in Congress; Governor of Massachusetts

Religious Affiliation:
Congregationalist

F ather of Democracy. Firebrand of the Revolution. These are among the many monikers worn by Samuel Adams, born in 1722 to Samuel Adams Sr. and Mary Fifield Adams. The senior Adams was the son of Captain John Adams, whose grandfather, Henry Adams, had emigrated to Massachusetts in 1638. Henry came from Barton St. David in Somersetshire, England with his wife, Edith Squire, and nine children. They were part of the great puritan migration of dissenters from the Church of England seeking to escape religious persecution. The fervency of the Adamses' religious beliefs lived on though the younger Samuel Adams, sometimes dubbed "the last Puritan," whose extreme radical political views—second-cousin John Adams characterizing him as having been "born a Rebel"—were inextricably intertwined with his Calvinistic religious sentiments.

Samuel Adams Sr. was a wealthy and prominent Boston citizen, active in local political affairs and a member of the Massachusetts colonial legislature. He was a devout Christian, a deacon in the Old South (Congregational) Church. In 1715, he was instrumental in the formation of a new Congregational church, known as the New South (or Summer Street) Church, and in procuring, as its first pastor, the Rev. Samuel Checkley. Rev. Checkley, whose own father had also been a deacon in the Old South Church, then ministered in the New South Church for the next fifty-one years. Rev. Checkley was a long-time friend of the elder Adams's and was related to him by marriage; after the death of Deacon Adams's mother, Captain John married the daughter of Anthony Checkley, the first provincial attorney general of Massachusetts. It was at the New South Church, by Rev. Checkley, his future father-in-law, that young Samuel Adams was baptized.

Adam's mother—whose father, Richard Fifield, had married into the illustrious Mather family of Congregational minsters—was a devout and pious woman, equally as religious as her husband. Together, they instilled in their children the puritan beliefs that guided Adams throughout his life. Prayers and Bible readings were a regular part of their everyday life, traditions that continued when, as a youngster, Adams was sent to the Boston Latin School. Boston Latin was a rigorous preparatory academy of great renown headed by Master John Lovell, whose sole criterion for admission was the ability to read verses from the Bible.

At the age of fourteen, Adams enrolled at Harvard College. It was then headed by Rev. Benjamin Wadsworth, a Congregational minister who had served for thirty years as pastor at Boston's First Church; Adams's father encouraged him to pursue the ministry. He graduated in 1740, but his interests shifted toward politics. Returning to Harvard, he was awarded a master's degree in 1743. By then, his revolutionary zeal was already emerging, as he presented his thesis, *Whether it be Lawful to resist the Supreme Magistrate, if the Commonwealth cannot otherwise be preserved*. He initially pursued the practice of law, but was dissuaded by his mother from that career path. He worked briefly in the counting house (bank) of Thomas Cushing, made an unsuccessful foray into the business world with a loan from his father, and then was brought into the family brewery business. This earned Adams the nickname, "Sammy the Maltster." But none of those pursuits proved to be his calling. While working at the brewery, Adams and a group of friends founded a newspaper called the *Public Advertiser* (or, by some accounts, the *Independent Advertiser*), which afforded Adams a platform from which to author, albeit anonymously, articles promoting his pro-liberty views and calling for heightened moral principles in society and government.

Soon, Adams was elected as a clerk of the Boston Market. In 1749, Rev. Checkley brought the Adams and Checkley families together in marriage once again, proudly officiating at Adams's wedding to his daughter, Elizabeth Checkley. Elizabeth's brother, also dubbed Rev. Samuel Checkley, was pastor of the Second (Congregational) (or Old North) Church, and his own daughter later married his successor in that pulpit, Rev. John Lathrop. Adams and Elizabeth shared much in common, not the least of which was their fervent Congregational faith, as well as the unfortunate circumstance that each was among only three of many siblings to survive to adulthood. In 1756, Adams was elected as a tax collector in Boston—giving rise among his detractors to the moniker, "Sammy the Publican." This was an odd but eye-opening pursuit by one who would later find himself among the instigators of the Boston Tea Party. The following year, having baptized Adams's children, Rev. Checkley was obliged to preside yet again; this time, it was at Elizabeth's funeral, shortly after she gave birth to a sixth (and stillborn) child. Seven years later, in 1764, he did Adams the honor of officiating at his second wedding ceremony, this time to Elizabeth Wells. This Elizabeth was the daughter of another long-time friend of Deacon Adams's, Francis Wells; her much younger brother, Thomas, married Adams's daughter, Hannah.

Adams's revolutionary activities steadily mounted, and with the passage by Great Britain of such measures as the Stamp Act in 1765, he became a key organizer of a resistance group, the Sons of Liberty. He conceived of and formed Boston's Committee of Correspondence to facilitate communications among members of the resistance in the various colonies. He gave the signal that unleashed the dumping of tea into the Boston Harbor in 1773. His enduring prayer was that Boston would become a "Christian Sparta." He authored numerous writings promoting the colonists' God-given rights and liberties. He was an ardent advocate of complete separation from the motherland, and a strenuous opponent of concession or compromise. Elected to the Massachusetts Assembly in 1765, he served there until his election in 1774 to the Provincial Council. Promoting the council as independent of Great Britain, and laying the groundwork for what was to come, Adams became the moral conscience of the revolution and soon—along with the council's president, John Hancock—among the most wanted men in the colonies. Forewarned by Paul Revere, they escaped capture in Lexington, and made their way to Philadelphia.

Adams also worked to create the Continental Congress, where he served as a guiding intellect and passionate advocate of independence from 1774 to 1781. Upon the opening of the Congress, and then a parishioner at the Brattle Street (Congregational) Church, Adams's puritanism revealed a conciliatory side; he adroitly diffused a potential controversy among the various religious denominations represented, by successfully proposing that an Episcopal clergyman offer the opening prayer. In 1776, Adams achieved his lifelong dream, as he transformed from radical agitator-in-chief to signer of the Declaration of Independence. He also helped craft (and signed) the Articles of Confederation. In 1781, he returned to Massachusetts as a member (and president) of the state Senate. He also served as a delegate to the Massachusetts state constitutional convention, where he helped frame the constitution of that state. Being opposed to a strong national government, he declined to attend the Constitutional Convention of 1787; but he was instrumental in securing the ratification by the state of Massachusetts of the resulting United States Constitution. And he later helped author the Bill of Rights. In 1789, he was elected lieutenant governor of Massachusetts, during which time he attended the Old South Church where his father had served as deacon. Upon the death of Governor Hancock in 1794, Adams succeeded to the governorship, where he served until 1797. Samuel Adams died in 1803, forever a Puritan and, as the original mixer of religion and politics, a believer in the indispensable role of virtue and religion in republican government.

In His Own Words:

A Writing by Samuel Adams in His Family Bible (upon the death of his wife, Elizabeth Checkley Adams) July 25, 1757[1]

> To her husband she was as sincere a Friend as she was a faithful Wife. . . . **She ran her Christian race with remarkable** steadiness and finished in triumph!

She left two small children. **God grant they may inherit her graces!**

Article by Samuel Adams, Signed As "Valerius Poplicola," *Boston Gazette*
October 25, 1771[2]

> [L]iberties . . . are originally from God and nature
> . . . . It is our duty therefore to contend for them
> whenever attempts are made to violate them.

Article by Samuel Adams, Signed As "Valerius Poplicola," *Boston Gazette*
October 5, 1772[3]

> The Religion and public Liberty of a People
> are intimately connected; their Interests are
> interwoven, they cannot subsist separately; and
> therefore they rise and fall together. For this
> Reason, it is always observable, that those who
> are combin'd to destroy the People's Liberties,
> practice every Art to poison their Morals.

***The Rights of the Colonists, A List of Violations of Rights and a Letter of Correspondence*, Authored by Samuel Adams and Adopted by the Town of Boston**
November 20, 1772[4]

> As neither reason requires, nor religeon permits
> the contrary, every Man living in or out of a state
> of civil society, has a right peaceably and quietly
> to worship God according to the dictates of his
> conscience. . . .
>
> Just and true liberty, equal and impartial liberty
> in matters spiritual and temporal, is a thing that

all Men are clearly entitled to, by the eternal and immutable laws Of God and nature . . . .

In the state of nature, every man is under God, Judge and sole Judge, of his own rights and the injuries done him: By entering into society, he agrees to an Arbiter or indifferent Judge between him and his neighbours; but he no more renounces his original right . . . .

If men through fear, fraud or mistake, should *in terms* renounce and give up any essential natural right, the eternal law of reason and the great end of society, would absolutely vacate such renunciation; the right to freedom being *the gift* of God Almighty, it is not in the power of Man to alienate this gift, and voluntarily become a slave—

The Rights of the Colonists as Christians . . . may be best understood by reading—and carefully studying the institutes of the great Lawgiver and head of the Christian Church: which are to be found clearly written and promulgated in the *New Testament*—

Oration by Samuel Adams, *On American Independence* August 1, 1776[5]

Heaven hath trusted us with the management of things for eternity, and man denies us ability to judge of the present, or to know from our feelings the experience that will make us happy. . . . **We have this day restored the Sovereign, to whom alone men ought to be obedient. He reigns in heaven, and with a propitious eye beholds his subjects assuming that freedom of thought and dignity of self-direction which he bestowed on them. From**

the rising to the setting the sun, may his kingdom come. . . .

Were the talents and virtues which Heaven has bestowed on men given merely to make them more obedient drudges, to be sacrificed to the follies and ambition of a few, or were not the noble gifts so equally dispensed with a divine purpose and law, that they should, as nearly as possible, be equally exerted, and the blessings of Providence be equally enjoyed by all? . . . The Deity, then, has not given any order or family of men authority over others, and if any men have given it, they only could give it for themselves. . . .

The Author of nature directs all his operations to the production of the greatest good, and has made human virtue to consist in a disposition and conduct which tends to the common felicity of his creatures. An abridgment of the natural freedom of man, by the institution of political societies, in vindicable only on this foot. . . .

These are instances of, I would say, an almost astonishing Providence in our favor; our success has staggered our enemies, and almost given faith to infidels; so that we may truly say, it is not our own arm which has saved us.

The hand of Heaven appears to have led us on to be, perhaps, humble instruments and means in the great providential dispensation which is completing. We have fled from the political Sodom; let us not look back, lest we perish and become a monument of infamy and derision to the world! . . .

And, brethren and fellow-countrymen, if it was ever granted to mortals to trace the designs of Providence, and interpret its manifestations in favor of their cause, we may, with humility of soul, cry out, "Not unto us, not unto us, but to Thy name be the praise." . . . And if we now cast our eyes over the nations of the earth, we shall find that instead of possessing the pure religion of the Gospel, they may be divided either into infidels, who deny the truth, or politicians, who make religion a stalking-horse for their ambition, or professors, who walk in the trammels of orthodoxy, and are more attentive to traditions and ordinances of men than to the oracles of truth.

The civil magistrate has everywhere contaminated religion by making it an engine of policy; and freedom of thought and the right of private judgment in matters of conscience, driven from every other corner of the earth, direct their course to this happy country as their last asylum. Let us cherish the noble guests, and shelter them under the wings of a *universal toleration.* Be this the seat of unbounded *religious freedom.* She will bring with her, in her train, industry, wisdom, and commerce. She thrives most when left to shoot forth in her natural luxuriance, and asks from human policy only not to be checked in her growth by artificial encouragements.

Thus, by the beneficence of Providence, we shall behold an empire arising, founded on the justice and the voluntary consent of the people, and giving full scope to the exercise of those faculties and rights which most ennoble our species. Besides the advantages of liberty and the most equal Constitution, Heaven has given us a country with every variety of climate and soil, pouring forth in abundance whatever is necessary for the support, comfort, and strength of a nation. Within our own borders we possess all the means of sustenance, defence, and commerce; at the same time these advantages are so distributed among the different States of this continent **as if Nature had in view to proclaim to us, Be united among yourselves, and you will want nothing from the rest of the world. . . .**

Countrymen! the men who now invite you to surrender your rights into their hands . . . are *the men* to whom we are exhorted to sacrifice **the blessings which Providence holds out to us — the *happiness*, the *dignity* of uncontrolled *freedom and independence*. . . . Go on, then, in your generous enterprise, with gratitude to Heaven for past success, and confidence of it in the future.**

Letter from Samuel Adams to His Wife, Elizabeth Adams December 26, 1776[6]

The name of the Lord (says the Scripture) is a strong tower; thither the righteous flee and are safe [Proverbs 18:10]. Let us secure His favor and He will lead us through the journey of this life and at length receive us to a better.

Address by Samuel Adams to Members of Congress September 1777[7]

Gentlemen, your spirits appear oppressed with the weight of the public calamities. Your sadness of countenance reveals your disquietude. A patriot may grieve at the distress of his country, but he will never despair of the commonwealth.

Our affairs, it is said, are desperate! If this be our language, they are indeed. If we wear long faces, long faces will become fashionable. The eyes of the people are upon us. The tone of their feelings is regulated by ours. If we despond, public confidence is destroyed, the people will no longer yield their support to a hopeless contest, and American liberty is no more. But we are not driven to such narrow straits. Though fortune has been unpropitious, our condition is not desperate. Our burdens, though grievous, can be borne. Our losses, though great, can be retrieved. Through the darkness which shrouds our prospects the ark of safety is visible. Despondency becomes not the dignity of our cause, nor the character of those who are its supporters.

Let us awaken then, and evince a different spirit, — a spirit that shall inspire the people with confidence in themselves and in us, — a spirit that will encourage them to persevere in this glorious struggle, until their rights and liberties shall be established on a rock. We have proclaimed to the world our determination "to die freemen, rather than to live slaves." **We have appealed to Heaven for the justice of our cause, and in Heaven have we placed our trust. Numerous have been the manifestations of God's providence in sustaining us. In the gloomy period of adversity, we have had "our cloud by day and pillar of fire by night."** [Referencing the **Book of Exodus, Chapter 13**]. **We have been reduced to distress, and the arm of Omnipotence has raised us up. Let us still rely in humble confidence on Him who is mighty to save. Good tidings will soon arrive. We shall never be abandoned by Heaven while we act worthy of its aid and protection.**

Letter from Samuel Adams to Richard Henry Lee
December 23, 1784[8]

If, my honord Friend, the leading Men in the United States would by Precept & Example disseminate thro' the lower Classes of People the Principles of Piety to God, Love to our Country and universal Benevolence, should we not secure the Favor of Heaven & the Honor & Esteem of the wise and virtuous Part of the World.

Letter from Samuel Adams to Richard Henry Lee
April 14, 1785[9]

I firmly believe that the benevolent Creator designd the republican Form of Government for Man. Will you venture so far as to say that all other Institutions that we know of are unnatural & Tend more or less to distress human Societies? Will the Lion ever associate with the Lamb or the Leopard with the Kid till our favorite principles shall be universally establishd?

Last Will and Testament of Samuel Adams, Attested December 29, 1790[10]

In the name of God, Amen. I, Samuel Adams of Boston, in the County of Suffolk, and Commonwealth of Massachusetts, Esquire, being, through Divine goodness, of sound and disposing mind and memory, and considering the uncertainty of human life, do make and ordain this to be my last will and testament, in manner and form following, viz.: Principally and first of all, I recommend my soul to that Almighty Being who gave it, and my body I commit to the dust, relying on the merits of Jesus Christ for a pardon of all my sins; and as to such worldly estate

as God hath been pleased to bestow upon me, I give, devise, and dispose of the same in the following manner . . . .

Address by Governor Samuel Adams to the Massachusetts Legislature
January 17, 1794[11]

It having pleased the Supreme Being, since your last meeting, in his holy Providence to remove from this transitory life our late excellent Governor Hancock, the multitude of his surveying fellow-citizens, who have often given strong testimonials of their approbation of his important services, while they drop a tear, may certainly profit by the recollection of his virtuous and patriotic example. . . .

Diffident as I am of my abilities, **I have yet felt myself constrained to undertake the performance of those duties, and the exercise of those powers and authorities in consequence of a sovereign act of GOD. To him I look for that wisdom which is profitable to direct. The Constitution must be my rule, and the true interest of my constituents, whose agents I am, my invariable object. . . .**

Among the objects of the Constitution of this Commonwealth, liberty and equality stand in a conspicuous light. It is the first article in the Declaration of Rights, — "all men are born free and equal, and have certain natural, essential, and inalienable rights." In the supposed state of nature, **all men are equally bound by the laws of nature, or, to speak more properly, the laws of the Creator. They are imprinted by the finger of God on the heart of man.**

Proclamation for a Day of Public Fasting, Humiliation and Prayer, by Governor Samuel Adams February 28, 1795[12]

Commonwealth of Massachusetts
By the Governor
A Proclamation
For a Day of PUBLIC FASTING,
HUMILIATION and PRAYER

THE supreme Ruler of the Universe, having been pleased, in the course of his Providence, to establish the Independence of the United States of America, and to cause them to assume their rank, amount the nations of the Earth, and bless them with Liberty, Peace and Plenty; we ought to be led by Religious feelings of Gratitude; and to walk before Him, in all Humility, according to his most Holy Law. — But, as the depravity of our Hearts has, in so many instances drawn us aside from the path of duty, so that we have frequently offended our Divine and Merciful Benefactor; it is therefore highly incumbent on us, according to the ancient and laudable practice of our pious Ancestors, to open the year by a public and solemn Fast. — That with true repentance and contrition of Heart, we may unitedly implore the forgiveness of our Sins, through the merits of Jesus Christ, and humbly supplicate our Heavenly Father, to grant us the aids of his Grace, for the amendment of our Hearts and Lives, and vouchsafe his smiles upon our temporal concerns:

I HAVE therefore thought fit to appoint, and with the advice and consent of the Council, I do hereby appoint Thursday, the Second Day of April next, to be observed as a Day of Public

Fasting, Humiliation and Prayer throughout this Commonwealth:—Calling upon the Ministers of the Gospel, of every Denomination, with their respective Congregations, to assemble on that Day, and devoutly implore the Divine forgiveness of our Sins,—To pray that the Light of the Gospel, and the rights of Conscience, may be continued to the people of United America; and that his Holy Word may be improved by them, so that the name of God may be exalted, and their own Liberty and Happiness secured.—That he would be graciously pleased to bless our Federal Government; that by a wise administration, it may be a sure guide and safe protection in national concerns, for the people who have established, and who support it—That He would continue to us the invaluable Blessings of Civil Liberty; guarding us against intestine commotions; and enabling the United States, in the exercise of such Governmental powers, as are devolved upon them, so that the honor and dignity of our Nation, upon the Sea and the Land, may be supported, and Peace with the other Powers of the World, upon safe and honorable terms, may be maintained.

That he would direct the administration of our Federal and State Governments, so that the lives, liberties and property of all the Citizens, and the just rights of the People, as Men and Citizens, may be forever acknowledged, and at all times defended, by Constitutions, founded upon equal rights; and by good and wholesome Laws, wisely and judiciously administered and duly executed.

That he would enable Legislators and Magistrates of this Commonwealth, to discharge the important duties incumbent on them, that the People may have good reason to feel themselves happy and safe, and **lead quiet and peaceable lives in all Godliness and Honesty.**

That he would incline the Natives of the Wilderness, to listen to reasonable offers of Peace, that tranquility and security may be established on the Frontiers Of our Country; — That he would graciously regard the Lives and Health of the People of this and our sister States, and preserve them from contagious and wasting diseases: To crown the ensuing Year with Plenty and Prosperity, by his blessing on our Husbandry, our Fisheries, our Commerce, and all the labor of our Hands—**to affect our minds with a sense of our entire dependence upon Him, and of his great goodness towards us, that when we may present ourselves before Him, at the close of the Year, with our thank-offerings, our Hearts may by his grace, be prepared to do it in a manner acceptable to Him.**

That He would be graciously pleased to establish the French Republic, and prosper others who are contending for the Rights of Men, and dispose all Nations to favor the same principles, and return to Peace and Friendship.

That He would in his great Mercy, remember the unhappy state of our Fellow-Citizens and others, who are groaning under bondage, in a foreign Land. That He would soften the Hearts of those who have led them captive, inclining that People to show them favor during their Captivity, and in His own due time open a door for their relief:—**And finally, that He would over-rule all the confusions that are in the Earth, of the speedy establishment of**

the Redeemer's Kingdom, which consisteth in Righteousness and Peace.

And I do recommend to the People of this Commonwealth, to abstain from all unnecessary Labor and Recreation on te said Day.

GIVEN at the Council-Chamber, in Boston, *this Twenty-eighth Day of February, in the Year of our Lord, One Thousand Seven Hundred and Ninety-five, and in the Nineteenth Year of the Independence of the United States of America.*

SAMUEL ADAMS
Attest: John Avery, jun. Secretary

GOD save the COMMONWEALTH of MASSACHUSETTS!

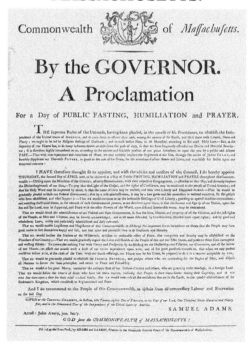

Proclamation for Day of Public Thanksgiving, by Governor Samuel Adams
October 6, 1796[13]

BY AUTHORITY.
Commonwealth of Massachusetts.
By the Governor
A PROCLAMATION
FOR A DAY OF PUBLIC THANKSGIVING

WHEREAS it has pleased God, the Father of all Mercies, to bestow upon us innumerable unmerited favors in the course of the year past; it highly becomes us duly to recollect his goodness, and, in a public and solemn manner, to express the grateful feelings of our hearts:

I have, therefore, thought fit, with the advice and consent of the Council, to appoint *Thursday*, the 15th day of *December* next, to be observed as a day of PUBLIC THANKSGIVING and PRAISE, to our Divine BENEFACTOR, thro' out this Commonwealth—Calling upon Ministers of the Gospel, with their respective Congregations, and the whole body of the people, religiously to observe said day by celebrating the praises of that all gracious Being of whose bounties we have experienced so large a share.

He hath prevented epidemical diseases from spreading, and afforded us a general state of health.

He hath regarded our pastures and fields with the eye of the most indulgent parent and rewarded the industry of our Husbandmen with a plentiful harvest.

Notwithstanding unreasonable obstructions to our trade on the seas, it has generally been prosperous and our fisheries successful.

Our civil constitutions of government, formed by ourselves and administered by men of our own *free election*, are by His Grace continued to us. And we still enjoy the inestimable blessings of the Gospel, and right of worshipping God according to His own institutions and the honest dictates of our consciences.

And, together with our thanksgiving, earnest supplication to God is hereby recommended, for the forgiveness of our sins which have rendered us unworthy of the least of His mercies; and that by the sanctifying influence of His Spirit, our hearts and manners may be corrected, and we become a reformed and happy people — That He would direct and prosper the administration of the Government of the United States, and of this and other States in the Union — That He would still afford his blessings on our Trade, Agriculture, Fisheries and all the labors of our hands — That he would smile upon our University, and all seminaries of learning — That tyranny and usurpation may everywhere come to an end — That the nations who are contending for true liberty may still be succeeded by His Almighty aid — That every nation and society of men may be inspired with the knowledge and feeling of their natural and just rights, and enabled to form such systems of Civil Government as shall be fully adapted to promote and establish their social security and happiness — And, finally, that in the course of God's Holy Providence, the great family of mankind may bow to the Scepter of the Prince of

Peace, so that mutual friendship and harmony may universally prevail.

And I do recommend to the people of this Commonwealth to abstain from all such labors and recreations as may not be consistent with the solemnity of the said day.

Given at the Council Chamber, in Boston, this sixth day of October, in the year of our Lord one thousand seven hundred and ninety six, and in the twenty-first year of the Independence of the United States of America.

SAMUEL ADAMS.
Attest. John Avery, Secretary.

GOD SAVE THE COMMONWEALTH OF MASSACHUSETTS.

91

Address by Governor Samuel Adams to the Massachusetts Legislature
January 27, 1797[14]

As Piety, Religion and Morality have a happy
influence on the minds of men, in their public as
well as private transactions, you will not think
it unseasonable, although I have frequently
done it, to bring to your remembrance the great
importance of encouraging our University, town
schools, and other seminaries of education, that
our children and youth while they are engaged in
the pursuit of useful science, may have their minds
impressed with a strong sense of the duties they
owe to their God, their instructors and each other,
so that when they arrive to a state of manhood,
and take a part in any public transactions, their
hearts having been deeply impressed in the course
of their education with the moral feelings — such
feelings may continue and have their due weight
through the whole of their future lives.

What follows is a
summary of an article
from contemporary American life . . .

nearly 250 years after
Samuel Adams
signed

the Declaration of Independence
and
the Articles of Confederation.

What Would Samuel Adams Think?

BLOG

CNN Anchor: 'Our Rights Do Not Come From God'

By Curtis Kalin | February 12, 2015 | 12:30pm EST

The constitutionality of same-sex marriage. That was the topic of a 2015 debate between Alabama Chief Justice Roy Moore and CNN anchor Chris Cuomo. When Chief Justice Moore took the position that rights cannot be handed down by men, Cuomo vociferously disagreed, declaring, "Our rights do not come from God, your honor, and you know that. They come from man. . . . That's your faith, that's my faith, but that's not our country. Our laws come from collective agreement and compromise."

Perhaps Cuomo's debate preparation failed to include a review of the Declaration of Independence:

"We hold these truths to be self-evident, that all men are created equal, **that they are endowed by their Creator with certain unalienable Rights, that among these are Life, Liberty and the pursuit of Happiness**. — That to secure these rights, Governments are instituted among Men, deriving their just powers from the consent of the governed . . . ."

https://www.cnsnews.com/blog/curtis-kalin/ cnn-anchor-our-rights-do-not-come-god.

Francis Dana
(1743-1811)

Signer of the Articles of Confederation

Highest Office Attained:
Representative in Congress; Chief Justice of Massachusetts

Religious Affiliation:
Congregationalist

T he great-grandson of an English immigrant, Francis Dana's religious and cultural heritage remains a subject of uncertainty. Some believe the Dana family originated in Italy and fled religious persecution. They arrived in England via France, where they were of like mind with the Huguenots; the Huguenots were followers of a new Protestant "Reformed" religion that came to follow the teachings of John Calvin. Regardless, Dana's great-grandfather, Richard Dana, was christened in Collegiate Church in Manchester, Lancashire, England in 1617, thus giving Dana some Anglican roots. But after Richard emigrated to Massachusetts in 1640, he and his wife, Anne Bullard Dana, were known to be active members of the First (Congregational) Church of Cambridge. Grandfather Daniel Dana was similarly active in the church; he was appointed in 1736 to a church committee that, according to Rev. Abiel Holmes (later, the church pastor), consisted "of wise, prudent and blameless Christians, a kind of privy council to the minister." The minister then was Rev. Nathaniel Appleton. The stage thus became set for later descriptions of Francis Dana as a "Puritan."

Francis Dana was born to Daniel's son, Richard Dana, and Lydia Trowbridge Dana in 1743. He was educated at the famed Boston Latin School, which had been established under the influence of Rev. John Cotton, a puritan reformist minister known today as the father of Congregationalism. There, Dana was schooled under the tutelage of Headmaster John Lovell, whose sole requirement for admission was the ability to read verses from the Bible. Dana followed the pathway to Harvard College that had been forged by his lawyer-father and his elder brother, Edmund. Graduating in 1762, he then studied law under his uncle, Judge Edmund Trowbridge, and met Elizabeth Ellery, whose mother was a sister of Mrs. Trowbridge. Elizabeth's family belonged to the Second Congregational Church of Newport, Rhode Island. Like the Danas, Judge Trowbridge was a member of the First (Congregational) Church of Cambridge; he also founded at Harvard the Alfred Professorship of Natural Religion, Moral Philosophy, and Civil Polity. He is said to have been the last of the judges of the Supreme Court of Massachusetts to have worn the scarlet robe and powdered wig.

In 1773, Dana and Elizabeth married, and for a time they made their home with the Trowbridges. Dana became an active member of the Sons of Liberty and a confidant of John Adams. The following year, he traveled to England, representing the Massachusetts patriots; he took with him confidential letters to Benjamin Franklin. During Dana's time away, Rev. Appleton met with many Cambridge families at Dana's home to comfort and pray with them over the growing political uncertainties. Unlike his brother, Edmund, who also had traveled to England, Dana returned to Massachusetts after two years; Edmund instead married into a family of English nobility, took holy orders in the Church of England, and remained in that country.

In 1776, Dana was elected to both the Massachusetts Provincial Council and the Continental Congress, and his father-in-law, William Ellery of Rhode Island, signed the Declaration of Independence. In 1778, Dana signed the Articles of Confederation (as did Ellery), and spent several months at Valley Forge with George Washington. For the next several years, he served on diplomatic missions, including as Minister to Russia, taking with him a young future president, John Quincy Adams, as his secretary. In 1783, upon his return to America, Dana was re-elected to the Continental Congress; he was also appointed by Governor John Hancock to the Massachusetts Supreme Court, where he later became chief justice. Due to his judicial duties, he declined appointment in 1787 to the convention that framed the new Constitution of the United States, but he later served as a member of the Massachusetts convention that ratified it.

In 1811, Francis Dana died, as he had lived, a puritan lawyer. John Adams served as a pall bearer at his funeral.

In His Own Words:

Letter from Francis Dana to John Adams (celebrating the Declaration of Independence)
July 28, 1776[1]

> The People shall be made the source of all Power and Authority within the State. A participation of foreign Influence has ever been distructive of the Harmony Peace and Happiness of Societies while it continued; too often has it ended in a final Tyranny. **That we are free from this political poison *at last*, I thank God.** The shackles are now thrown away, and I doubt not the public mind will expand sufficiently to comprehend the grand objects presenting themselves to our view. Our former subordinate state cramped the Genius of this people. It had its bounds marked out, beyond which it was afraid to ramble forth. It may now range with freedom.

Journal Entry by Francis Dana (regarding diplomatic voyage with John Adams)
November 26, 1779[2]

> There were about thirty souls on board the *Chasse Marce*, one a woman. **Heaven protect them from further harm.**

Journal Entry by Francis Dana (upon arriving in Spain)
December 8, 1779[3]

> Before we entered the harbour we were obliged to set a third pump to work, and for the greater part of the time since her arrival in the harbour, four pumps

have been going, and our Ship there makes 7 1/2 feet of water in one hour. **We have great reason therefore to thank Heaven for our safe arrival** in this place tho it will occasion us a tour of not less than 900 miles from hence to Paris.

Recounting by Francis Dana of Travels (while on diplomatic mission to Spain) c. December 31, 1779[4]

From Galiego to Lebraro you almost constantly rise, for seven Leagues, mountain after mountain and when you have ascended to the pinacle (Lebraro) **it may be said you enter the region of the Gods. When we passed a mountain about two miles short of Lebraro, on all sides there opened upon us a prospect the most sublime imagination can conceive, or I believe, the world exhibits; it must be seen to be felt; here was such a magnificent display of the great works of Nature's God as filled the soul with astonishment and veneration.** The Day was fine, and the Sun shone in all his glory, and was about to close the scene. Having happily arrived to this most remarkable point of this World, we closed the year this evening with joy and gratitude. The next morning (January 1st 1780) . . . we begun our progress down the mountains. The first we descended was very long, steep, and difficult of passage; the road being rockey, and running upon the edge of enormous precipices, that accident of overturning a carriage or starting of a Mule, on *one* side, wou'd have hurled us to the bottom of the Creation.

Letter from Francis Dana to His Father-in-Law, William Ellery (referring to Benjamin Franklin) March 16, 1780[5]

I presume you will have new work carved out for you, upon the arrival of Dr. Lee and Mr. Izard, both of whom will shortly embark for America. Their weapons, I understand, are pointed not only against Mr. Dean, but at the head of the *old Gentleman*. In these disputes we take no part here, being determined not to entangle ourselves in their animosities. I have however my private opinion regarding them. **I hope in God, Congress will not again be thrown into parties about this business, but that an inquiry into it, will be conducted with deliberation, and without respect to persons.**

Letter from Francis Dana to Judge Theophilus Parsons 1780[6]

No country, it appears to me, can be more benefitted in future by this than America, **whose wisdom I hope in God it will be** to hold herself free from the entangled system of Europe and all their wars.

Letter from Francis Dana to James Lovell (regarding rumors in European chancellories) August 23, 1780[7]

I hear many curious doctrines & Prophecies among the Politicians. One set says, America will quit France. Another that France and Spain will desert America, a third, that Spain will abandon France and America. A fourth, that America has the Interest of almost all Europe against her, a fifth, that America will become the great manufacturing Country, and thus distress Europe, a sixth, that America will become a military and naval power that will be terrible to Europe. To such profound Politicians, I would say, **America will be that great and respectable Power, for which Heaven has bitten her, in spight of all who fear, or hate her.**

Letter from Francis Dana to Count Vergennes November 1780[8]

> **May Heaven preserve us from Kings, Princes, and Stadtholders. The People are the best Guardians of their own Liberties and Interests.**

Letter from Francis Dana to John Adams January 1781[9]

> I cannot yet learn what assistance American may hope for in the approaching campaign. **I pray God she may not be again flattered by any false hopes.** Let our Allies give essential Aid, or withdraw all they have sent: When our Country will see they must work out their own political Salvation.

Letter from Francis Dana to John Adams (regarding effort to seek recognition by Austria) March 16, 1783[10]

> You have conferred additional obligations upon, or to express myself otherwise, you have rendered additional services to your Country by breaking to pieces Chains forged to hold it in a state of subserviency to the Interests of others. **God & your Country will approve the measure.**

Letter from Francis Dana to John Adams (regarding efforts as Minister to Russia)
May 1, 1783[11]

> The time of my departure will depend upon the Answer I may receive to my Memorial. I have no intention to sacrifice another Year of my life, in the manner I have already done near Two Years of it in this Country. **I hope Almighty God has created me for some more useful purpose.** If not, I shou'd be ashamed of my Existence.

Letter from Francis Dana to John Adams (while in St. Petersbourg, referring to John Quincy Adams)
July 29, 1783[12]

> **And may God grant I may soon have the pleasure of meeting you in our Country, and all Friends well — I will take Master John's things under my own care.**

Statement by Francis Dana (regarding the death of George Washington)
February 1800[13]

> **The late afflictive bereavement with which it hath pleased the Ruler of the Universe to visit our Nation,** has been generally received with that sincere & deep sorrow which super eminent usefulness demanded from every friend of our Country.

> Its brightest luminary is extinguished. The noblest Millar in the Temple of American Liberty is removed: And the Rock of our Union seems rent in twain.

> Not to see that a new danger threatens *us*, our Country would prove a political blindness. To dispair

of the Commonwealth without a great effort to save it, [would be] a disgraceful timidity.

Letter from Francis Dana to John Quincy Adams (regarding the death of his wife, Elizabeth Ellery Dana) September 6, 1807[14]

I have now to inform you that it hath pleased God who gave her to me as the greatest comfort of my life, to take her away, leaving myself, & our Children overwhelmed with the affliction at our irreparable loss. To me she was everything a wife could be. She died this day week, the 30th of Aug.: about 3:55 P.M., after a painful sickness, having completed the 56 year of her age on the 24 of the month, as she did the 34th of our connubial connection on the 5th.

What follows is a
summary of an article
from contemporary American life . . .

nearly 250 years after
Francis Dana
signed

the Articles of Confederation.

What Would Francis Dana Think?

FAITH · Published February 7, 2016

'God Bless America' signs fly after atheist group targets post office banner

By | Fox News

After the tragic events of September 11, 2001, patriotic employees of the post office in Pittsburg, Kansas proudly erected a banner: "God Bless America." Fifteen years later, the Freedom From Religion Foundation filed suit. The banner was removed.

Many Pittsburg residents were incensed. A local business, Jake's Fireworks, printed twelve hundred yard signs and three hundred banners proclaiming, "God Bless America." It offered them for free, and within forty-five minutes all were claimed.

Said Senator Jerry Moran (R-KS), the Constitution guarantees "freedom of religion, not freedom from religion." He added, "It is outrageous that some would aim to divide a community over a banner that has been proudly displayed since Sept. 11, 2001. I commend the Pittsburg community for rejecting this decision and I stand with them."

https://www.foxnews.com/us/god-bless-america-signs-fly-after-atheist-group-targets-post-office-banner.

Elbridge Gerry
(1744-1814)

*Signer of the Declaration of Independence and
the Articles of Confederation*

Highest Office Attained:
Vice President of the United States

Religious Affiliation:
Congregationalist; Episcopalian

E lbridge Gerry was born in 1744 in the oceanside town of Marblehead, Massachusetts. His father, Captain Thomas Gerry, was a very successful merchant and sea captain who had immigrated from Newton Abbott, Devonshire, England in 1730. His mother, Elizabeth Greenleaf Gerry, was the daughter of another very successful Boston merchant, and the great-granddaughter of Edmond Greenleaf, an immigrant from England in 1632.

The Gerry family faithfully attended the First Congregational Church in Marblehead, then pastored by Rev. John Barnard. Gerry was tutored as a child, and enrolled at Harvard College at the age of fourteen. There, he encountered another Marblehead Congregationalist, Rev. Edward Holyoke, who had been appointed president of Harvard in 1737. Years before, Rev. Holyoke and Rev. Barnard each had sought to assume the ministry of the First Congregational Church; upon Rev. Barnard's selection, Rev. Holyoke and a number of parishioners withdrew from the church to form the Second Congregational Church of Marblehead. Rev. Holyoke served as pastor there until his appointment to the Harvard presidency.

By the age of twenty, Gerry had earned both undergraduate and graduate degrees from Harvard, arguing in his master's thesis that the colonies should resist the recently-passed Stamp Act. These early political views laid the foundation for Gerry's later public service to the unfolding new nation. After college, Gerry returned to Marblehead, joining his father and two older brothers in the family business; this earned Gerry a considerable fortune. He also became increasingly active in the patriot movement, and, in 1771, was elected to the Massachusetts General Court and then to its successor, the Provincial Congress. There, he became a staunch ally of John and Samuel Adams. In 1775,

Gerry was elected to the Continental Congress, where he was regarded as one of the boldest spokesmen for independence. He proudly cast a vote in favor of, and signed, the Declaration of Independence; he also signed the Articles of Confederation that initially governed the new nation.

After a brief hiatus, Gerry returned to the Congress in 1783. While serving there in New York, he fell in love with a much younger Ann Thompson; Ann was the daughter of shipping magnate James Thompson and Catharine Walton Thompson. James had immigrated from Ireland, and Ann was educated there. Catharine's parents, Jacob Walton and Maria Beekman Walton, both came from prominent colonial families in New York. They had raised their family in the Dutch Reformed Church in New York City, giving Ann some historical and cultural affinity with James, whose own "Irish" family had originated in Holland.

Elbridge and Ann Thompson Gerry were married, however, at Trinity Episcopal Church in New York in 1786; Gerry converted to Episcopalianism. He returned to Massachusetts, where he purchased a former Tory estate in Cambridge and served in the state legislature; Ann bore him ten children. In 1787, he was elected as a delegate to the Constitutional Convention; he favored amending the Articles of Confederation, but initially opposed (and did not sign) the proposed constitution because he believed it provided too much power to the national government and because it lacked a bill of rights. He was again elected to the Congress; there, he supported the new United States Constitution and was instrumental in drafting what became the Bill of Rights. His proposed language, "[N]o religious doctrine shall be established by law," contributed toward what became the First Amendment. He later served as an envoy to France and then as governor of Massachusetts. It was during his tenure in that position that a redistricting bill would forever tarnish his name with the moniker of the "gerrymander."

In 1812, Gerry was nominated to fill a vacancy in the office of Vice President of the United States. He served briefly in that position under President James Madison, but died while en route to preside over the Senate in 1814. He was buried in the Congressional Cemetery in Washington DC, where a monument was erected bearing words that Gerry spoke and tried to live by: "It is the duty of every man, though he may have but one day to live, to devote that day to the good of his country."

In His Own Words:

Letter from Elbridge Gerry to His Wife, Ann Thompson Gerry August 14, 1787[1]

> I am very anxious for the Health of my dearest Girl and her lovely Infant in consequence of your letter of the 12th recd this Day. . . . I was writing to you on Sunday Morning, but I should have Spent the Day in Festivity, had I known it had been your Birth Day. **God Grant my lovely Nancy [then a term of affection], You may Live to see birth Days repeated, until Satiated with the Happiness of this Life.**

Observations, **by Elbridge Gerry 1788**[2]

> Self defence is a primary law of nature, which no subsequent law of society can abolish; this primaeval principle, **the immediate gift of the Creator, obliges every one to remonstrate against the strides of ambition, and a wanton lust of domination, and to resist the first approaches of tyranny, which at this day threaten to sweep away the rights for which the brave sons of America have fought with an heroism scarcely paralleled even in ancient republicks.**

Proclamation for a Day of Thanksgiving and Praise, by
Governor Elbridge Gerry
October 24, 1810[3]

> [W]ith one heart and voice we may prostrate
> ourselves at the throne of heavenly grace and
> present to our Great Benefactor sincere and
> unfeigned thanks for His infinite goodness and
> mercy towards us from our birth to the present
> moment for having above all things illuminated us
> by the Gospel of Jesus Christ, presenting to our
> view the happy prospect of a blessed immortality.

Proclamation for a Day of Fasting and Prayer, by Governor
Elbridge Gerry
March 13, 1811[4]

> And for our unparalleled ingratitude to that
> Adorable Being Who has seated us in a land
> irradiated by the cheering beams of the Gospel
> of Jesus Christ . . . let us fall prostrate before
> offended Deity, confess sincerely and penitently
> our manifold sins and our unworthiness of the
> least of His Divine favors, fervently implore His
> pardon through the merits of our mediator.

Proclamation for a Day of Public Thanksgiving and Praise, by
Governor Elbridge Gerry
October 22, 1811[5]

COMMONWEALTH OF MASSACHUSETTS
By His Excellency,
Elbridge Gerry, Esquire,
Governor of the Commonwealth of Massachusetts
A PROCLAMATION
FOR A DAY OF
PUBLIC THANKSGIVING AND PRAISE.

"The Lord reigneth, let the earth," let all creation, "rejoice." The innumerable blessings conferred by our divine benefactor, during the present and in every preceding year, on the inhabitants of this Commonwealth, proclaim their duty, to offer to Him, at all times, with unbounded gratitude, their cheerful acknowledgments of His perpetual favors. To implore, with the deepest humility, His pardon of their multiplied and aggravated offenses, to resolve, with unfeigned sincerity, on an implicit obedience to His sovereign will, and to supplicate, with true devotion, His indispensable aid, in every religious, moral, and lawful pursuit.

Impressed by these *considerations*, and by the usage of our venerable Ancestors, at the close of harvest, I have thought fit, by the advice of the council, to appoint, and I do hereby appoint THURSDAY, the TWENTY-FIRST of NOVEMBER next, to be a day of Public THANKSGIVING, PRAISE, and PRAYER, throughout this Commonwealth; calling on and requesting the ministers and people of every religious denomination, to meet on that day in their respective sanctuaries, that with unanimity and fervor, we may present our unfeigned praises for all the mercies we have received of our Bountiful Creator, who has continued to us the inestimable blessings of the gospel of Jesus Christ, blessings not confined to time, but extended to *eternity*, who has confirmed to us our federal and State constitutions, which secure the enjoyment of our lives, liberties and property, who continues to bless us with a National Government and Administration, whose wisdom, virtue, and firmness have not been circumvented, corrupted or appalled by the arts, seductions, or threats of foreign or domestic foes, but whose patriotic efforts have uniformly and manifestly resulted from an ardent desire to promote the public welfare and happiness, who has not punished our ungrateful murmurs, discontents and other crimes, as He has those of distant nations, by war and its dire effects; but **has preserved to us peace, the greatest of national blessings, who has favored us with a Clergy, (with few exceptions,) whose conduct, is influenced by the mild, benign and benevolent principles of the Gospel; and whose example is a constant admonition to such pastors and professors of Christianity, as are too much under the guidance of passion, prejudice, and worldly delusion,** Who has enabled us from unavoidable spoliations to derive permanent benefits, by gradually diminishing our dependence on foreign markets, for necessary supplies; by rapidly increasing our manufactures thereof; and by thus preventing in future the plunder of such property by avaricious nations, who has not visited us, as He has other countries, with plague, pestilence or famine; but has kindly preserved to us a great degree of health, and crowned with plenty the labors of our industrious husbandmen, Who has increased the martial ardor and discipline of our militia, and enables us to smile at the menaces of mighty potentates, **Who continues to us the due administration of justice, the full and free exercise of our civil religious rights, and the numerous blessing which have resulted from them, Who has prospered in a remarkable degree our Schools, Academies and Colleges; those inestimable sources of public information and happiness,** who has protected so great a portion of the property of our merchants, when exposed to the depredations of perfidious governments, Who has granted success to our enterprising fishermen, prospered our ingenious mechanics, and loaded us with His boundless munificence.

And whilst with circumscribed views, we contemplate that Incomprehensible Being whose infinite wisdom and power are displayed in the creation, formation, combination and government of all material substances, animate or inanimate, minute or massive, and in the order and offices prescribed for and performed by the various parts of the Universe, Whose omnipresence is excluded, by neither spirit or matter; but fills all creation and space, let us acknowledge our dependence on His infinite goodness and mercy, for every moment of our existence; consider that all our thoughts, words and actions are open to His view; be convinced that in His presence we are mere nullities; and approach Him with solemn awe and reverence, whilst we humbly solicit, that He will freely pardon our numberless sins and iniquities, that He will be pleased to continue to us the unmerited favors, spiritual and temporal, which we now enjoy, that He will extend throughout the globe, the celestial blessing of the gospel of Christ, that He will place our National and State governments under His wise and holy protection; and direct them always to pursue the true interest and happiness of the people, that He will revive, increase, and protect our commerce, and continue His smiles on our husbandmen, manufacturers, mechanics, fishermen, and every description and individual of the inhabitants of this State and Nation, that He will preserve in health, and long continue the valuable life of the President of United States, that He will restore to the citizens of this commonwealth those indispensable sources of enjoyment and happiness, their wonted benevolence and affection for each other, long interrupted by political, casual, and uncontrollable events, that He will promote the progress of useful arts and sciences, that He will declare to the mighty warriors and destroyers of human felicity, "thus far has thou gone, but thou shalt go no farther," and, that health, peace, and happiness may pervade all nations of the earth.

And I do earnestly recommend to the Citizens of the Commonwealth to enjoy this festival rationally, and to abstain from unnecessary labor, and from recreations inconsistent with their duty on that day.

Given at the council chamber in Boston this twenty-second day of October, in the year of our Lord one thousand eight hundred and eleven, and in the thirty-sixth year of the Independence of the United States.

E. GERRY.

By His Excellency the Governor, with the advice and consent of the Council.

BENJAMIN HOMANS, *Secretary.*

God Save the Commonwealth of Massachusetts.

Proclamation for a Day of Fasting and Prayer, by Governor
Elbridge Gerry
March 6, 1812[6]

> And deeply impressed with a scene of our
> unparalleled ingratitude, let us contemplate the
> blessings which have flowed from the unlimited
> grave and favor of offended Deity, that we are still
> permitted to enjoy the first of Heaven's blessings:
> the Gospel of Jesus Christ.

What follows is a
summary of an article
from contemporary American life . . .

nearly 250 years after
Elbridge Gerry
signed

the Declaration of Independence
and
the Articles of Confederation.

What Would Elbridge Gerry Think?

Long-standing cross removed by DNR from state land after complaint

Updated Jan 30, 2019; Posted May 15, 2018

By **Taylor DesOrmeau | tdesorme@mlive.com**

Since 1938, churches affiliated with the Grass Lake Ministerial Association in Jackson County, Michigan have gathered every year for an Easter service in the Waterloo Recreation Area. In the early years, they brought with them a temporary cross, and in 1950 they erected a permanent one.

But in 2018, sixty-eight years later, the Michigan Association of Civil Rights Activists complained to the Michigan Department of Natural Resources. The problem? Waterloo Recreation Area is state-owned land. The simple white cross has now been removed from its long-standing location on Sackrider Hill.

https://www.mlive.com/news/jackson/2018/05/longstanding_cross_removed_fro.html.

Nathaniel Gorham
(1738-1796)

Signer of the United States Constitution

Highest Office Attained:
President of the United States in Congress Assembled

Religious Affiliation:
Congregationalist

Nathaniel Gorham grew up in Charlestown, Massachusetts, the son of Nathaniel Gorham Sr., a ship captain of modest means. His ancestor, Ralph Gorham, had emigrated with his wife and children from Benefield, Northamptonshire, England in 1635. Among Ralph's children was another young, future ship captain, John Gorham, Nathaniel's great-great-grandfather; John was baptized in the Benefield Parish (Anglican) Church but raised as a Puritan in America. Nathaniel's roots also extend to the *Mayflower*, as Captain John married Desire Howland; her puritan parents and grandparents had earlier traversed the seas aboard that renowned vessel in 1620, settling in Plymouth, Massachusetts. Three generations later, Nathaniel was baptized and raised in the family's Congregationalist traditions at the First Church in Charlestown.

As a child, Nathaniel's public education included the Latin and Greek language instruction that qualified him for university admission. However, at the age of fifteen, he was instead sent to New London, Connecticut, where he served an apprenticeship with merchant Nathaniel Coffin and learned the export/import business. In 1759, he returned to Charlestown and opened his own successful business.

Meanwhile, Nathaniel's brother, John Gorham, attended Harvard College with Charles Coffin; this led to the introduction of the Gorham brothers' sister, Mary Gorham, to Charles's brother, Paul. The two subsequently wed and moved to Buxton, Maine, where Rev. Paul Coffin pastored the local Congregational church. Preceding Rev. Paul as Congregational church leaders were his grandfather, Hon. Nathaniel Coffin, and great-grandfather, Tristram Coffin; both were deacons at the First (Congregational) Church of Newbury, Massachusetts. And his uncle, Rev. Enoch Coffin, was pastor of the Congregational church in Concord. How precisely this branch of the Coffin family was related to the Nathaniel Coffin for whom Nathaniel Gorham apprenticed in New London is unclear. Indeed, the Coffin family was greatly fragmented during the revolutionary period, some being puritanical Congregationalists, others becoming Quakers, and still others who were staunch Anglican loyalists; the latter most notably included a Nathaniel Coffin who served as receiver general and cashier (tax collector) of his majesty's customs at the port of Boston.

In 1763, Gorham wed Rebecca Call, daughter of baker Caleb Call and Rebecca Stimson, and a maternal descendant of Rev. John Maverick; Rev. Maverick was an Anglican priest, who, while still in England, joined with others of puritan leanings to form a Congregational church seeking religious freedom in America. Rev. Maverick performed daily religious services during their ten-week voyage to America, and became one of the original pastors of the new Congregational church in Dorchester. His son, Elias, became a prominent early member of the First (Congregational) Church in Charlestown, and five generations later, the Gorhams also raised their nine children in the Congregational church. Son Stephen became a founder of Harvard Church, also known as the Second Congregational Church of Charlestown; daughter Elizabeth also joined that church. Son Benjamin later represented Massachusetts in Congress. One of daughter Ann's children later married Charles Francis Adams, the son of future President John Quincy Adams.

In 1771, Gorham was elected to the colonial legislature, where he served in both houses, including as Speaker of the lower house; there he developed a reputation as an ardent patriot. He served in the Provincial Congress, and during the revolutionary war put his business and administrative talents to use organizing military logistics and manpower as a member of the Massachusetts board of war. In 1779, he was a delegate to the Massachusetts constitutional convention, playing an important role in drafting the Massachusetts constitution. In 1782, he was selected as a delegate to the Continental Congress, where he again rose to a position of leadership, serving for a time under the Articles of Confederation as the eighth President of the United States in Congress Assembled.

Gorham later served as a judge of the Middlesex County Court of Common Pleas, and on the Governor's Council, advising the state's chief executive. In 1787, he was a delegate to the Constitutional Convention, where he approved and affixed his signature to the United States Constitution. He advocated for states to ratify the Constitution by conventions, rather than through state legislatures, because some legislatures excluded clergymen, and he believed that clergyman "are generally friends to good Government" and that "their services were found to be valuable in the formation & establishment of the Constitution of Massachusetts." He later was instrumental in securing the ratification of the Constitution by the state of Massachusetts. Gorham died in 1796, in death as in life a puritan Congregationalist.

In His Own Words:

Letter from Town Clerk of Charlestown to Committee of Correspondence of the Town of Boston, Drafted by Nathaniel Gorham, Samuel Sweetser, and Richard Devens December 28, 1772[1]

> [I]t gives us great pleasure to receive the thoughts of our brethren, upon the situation of public affairs at this alarming season. We agree with them, that our rights are in many instances broken in upon and invaded, and that it is our desire and intention to cooperate with our brethren in every part of the province, in all proper and legal measure, for the recovery of such as are wrested from us, and for the security of such as we still enjoy, **sincerely hoping, that the all-wise God will direct to such measures as shall be effectual for that purpose**.

Letter from the Inhabitants of the Town of Charlestown, Massachusetts to the Inhabitants of the Town of Boston,

Massachusetts, Drafted by Nathaniel Gorham, Seth Sweetser, and Isaac Foster Jr.
August 12, 1774[2]

> A most alarming crisis in our public affairs is at hand, and **most earnestly we pray the Author and Giver of every good and perfect gift, to endue you with that wisdom which is profitable to direct to such measures as may be most for His glory and the lasting happiness of us and our posterity. . . .**

> Persevere in the glorious cause of liberty you are engaged in. You may be sure of all the assistance we can give you. **Let us all, as is our duty, unite in constant, fervent prayers to Almighty God, our father's God, who is wonderful in council and mighty in working, for his direction to take, and assistance** in prosecuting such measures as have a tendency to extricate us out of our difficulties, and then we may humbly hope our endeavors will be crowned with success.

Massachusetts Constitution of 1780, Drafted in Part by Nathaniel Gorham[3]

> **Any person chosen governor, or lieutenant-governor, counsellor, senator, or representative, and accepting the trust, shall before he proceed to execute the duties of his place or office, take, make and subscribe the following declaration, viz. "I, _____, do declare, that I believe the Christian religion, and have a firm persuasion of its truth."**

Resolution of Massachusetts Legislature, Signed by Nathaniel Gorham, Speaker
July 4, 1782[4]

COMMONWEALTH OF MASSACHUSETTS, IN SENATE, July 4th 1782.

Whereas the King of Great Britain, despairing to effect the subjugation of the United States of North America by menaces and the violence of a cruel and vindictive war, entertains the idea of effecting his purpose by artfully disseminating the seeds of disunion among ourselves, and detaching some of these United States, or some bodies of men therein, from the common cause, and from a connection with our illustrious ally, —

Resolved unanimously, That every idea of deviating from the treaty of the United States with his most Christian Majesty in the smallest article, or of listening to the proposals of accommodation with the Court of Great Britain in a partial and separate capacity, shall forever be rejected by us with the greatest abhorrence and detestation. And as we engaged in the present war with a solemn determination to secure, if possible. the **rich blessings of freedom** to the present and future generations, — a determination which we are firmly persuaded was **suitable to the dignity of our nation and the precepts of our religion**, and which we therefore reflect on with the highest satisfaction, — so will we persevere in our utmost exertions to support the just and necessary war we are engaged in; and, **with the aid of that almighty and most merciful Being who has ever appeared for us in our distress, we will prosecute the war with unremitting ardor, until the independence of the United States shall be fully recognized and established.**

Sent down for concurrence,
SAM. ADAMS, *President*.
IN THE HOUSE OF REPRESENTATIVES,
July 4th, 1782.
Read and unanimously concurred in,
NATHANIEL GORHAM, *Speaker*.
Approved: JOHN HANCOCK.

What follows is a
summary of an article
from contemporary American life . . .

nearly 250 years after
Nathaniel Gorham
signed

the United States Constitution.

What Would Nathaniel Gorham Think?

'Merry Christmas' Sign Removed After Complaint In Marshfield

By Bill Shields, WBZ-TV

By Bill Shields   December 18, 2014 at 6:38 pm   Filed Under: Bill Shields, Christmas, DPW, Merry Christmas, Marshfield, Sign

In Marshfield, Massachusetts, the local school district decided that it would be a good idea to change the name of the school's "Christmas Break" to "Holiday Break." Some residents disagreed with the change. Said one, "It's a Christmas holiday, it's a national holiday, not some random holiday."

So, other residents, who happened to work for the city's department of public works, decided to put an electronic sign on a friend's property, where it would be visible on the main road through town. Its message: "Merry Christmas." After a complaint, Marshfield officials decided that the sign had to come down. A building commissioner claimed that the problem was not with the sign's message, but rather that "the sign has to conform to size regulations, among other factors."

Next year, residents plan to erect a large banner. Said one DPW worker, "There are fewer regulations about banners."

https://boston.cbslocal.com/2014/12/18/ merry-christmas-sign-removed-after-complaint-in-marshfield/.

John Hancock
(1737-1793)

*Signer of the Declaration of Independence and
the Articles of Confederation*

Highest Office Attained:
President of the United States in Congress Assembled

Religious Affiliation:
Congregationalist

J ohn Hancock, whose iconic signature most prominently adorns the Declaration of Independence, was born into a distinguished family of Congregational ministers in 1737. A century earlier, his ancestor, puritan farmer Nathaniel Hancock, had fled the religious persecution of the Church of England in his native Padiham, Lancashire, England; he settled in Cambridge, Massachusetts in 1634.

Signer Hancock's father, Rev. John Hancock, had become pastor of the First (Congregational) Church in Braintree in 1726, at the age of only twenty-four. There, he baptized, among others, a young future president, John Adams. Rev. Hancock's father, also of the same name as the signer, was himself a minister of the Congregational church, pastoring in Lexington beginning in 1698 and for the next fifty-five years. Grandfather John, whose own shoemaker-father, a second Nathaniel Hancock, had served as a deacon at the First (Congregational) Church in Cambridge, attained such a respected stature that he bore the informal title, "Bishop." In 1700, Bishop Hancock married Elizabeth Clarke; she was the daughter of Rev. Thomas Clarke of Chelmsford and the maternal granddaughter of Rev. Edward Bulkley of Concord. It is thus perhaps not surprising that Rev. Hancock, father of the signer, would follow the well-worn family pathway into the ministry. Indeed, Rev. Hancock's elder brother, Ebenezer, had earlier joined the ministry as co-pastor with his father, Bishop Hancock, in Lexington; and his two sisters, Elizabeth and Lucy, each married ministers, Rev. Jonathan Bowman of Dorchester and Rev. Nicholas Bowes of Bedford.

Ebenezer died, however, in 1740, leaving Bishop Hancock to pastor on in Lexington without him; and any hopes that Rev. John may have had for his son John to follow in the family footsteps may have been dashed by his own untimely passing in 1744.

Hancock, the signer, was then only seven years old. Upon Rev. John's passing, young John moved initially to Lexington, where he lived in the parsonage with Bishop Hancock and Elizabeth. But, concerned for Hancock's future, and aware of his own increasing age, Bishop Hancock sent his grandson to Boston to live with a third son — Hancock's uncle, Thomas Hancock — and his wife, Lydia Henchman, who were themselves childless. Although he regularly visited his grandparents at the parsonage, Hancock was from that time raised by his aunt and uncle, who, as a successful businessman, had become one of the wealthiest men in the colonies.

Now living in Boston, Hancock enrolled at the celebrated Boston Latin School, which had been established under the influence of Rev. John Cotton, a puritan reformist minister known today as the father of Congregationalism. He attended during the tenure of Headmaster John Lovell, whose sole requirement for admission was the ability to read verses from the Bible. After later graduating from Harvard College in 1754 at the age of seventeen, and spending four years in England studying commerce, Hancock took over the family business upon his uncle's death; he inherited one of the largest fortunes in Massachusetts, a fortune that Hancock would later tap to help fund and provide supplies for the revolutionary army headed by General (and future President) George Washington.

Hancock was elected in 1765 as a selectman in Boston, and in 1766 to the Massachusetts House of Representatives. With the passage by Great Britain of the Stamp Act and other oppressive measures, Hancock became increasingly active in the patriot movement, joining with Samuel Adams and the Sons of Liberty in opposing the British. In 1774, Hancock was elected president of the newly-formed Massachusetts Provincial Congress, a body that deemed itself autonomous of the motherland. Hancock and Adams soon became the most wanted men of British authorities. As they hid out in Hancock's Lexington home, it was Paul Revere's warning, by his famous midnight ride, that thwarted their impending arrest.

Hancock was elected to the Continental Congress, and in 1775 became its president. In that capacity, he became the first to sign the Declaration of Independence, boldly and prominently affixing his now-famous signature in defiance of British oppression. That same year, he wed Dorothy Quincy; she was a member of a prominent Boston family whose members included Dorothy's great-grandfather, Rev. Josiah Flynt, and Abigail Adams, John Adams's wife. The Quincys, like the Hancocks, were devout Christians, active in Congregational church affairs since puritan ancestor Edmund Quincy joined the First (Congregational) Church in 1633. Hancock and Dorothy had two children, neither of whom lived to adulthood. He served as governor of Massachusetts from 1780 to 1785 and from 1785 until his death in 1793 at the age of fifty-six.

In His Own Words:

Address to the Inhabitants of the Massachusetts Bay, by the Second Provincial Congress of Massachusetts, John Hancock, President
February 9, 1775[1]

When a people entitled to that freedom, which your ancestors have nobly preserved, as the highest inheritance of their children, are invaded by the hand of oppression, and trampled on by the merciless feet of tyranny, **resistance** is so far from being criminal, that it **becomes the christian and social duty of each individual**.

When you see the lives of your fellow men, in other nations, sported with and destroyed, and their estates confiscated by their prince, only to gratify the caprice, ambition, or avarice of a tyrant, **you ought to entertain and cultivate in your minds, the highest gratitude to the Supreme Being, of this having placed you under such a form of government, as,** when duly administered, gives the meanest peasant the same security in his life and property, as his sovereign has in his crown. . . .

Your conduct hitherto, under the severest trials, has been worthy of you as men and christians, and, notwithstanding the pains that have been taken by your enemies, to inculcate the doctrines of non-resistance and passive obedience, and, by every art, to delude and terrify you, the whole continent of America has, this day, cause to rejoice in your firmness. We trust you will still continue steadfast, and having regard to the dignity of your characters as freemen, and those generous sentiments resulting from your natural and political connections, you will never submit your necks to the galling yoke of despotism prepared for you; but with a proper sense of your dependance on God, nobly defend those rights which Heaven gave, and no man ought to take from us.

Resolution for Day of Public Humiliation, Fasting, and Prayer, by the Second Provincial Congress of Massachusetts, John Hancock, President
April 15, 1775[2]

Whereas it hath pleased the righteous Sovereign of the universe, in just indignation against the sins of a people long blessed with inestimable privileges, civil and religious, to suffer the plots of wicked men, on both sides of the Atlantic, who for many years, have incessantly labored to sap the foundation of our public liberties, so far to succeed, that we see the New England colonies reduced to the ungracious alternative of a tame submission to a state of absolute vassalage to the will of a despotic minister, or of preparing themselves to defend, at the hazard of their lives, the inalienable rights of themselves and posterity against the avowed hostilities of their parent state, who openly threaten to wrest them from their hands, by fire and sword;

In circumstances dark as these, it becomes us, as men and christians, to reflect, that whilst every prudent measure should be taken to ward off the impending judgments, or prepare to act a proper part under them when they come; **at the same time, all confidence must be withheld from the means we use, and repose only on that God, who rules in the armies of heaven, and without whose blessing, the best human councils are but foolishness, and all created power vanity.**

It is the happiness of this church that when the powers of earth and hell combine against it, and those who should be nursing fathers become its persecutors, then the throne of grace is of the easiest access, and **its appeal thither is graciously invited by that Father of mercies, who has assured it that when his children ask bread he will not give them a stone.**

Therefore, **in compliance with the laudable practice of the people of God in all ages, with humble regard to the steps of Divine Providence** towards this oppressed, threatened, and endangered people, and especially in obedience to the command of Heaven, that binds us to call on him in the day of trouble.

Resolved, That it be, and hereby is, recommended to the good people of this colony, of all denominations, that Thursday, the eleventh day of May next, be set apart as a **day of public humiliation, fasting, and prayer;** that a total abstinence from servile labor and recreation be observed, and **all their**

religious assemblies solemnly convened, to
humble themselves before God, under the heavy
judgments felt and feared, to confess the sins they
have deserved them; to implore the forgiveness
of all our transgressions, a spirit of repentance
and reformation, and a blessing on the husbandry,
manufactures, and other lawful employments
of this people; and especially, that the union of
the American colonies in defence of their rights,
for which, hitherto, we desire to thank Almighty
God, may be preserved and confirmed; that
the Provincial, and especially the Continental
Congresses, may be directed to such measures
as God will countenance: that the people of Great
Britain and their rulers may have their eyes opened to
discern the things that shall make for the peace of the
nation and all its connections: and that America may
soon behold a gracious interposition of Heaven, for
the redress of her many grievances, the restoration
of all her invaded liberties, and their security to the
latest generations.

Ordered, That the foregoing be copied, authenticated,
and sent to all the religious assemblies in this colony.

Letter from John Hancock to His Fiancée, Dorothy Quincy May 7, 1775[3]

I beg you will write me to acquaint me with every
circumstance relative to that dear aunt of mine. Write
lengthy and often. . . . Pray let me hear from you by
every post. **God bless you, my dear girl**[.]

Letter from John Hancock, President of Congress, to General George Washington
September 8, 1776[4]

> My most ardent and incessant wishes attend you, that you may still rise superiour to every difficulty, and that your great and virtuous exertions on behalf of your country may be crowned with that success which, from the Supreme Being's love of justice, and the righteousness of our cause, in conjunction with our own endeavours, it is not irrational to expect.

Public Statement by Governor John Hancock
November 2, 1780[5]

> Sensible of the importance of Christian piety and virtue to the order and happiness of a state, I cannot but earnestly commend to you every measure for their support and encouragement. . . . [T]he very existence of the republics . . . depend much upon the public institutions of religion.

***Proclamation For a Day of Thanksgiving*, by Governor John Hancock**
October 28, 1784[6]

> COMMONWEALTH OF MASSACHUSETTS.
> By His Excellency JOHN HANCOCK, Esquire, Governour of the Commonwealth of Massachusetts,
>
> A PROCLAMATION,
> For a Day of THANKSGIVING.
>
> *It being our indispensable duty as a people, in a public and religious manner, to acknowledge the preserving and Governing providence of Almighty God, and more*

especially to celebrate the Divine Goodness in the various blessings conferred upon us in the course of the year past.

I have therefore thought fit, with the advice and consent of the Council, to appoint, and do hereby appoint THURSDAY the Twenty-Fifth Day of NOVEMBER next, **to be religiously observed as a Day of THANKSGIVING** throughout this Commonwealth; hereby **calling upon Ministers and people of all denominations, in their several assemblies, to unite with grateful hearts in celebrating the Praises of Almighty GOD, of His great goodness and bounty vouchsafed to a sinful and unworthy people; particularly for the great and signal interpositions of His Providence in behalf of the United States in the course of the late contest**, and that after being rescued from the dangers and calamities of war; peace has been restored to us, and that our public affairs are in so promising and happy a situation; for granting to us a plentiful harvest in the great abundance of the fruits of the earth; for the general health enjoyed throughout this State during the course of the year, and preventing epidemical and mortal distempers from spreading among us; reviving our trade, navigation and fishery and protecting the same from the insults of Pirates and other disasters; for directing and succeeding our public Councils, and **above all for continuing to us the light of the blessed Gospel, and securing to us our religious and civil liberties and privileges. And to join with their praises their earnest and humble supplications to Almighty GOD, for the pardon of our past ingratitude and other transgressions; and that He would grant that all instances of the Divine goodness may have an effectual influence for working a general reformation in all orders of** persons among us; that so we may be that happy people, whose GOD is the LORD, and that ALL nations may bow to the scepter of our LORD and SAVIOR JESUS CHRIST, and that the whole Earth may be filled with His Glory.

GIVEN at the Council-Chamber in Boston, the 28th day of October, in the Year of our Lord, one Thousand seven hundred and eighty-four, and in the ninth year of the Independence of the United Sates of America.

JOHN HANCOCK.
By his Excellency's Command,
JOHN AVERY, Jun. Secretary

GOD save the Commonwealth of MASSACHUSETTS.

COMMONWEALTH OF MASSACHUSETTS.
By his Excellency JOHN HANCOCK, Esquire,
Governour of the Commonwealth of Massachusetts,

A PROCLAMATION,

For a Day of THANKSGIVING.

IT being our indispensable duty as a people, in a publick and religious manner, to acknowledge the preserving and Governing providence of Almighty God, and more especially to celebrate the Divine Goodness in the various blessings conferred upon us in the course of the year past.

I have therefore thought fit, with the advice and consent of the Council, to appoint, and do hereby appoint THURSDAY the Twenty-Fifth Day of NOVEMBER next, to be religiously observed as a Day of THANKSGIVING throughout this Commonwealth ; hereby calling upon Ministers and people of all denominations, in their several assemblies, to unite with grateful hearts in celebrating the Praises of Almighty GOD, for his great goodness and bounty vouchsafed to a sinful and unworthy people ; particularly for the great and signal interpositions of his Providence in behalf of the United States in the course of the late contest, and that after being rescued from the dangers and calamities of war ; peace has been restored to us, and that our publick affairs are in so promising and happy a situation ; for granting to us a plentiful harvest in the great abundance of the fruits of the earth ; for the general health enjoyed throughout this State during the course of the year, and preventing epidemical and mortal distempers from spreading among us ; reviving our trade, navigation and fishery, and protecting the same from the insults of Pirates and other disasters ; for directing and succeeding our publick Councils, and above all for continuing to us the light of the blessed Gospel, and securing to us our religious and civil liberties and privileges. And to join with their praises their earnest and humble supplications to Almighty GOD, for the pardon of our past ingratitude and other transgressions; and that he would grant that all instances of the divine goodness may have an effectual influence for working a general reformation in all orders of persons among us ; that so we may be that happy people whose GOD is the LORD, and that ALL nations may bow to the Sceptre of our LORD and SAVIOUR JESUS CHRIST, and that the whole Earth may be filled with his Glory.

GIVEN at the Council-Chamber, in Boston, the 28th day of October, in the Year of our Lord, one Thousand seven hundred and eighty-four, and in the ninth year of the Independence of the United States of America.

JOHN HANCOCK.

By his Excellency's Command,
JOHN AVERY, jun. Secy.
GOD save the Commonwealth of MASSACHUSETTS.

Proclamation For a Day of Thanksgiving,
by Governor John Hancock
October 5, 1791[7]

Commonwealth of Massachusetts.
BY His EXCELLENCY
John Hancock, Esq.
GOVERNOR of the COMMONWEALTH
of Massachusetts.
A PROCLAMATION,
For a Day of Public Thanksgiving.

In consideration of the many undeserved Blessings conferred upon us by GOD, the Father of all Mercies; it becomes us no only in our private and usual devotion, to express our obligations to Him, as well as our dependence upon Him; but also specially to set a part a Day to be employed for this great and important Purpose:

I HAVE therefore thought fit to appoint, and by the advice and consent of the Council, do hereby accordingly appoint, THURSDAY, the seventeenth of *November* next, to be observed as a **Day of Public THANKSGIVING and PRAISE, throughout this Commonwealth:** — Hereby calling upon **Ministers and People of every denomination, to assemble on the said Day** — and in the name of the **Great Mediator, devoutly and sincerely offer to Almighty God, the gratitude of our Hearts, for all his goodness towards us;** more especially in that **HE has been pleased to continue to us so a great a measure of Health** — to cause the Earth plentifully to yield her increase, so that we are supplied with the Necessaries, and the Comforts of Life — to prosper our Merchandise and Fishery — **And above all, not only to continue to us the enjoyment of our**

civil Rights and Liberties; but the great and most important Blessing, the Gospel of Jesus Christ: And together with our cordial acknowledgments, I do earnestly recommend, that we may **join the penitent confession of our Sins, and implore the further continuance of the Divine Protection, and Blessings of Heaven upon this People;** especially that He would be graciously pleased to direct, and prosper the Administration of the Federal Government, and of this, and the other States in the Union — to afford Him further Smiles on our Agriculture and Fisheries, Commerce and Manufactures — To prosper our University and all Seminaries of Learning — To bless the virtuously struggling for the Rights of Men — so that universal Happiness may be Allies of the United States, and **to afford his Almighty Aid to all People, who are established in the World; that all may bow to the Scepter of our LORD JESUS CHRIST, and the whole Earth be filled with his Glory.**

And I do also earnestly recommend to the good People of this Commonwealth, to abstain from all servile Labor and Recreation, inconsistent with the solemnity of the said day.

Given at the Council-Chamber, in Boston, the fifth Day of October, in the Year of our Lord, One Thousand Seven Hundred and Ninety-One, and in the sixteenth Year of the Independence of the United States of America.

JOHN HANCOCK.
By his Excellency's Command,
JOHN AVERY, jun. Sec'y

GOD save the Commonwealth of MASSACHUSETTS!!

Commonwealth of *Massachusetts*.

BY HIS EXCELLENCY

John Hancock, Esq.

GOVERNOR of the COMMONWEALTH
of *Massachusetts*.

A PROCLAMATION,

For a Day of Public THANKSGIVING.

IN consideration of the many undeserved Blessings confered upon us by GOD, the Father of all Mercies; it becomes us not only in our private and usual devotion, to express our obligations to HIM, as well as our dependence upon HIM; but also specially to set a part a Day to be employed for this great and important Purpose:

I HAVE therefore thought fit to appoint, and by the advice and consent of the Council, do hereby accordingly appoint, THURSDAY, the SEVENTEENTH of *November* next, to be observed as a Day of Public THANKSGIVING and PRAISE, throughout this Commonwealth :— Hereby calling upon Ministers and People of every denomination, to assemble on the said Day—and in the name of the GREAT MEDIATOR, devoutly and sincerely offer to ALMIGHTY GOD, the gratitude of our Hearts, for all his goodness towards us; more especially in that HE has been pleased to continue to us so great a measure of Health—to cause the Earth plentifully to yield her increase, so that we are supplied with the Necessaries, and the Comforts of Life—to prosper our Merchandize and Fishery—And above all, not only to continue to us the enjoyment of our civil Rights and Liberties; but the great and most important Blessing, the Gospel of JESUS CHRIST: And together with our cordial acknowledgements, I do earnestly recommend, that we may join the penitent confession of our Sins, and implore the further continuance of the Divine Protection, and the Blessings of HEAVEN upon this People; especially that He would be graciously pleased to direct, and prosper the Administration of the Federal Government, and of this, and the other States in the Union—To afford His further Smiles on our Agriculture and Fisheries, Commerce and Manufactures—To prosper our University and all Seminaries of Learning—To bless the Allies of the United States, and to afford his Almighty Aid to all People, who are virtuously struggling for the Rights of Men—so that universal Happiness may be established in the World; that all may bow to the Scepter of our LORD JESUS CHRIST, and the whole Earth be filled with his Glory.

And I do also earnestly recommend to the good People of this Commonwealth, to abstain from all servile Labour and Recreation, inconsistent with the solemnity of the said Day.

GIVEN at the Council-Chamber, in Boston, *the fifth Day of October, in the Year of our* LORD, *One Thousand seven Hundred and Ninety-One, and in the sixteenth Year of the Independence of the* United States *of* America.

JOHN HANCOCK.

By his Excellency's Command,

JOHN AVERY, jun. Sec'y.

GOD *save the Commonwealth of* MASSACHUSETTS ! !

Will of John Hancock[8]

I John Hancock, . . . being advanced in years and being of perfect mind and memory-**thanks be given to God**—therefore calling to mind the mortality of my body and knowing it is appointed for all men once to die [Hebrews 9:27], do make and ordain this my last will and testament . . . **Principally and first of all, I give and recommend my soul into the hands of God that gave it**: and my body I recommend to the earth . . . nothing doubting but **at the general resurrection I shall receive the same again by the mercy and power of God.**

What follows is a
summary of an article
from contemporary American life . . .

nearly 250 years after
John Hancock
signed

the Declaration of Independence
and
the Articles of Confederation.

What Would John Hancock Think?

Atheists Lose Lawsuit to Stop House of Representatives From Opening in Prayer

NATIONAL   CORTNEY O'BRIEN   OCT 12, 2017 | 10:50AM   WASHINGTON, DC

From its inception, the United States House of Representatives has opened its proceedings in prayer. But that didn't stop the Freedom From Religion Foundation's president from suing House Chaplain Patrick Conroy—on the National Day of Prayer, no less—for "violating his rights" under the United States Constitution and the Religious Freedom Restoration Act.

But the court dismissed the suit. A grateful Speaker Paul Ryan responded, "Since the first session of the Continental Congress, our nation's legislature has opened with a prayer to God. Today, that tradition was upheld and the freedom to exercise religion was vindicated. The court rightfully dismissed the claims of an atheist that he had the right to deliver a secular invocation in place of the opening prayer. Recently, especially following the return of Majority Whip Steve Scalise, this institution has been reminded about the power of prayer. I commend the District Court for its decision, and I am grateful that the People's House can continue to begin its work each day as we have for centuries: taking a moment to pray to God."

https://www.lifenews.com/2017/10/12/atheists-lose-lawsuit-to-stop-house-of-representatives-from-opening-in-prayer/.

Samuel Holten
(1738-1816)

Signer of the Articles of Confederation

Highest Office Attained:
Representative in Congress

Religious Affiliation:
Congregationalist

A devout Christian, Samuel Holten was a lifelong member of the First (Congregational) Church in Danvers, Massachusetts. His ancestors had emigrated from England in the early 1600s, settling in what was then known as Salem Village. His great-great-grandparents, Edward and Bridget Haste Houlton, hailed from Nayland, in Suffolk County, England. In 1641, at the age of twenty, their son, Joseph Houlton, who later contributed land for the church parsonage, worked as a servant to Richard Ingersoll. Ingersoll had emigrated in 1629 on the *Mayflower 2* from Bedfordshire, England as part of the great puritan migration. Accompanying him were his wife, Agnes (Ann) Langlye Ingersoll, and their children; one of them, daughter Sarah, married Joseph in 1651. Sarah's parents had been married in 1611 at St. Swithins (Anglican) Church in Sandy, England. But, by 1636, they, like the Houltons, were active in the Congregational church in Salem; Richard held a church office that directed him to "walk forth in the time of God's worship, to take notice of such as either lie about the meeting house without attending to the word or ordinances, or that lie at home or in the fields."

In 1672, a number of local farmers desired a new and closer meetinghouse. One of them, Captain Thomas Flint, a man of great religious faith, prepared a petition and worked diligently to gather support; being skilled in carpentry, Flint was chosen to construct the church. Ultimately, this effort gave birth to the First Church of Salem Village (now, Danvers). There, future generations of Flints and Holtens would worship, beginning with Flint's daughter, Abigail Flint; she, in 1688, married Joseph Houlton's son, Henry, the grandfather of Holten the signer.

It was during this era that Salem Village experienced its darkest chapter. With the formal organization of the church in 1689 as the Church of Christ at Salem Village, came a new pastor, Rev. Samuel Parris. In 1692, not long after Rev. Parris came to occupy its pulpit, the church endured what became known as the Salem Witchcraft Delusion. And Holten's forbears found themselves in the midst of it. Indeed, Joseph Houlton and Captain Flint are identified as among the accusers of alleged witches; and one of Joseph's sons, Benjamin Houlton, who had taken ill and died in 1689 following the straying of his pigs onto a neighbor's property, was claimed by some to have been a victim of an alleged witch, neighbor Rebecca Nurse. Benjamin's wife Sarah's testimony was used against Nurse, and Nurse was later executed, notwithstanding that Joseph, widow Sarah, and Joseph's son, Joseph Jr., all signed an affidavit that they "never had any cause or grounds to suspect her of any such thing as she is now accused of."

In 1696, the church rid itself of Rev. Parris, engaged in much prayer and fasting, and within two years found reconciliation and healing in the work of its new pastor, Rev. Joseph Green. Among the members of the committee that sought out Rev. Green was none other than Holten's great-grandfather, Captain Flint. Over the next seventeen years, Rev. Green worked tirelessly to mend the broken church, and to overcome past evil with good. It was during Rev. Green's pastorate, in 1704, that Holten's parents, Samuel Holten Sr. and Hannah Gardner Holten, were married. The Gardners also worshipped at First Church; but Hannah's father and grandfather, John and Samuel Gardner, were among those who, in 1709, petitioned for a new meeting-house to be located in what was known as the Middle Precinct, located between Salem and Salem Village. Rev. Green's restorative pastorate continued until his death in 1715, and the church then (and for more than fifty years) continued its return to reasoned, theological discourse under the tutelage of his successor, Rev. Peter Clark.

Born during the pastorate of Rev. Clark in 1738, Holten suffered from poor health as a youngster. This prevented him from pursuing the collegiate path that his parents initially had intended for him. Instead, he schooled under the auspices of Rev.

Clark, and then went on to study medicine with Dr. Jonathan Prince Sr.; Dr. Prince also schooled his own son, Dr. Jonathan Prince Jr., later the husband of Holten's sister, Lydia. At the age of eighteen, Holten left what by then had become the sepa-rately-incorporated town of Danvers and began the practice of medicine in Gloucester. But he returned to his hometown just two years later with his bride, Mary Warner Holten. Mary's father, Philemon Warner, was a noted elder and deacon of the First (Congregational) Church of Gloucester.

Although medicine was Holten's profession, and he later was among the incorporators of the Massachusetts Medical Society, it proved not to be his true calling. By 1775, he had given it up completely, devoting himself entirely to public service and the cause of the revolution. For more than twenty years, Holten served his community in local offices, including as selectman, town clerk, and treasurer; he also served on the board of the Overseers of the Poor. And he represented Danvers for many years in the Massachusetts colonial legislature (as had his father-in-law, John Gardner) and in the Provincial Congress. An ardent patriot, he joined the Sons of Liberty, helped lead anti-British efforts in Danvers, and worked with the Committee of Correspondence to coordinate such efforts between communi-ties. He was elected to the Continental Congress, served on the Committee of Safety and the Governor's Council, and became a first major in the First Essex County Regiment. While serving in the Congress in 1778, he helped draft — and signed — the Articles of Confederation; and in 1785, he briefly served as the presiding officer of that body. The diary he kept during his congressional years is replete with references to the worship services (often more than one) he attended on sabbath days, and to the min-isters whose words were imparted to him. He also served as a delegate to the Massachusetts convention to frame a new state constitution, and as a judge (and chief justice) for more than thirty years.

When in Danvers, Holten was at home in what is known today as the Judge Samuel Holten House, which had been acquired by his father from the descendants of his deceased kin, Benjamin

Houlton of the forsaken era gone by; it was located on a site once owned by ancestor Richard Ingersoll. A regular attendee of the First Church, Judge Holten was so revered in the community that parishioners would stand until he took his seat in the pews, and would await his departure before taking their own. Holten often received visiting clergyman as his houseguests, and was a close friend of Rev. Benjamin Wadsworth's, who assumed the pastorate of the church in 1772. In 1812, the two helped form the Massachusetts Society for the Suppression of Intemperance, and thereafter they formed the Danvers Moral Society; Holten served as its president and Rev. Wadsworth as its vice president. Holten passed into eternity in Danvers in 1816.

In His Own Words:

Proclamation For A Public Thanksgiving, by Samuel Holten and Others
November 4, 1775[1]

A Proclamation For A Public Thanksgiving

ALTHOUGH in consequence of the unnatural, cruel, and barbarous measures adopted and pursued by the British Administration, great and distressing calamities are brought upon our oppressed country, and on this colony in particular, we feel the dreadful effects of civil war, by which America is stained with the blood of her valiant sons, who have bravely fallen in the laudable defence of our rights and privileges; our capital, once the seat of justice, opulence and virtue, is unjustly wrested from its proper owners, who are obliged to flee from the iron hand of tyranny, or are held in the unrelenting arms of oppression; our seaports greatly distressed, and towns burnt by the foes, who have acted the part of barbarous incendiaries. And although **the wise and holy Governor of the world has, in his**

righteous providence, sent droughts into this colony, and wasting sickness into many of our towns, yet **we have the greatest reason to adore and praise the Supreme Disposer of events, who deals infinitely better with us than we deserve; and amidst all his judgments hath remembered mercy**, by causing the voice of health again to be heard amongst us. Instead of famine, affording to an ungrateful people a competency of the necessaries and comforts of life, in remarkably preserving and protecting our troops, when in apparent danger, while our enemies, with all their boasted skill and strength, have met with loss, disappointment, and defeat; and, **in the course of his good providence, the Father of Mercies hath bestowed upon us many other favors, which call for our grateful Acknowledgments.**

Therefore we have thought fit, with the advice of the Council and House of Representatives, to appoint Thursday the twenty-third Day of November (inst.) to be observed as a **day of public THANKSGIVING, throughout this colony, hereby calling upon ministers and people, to meet for religious worship on said day, and devoutly to offer up their unfeigned praises to Almighty God, the source and benevolent bestower of all good**, for his affording the necessary means of subsistence, though our commerce has been prevented, and the supplies from the fishery denied us. That such a measure of health is enjoyed among us, that the lives of our officers and soldiers have been so remarkably preserved, while our enemies have fell before them. That the vigorous efforts which have been used to excite the savage vengeance of the wilderness, and rouse the Indians to arms, that an unavoidable destruction might come upon our frontiers, have been almost miraculously defeated. That our unnatural enemies, instead of ravaging the country with uncontrolled sway, are confined within such narrow limits, to their own mortification and distress, environed by an American army, brave and determined. That such a band of union, founded upon the best principles, unites the American colonies. That our rights and privileges, both civil and religious, are so far preserved to us, notwithstanding all the attempts of our barbarous enemies to deprive us of them.

And to offer up humble and fervent prayers to Almighty God for the Whole British Empire, especially for the United American Colonies, that he would bless our civil rulers, and lead them into wise and prudent measures in this dark and difficult day. **That he would** endow our General Court with all that wisdom which is profitable to direct. **That he would** graciously smile upon our endeavours to restore peace, preserve our rights and privileges, and hand them down to posterity. **That he would** give wisdom to the American Congress, equal to their important station. **That he would** direct the Generals, and the American armies, wherever employed, and give them success and victory. **That he would** preserve and strengthen the harmony of the United Colonies. **That he would** pour out his Spirit upon all orders of men through the land, bring us to a hearty repentance and reformation; purity and sanctify all his churches. **That he would** make our's Emanuel's land. **That he would spread the knowledge of the Redeemer through the whole earth, and fill the world with his glory.** — And all servile labor is forbidden on said day.

Given under our Hands at the Council-Chamber in Watertown, the fourth day of November, in the year of our Lord, one thousand seven hundred and seventy-five.

By their honor's command, PEREZ MORTON, Dep. Sec. James Otis, Walter Spooner, Caleb Cushing, Joseph Gerrish, John Whetcome, Jedediah Foster, James Prescott, Eldad Taylor, Benjamin Lincoln, Michael Farley, Joseph Palmer, Samuel Holten, Jabez Fisher, Moses Gill, Benjamin White.

GOD Save the PEOPLE.

A PROCLAMATION for a public Thanksgiving.

ALTHOUGH, in consequence of the unnatural, cruel, and barbarous measures adopted and pursued by the British Administration, great and distressing calamities are brought upon our oppressed country, and on this colony in particular, we feel the dreadful effects of civil war, by which America is stained with the blood of her valiant sons, who have bravely fallen in the laudable defence of our rights and privileges; our capital, once the seat of justice, opulence and virtue, is unjustly wrested from its proper owners, who are obliged to flee from the iron hand of tyranny, or are held in the unrelenting arms of oppression; our seaports greatly distressed, and towns burnt by the foes, who have acted the part of barbarous incendiaries. And although the wise and holy Governor of the world has, in his righteous providence, sent droughts into this colony, and wasting sickness into many of our towns, yet we have the greatest reason to adore and praise the Supreme Disposer of events, who deals infinitely better with us than we deserve; and amidst all his judgments hath remembered mercy, by causing the voice of health again to be heard amongst us. Instead of famine, affording to an ungrateful people a competency of the necessaries and comforts of life, in remarkably preserving and protecting our troops, when in apparent danger, while our enemies, with all their boasted skill and strength, have met with loss, disappointment, and defeat; and, in the course of his good providence, the Father of Mercies hath bestowed upon us many other favors, which call for our grateful acknowledgements.——

Therefore we have thought fit, with the advice of the Council and House of Representatives, to appoint Thursday the twenty-third day of November (inst.) to be observed as a day of public THANKSGIVING throughout this colony, hereby calling upon ministers and people to meet for religious worship on said day, and devoutly to offer up their unfeigned praises to Almighty God, the source and benevolent bestower of all good, for his affording the necessary means of subsistance, though our commerce has been prevented, and the supplies from the fishery denied us. That such a measure of health is enjoyed among us, that the lives of our officers and soldiers have been so remarkably preserved, while our enemies have fell before them. That the vigorous efforts which have been used to excise the savage vengeance of the wilderness, and rouse the Indians to arms, that an unavoidable destruction might come upon our frontiers, have been almost miraculously defeated. That our unnatural enemies, instead of ravaging the country with uncontrouled fury, are confined within such narrow limits, to their great mortification and distress, environed by an American army, brave and determined. That such a band of union, founded upon the best principles, unites the American colonies. That our rights and privileges, both civil and religious, are so far preserved to us, notwithstanding all the attempts of our barbarous enemies to deprive us of them.——

And to offer up humble and fervent prayers to Almighty God for the whole British empire, especially for the United American Colonies, that he would bless our civil rulers, and lead them into wise and prudent measures in this dark and difficult day. That he would endow our General Court with all that wisdom which is profitable to direct. That he would graciously smile upon our endeavours to restore peace, preserve our rights and privileges, and hand them down to posterity. That he would give wisdom to the American Congress, equal to their important station. That he would direct the Generals and the American armies, wherever employed, and give them success and victory. That he would preserve and strengthen the harmony of the United Colonies. That he would pour out his spirit upon all orders of men through the land, bring us to a hearty repentance and reformation, purify and sanctify all his churches. That he would make our's Emanuel's land. That he would spread the knowledge of the Redeemer through the whole earth, and fill the world with his glory.——And all servile labor is forbidden on said day.

Given under our hands at the Council Chamber in Watertown, the fourth day of November, in the year of our Lord one thousand seven hundred and seventy-five.

By their honors command, PEREZ MORTON, Dep. Sec. James Otis, Walter Spooner, Caleb Cushing, Joseph Gerrish, John Whetcomb, Jedediah Foster, James Prescott, Eldad Taylor, Benjamin Lincoln, Michael Farley, Joseph Palmer, Samuel Holten, Jabez Fisher, Moses Gill, Benjamin White.

GOD save the PEOPLE.

Letter from Samuel Holten to Daniel Putnam July 15, 1776[2]

The Congress have sent us their Declaration, declaring the Colonies independent States; and the General informs us of his ordering three of the Regiments of the Continental troops at or near Boston to march immediately to Ticonderoga, so that I suppose the Court must be called together again immediately. Give my kind regards to Capt. Flint and Lieut. Putnam, and let them know from me that I desire them to exert themselves for their distressed country, for we have everything to get or everything to lose. We have not a day to lose, no, not even an hour. **Independency is the best news I ever heard, and as I trust our cause is just, we ought to put our trust in the God of Armies, and not fear what man can do in an unjust cause.**

Letter from Samuel Holten to General David Putnam April 13, 1779[3]

Since I have been in the southern states, I have had opportunity of being acquainted with many of the principal people and have made myself somewhat acquainted with the institutions and Laws under which they have lived; and **I am fully convinced that it is owing under providence to the care our fore-fathers took in New England in enacting such a good code of Laws, both to preserve our civil and religious liberties, that the people in this land are not now in a state of abject Slavery.**

I have ever considered this war as a judgment of heaven upon us for our sins, as a people, and I'm very sure if there was a general reformation, we should soon see our difficulties removed; but the growing vices of the times gives me great concern.

As I have the pleasure of corresponding with a number of the clergy in New England, they all give me the following account that they apprehend there is great danger of a general failure of the

support of the gospel; I cant yet bring myself to believe that my countrymen in New England are so far degenerated; but if such an event should take place, and our churches be dispersed, I fear we shall be a ruined people indeed; you may suppose it gives me real concern for the church of which I have the honor of being a member; and permit me sir to ask whither you think our Rev. and worthy friend Mr. Wadsworth, is encouraged and supported in the great work of the ministry as he ought to be; I do not pretend to know, for tho' I correspond with him, I take it he has too tender a regard for his people to make complaints against them, but from my knowledge of you as a supporter of the church, are the reasons of my writing thus freely.

Letter from Samuel Holten to Colonel Enoch Putnam August 21, 1783[4]

You must be sensible that there have been a large number of persons in all parts of the United States that have been inimical to us from the beginning of the contest, and as we are not now at war with the common enemy, so we are apt to be off our guard respecting those people who now dare to come forward in public life and find fault with things that have been done by Congress in years past which has been a means under God of saving this people from ruin; and some have influence enough to procure seats in our general assemblies, and that gives them great opportunities to find fault with the doings of Congress and endeavor to counteract their proceedings; and what gives these sort of people great advantage at this time is the good people being burthened with the charge of the war. They tell them it is owing to misconduct in our public affairs, and that they can set things right and relieve them of their taxes, and it is not to be wondered at that sundry of the good people believe them. But it is impossible to make those inimical people like our new republican governments. From their hearts they wish to destroy them, and yet hope we shall be obliged to fall under the British government, or at least some of the states, if they can divide us in our public councils. No doubt you have heard that the state of Massachusetts has publicly remonstrated against the proceedings of Congress in two instances. I have not time to enlarge on this subject, but beloved Hutchinson can inform you more of this matter.

The remonstrance has been read in Congress, and I shall spare no pains in endeavoring to prevent any disputes between Congress and the state I have the honor to represent, as I foresee the consequences. **God grant that this people may not again be involved in all the horrors of war.**

Letter from Samuel Holten to His Son-in-Law, Luke Webster October 2, 1783[5]

[H]appiness doth not consist in the abundance of the things we possess in this life, but in virtue & religion added to a contented mind. By the leave of providence I expect to be at home toward the last of Novr.

Letter from Samuel Holten to His Son-in-Law, John Kettell October 9, 1783[6]

It is to be lamented that the State I have the honor to represent, are so dissatisfied with the proceedings of Congress, when I am sure both Congress & the state, are indeavoring to promote our national happiness; I shall continue my indeavors, while I tarry, to make things more agreeable to both; **God grant that the union may not be dissolved, & the good people again involved in all the horrors of war.**

What follows is a
summary of an article
from contemporary American life . . .

nearly 250 years after
Samuel Holten
signed

the Articles of Confederation.

What Would Samuel Holten Think?

NEWS | DECEMBER 01, 2018

Group demands removal of Christmas display of three wise men, star, from Michigan school building

For more than forty years, it has been a tradition in Newaygo, Michigan to mount a Christmas display atop a school district building. But the Michigan Association of Civil Rights Activists demanded that it be taken down. Its offense? It depicts three wise men and a star. According to the MACRA, "You have a public school that's promoting the story of the Christian Nativity and that's not permitted under the Constitution."

https://www.theblaze.com/news/2018/12/01/group-demands-removal-of-christmas-display-of-three-wise-men-star-from-michigan-school-building.

Rufus King
(1755-1827)

Signer of the United States Constitution

Highest Office Attained:
United States Senator

Religious Affiliation:
Congregationalist; Episcopalian

A Congregationalist-turned-Episcopalian, Rufus King was born in 1755 in Dunstan Landing, now part of Scarborough, Maine; it was then part of Massachusetts. His grandfather, John King, had emigrated to Boston from Kent, England in the late 1600's. And his father, Richard King, had settled in Dunstan Landing in 1748; he soon became a successful merchant and one of its most prominent citizens. King's paternal grandmother, Mary Stowell King, was the granddaughter of Samuel Stowell, who, along with puritan Rev. Peter Hobart, was one of the early English settlers of Hingham, Massachusetts. King's mother, Isabella Brandon King, died when King was only four years old, leaving King and his two younger sisters to be raised by Isabella's cousin, Mary Parker. Mary later married King's father and bore him five more children; they included William King, the first Governor of Maine, and Cyrus King, a congressman from Massachusetts. Mary, a strict Puritan, governed her family according to the Ten Commandments, the Golden Rule, and the Sermon on the Mount; and regular family attendance at the Second (Congregational) Church, then pastored by Rev. Richard Elvins—a disciple of the evangelical Rev. George Whitefield—was mandatory.

At the age of twelve, Rufus King was enrolled in Dummer School (later, Dummer Academy, and now, The Governor's Academy); it was the first private chartered school in New England. Among the founders of Dummer School, which was located in Byfield, Massachusetts, was Rev. Moses Parsons, Byfield's Congregational minister; the property for the school had been willed for that purpose by Governor William Dummer, himself a man of firm religious faith. King studied under the school's preceptor (headmaster), Rev. Samuel Moody, who was referred to Rev. Parsons for that position by Rev. Whitefield.

Master Moody was a Godly man who hailed from a family of Congregational ministers and who was himself, like many Dummer headmasters and trustees over the years, ordained in the Congregationalist traditions. From the opening of its doors under Master Moody, the pupils of Dummer School began their day with devotional services and a sermon from Pastor Parsons.

In 1773, King entered Harvard College; he graduated at the head of his class, distinguishing himself in mathematics, language, and oratory. He became an ardent supporter of the American cause. But beyond preparing him for a career in law and public service, Harvard altered the religious direction of King's life as well. There, he was exposed to the grandeur of the Anglican religious traditions as practiced at nearby Christ (Episcopal) Church in Cambridge. The attraction was so great for King that his Congregationalist father requested of the president of Harvard that King "be permitted to attend public Worship after the manner of the Church of England."

Following Harvard in 1777, King served briefly as a general's aide during the war for independence, and moved to Newburyport, not far from Byfield. He studied law under another Dummer School alumnus, Theophilus Parsons; Parsons, later the chief justice of Massachusetts, was the son of Rev. Parsons. King opened his own law practice in Newburyport in 1780, and soon was elected to the Massachusetts legislature. He also became an active member of St. Paul's (Episcopal) Church, where he served as a warden. In 1784, King was elected to the Congress, where he represented Massachusetts under the Articles of Confederation. During that time, he boarded with the family of John Alsop, a wealthy New York City merchant who previously had served as a member of the Continental Congress; Alsop, however, had favored reconciliation with Great Britain, did not vote for independence, and instead resigned his seat in the Congress. King made the acquaintance of Alsop's daughter, Mary, whom he wed in 1786 at the Trinity (Episcopal) Church where Alsop was then a vestryman. She later bore King seven children. Among them were John Alsop King, who became governor of New York; Charles King, who became the president of Columbia College; James Gore King, a congressman from New Jersey; and Edward King, Speaker of the Ohio House of Representatives.

While in Congress, King championed the principle of state aid to religious institutions. Because he regarded the church as necessary to ensuring morality and as the foundation of social order, he advocated, for example, for land grants and ordinances that would require portions of property to be "given perpetually for the purposes of religion." In 1787, King served as a Massachusetts delegate to the Constitutional Convention; there, he helped craft, and signed, the United States Constitution. He also served as a delegate to the Massachusetts state convention that ratified the Constitution.

King then moved to New York, where he was quickly elected to that state's legislature. In 1789, he was chosen as one of New York's first United States senators under the new Constitution to which King was a Massachusetts signatory. He became a devoted member of Trinity Church, where he served, as he had at St. Paul's Church in Newburyport, as a warden and vestryman. He also served, on five occasions, as a lay delegate to state conventions of the Protestant Episcopal Church. And he served on several important diocesan committees, served as a member of the Society for Promoting Religion and Learning in the State of New York, and was offered an appointment to the board of the American Bible Society. He was also for many years a trustee of Columbia College, which maintained a close connection with Trinity Church.

In 1796, King left the Senate to become United States Minister to Great Britain, a post he held until 1803. The following year, he was unsuccessful as the Federalist candidate for Vice President of the United States (the presidential candidate being Charles Cotesworth Pinckney). He purchased an estate in the Long Island village of Jamaica, and there contented himself for a time with agricultural pursuits. He also joined Grace (Episcopal) Church, where he again was an active and enthusiastic member, once again serving as a church warden.

In 1813, King was elected to a second stint in the United States Senate. Three years later, he was unsuccessful as a candidate for governor of New York, but was nominated as the Federalist candidate for President of the United States; he lost that election, however, to James Monroe. An ardent opponent of slavery, he supported the Missouri Compromise in 1820, permitting Maine to enter the union as a free state; his brother, William King, then became that state's first governor. King remained in the Senate until 1825, at which time he briefly accepted re-appointment as Minister to Great Britain; he returned home in 1826 due to ill health. Upon his death in 1827, his family fulfilled his request to be buried in the cemetery of his beloved Grace Church.

In His Own Words:

Draft of Address by Rufus King (in answer to a speech to Congress by President George Washington) December 10, 1795[1]

> Circumstances thus every way auspicious demand our gratitude, and **sincere acknowledgements to Almighty God**, and require that we should unite our efforts in imitation of your enlightened, firm and persevering example to establish and preserve the peace, freedom and prosperity of our country.

Letter from Rufus King to Russian Envoy, Count Woronzow, May 24, 1799[2]

> [I]t will afford me the greatest satisfaction to see **the cause of Order and of Religion in America supported and strengthened** as it would be by a public intercourse and connexion between the Governments of our two Countries.

Letter from Rufus King to Rev. John Mitchell Mason (regarding a pitchfork injury to King's son, Frederick) July 28, 1808[3]

I have received your friendly letter of yesterday and both Mrs. King & myself are heartily thankful to you for the kind wishes and consoling Reflexions that it contains. Tho' the poor child's wound was extremely hazardous, and the danger is not yet passed, **he has, thanks to God, suffered very little pain; and as no unfavourable symptom has hitherto occurred, we are encouraged to hope that it may be the merciful will of the Almighty that his dear life shall be spared to us.**

Speech by Rufus King February 11, 1820[4]

Mr. President I have yet to learn that one man can make a slave of another; if one man cannot do so, no number of individuals can have any better right to do it, and **I hold that all laws and compacts imposing any such condition upon any human being are absolutely void, because contrary to the law of nature, which is the law of God, by which he makes his way known to man, and is paramount to all human control.**

Letter from Rufus King to Christopher Gore February 17, 1820[5]

[T]he broad principles of the law of nature, a law **established by the Creator, which has existed from the beginning, extends over the whole globe, is everywhere, and at all times, binding upon making;** A law which applies to nations, because their members are still men; **a law which is the foundation of all** constitutional, conventional & civil laws, none of which are valid if contrary to the law of nature; that according to this law all men are born free, and justly entitled to the possession of life and liberty and to the free pursuit of happiness. Hence that man could not enslave man; and that states could not make them slaves, since they could not possess any authority except that wh. naturally belongs to man.

Speech by Rufus King
October 30, 1821[6]

The laws of every nation in Christendom have for ages acknowledged and protected the Christian religion—and in virtue of the laws and statutes of England the Christian religion, for many centuries, has been acknowledged and established in that nation. . . .

The fair import of the several provisions, taken in connection with each other, must be, that **the laws of the state do so far recognize and establish the Christian religion**, (comprehending all denominations of Christians, without distinction or preference,) as portion of the law of the land, that defamatory, scandalous, or blasphemous attacks upon the same, may and should be restrained and punished.

While all mankind are by our constitution tolerated, and free to enjoy religious profession and worship within this state, yet **the religious professions of the Pagan, the Mahomedan, and the Christian, are not, in the eye of the law, of equal truth and excellence.**

According to the Christian system, men pass into a future state of existence, when the deeds of their

life become the subject of rewards or punishment — the moral law rests upon the truth of this doctrine, without which it has no sufficient sanction. Our laws constantly refer to this revelation, and by the oath which they prescribe, we appeal to the Supreme Being, so to deal with us hereafter, as we observe the obligation of our oaths.

The Pagan world were, and are, without the mighty influence of this principle, which is proclaimed in the Christian system — their morals were destitute of its powerful sanction, while their oaths neither awakened the hopes, nor the fears which a belief in Christianity inspires.

While the constitution tolerates the religious preferences and worship of all men, it does more in behalf of the religion of the gospel — and by acknowledging, and in a certain sense, incorporating its truths into the laws of the land, we are restrained from adopting the proposed amendment, whereby the Christian religion may lose that security which every other Christian nation is anxious to afford to it.

Diary Entry by Rufus King (as his death approached) January 1, 1827[7]

God grant in his mercy it may be a short one. I desire to die, when his mercy permits, and hope I discover no improper impatience; I submit to God's will, as is my duty.

What follows is a
summary of an article
from contemporary American life . . .

nearly 250 years after
Rufus King
signed

the United States Constitution.

What Would Rufus King Think?

TODD STARNES · Published May 16, 2017

School: Offering to pray for a colleague is unacceptable

OPINION By Todd Starnes, | Fox News

Toni Richardson attended the same church as one of her co-workers at the Augusta School District in Augusta, Maine. The co-worker shared with Toni the difficulty he was experiencing adjusting to his new job. So, Toni told her co-worker that she would pray for him.

No problem, right? After all, it seems the caring and "Christian" thing to do. Ah, but the private conversation took place in a public-school building!

When the school district learned of Toni's offense, it launched an investigation, followed up by a "coaching memorandum" that concluded that Toni may have "imposed some strong religious/spiritual belief system" on her co-worker. It advised her that "[s]tating, 'I will pray for you,' and 'you were in my prayers' is not acceptable — even if that other person attends the same church as you." It warned, "in the future, it is imperative you do not use phrases that integrate public and private belief systems when in the public schools"; instructed her to make "no reference to your spiritual or religious belief"; and advised that "[i]f you have any additional interactions that are deemed unprofessional by administration, you will be subject to disciplinary action and/or possibly dismissal."

https://www.foxnews.com/opinion/ school-offering-to-pray-for-a-colleague-is-unacceptable.

James Lovell
(1737-1814)

[Portrait Unavailable]

Signer of the Articles of Confederation

Highest Office Attained:
Representative in Congress

Religious Affiliation:
Congregationalist

T he revolutionary cause sometimes divided families, and that is perhaps nowhere better demonstrated than in the life of James Lovell. And that life further reflects how religious traditions affected political allegiances during the turbulent times of our country's birth.

James Lovell was born in Boston in 1737. There, like many others of later renown, he attended the rigorous Boston Latin school. The stern headmaster at the school at that time (and for nearly forty years) was none other than young Lovell's father, John Lovell. Although a public academic institution, indeed the first in the United States, the Boston Latin School was established under the influence of Rev. John Cotton, a puritan reformist minister known today as the father of Congregationalism. The only requirement for admission during Headmaster Lovell's tenure was the ability to read verses from the Bible.

Following his graduation from Harvard in 1756, Lovell returned to Boston Latin, and worked for many years as an assistant to his father. He also served as the master of the North Grammar School in Boston. A respected academic, Lovell became sought out as an orator. In 1760, he delivered an oration in Latin to the memory of Henry Flint, who for more than half a century had taught at Harvard. The son of a minister, Flint also briefly served as pastor of the First Congregational Church of Norwich, and during his time at Harvard authored such works as *The Doctrine of the Last Judgment, Asserted and Explained* (1714).

As relations with Great Britain deteriorated, Lovell became a fervent patriot. Here he split with his father, the headmaster, who remained a strong loyalist. In 1771, against the advice of his father, Lovell delivered the first oration to Bostonians to commemorate the Bloody Massacre that had occurred there just a year earlier. He offered that commemoration from the

Old South (Congregational) Church, following a fervent prayer by Rev. Charles Chauncy, pastor of the First (Congregational) Church; First Church was where Rev. Cotton formerly had ministered and where numerous headmasters of Boston Latin, possibly including John Lovell, were members.

James Lovell also experienced Episcopalian influences. In 1760, he married Mary Middleton, who came from a family of strong Anglican traditions. Her family originated in Scotland; two of her ancestors, Alexander Middleton and his son, George Middleton, were Anglican ministers. Each had served as principal of King's College in Aberdeen, where George also served as dean of the Diocese of Aberdeen. It is perhaps not surprising, therefore, that Lovell and Mary were married at Trinity (Episcopal) Church in Boston.

Notwithstanding those influences, and the pressures on those of the Anglican tradition to remain loyal to the mother country, Lovell was an ardent patriot; indeed, following the Battle of Bunker Hill in 1775, he was taken into custody, imprisoned in Halifax, Nova Scotia, and held there until achieving his release in a prisoner exchange in late 1776.

The patriot Lovell was not the only member of his family to travel to Nova Scotia; his father did so not long after, although under far different circumstances. As the siege of Boston ended, with the rebels claiming victory, General Washington negotiated an evacuation of loyalists from the city. Among those seeking refuge in Nova Scotia was the former headmaster, John Lovell; others included Rev. William Walker, rector at Trinity (Episcopal) Church (where Lovell and Mary had wed), and Rev. Mather Byles Jr., rector of Christ (Episcopal) Church in Boston.

The turbulent times nearly placed James Lovell in his own pulpit. Rev. Byles was the son of Rev. Mather Byles Sr., the longtime minister at Boston's Hollis Street (or Eighth Congregational) Church; he counted among his kin the famous Rev. John Cotton and Rev. Cotton Mather. Rev. Byles Jr. had himself been a Congregational minister in New London, Connecticut. But upon receiving an invitation to become the rector at Boston's Christ (Episcopal) Church in 1768, Rev. Byles

Jr. traveled to London, was re-ordained a priest of the Anglican Church, and embarked on a new ministry at Christ Church. He remained there until his flight to Nova Scotia, but, in 1771, was nearly forced to depart the church. His loyalist views were at odds with much of his congregation, which tended toward independence more than most Episcopalians. They threatened to dismiss him from their pulpit, and to replace him with none other than James Lovell, although they knew they would have to ordain him through the Congregational Church and would lose their Episcopalian status. They even induced Lovell to officiate in the church on the Sabbath, allowing him to omit portions of the liturgy as he saw fit. But Rev. Byles capitulated, and Lovell's formal ministry went no farther.

Upon his release from British prisons in 1776, Lovell returned to Boston and was quickly elected to the Continental Congress. He served there from 1777 to 1782, signing the Articles of Confederation as a delegate from Massachusetts, and serving on the Committee of Foreign Correspondence. He later served as a collector of taxes, as a customs officer, and as a naval officer of the ports of Boston and Charlestown. James Lovell died in 1814.

In His Own Words:

***An Oration Delivered by James Lovell, A.M., at the Request of the Inhabitants of the Town of Boston, to Commemorate the Bloody Tragedy of the Fifth of March, 1770* (relating to the "Boston Massacre")**
April 2, 1771[1]

> The horrid bloody scene we here commemorate, whatever were the causes which concurred to bring it on that dreadful night, must lead the pious and humane of every order to some suitable reflections. **The pious will adore the conduct of that BEING who is unsearchable in all his ways, and without whose knowledge not a single sparrow falls, in**

permitting an immortal soul to be hurried by the flying ball, the messenger of death, in the twinkling of an eye, to meet the awful Judge of all it's secret actions. The humane, from having often thought with pleasing rapture on the endearing scenes of social life, in all it's amiable relations, will lament with heart-felt pangs their sudden dissolution by the indiscretion, rage and vengeance of untruly human passions.

But, let us leave that shocking close of one continued course of rancor and dispute from the first moment that the troops arrived in town: that course will now be represented by your own reflexions to much more solid, useful purpose than by any artful language. I hope, however, that Heaven has yet in store such happiness, for this afflicted town and province, as will in time wear out the memory of all our former troubles. . . .

May the allies and beneficent RULER OF THE UNIVERSE preserve our *lives* and *health*, and prosper all our lawful *endeavours in the glorious cause of* FREEDOM.

James Lovell's Draft of the Reverse Side of the Proposed Great Seal of the United States (prepared during consideration of the Articles of Confederation) 1776[2]

On the other side of the said Great Seal should be the following Device. Pharoah sitting in an open Chariot, a Crown on his head and a Sword in his hand passing through the divided Waters of the Red Sea in pursuit of the Israelites: **Rays from a Pillow of Fire in the Cloud, expressive of the divine Presence and Command, beaming on Moses who stands on the**

Shore, and extending his hand over the Sea, causes it to overwhelm Pharoah.

Motto. Rebellion to Tyrants is Obedience to God.

Letter from James Lovell and Other Massachusetts Delegates to James Warren, Speaker of the Massachusetts House of Representatives (regarding Charlestown petition for compensation for losses of war)
May 21, 1777[3]

In the mean Time, our Brethren and Neighbors, virtuously struggling together with us for every Thing that is valuable, and reduced from Prosperity to Adversity by the cruel Stroke of War, must not be left to suffer unnoticed. **This would be plainly repugnant to the dictates of Humanity, to the Precepts of Christian Charity to the Rules of common Justice and the soundest policy;** — a Chain of Motives which doubtless produced the Grants already made by the General Assembly of our State for the immediate Subsistence of these sufferers.

Letter from James Lovell and Richard Henry Lee to William Lee
October 28, 1778[4]

With hearty prayers for your welfare, we are, sir, your affectionate friends.

Letter from James Lovell to Richard Henry Lee
July 17, 1779[5]

An honest man's the noblest work of God.

Letter from James Lovell to John Jay
July 11, 1780[6]

By a letter from Messrs. Gardoqui and Sons, of May 3d, received yesterday, I have the pleasure of knowing you were then well. In a postscript to one of his former of February 24th, the P.S. not dated, he says he hears of you *every week*. This creates a chagrin, as we have none of your favours later than March 3d. **You are not to suppose that I dare to *complain*; I have read my Bible to better purpose. I am not entitled to throw the "first stones,"** but I have as good a title as anybody to palliate my own faults, and to shift them upon others.

What follows is a
summary of an article
from contemporary American life . . .

nearly 250 years after
James Lovell
signed

the Articles of Confederation.

What Would James Lovell Think?

Judge Orders School District to Halt Prayers, Bible Reading after ACLU Suit

Michael Foust | *ChristianHeadlines.com Contributor* | Friday, September 18, 2020

Apparently, the Smith County School System in Tennessee allowed too much religion. The American Civil Liberties Union sued, and the school district ultimately agreed to a consent decree. The district's sin? According to the consent decree, the district had allowed coaches and students to pray before sporting events; fifth-graders to receive free Bibles from the Gideons; a mural in the weight-training room depicting a cross and the national motto, "In God We Trust"; the display of hallway signs containing Bible verses; the reading of Bible verses to students; and the use of a public-address system at graduations and football games to request attendees to bow their heads in prayer. The consent decree continued, "Some of these practices and customs and others alleged in the Complaint (a) endorse and promote religion, (b) have the purpose or effect of advancing religion, and/or (c) coerce religious exercise either directly or indirectly, in violation of the Establishment Clause of the First Amendment."

The school district and its employees are now forbidden from "promoting, advancing, endorsing, participating in, or causing Prayers during or in conjunction with School Events for any school within the School District," from promoting "their personal religious beliefs to students in class or during or in conjunction with a School Event," and they "shall not cite to, read or assign readings from the Bible, a sacred text or a sermon absent a legitimate non-religious, educational objective."

https://www.christianheadlines.com/contributors/michael-foust/judge-orders-school-district-to-halt-prayers-bible-reading-after-aclu-suit.html.

Robert Treat Paine
(1731-1814)

Signer of the Declaration of Independence

Highest Office Attained:
Representative in Congress; Justice of Massachusetts Supreme Court

Religious Affiliation:
Congregationalist; Unitarian

B efore turning to the law, Robert Treat Paine contemplated the ministry, one of many ways in which he emulated his Congregationalist-clergyman father. Paine was born in Boston in 1731 to Rev. Thomas Paine and Eunice Treat Paine, who were married in 1721 by Rev. Peter Thatcher of the New North (Congregational) Church in Boston. Paine's father had himself been the pastor of the Congregational church in nearby Weymouth. But after moving to Boston shortly before Paine's birth, Rev. Paine and his Weymouth church gradually parted ways; Rev. Paine then transitioned his career to that of a merchant. Paine's paternal roots reach back to his immigrant great-grandfather, Thomas Paine, whose own father, Thomas Payne, was an Anglican priest in Hernhill, Kent, England; another paternal ancestor was Stephen Hopkins, a passenger on the *Mayflower*.

Paine's mother, Eunice, was the daughter of Rev. Samuel Treat and Abigail Willard. Rev. Treat was the first pastor of the Congregational church in Eastham, Massachusetts, where he was known for preaching "hellfire and damnation"; he was the son of Robert Treat, Paine's namesake, who was both the governor of Connecticut and the founder of Newark, New Jersey. Paine was baptized by Rev. Thomas Prince in the Old South (Congregational) Church in Boston, where Abigail's own father, Rev. Samuel Willard, had earlier served as pastor while simultaneously serving for a time as acting president of Harvard College. Abigail's puritan, maternal grandfather, Rev. John Sherman, had served as the first pastor of the Congregational church in Wethersfield, Connecticut, and later as pastor of the Congregational church in Watertown, Massachusetts.

As a child, Paine attended the acclaimed Boston Latin School, where he studied, as did John Adams, John Hancock, and other important founders, under headmaster John Lovell. Lovell was known for having one criterion for admission to his school: the ability to read verses from the Bible. At the age of fourteen, Paine entered Harvard, where he lived with the college chaplain and long-time pastor of the First (Congregational) Church of Cambridge, Rev. Nathaniel Appleton. During that time, he joined the Old South Church, where his grandfather had formerly served as pastor. Following Harvard, Paine worked briefly as an usher at Boston Latin, and as a teacher in Lunenberg. At the age of twenty-one, he turned sea captain and merchant and, like his father, traveled the world from the Carolinas to Spain, followed by a whaling expedition to Greenland.

Upon returning to Massachusetts in 1755, Paine began studying law in Lancaster with his mother's cousin, Samuel Willard, a judge of the Court of Common Pleas in Lancaster. The study of law was also a pursuit that his father, the former Rev. Paine, was pursuing at that time late in his own life. Paine had not yet abandoned thoughts of the ministry, however, as he accepted an offer to preach for six weeks in Shirley and a position as chaplain of a regiment during the French and Indian War. But, in 1756, he resumed the study of law under Boston lawyer Benjamin Pratt, later the chief justice of New York. Upon his admission to the bar, he settled in Taunton, where he established a successful law practice and served as a justice of the peace.

Paine became increasingly active in the patriot movement, and, in 1770, prosecuted British soldiers (who were defended by John Adams) for their conduct during the Boston Massacre. That same year, he married Sally Cobb, sister of General David Cobb; General Cobb later served as an aide to General George Washington, a representative in Congress, and lieutenant governor of Massachusetts. Together, Paine and Sally had eight children who were baptized by Rev. Caleb Turner of the First (Congregational) Church in Taunton. Paine also, like Adams, became a follower of Rev. Jonathan Mayhew, pastor of the Old

West (Congregational) Church in Boston, an early forerunner of Unitarianism and decrier of "taxation without representation."

Beginning in 1774, Paine represented Taunton in the Provincial Congress, as well as in the Massachusetts General Court (legislature), including as Speaker of the House of Representatives. Paine also was elected to the Continental Congress, where he was a vocal and active member; his penchant for objecting to others' proposals earned him the moniker, "Objection-Maker." Although initially hopeful that negotiations with Great Britain would prove fruitful, Paine ultimately, while calling for the support of God, proudly voted in favor of independence and signed the Declaration of Independence. He assisted in drafting the Massachusetts state constitution, served as a delegate to its constitutional convention, and served on the Governor's Council. He was elected attorney general of Massachusetts, a position he held from 1777 until 1790, when Governor John Hancock appointed him to be an associate justice of the Massachusetts Supreme Court. Paine held that position until he retired in 1804. He accepted his final public post as counselor of Massachusetts, and was a founder of the American Academy of Arts and Sciences.

Having moved with his family to Boston in 1780, Paine joined the First (Congregational) Church of Boston, and he followed it into Unitarianism. Throughout his life, he was known to be a devout Christian and an unfailing attendee of church services, who viewed the holy scriptures as instruction to mankind of their earthly duties. He died in 1814, his abiding religious faith and trust in God being operative not only throughout his earthly life, but as he offered a Christian blessing to his survivors while passing into his heavenly life.

In His Own Words:

Robert Treat Paine's Confession of Faith
1749[1]

> I desire to bless and praise the name of God most high for appointing me my birth in a land of Gospel Light where the glorious tidings of a Savior and of pardon and salvation through Him have been continually sounding in mine ears. . . .
>
> I believe the Bible to be the written word of God and to contain in it the whole rule of faith and manners.

Letter from Robert Treat Paine to Joseph Palmer
July 6, 1776[2]

> The day before yesterday the declaration of American independency was voted by twelve colonies, agreeable to the sense of the constituents, and New York was silent, till their new convention (which sits next week) express their assent, of which we have some doubt. Thus the issue is joined; and it is our comfortable reflection, that if by struggling we can avoid that servile subjection which Britain demanded, we remain a free and happy people; but **if, through the frowns of Providence, we sink in the struggle, we do but remain the wretched people we should have been without this declaration. Our hearts are full, our hands are full; may God, in whom we trust, support us.**

Last Will and Testament of Robert Treat Paine, attested May 11, 1814[3]

When I consider that this instrument contemplates my departure from this life and all earthly enjoyments and my entrance on another state of existence, **I am constrained to express my adoration of the Supreme Being, the Author of my existence, in full belief of his Providential goodness and His forgiving mercy revealed to the world through Jesus Christ, through whom I hope for never ending happiness in a future state, acknowledging with grateful remembrance the happiness I have enjoyed in my passage through a long life.**

What follows is a
summary of an article
from contemporary American life . . .

nearly 250 years after
Robert Treat Paine
signed

the Declaration of Independence.

What Would Robert Treat Paine Think?

TODD STARNES · Published November 3, 2015

Might offend non-Christians? Man told to remove Christmas display

The West Hayden Estates First Addition Homeowners Association in Hayden, Idaho threatened Jeremy Morris with a lawsuit if he didn't take down his lavish Christmas display—complete with a Living Nativity featuring Dolly the Camel. Why? As the association explained in a certified letter, "I am somewhat hesitant in bringing up the fact that some of our residents are non-Christians or of another faith and I don't even want to think of the problems that could bring up." So much for the proceeds that Jeremy donated to charities serving cancer patients and homeless children.

http://www.foxnews.com/opinion/2015/11/03/might-offend-non-christians-man-told-to-remove-christmas-display.html?intcmp=hplnws.

Chapter Three:

New Hampshire Signers

Josiah Bartlett
(1729-1795)

Signer of the Declaration of Independence and
the Articles of Confederation

Highest Office Attained:
Representative in Congress; President of New Hampshire; Chief Justice of New Hampshire

Religious Affiliation:
Congregationalist

J osiah Bartlett's lineage traces back to Adam Barttelot, who, in 1066, accompanied William the Conqueror of Normandy to establish William's reign in England; he was awarded a tract of land in what became the village of Stopham. Generations later, in 1635, Josiah's great-great-grandfather, Richard Bartlett, emigrated to Newbury, Massachusetts; he operated a ferry between Newbury and nearby Amesbury—later, the site of Josiah's birth. Among the possessions that Richard, a church elder, brought with him was a Breeches Bible—a version of the Geneva Bible that was translated by Protestant scholars influenced by John Calvin. It was inscribed with the birthdates of Richard's family members, one being Bartlett's great-grandfather, Richard Jr., who was then fourteen years old. Richard Jr., who served in the colonial legislature, begat another Richard; this Richard's son, Stephen, was Bartlett's father.

As a child, Bartlett was raised in a puritan and Calvinistic family, attending the First (Congregational) Church of Christ in Amesbury, where his father was a deacon. He was schooled in Latin and Greek by a maternal relative, Rev. John Webster, and at the age of sixteen began the study of medicine with another relative, Dr. Nehemiah Ordway. Dr. Ordway was the son of Deacon John Ordway and the father of a minister, Rev. Nehemiah Ordway. In 1750, at the age of twenty-one, Bartlett established his medical practice in Kingston, New Hampshire. He lived with Rev. Joseph Seccombe in the parsonage of the First (Congregational) Church until his marriage in 1754 to his cousin, Mary Bartlett.

Bartlett was like a son to Rev. Seccombe, and his involvement in the church continued after the pastor's death in 1760. Over the years, he actively opposed the pastorates of certain ministers who were proposed for the church. But, in 1776, he assented to a call to Rev. Elihu Thayer; Rev. Thayer later would deliver Bartlett's eulogy. Bartlett raised his children in the church, and his son, Levi, was sent to Dummer Academy to study under its preceptor, Rev. Samuel Moody.

During that time, Bartlett's career took him from medicine to the world of politics. In 1757, he became a town selectman. In 1765, he was elected to the New Hampshire legislature, and he was soon appointed by loyalist Governor John Wentworth as a justice of the peace and as a commander in the local militia. But notwithstanding those appointments, Bartlett became an ardent patriot and proponent of colonial interests. He was chosen as a delegate to the Continental Congress in 1774, but was forced to decline the seat after his home was burned, presumably by loyalists opposed to his support of the coming revolution.

In 1775, he was again elected to the Congress; the following year, his vote was the first recorded in favor of independence. He was the second, after John Hancock, the president of the Congress, to affix his signature to the Declaration of Independence. And he later also helped draft—and became the first to vote for and sign—the Articles of Confederation that would initially govern the new nation.

In 1780, he was appointed chief justice of the Court of Common Pleas, and he later served on the New Hampshire Supreme Court, including as its chief justice. He was an active member of the convention that framed the United States Constitution, and was chosen for but declined the office of senator in the first United States Congress. In 1788, he served as a delegate and temporary chairman of the New Hampshire state convention, where he strongly advocated in favor of the ratification of the Constitution. In 1790, he was elected the first president (later, governor) of the state of New Hampshire. Following the 1792 re-election of President George Washington, he served as a presidential elector.

While the cause of the revolution became his life's work, Dr. Bartlett never forgot his initial calling. During the war for independence, he applied his medical skills on behalf of the revolutionary fighters. And while serving as president of New Hampshire, he would help found the New Hampshire Medical Society; he signed the charter establishing the society, and he served as its first president. At all times, he approached his profession not through the lens of traditional medical rules, but with an eye toward the laws of nature flowing from the love of God in all of His creation.

A lifelong and devout Christian, Josiah Bartlett is said to have leaned later in life toward the Universalist Church—which promoted the view that all people would be saved—that was beginning to make inroads upon the prevailing Congregationalism. Upon his death in 1795, he was buried in the Universalist Plains Church cemetery in Kingston.

In His Own Words:

Letter from Josiah Bartlett to His Son, Levi Bartlett June 17, 1776[1]

> My Dear Son. I Send this with my love to you and hope it will find you well as it leaves me. Your mother has wrote to me that She hears you are well and like being at School. I hope you will take Care to behave So as to have the good will of your Master & School Mates that I may have the pleasure to hear of your good behavior and that you make a wise improvement of your time to gain learning that the Cost I am at for you may not be in vain.
>
> **You have now an opportunity to gain learning & to fit your self for whatever Station in life it may please God to place you.** If you now neglect the prize put into your hands you will have Cause to repent it all your Days.
>
> **That you may remember that all favors and Blessings Come from the Supreme father of all,**

who is good to all, & his tender mercies are over all his works, and that God will take you under his holy protection is the ardent prayer of your affectionate father.

Josiah Bartlett
Give my Regards to Master Moody

Letter from Josiah Bartlett to His Wife, Mary Bartlett June 24, 1776[2]

I have been for about a week on a Committe of one member from Each Colony to form a Confederation or Charter of firm & Everlasting Union of all the united Colonies: It is a matter of the greatest Consequence & requires the greatest Care in forming it: when it is agreed to by the Committe, it will be laid before the Congress & when they have agreed to it, it will be sent to Each Colony to be by them ratified & Confirmed. **May God grant us wisdom to form a happy Constitution, as the happiness of America to all future Generations Depend on it. . . .**

I hope kind Providence will order all things for the best, and if Sometimes affairs turn out Contrary to our wishes, we must make our selves Easy & Contented, as we are not Certain what is for the best.

Letter from Josiah Bartlett to His Wife, Mary Bartlett July 14, 1776[3]

But **I hope and trust that the Supreme Disposer of all Events, who loveth Justice & hateth iniquity will Continue to favor our righteous Cause and that the wickedness of our Enemies will fall on their own heads.**

I am glad to hear you & my family are well. I am so at this time & may we all Continue so **till it shall please Providence to return to you again** in Due time.

I Can inform you that the greatest preparations are making to oppose the Powerful army that are now or will soon be near New York. **I hope it will be Done Successfully however that Depends on Divine Providence whose ways are unsearchable by human beings.**

Letter from Josiah Bartlett to William Whipple December 15, 1776[4]

I am very loth to go on to raise men Contrary to the Resolves of Congress which has hitherto been held here as Sacred yet **I think the Salvation of the Country Depends (under God) on an army.**

Letter from Josiah Bartlett to Militia Colonels May 3, 1777[5]

Yet if the Country will now Exert themselves like men of Spirit & Resolution, I firmly believe, that God who has hitherto saved the Americans, will now Assist their Endeavours and a few Struggles more fix their Liberties on a Solid Basis.

Letter from Josiah Bartlett to His Wife, Mary Bartlett July 14, 1778[6]

By the favor of Heaven I have had my health as well since I Came from Home as I had it for some time & I think rather better than usual. Hope it will be Continued if for the best. God Grant you & the Rest of my family may Enjoy an Equal share of Health of Body & peace & Contentment of mind.

Letter from Josiah Bartlett to William Whipple
August 21, 1779[7]

I am of your opinion that we ought not put too much dependence on foreign alliance, but on Heaven and our own exertions.

Letter from Josiah Bartlett to the Members of the New Hampshire Senate and House of Representatives
June 9, 1790[8]

Through the partiality of my fellow Citizens I have been called in various Stations & employments to manifest my love and attachment to my country in times of danger & distress and **the best part of my life has been spent in support of a cause which it hath pleased divine Providence to crown with success. That our Country is now free and that we have now the means of attaining all the blessings & advantages resulting from a free & equal Government we are under Heaven indebted to the valour & patriotism of our citizens as yet unparralleled in the Annals of History.** And it is peculiarly grateful to me in the evening of my days to be called by *such* Citizens to the chief seat in Government.

Letter from President Josiah Bartlett to the Members of the New Hampshire Senate and House of Representatives
June 3, 1791[9]

The peace harmony and good order that prevails among us: The Diminution of our late burdensome direct Taxes, the rapid increase of our agriculture & manufacturg, the freedom of Commerce & advantage of fisheries, all conspire to afford us the agreable prospect (if we are not wanting to ourselves) of future ease and Prosperity connected with Civil and Religious Liberty as the happy effects **(under the Smiles of Divine Providence)** of the noble Exertions of the Citizens of the United States in the great cause of Freedom and their Country and as in those Exertions the Citizens of this State in proportion to their numbers and abilities have had at least an equal Share with those of the other States in general, So they have a right to Expect in the Same proportion an Equal Share in all the advantages arising from those Exertions.

Letter from President Josiah Bartlett to the Members of the New Hampshire Senate and House of Representatives November 30, 1791[10]

It afford me peculiar satisfaction at this time to meet the two Houses of the Legislature at this Antient seat of Government of the late Province now state of New Hampshire as it brings to mind the many important Scenes through which we have been conducted in the course of a few years past and which by **(divine goodness)** has terminated in the happy privilege we now enjoy of enacting such Laws as shall be most conducive to the happiness and prosperity of the state with out the controul of a foreign jurisdiction.

Indulged by Providence with so great a blessing it becomes our Indispensible duty in enacting laws and making regulations to consult the general good of the Community and to use our best endeavours both by precept and example to cultivate the principles of virtue and morality of justice and patriotism to encourage a spirit of Industry and Economy and the Increase of Learning and useful knowledge through the state which will be the best means to procure a cordial Submission to the equitable Laws of the

Community and greatly promote the happiness and tranquility of this rising republic.

Proclamation for Day of Thanksgiving, by Governor Josiah Bartlett
October 26, 1793[11]

By His Excellency
Josiah Bartlett, Esquire,
Governor and Commander in Chief of the
State of New Hampshire.

A PROCLAMATION, For A Public THANKSGIVING.

The many favors the inhabitants of this State have been made the subjects of in the court of the current year, **call for a public return of sincerer gratitude and praise to that Being from whom all our mercies flow;** — And the Legislature having appointed Thursday the Twenty First day of November next, to be observed as a **day of public Thanksgiving** throughout this State:

I have thought fit, by and with the advice of Council, to issue this Proclamation, exhorting the people of every denomination to **dedicate said day to the duties of thanksgiving and praise, and to devote a reasonable part thereof in their respective places of public worship in a social manner, with grateful hearts and united voices in returning our most humble and hearty thanks to Almighty God for the unmerited favors He has been graciously pleased to confer upon us in the course of the present year now drawing to a close.**

In a particular manner, **that He was graciously pleased to appear for us in the course of the**

summer past when, by reason of a severe and early drought, the hope of the husbandman seemed likely to be cut off and we were threatened with a great and general scarcity of the necessary fruits and of the field, that **in the midst of judgment He remembered mercy** and by sending plentiful showers of rain, the decaying and almost dying fruits of the earth were greatly revived; and that He has been pleased so to order the latter part of the season, that **we are still blessed** with a competent supply of the most of the necessary fruits of the field.

That He had been pleased to continue to us the inestimable blessings of civil and religious liberty.

That notwithstanding the tumults and confusions of the contending nations, **we still enjoy the blessing of peace and good government.**

That we have been favored with a general measure of health, and that no waiting and pestilential disease has been suffered to prevail among us.

And together with our thanksgiving, let us entreat the Father of Mercies, to continue us the blessings we now enjoy, and bestow upon us all further needed favors.

That it would please Him still to have these United States under His Holy protection and guidance — that He would inspire those who have the management of all our public affairs with all that wisdom, prudence and integrity that is necessary to the faithful discharge of their important trusts, that all their determinations may tend to promote the real happiness and prosperity of this great and rising Republic, and that all people may be

disposed to afflict in carrying such determinations into effect.

That it would please God to over-rule the tumults and confusions among the nations, in such a manner as shall **subserve to His own Glory** and the best good and happiness of mankind, and that in His own due time, He would calm the angry passions of the contending nations and say to them, peace, be still.

That God would be pleased to look down with an eye of compassion upon the whole human race, and dispel those clouds of ignorance, superstition and bigotry that overspread so great a part of the world, **and that the knowledge of and reverential love and regard to the One God and Father, of all, and a true benevolence and good will to their fellow men, may pervade the hearts, and influence the lives of all mankind, and all Nations, Languages and Tongues be brought to join in singing, Glory to God in the highest, on Earth Peace and good will to men.**

It is recommended and expected, that all persons abstain from all servile labor and such recreations as are unbecoming the solemnity of said day.

Given at the Council Chamber in Exeter, the Fifth day of October, in the year of our Lord, one thousand, seven hundred and ninety three and of the Sovereignty and Independence of the United states of America the Eighteenth.

Josiah Bartlett.
By His Excellency's command,
with the advice of Council,
JOSEPH PEARSON, *Sec'ry.*

BY HIS EXCELLENCY
JOSIAH BARTLETT, Esquire,
Governour and Commander in Chief of the
State of New-Hampshire.

A PROCLAMATION,
FOR A PUBLIC
THANKSGIVING.

THE many favours the inhabitants of this
State have been made the subjects of in
the course of the current year, call for a public return of sincere gratitude and praise to that
Being from whom all our mercies flow;—And
the Legislature having appointed Thursday the
Twenty First day of November next, to be
observed as a day of public Thanksgiving
throughout this State:

I have thought fit, by and with the advice
of Council, to issue this Proclamation, exhorting the people of every denomination to dedicate said day to the duties of thanksgiving
and praise, and to devote a reasonable part
thereof in their respective places of public
worship, in a social manner, with grateful
hearts and united voices in returning our most
humble and hearty thanks to Almighty God
for the unmerited favours he has been graciously pleased to confer upon us in the course
of the present year now drawing to a close.

In a particular manner, that he was graciously pleased to appear for us in the course of
the summer past, when by reason of a severe
and early drought, the hope of the husbandman seemed likely to be cut off, and we were
threatened with a great and general scarcity of
the necessary fruits of the field, that in the
midst of judgment he remembered mercy, and
by sending plentiful showers of rain, the decaying and almost dying fruits of the earth
were greatly revived; and that he has been
pleased so to order the latter part of the season,
that we are still blessed with a competent supply of most of the necessary fruits of the field.

That he has been pleased to continue to us
the inestimable blessings of civil and religious

liberty.

That notwithstanding the tumults and confusions of the contending nations, we still enjoy the blessing of peace and good government.

That we have been favoured with a general measure of health, and that no wasting and
pestilential disease has been suffered to prevail
among us.

And together with our thanksgivings, let us
entreat the Father of mercies, to continue to us
the blessings we now enjoy, and bestow upon
us all further needful favours.

That it would please him still to have these
United States under his holy protection and
guidance;—That he would inspire those who
have the management of all our public affairs
with all that wisdom, prudence and integrity
that is necessary to the faithful discharge of
their important trusts, that all their determinations may tend to promote the real happiness
and prosperity of this great and rising Republic, and that all people may be disposed to assist in carrying such determinations into effect.

That it would please God to over-rule
the tumults and confusions among the nations,
in such a manner as shall subserve to his own
Glory and the best good and happiness of mankind, and that in his own due time, he would
calm the angry passions of the contending nations and say to them, peace, be still.

That God would be pleased to look down
with an eye of compassion upon the whole human race, and dispel those clouds of ignorance,
superstition and bigotry that overspread so great
a part of the world, and that the knowledge of,
and a reverential love and regard to the One

God and Father of all, and a true benevolence
and good will to their fellow-men, may pervade the hearts, and influence the lives of all
mankind, and all Nations, languages and
Tongues be brought to join in singing, Glory to God in the highest, on Earth Peace and
good will to men.

It is recommended and expected, that all persons abstain from all servile labour, and such
recreations as are unbecoming the solemnity of
said day.

GIVEN at the Council Chamber in Exeter, the
Fifth day of October, in the year of our LORD,
one thousand, seven hundred and ninety-three and
of the Sovereignty and Independence of the United States of America the Eighteenth.

Josiah Bartlett.

By His Excellency's command,
with advice of Council,
JOSEPH PEARSON, Secry.

Will of Josiah Bartlett
February 25, 1795[12]

I Josiah Bartlett of Kingstown in the County of
Rockingham and State of Newhampshire Esquire,
being at this time of a sound mind, Do make & ordain
this my last Will and Testament, that is to Say, **Firstly
I Commit my Soul into the hands of GOD its great
and benevolent Author** and my body to the Earth to
be buried in a decent manner.

What follows is a
summary of an article
from contemporary American life . . .

nearly 250 years after
Josiah Bartlett
signed

the Declaration of Independence
and
the Articles of Confederation.

What Would Josiah Bartlett Think?

Texas Teens Stand up to Atheists and Defend Christian Flag

Todd Starnes
Oct 22, 2017

Three flags have flown outside LaPoynor High School in LaRue, Texas for as long as anyone can remember. The first is Old Glory—the red, white, and blue of the United States of America. The second is the Texas state flag. And the third—white, with a red cross over a blue field—is the Christian flag. But while residents of LaRue may cherish their flags, the Wisconsin-based Freedom From Religion Foundation demanded that the Christian flag be removed. Said the FFRF, "The District must immediately remove the Christian flag from school grounds. In addition, the District must ensure that its staff members are not organizing, promoting, or participating in religious events while acting in their official capacities."

While school officials pondered what to do, students at the high school stood up for themselves, purchased Christian flags of their own, and proudly displayed them in the beds of their pickup trucks as they lined the high school parking lot. Said one high school junior, "They can try to take it, but we're going to fight for it." Another local resident summed up the feelings of many at a school board meeting: "The Freedom From Religion organization really has a distorted and inaccurate view of the separation of church and state in the First Amendment. Matter fact I'd like to say that their viewpoint is probably void and alien to that of our founding fathers."

https://www.toddstarnes.com/uncategorized/texas-teens-stand-up-to-atheists-and-defend-christian-flag/.

Nicholas Gilman
(1755-1814)

Signer of the United States Constitution

Highest Office Attained:
United States Senator

Religious Affiliation:
Congregationalist

Nicholas Gilman hailed from a family that was puritan and Congregationalist to its core. His paternal ancestry is traced to Edward Gilman (or perhaps Gyllman), who was born in 1530 in Norfolk, England. His maternal ancestry includes Rev. John Rogers ("Roaring John"), who was born in 1571 in Moulsham, Essex, England; he became a fiery preacher in the town of Dedham. Roaring John's grandfather, Rev. John Rogers, was prebendary of St. Paul's; vicar of St. Sepulchre's; and a reader of divinity. In 1555, he became the first martyr burned during Queen Mary's reign of brutality. The resulting growth of Puritanism would thereafter take root in both the Gilman and Rogers families; they would later come together in Exeter, New Hampshire, and would officially be joined upon the marriage of Gilman's parents, Nicholas Gilman Sr. and Ann Taylor, in 1752.

Edward Gilman's grandson, also named Edward, was a leader in the community in Hingham, Norfolk, England in the early 1600s. He was an active member of the local parish church, St. Andrews, then led by Rev. Robert Peck, its vicar; Rev. Peck is believed to have been Edward's cousin. Although the Church of England had by then broken from the Catholic Church, many Anglicans felt that the reforms had not gone far enough. Rev. Peck was among them, and his puritan ideas greatly influenced the parishioners at St. Andrews. In 1638, facing prosecution in the church courts, Rev. Peck chose to depart England for the New World; a significant number of his parishioners, the Gilman family among them, accompanied him. Others who made the journey included ancestors of future President Abraham Lincoln.

Sailing aboard the *Diligent*, Edward and his family settled initially in what became known as Hingham, Massachusetts. By about 1648, after brief residencies in Rehoboth and Ipswich,

Massachusetts, they had established themselves in Exeter, New Hampshire. Edward's three grown sons, Edward Jr., John, and Moses, accompanied him there; they initially followed him into the business of sawmilling.

Son John Gilman (known as Councilor John) also became active in public affairs. He served as a captain in the local militia; as an Exeter selectman; as a member of the New Hampshire Colony Council; and in the New Hampshire Assembly, including as its Speaker. Baptized at St. Andrews, his activities on behalf of the Congregational church in Exeter included serving on a committee in 1693 that called Rev. John Clarke to be its second pastor. Rev. Clarke's sister, Sarah, later would marry Councilor John's son, Judge Nicholas Gilman; it was their great-grandson, Nicholas Gilman, who would come to sign the United States Constitution.

In 1727, Royal Governor John Wentworth granted a charter to the new town of Gilmanton (then, Gilmantown), New Hampshire, twenty-four of whose proprietors bore the name Gilman. Among them were Judge Gilman; his son, Daniel; and his grandson, Nicholas. The charter was conditioned on the building of a meetinghouse for the worship of God within four years. Notwithstanding their proprietorship of Gilmanton, Daniel's branch of the Gilman family continued to reside in Exeter.

In 1743, signer Nicholas Gilman's grandfather, the same Daniel Gilman, was among those in Exeter who were sympa-thetic to the views of Rev. George Whitefield, leader of the Great Awakening movement. They formed the second Congregational church, which Rev. Daniel Rogers came to pastor. Daniel Gilman willed the use of his silver tankard to "the church of Christ in Exeter whereof the Rev'd Daniel Rogers is pastor"; Daniel later died of apoplexy while in church. Another friend of Rev. Whitefield's was Daniel Gilman's brother, Rev. Nicholas Gilman, pastor of the Congregational church in Durham, New Hampshire; Rev. Gilman's son, Rev. Tristram Gilman, came to pastor the Congregational church in Yarmouth, Maine.

Rev. Rogers was the son of a famous Ipswich pastor, Rev. John Rogers, whose father—also named Rev. John Rogers—was president of Harvard College. President Rogers's father was Rev. Nathaniel Rogers of Ipswich, England; and his father was none other than "Roaring John," the puritan ancestor of signer Nicholas's mother, Ann (Taylor) Gilman. Ann was born to Rev. John Taylor of Milton, Massachusetts and Elizabeth (Rogers) Taylor; Elizabeth's father, Rev. Nathaniel Rogers, was the pastor of the Congregational church in Portsmouth, New Hampshire and the uncle of Rev. Rogers of Exeter.

In 1752, Ann married Nicholas Gilman Sr., the signer's father. Nicholas Sr. was exceedingly influential in Exeter and beyond. A shipbuilder and merchant, Nicholas Sr. became a leader in the patriot movement. He served as a commander of a New Hampshire militia regiment, became treasurer and councilor of New Hampshire, and was a member of its Committee of Safety. Described as the "Brains of the Revolution in New Hampshire," he passed along to his sons his great passion for liberty. Eldest son John Taylor Gilman succeeded his father as treasurer of New Hampshire and served the public in numerous other roles; he was a representative in the Continental Congress and a long-standing governor of New Hampshire. Youngest son Nathaniel held office in the state legislature, and also served as state treasurer. And Nicholas Jr. served in both houses of the national legislature and became signatory to the nation's Constitution.

Born in Exeter in 1755, Nicholas Gilman Jr. served as a captain in the New Hampshire regiment of the Continental Army during the war for independence, and as senior deputy adjutant general on the staff of General George Washington. He then was elected to the Continental Congress, represented New Hampshire during the Constitutional Convention, and upon becoming a signatory to the Constitution, helped secure its ratification by the State of New Hampshire. He later served in the United States House of Representatives, as a presidential elector, and in the New Hampshire state legislature. In 1804, he was elected to the United States Senate; he served there until his death in 1814, having never married, at the age of fifty-eight. A puritan Congregationalist to the end, he was buried in the Winter Street Cemetery in Exeter, located on land that had been willed to the town by his great-great-grandfather, Councilman John.

In His Own Words:

Letter from Nicholas Gilman to John Langdon
October 30, 1787[1]

> Should there be a War in Europe it would be peculiarly unfortunate for us not to have an efficient Government by which we might be enabled to avail ourselves of the advantages that would open to us. It seems as tho. nothing but a consideration of the wretched state of the finances of France and England now smothers the flame and should the report of Cornwallace's having sunk the french Vessel in Calcutta prove true; there is some reason to believe it will soon burst forth. **Be these things as they may I pray GOD to give us a further respite with Wisdom to improve the present Glorious opportunity to become great and happy.**

Congressional Resolution Regarding Congressional Oath of Office, Adopted on Motion by Representative Nicholas Gilman (and others)
April 6, 1789[2]

> Resolved, That the form of the oath to be taken by the members of this Houses, as required by the third clause of the sixth article of the Constitution of Government of the United States, be as followeth, to wit: "I, A B a Representative of the United States in the Congress thereof, **do solemnly swear (or affirm, as the case may be) in the presence of Almighty**

GOD, that I will support the Constitution of the United States. So help me GOD."

MONDAY APRIL 6.

Another member, to wit, Daniel Carroll, from Maryland, appeared and took his seat.
On motion,
Ordered, That leave be given to bring in a bill to regulate the taking the oath or affirmation prescribed by the sixth article of the Constitution; and that Mr. White, Mr. Madison, Mr. Trumbull, Mr. Gilman, and Mr. Cadwalader, do prepare and bring in the same.
On motion,
Resolved, That the form of the oath to be taken by the members of this House, as. required by the third clause of the sixth article of the Constitution of Government of the United States, be as followeth, to wit: "I, A B a Representative of the United " States in the Congress thereof, do solemnly swear (or affirm, as the case may be) in " the presence of Almighty GOD, that I will support the Constitution of the United " States. So help me GOD."

Congressional Address, as Passed by House of Representatives (Representative Nicholas Gilman Voting in Favor), to be Delivered to President George Washington upon his Impending Retirement
December 15, 1796[3]

When we advert to the internal situation of the United States, we deem it equally natural and becoming to compare the present period with that immediately antecedent to the operation of the Government, and to contrast it with the calamities in which the state of war still involves several of the European nations, as the reflections deduced from both, tend to justify as well as to excite a warmer admiration of our free Constitution, and **to exalt our minds to a more fervent and grateful sense of piety towards Almighty God, for the beneficence of his providence, by which its administration has been hitherto so remarkably distinguished. . . .**

The spectacle of a free and enlightened Nation offering, by its Representatives, the tribute of unfeigned approbation to its First Citizen, however novel and interesting it may be, **derives all its lustre (a lustre which accident or enthusiasm could not bestow, and which adulation would tarnish,) from the trancedent merit of which it is the voluntary testimony.**

May you long enjoy that liberty which is so dear to you, and to which your name will ever be so dear: **May your own virtues and a Nation's prayers obtain the happiest sunshine for the decline of your days, and the choicest of future blessings.** For our country's sake; for the sake of Republican liberty; it is our earnest wish that your example may be the guide of your successors; and thus, after being the ornament and safeguard of the present age, become the patrimony of our descendants.

Congressional Resolution Requesting President to Recommend Day of Public Humiliation and Prayer, Approved by Congress (including Representative Nicholas Gilman) July 16, 1813[4]

The **resolution requesting the President of the United States to recommend a day of public humiliation and prayer** . . . passed, as follows:

It being a duty peculiarly incumbent in a time of public calamity and war, humbly and devoutly to acknowledge our dependence on Almighty God, and to implore his aid and protection: therefore,

«**Resolved**, by the Senate and House of Representatives of the United States of America, in Congress assembled, That a joint committee of both Houses wait on the President of the United States and **request that he recommend a day of public humiliation and prayer, to be observed** by the people of the United States with religious solemnity, and the offering of fervent supplications to Almighty God for the safety and welfare of these states, his blessing on their arms, and the speedy restoration of peace.»

What follows is a
summary of an article
from contemporary American life . . .

nearly 250 years after
Nicholas Gilman
signed

the United States Constitution.

What Would Nicholas Gilman Think?

PENTAGON MAY COURT MARTIAL SOLDIERS WHO SHARE CHRISTIAN FAITH

by KEN KLUKOWSKI | 1 May 2013 | 11,797

Pentagon officials in the Obama Administration announced that "Religious proselytization is not permitted within the Department of Defense . . . Court martials and non-judicial punishments are decided on a case-by-case basis . . . ." The statement was issued after Pentagon appointees met with Mikey Weinstein of the Military Religious Freedom Foundation, who contends that Christians (and even military chaplains) commit "treason" and "spiritual rape" by sharing their Christian faith in the military and that they are "enemies of the Constitution."

http://www.breitbart.com/national-security/2013/05/01/breaking-pentagon-confirms-will-court-martial-soldiers-who-share-christian-faith/.

John Langdon
(1741-1819)

Signer of the United States Constitution

Highest Office Attained:
United States Senator; Governor of New Hampshire

Religious Affiliation:
Congregationalist

J ohn Langdon's ancestors hailed from England, his great-great-grandfather, Tobias Langdon I, having been born in Cornwall in 1631. In 1656, having settled in New Hampshire, Tobias married Elizabeth Sherburne in the Old South Church of Portsmouth. Her parents, Henry Sherburne and Rebecca Gibbons Sherburne, had emigrated from Odiham, Hampshire, England in 1632, traveling with Captain John Mason as part of the great puritan migration.

The town of Portsmouth, however, unlike many other New England communities, was settled not as a bastion of religious freedom, but rather as a center of commerce. And the church in Portsmouth initially preserved the traditions of the Church of England. It was built upon land originally deeded to, among others, the same Henry Sherburne—who also was one of the church wardens—and a John Landen (or Langden)—likely Tobias's father or other kin of signer Langdon. The church's Anglican traditions were short-lived, however. The first minister of the church, Rev. Richard Gibson, was charged by the royal governor of Massachusetts with conducting baptisms and mar-riages without authority, and by 1642 he was forced to resign and return to England. The Anglicans in what was originally known as Strawbery Banke were thus left without a church.

For a time, church services proceeded unsanctioned by any established church, but beginning in 1658 they were led by a Congregationalist, Rev. Joseph Moodey. Upon his ordination in 1671, the Church of Christ in Portsmouth was formally estab-lished, and the pastorate of Rev. Moodey continued there until his death in 1697. At one point, however, the English provin-cial governor, Edward Cranfield, demanded that Rev. Moodey perform communion in the Anglican manner; upon his refusal, Governor Cranfield imprisoned the pastor for thirteen weeks.

211

Rev. Moodey was succeeded in the pulpit by Rev. Nathaniel Rogers; he was presiding over the church when, in 1713, it split into two parishes—the north parish and the south parish. The ministry of Rev. Rogers then continued in the north parish, and the Langdons were among the parishioners who followed him there. This included Langdon's grandfather, Tobias Langdon II—a deacon in the church—and his son, a young John Langdon Sr.—the father of the signer. In 1775, Rev. Rogers's successor in that church, Rev. Jabez Fitch, delivered the funeral sermon for Langdon's great-great-grandmother, Elizabeth.

Langdon's mother, Mary Hall Langdon, came from a prominent Congregationalist family in Exeter, New Hampshire. She was descended from Thomas Dudley, the second governor of the Massachusetts Bay colony. Mary's parents, Josiah Hall and Mary Woodbury Hall, were married in the Exeter Congregational Church.

A lifelong attendee of Portsmouth's north church, Langdon was educated in the celebrated Latin grammar school run by a respected south parish parishioner, Major Samuel Hale. He then worked as an apprentice in the business of a prominent merchant, Daniel Rindge, and later saw the world as a ship's captain. Eventually, he owned a fleet of vessels and became a successful, international sea merchant. British control over the shipping industry negatively impacted his business interests, however, influencing him to become an early supporter of the growing revolutionary fervor. He became a selectman in Portsmouth, and served on New Hampshire's Committee of Correspondence. He became a leader of the Sons of Liberty, and participated in the seizure of British munitions in 1774. That same year, he and his brother, Woodbury Langdon, were both elected to the New Hampshire legislature. In 1775, Langdon was elected to the Continental Congress. He was also a driving force in securing for New Hampshire the distinction among the states of being the first to craft a state constitution. The following year, and although a vigorous supporter of the revolution, Langdon left the Congress shortly before the vote was taken to declare independence. Instead, his support for the patriot cause took him in a different direction, as he was asked to oversee the construction of several warships; one of them, the *Ranger*, was captained by John Paul Jones. He also assumed the position of marine agent for New Hampshire, the primary national government official within the state.

In 1777, Langdon began serving as the Speaker of the lower assembly of the New Hampshire legislature. He also took an active role in organizing the New Hampshire militia, in which he served as a colonel. The same year, he married Elizabeth Sherburne, twenty-two years his junior; she shared with Langdon the heritage of their common great-great-grandparents, the same Henry and Rebecca Gibbons Sherburne. Elizabeth also shared common maternal grandparents, Robert and Dorcas Hammond Cutt, with General William Whipple, a signer of the Declaration of Independence; Whipple had married Elizabeth's Aunt Katharine, and he thus became Langdon's uncle by marriage. The Langdons raised their children in the north parish church; they were christened there by the respected Congregational minister, Rev. Ezra Stiles, who briefly pastored the church before assuming the presidency of Yale College.

Following the war, Langdon continued his service in the state legislature, but gave up his seat in the Congress. He then served as governor of the state, actively represented New Hampshire in the constitutional convention that framed the United States Constitution that bears his signature, and was a delegate to the state's ratifying convention. In 1789, Langdon left the governorship to assume a new role as one of New Hampshire's first senators under the new national Constitution. He served as the first president of the Senate. In that role, he presided over its initial session called to count the electoral votes cast for president and vice president; and he had the honor of informing George Washington that he had been elected as the first President of the United States, and of administering the oath of office to him. Later that year, Langdon welcomed President Washington to Portsmouth, and hosted him for services at the north parish church. Langdon retired from the Senate in 1801, declined President Thomas Jefferson's offer to become secretary of the navy, and returned to New Hampshire to again serve in the state legislature, as Speaker, and as governor.

After Langdon's brother, then-Justice Woodbury Langdon, died in 1805, Langdon's thoughts turned more than ever toward God. Always known as a Christian in the Calvinist tradition, Langdon devoted the rest of his years purely to religious endeavors. He cultivated the acquaintance of ministers of various denominations. During the pastorate of Rev. Joseph Buckminster, he and his wife (and his sister, Elizabeth Barrell) formally joined the membership of the north parish church that he had long attended; he served the church as a warden. He co-founded the New Hampshire Bible Society, serving as its first president. He also served as a vice-president of the American Bible Society; its mission was to distribute Bibles, especially among the poor and needy.

In 1812, Langdon declined nomination for the office of Vice President of the United States. He passed into eternity in 1819, six years after his beloved Elizabeth, and was buried in Portsmouth's north burial grounds.

In His Own Words:

Letter from John Langton (and Josiah Bartlett) to New Hampshire Convention (upon approval by Continental Congress of petition to form a state government) November 1775[1]

> We think we can say without any boasting that we have done our duty in this matter, by paying constant attention, for a long time, not only in the house, but in private conversation with members, to clear up any doubts they might have. **We can't help rejoicing to see this as a groundwork of our government, and hope by the Blessing of Divine Providence, never to return to our despotick state.**

Letter from John Langdon to James Monroe
April 12, 1776[2]

> [T]hanks to good Providence, the day is at hand when United America will see her True friends.

Proclamation for a Public Thanksgiving, by President Meshech Weare and Speaker John Langdon
November 19, 1778[3]

Proclamation for a Public Thanksgiving.

The mercies which, notwith-standing our great Unworthiness, we are constantly receiving at the Hands of Almighty God, ought ever to remind us of our obligations to him; and it becomes our especial duty at the Close of a year, to unite together in rendering thanks to the Divine Dispenser of all good for the bounties of his providence conferred on us in the course thereof.

We have therefore thought fit to appoint and accordingly do appoint Thursday the Tenth day of December next to be observed as a **day of Public Thanksgiving** throughout this state — **hereby calling upon Ministers and People of all Denominations to meet for religious Worship on said day and** <u>Devoutly</u> **to offer up their unfeigned Praises to Almighty God, the Source and Benevolent bestower of all good, who in the midst of Judgment hath been graciously pleased to remember great mercy — for** his affording the necessary means of Subsistence though our commerce has been so greatly obstructed in that such a measure of health has been and is still enjoyed among us — **that** the lives of our officers and soldiers has been preserved — **that**, notwithstanding the threatening aspects of

Providence the last summer he hath dispensed to us the Fruits of the earth in such quantity, as will enable us cheerfully to wait his further Bounty — **That** the attempts of our enemies have in a great measure proved abortive — **That** our rights and privileges, both civil and Religious, are yet presented to us, notwithstanding all the Endeavors of our barbarous Enemies to deprive us of them.

At the same time, to offer up humble and fervent Prayers to Almighty God for these free Sovereign and Independent States. That he would commiserate us in our present Distresses, and deliver us out of the hands of our enemies – **That** he would enable us to recover our rights and Properties by them unjustly invaded — **That** he would keep all Sin out of our camps, as well as from the whole Community, and make us a penitent and reformed people — **That** he would Inspire our officers with conduct and resolution, and our soldiers with faithfulness and courage; and **that as the Captain of our Salvation**, he would lead them on to Success and Victory — **That** he would graciously Divest our the Counsels and prosper the Just arms of these States for restoring and establishing Peace — and **that the divine Promises and predictions of the universal and Spiritual Reign of our Lord and Savior Jesus Christ, the prince of Peace, may be speedily accomplished.** — And all Servile Labor is forbidden on Said day.

State of New Hampshire November 19th, 1778
By order of the Council and Assembly
E. Thompson Secry
M Weare President
John Langdon Speaker
God save the United States of America.

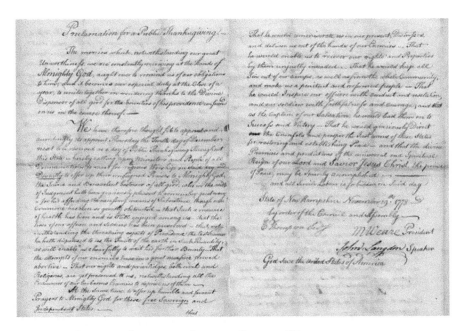

Letter from John Langdon to James Monroe December 5, 1794[4]

It is with Infinite satisfaction I hear the generous and kind Reception you have met with from the National Assembly of France. The Intrepidity, Justice, and Magnanimity of that great Nation Astonishes the Universe; **I pray God they may finally prevail over all their enemies**, and establish such a Government as shall conduce to their lasting happiness and an example to the rest of the World. . . . We are every day entertained and gratified with the Amazing Successes of France, in which the great Body of the people of this Country most righteously Rejoice; and **I most Religiously wish our Government would do more then barely to Rejoice. However, I believe it is Intended by good Providence that France shall have all the honor and Glory of Saving not only themselves but the Rest of the World from Despotism.**

Proclamation for a Day of Thanksgiving and Prayer, by Governor John Langdon
October 10, 1805[5]

STATE OF NEW HAMPSHIRE.
BY THE GOVERNOR.
A PROCLAMATION.

It has been customary for the citizens of this state, at the recommendations of the supreme executive authority, to set **apart a certain day near the close of the year for the purpose of publicly recognizing their dependence upon Almighty God for protection, and that they might express their gratitude to Him for all blessings and mercies received and implore a continuance of them;** — I therefore, in conformity to this laudable and long established practice, do by and with the advice of the council, appoint THURSDAY THE TWENTY-EIGHTH DAY OF NOVEMBER NEXT to be observed as a **day of PUBLIC THANKSGIVING AND PRAYER** throughout this state, hereby **exhorting the people of all sects and denominations to assemble with their pastors and religious teachers, at their respective places of public worship on that day, and devote a reasonable part thereof in praising and adoring Almighty God, and in offering up our thanks to Him as the great author of every good and perfect gift, for the many favors that he has been pleased to bestow upon us as individuals during the past year; as also for the gracious exercise of his guardian care over the great and general concerns of our common country. That** although the earth has been visited by a severe and early drought, yet **that** by his blessing we are favored with a competency of the fruits of the field, for the supplies of another year. **That** we have not been afflicted with those contagious diseases that have visited some of the cities of our sister states, but have enjoyed a general measure of health.

That the life and health of the President of the United States have been preserved; **that** our civil and religious liberties are secure; and that no internal causes have occurred to disturb the peace and harmony of our land. **For** the termination of our contest with one of the African powers; the liberation of our fellow-citizens from bondage, and their restoration to the arms of their country, and the sweets of liberty. **For** his smiles on our commerce, navigation and fisheries, and **for** that prosperity that has generally prevailed. **But above all, for the inestimable blessings of the gospel of peace and salvation, the means of grace and hopes of future glory, through the merits of a crucified Savior.**

And while our mouths are filled with praise and thanksgiving, let us supplicate our heavenly benefactor, that he would penetrate our hearts as well with a due sense of his goodness, as of our own unworthiness, and continue to us all the blessings that we now enjoy, and bestow upon us all such addition favors as may be for our good. That he would be pleased to keep the government of the United States under his protection; **bless** our nations in all its internal and external concerns, and **inspire** all in authority with wisdom, and with a patriotic regard to its welfare and honor. **That** he would command the pestilence that now scourges some of the cities of our country to cease its desolations, and make those cities rejoice in the return of health, and in **the mercies of the Lord. That** he would particularly keep this state under **his holy and superintending care, smile** upon its agriculture, commerce, and fisheries, and **bless** the labors of the laborer in every walk and department of life. **That** he would cherish our university, our academies and schools, and all our institutions for promoting improvements in knowledge, usefulness, and virtue. **That** he would preside in all our courts and **inspire** those who make, and those who administer the laws, **with his divine wisdom**; and make every branch of our civil government sub serve the best interests of the people. **That he would bless the means used for the promulgation of his word, and make pure religion and morality more and more abound.** And it is hereby earnestly recommended that all persons abstain from labor and recreation unbecoming the solemnities of the day.

Given at the council chamber in Portsmouth, this tenth day of October, in the year of our Lord, one thousand eight hundred and five, and of the independence of the United States of America, the thirtieth.

JOHN LANGDON
By His Excellency's Command, with advice of council.

Letter from John Langdon to Thomas Jefferson
February 18, 1810[6]

I look back often, with pleasure, when I call to my recollection, the happy hours I have passed, while I had the honor of associating with you S^r in our General Govm^t although **we had every thing to contend with yet kind Providence gave us the Victory**.

Letter from John Langdon to Congressman Harper (describing his feelings toward President James Madison, upon declining nomination as vice president)
June 15, 1812[7]

I should have thought it an honor & it would have been my highest pleasure to serve my country in any station while my great and good friend Mr. Madison continued in the presidency, as **I consider him one of our greatest statesmen, an ornament to our Country and above all *the noblest work of God, an honest man*.**

John Langdon's Last Will and Testament[8]

In the name of God, Amen. I, John Langdon, . . . considering the uncertainty of life and that it is appointed unto all men once to die [**Hebrews 9:27**], do make, ordain and publish this my last will and testament in manner following, that is to say — First: **I commend my soul to the infinite mercies of God in Christ Jesus, the beloved Son of the Father, who died and rose again that He might be the Lord of the dead and of the living . . . professing to believe and hope in the joyful Scripture doctrine of a resurrection to eternal life.**

What follows is a
summary of an article
from contemporary American life . . .

nearly 250 years after
John Langdon
signed

the United States Constitution.

What Would John Langdon Think?

TODD STARNES · Published August 17, 2016

Air Force officer faces investigation over Bible on his desk

OPINION By Todd Starnes, | Fox News

Air Force Major Steve Lewis, a supervisor at the Reserve National Security Space Institute at Peterson Air Force Base in Colorado Springs, found himself under investigation. His infraction? The open Bible on his desk.

The Military Religious Freedom Foundation demanded that Major Lewis be "aggressively punished" for "harboring and encouraging a truly abhorrent example of First Amendment civil rights violations." Said the MRFF, "It's not his desk. That desk belongs to the American people, to the U.S. military."

According to Colonel Damon Feltman, the commander of the 310th Space Wing, Major Lewis "removed the Bible voluntarily because he didn't want this to cause attention or disruption to his unit." Colonel Feltman later "performed a walk-through of the office and everything seemed to be in compliance with Air Force regulation."

*https://www.foxnews.com/opinion/
air-force-officer-faces-investigation-over-bible-on-his-desk.*

Matthew Thornton
(1714-1803)

Signer of the Declaration of Independence

Highest Office Attained:
Representative in Congress

Religious Affiliation:
Presbyterian

Of English ancestry, Matthew Thornton was born in pre-
dominantly-Catholic northern Ireland in 1714, emigrating
to America with his family at the age of three. Thornton's parents,
James and Elizabeth Jenkins Thornton, were among the Scots-
Irish Presbyterians who sought refuge in the religious freedoms
afforded in the colonies. Led by Rev. Edward Fitzgerald, they
initially settled in what is now Wiscasset, Maine, but soon established themselves in Worcester, Massachusetts. There, young
Matthew was educated in the schools that later would employ
future President John Adams as a teacher.

Religious intolerance followed the Thorntons, however,
although the source of that intolerance now was the Puritans
of the prevailing Congregational church. The denominational differences were not principally doctrinal in nature, but
rather related to the form of church governance. But while the
Congregationalists of Worcester allowed Presbyterian services
to take place, they relegated them to an old garrison house
known as the "Old Fort." And the Presbyterian community in
Worcester was taxed to support the local Congregational ministry. In 1733, the Presbyterians were assigned seats in the First
Parish (Congregational) Church, but they were not allowed to
hold their own services there. In 1736, wishing to support the
ministry of Rev. William Johnston as their own pastor, they
petitioned for relief from the burden of Congregational taxation.
The rejection of their petition gave rise to another Presbyterian
exodus, this time from Worcester, again in search of religious
tolerance. In 1738, James Thornton was among the organizers
of a new town, later called Pelham, New Hampshire, that would
be of the Presbyterian persuasion.

Son Matthew Thornton soon embarked upon the study of
medicine in Leicester, Massachusetts. He apprenticed under the

tutelage of a Leicester physician, although authorities differ over whether this was a relative by the name of Dr. Grout or the Rev. Dr. Thomas Green; Dr. Green, in addition to being a prominent physician, was the pastor of the Baptist church in Leicester.

In 1740, Thornton established what became a thriving medical practice in Londonderry, New Hampshire. It was there that he would reside for many years, and where he would later rise to prominence in the cause for independence. In 1745, he volunteered his services as a surgeon on behalf of the New Hampshire regiment supporting the British campaign against the French stronghold of Fort Louisbourg in Cape Breton, Canada. Following that campaign, Thornton returned to his medical practice in Londonderry, and also became increasingly active in political affairs. In 1758, he was elected to represent Londonderry in the provincial legislature, where he served until 1762.

Meanwhile, in 1760, Thornton married Hannah Jack, the daughter of Andrew and Mary Morison Jack of Chester, New Hampshire. Like the Thorntons, the Jacks were Scots-Irish Presbyterians, and like Worcester, Chester had been the site of dissension between the Presbyterians and the prevailing Congregationalists. The Presbyterians of Chester were successful, however, in establishing their own church, and Andrew later was a warden in that church during the ministry of Rev. John Wilson. At the time of Hannah's marriage to Thornton, she was but eighteen years of age; he was forty-six. Thornton is said to have promised Hannah as a child, as a reward for taking some medicine, that he would wait for and marry her. The Thorntons would have five children, four of whom would live to adulthood.

In 1770, Thornton became a selectman for the town of Londonderry. Shortly thereafter, he was appointed judge of the Court of Common Pleas and a justice of the peace. He was also commissioned by loyalist Governor John Wentworth as a colonel of the Londonderry militia regiment, a commission that would be renewed by the Provincial Congress in 1775 after Governor Wentworth fled New Hampshire.

While in Londonderry, Thornton was also active in church matters. By that time, the Presbyterian church in Londonderry had separated into two parishes, the First (East) Parish, led by Rev. David MacGregor, and the Second (West) Parish, led by Rev. William Davidson. In establishing the West Parish, the provincial legislature had provided for the taxation of parishioners based on where they worshipped, rather than where they resided. But tensions developed as certain parishioners residing in the East Parish preferred to worship with Rev. Davidson, and certain parishioners residing in the West Parish preferred to worship with Rev. MacGregor. By 1773, petitions and counter-petitions were submitted to the legislature to address the matter; among the petition signers was Thornton, as a member of the committee representing the interests of the East Parish. He also served as a member of its building committee.

In 1775, Thornton was elected as a delegate to the Provincial Congress; he was then chosen to serve as its president. He additionally served as chairman of the colony's Committee of Safety, and as chairman of a committee to develop a plan of government. The committee's subsequent proposal comprised the first written constitution adopted by any of the American colonies. Upon the adoption of that proposal in early 1776, the Provincial Congress became the New Hampshire House of Representatives, and Thornton was elected Speaker — a position later also held by his grandson, James Bonaparte Thornton.

Also in 1776, Thornton was elected to the Continental Congress. He did not arrive there until November of that year, after the vote in favor of independence had been taken; he nonetheless became a signatory to the Declaration of Independence. He was also appointed chief justice of the Court of Common Pleas and justice of the newly formed New Hampshire Superior (Supreme) Court.

During this time, Thornton's duties took him to Exeter, and he relocated there for a time, selling his home in Londonderry — and his pew in the East Parish church — in 1779. In 1780, he moved to Merrimack, New Hampshire, purchasing a former loyalist estate. He retired from his medical practice, and from the judiciary, but again was elected to the state House of Representatives and the state Senate; he also served as councilor to New Hampshire. In 1786, wife Hannah passed away at the age of forty-four. Thereafter, Thornton devoted himself to his farm, operated a ferry on the Merrimack River, and authored political articles and philosophical works.

While in Merrimack, Thornton attended a church pastored by Rev. Jacob Burnap. While the church was Congregational in its orthodoxy, it was the only church in Merrimack at the time, and Rev. Burnap was known as one who was determined not to confine religion to a single denomination. Upon Thornton's death in 1803 at the age of eighty-nine, Rev. Burnap delivered a funeral sermon extolling Thornton's steadfast worship and regard for religious institutions. Thornton was buried in an area that became known as Thornton's Ferry, his grave marked by a stone describing him simply as, "An Honest Man."

In His Own Words:

Letter from Matthew Thornton, President of New Hampshire Provincial Congress, to Continental Congress
May 23, 1775[1]

> **We will not conceal that many among us are disposed to conclude that the voice of God and Nature to us,** since the late hostile design and conduct of Great Britain, is, *that we are bound to look to our whole political affairs.* . . .

> We trust we shall keep this alone in view until we hear the united plan of the Colonies in the General Council, **which we pray and trust may be under the influence of Heaven.**

Letter from Matthew Thornton, President of New Hampshire Provincial Congress, to the Inhabitants of the Colony of New Hampshire
June 2, 1775[2]

To the Inhabitants of the
Colony of New Hampshire:

Friends and Brethren: You must all be sensible that the affairs of America have at length come to a very affecting and alarming crisis. . . . **Duty to** *God*, to ourselves, to Posterity, enforced *by the cries of slaughtered Innocents*, have urged us to take up Arms in our Defence. Such a day as this was never before known, either to us or to our Fathers. You will give us leave therefore — in whom you have reposed special confidence — as your representative body, to suggest a few things which call for the serious attention of everyone who has the true interest of *America* at heart. **We would therefore recommend to the Colony at large to cultivate that Christian Union, Harmony and tender affection which is the only foundation upon which our invaluable privileges can rest with any security, or our public measures be pursued with the least prospect of success. . . .**

We further recommend a serious and steady regard to the rules of *temperance, sobriety* **and** *righteousness*, and that those Laws which have heretofore been our security and defense from the hand of violence may still answer all their former valuable purposes, though persons of vicious and corrupt minds would willingly take advantage from our present situation.

In a word, we seriously and earnestly recommend the practice of that pure and undefiled *religion* which embalmed the memory of our pious ancestors, as that alone upon which we can build a solid hope and confidence in the *Divine protection* and *favor*, without whose *blessing* all the measures of safety we have or can propose will end in our shame and disappointment.

MATTHEW THORNTON, *President*.

Letter from Matthew Thornton to Meshech Weare December 29, 1781[3]

The Vermont affair grieves me more than our war with Great Britain. Heathens were shocked when brother killed brother in battle; **how much more ought Christians to shudder at the very thought of brother killing brother about a line of jurisdiction.** For mercy's sake, Sir, if possible, prevent every hostile measure until the honble. Continental Congress explicitly fixes their bounds, and informs them what to depend upon and New Hampshire how to conduct. Taking one man may begin a war, but **when or how it will end the Great Ruler only knows.**

Title of Philosophical Work Authored by Matthew Thornton in Last Years of Life c. 1800[4]

Paradise Lost; or the Origin of the Evil called Sin examined; or how it ever did or ever can come to pass, that a creature should or could do anything unfit or improper for that creature to do; or how it ever did, or ever can come to pass, that a creature should or could omit, or leave undone what that creature ought to have done, or was fit and proper for that creature to do; or how it ever was, or can be possible for a creature to displease the Creator in Thought, Word or Action.

Funeral Sermon by Rev. Jacob Burnap
(upon the death of Matthew Thornton)
1803[5]

You were, on the last Lord's day, called to follow to
the grave and deposit in the dust, the remains of a
man venerable for his age and skill in his profession
and for the several very important and honorable
offices he has sustained; — noted for the knowledge
he had acquired and his quick penetration into
matters of abstruse speculation; **exemplary for his
regard to the public institutions of religion, and
for his constancy in attending the public worship,
where he trod the courts of the house of God with
steps tottering with age and infirmity.**

What follows is a
summary of an article
from contemporary American life . . .

nearly 250 years after
Matthew Thornton
signed

the Declaration of Independence.

What Would Matthew Thornton Think?

TODD STARNES · Published February 29, 2016

Bible removed from POW/MIA display inside VA clinic

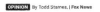 

OPINION By Todd Starnes, | Fox News

A Veteran's Administration outpatient clinic in Akron, Ohio honored service members with a "Missing Man Table" dedicated to prisoners of war and those missing in action. Among the items featured in the POW/MIA display were a Bible and a framed Bible verse. This was in line with the United States Navy's Missing Man Table & Honors Ceremony, which states that "The Bible represents faith in a higher power and the pledge to our country, founded as one nation under God." Indeed, the Chaplain Alliance for Religious Liberty (CARL) says that "MIA/POW tables have been part of military tradition for generations. They have always included certain elements including a Bible."

But the Military Religious Freedom Foundation objected, complaining that the inclusion of the Bible and Bible verse were unconstitutional. The clinic capitulated and removed the offensive items. Responded CARL, "It is a sad day when the Veteran's Administration caves to one narrow view of the proper way to honor the courage and sacrifice of those who have dedicated their lives in service of their country. Many have died to protect the right of Americans to have and read the Bible. Surely we can honor their sacrifice by allowing a Bible at their table of remembrance."

https://www.foxnews.com/opinion/bible-removed-from-pow-mia-display-inside-va-clinic.

John Wentworth Jr.
(1745-1787)

[Portrait Unavailable]

Signer of the Articles of Confederation

Highest Office Attained:
Representative in Congress

Religious Affiliation:
Congregationalist

Descended from an English family of great nobility and wealth, John Wentworth Jr. applied his family tradition of public service to the cause of the American revolution. His ancestry can be traced to 1066—a time that pre-dated the use of surnames—when ancestor Reginald (or Rynold) de Wynterwade held the lordship of Wentworth, in the Wapentake of Strafford, which was located in the West Riding region of Yorkshire, England. The succeeding generations produced numerous knights, barons, and earls all by then bearing the name "Wentworth."

The influence of the Wentworths extended also to matters of religion. In the late 1100s, ancestor Hugh Wentworth donated eleven acres of land to the Monk Bretton priory; Monk Bretton was a monastery then of the French Order of Cluny, whose monks followed the sixth-century Rule of St. Benedict. In 1538, when King Henry VIII took control of monastic estates, the Monk Bretton priory that had been established with the aid of ancestor Hugh was closed. But Thomas Wentworth, the high sheriff of York, stepped in to acquire the north aisle columns of the monastery; he used them to construct the Wentworth Old Church in the village of Wentworth.

Meanwhile, in 1338, Hugh's great-great-grandson, Richard Wentworth, was elevated from his position as prebendary of St. Paul's Cathedral to become both the Bishop of London and the Lord High Chancellor of England. The former position was exceeded in authority only by the Archbishops of Canterbury and York, and the latter position was exceeded only by the king. Richard was the brother of signer-Wentworth's direct ancestor, William Wentworth.

Eleven generations later came William Wentworth, later known as Elder William, the progenitor of the Wentworth family in America. Elder William emigrated in the late 1620s or early 1630s, settling in Exeter, New Hampshire. He had been a parishioner of Rev. John Wheelwright while in England, and shared a distant but important familial connection with him as well. Elder William was a distant cousin of Anne (Marbury) Hutchinson—later, along with Rev. Wheelwright himself, a celebrated if controversial religious figure in New England. Anne's father, Rev. Francis Marbury, was the brother of Elder William's grandmother, Catherine (Marbury) Wentworth. And Anne's sister-in-law, Susanna Hutchinson, was also Rev. Wheelwright's sister-in-law. Elder William's aunt, Anne Wentworth Lawson, married Rev. John Lawson. And all of these connections eventually would coalesce in the founding of Exeter.

Rev. Wheelwright had been the vicar of Bilsby, having succeeded his father-in-law, Rev. Thomas Storre, in that position. But Rev. Wheelwright's religious convictions eventually led him into the ranks of the Puritans. Following him into Puritanism were Elder William and other members of the Wentworth family. To secure greater religious freedom, they made their way to America. Rev. Wheelwright soon became the pastor at the Mount Wollaston (Congregational) Church in what is now Quincy, Massachusetts; Anne Hutchinson accompanied him there. The two became leading figures in the Antinomian movement—which challenged the continued force of the Law of Moses. This ultimately led to Rev. Wheelwright's conviction of contempt and sedition, notwithstanding the support of the noted Congregationalist, Rev. John Cotton; he was then banished from the Mount Wollaston church.

Fate thus brought Rev. Wheelwright to New Hampshire. He joined with Elder William and others (including his Lawson cousins), to found the town of Exeter with a form of government agreeable to the will of God. The first order of business was to establish a place of worship. But while the Congregationalists of New Hampshire were puritan and Calvinistic in their doctrines, they were not the Puritans of Massachusetts; indeed, they retained much affinity to the traditions of the Anglican Church.

By 1650, Elder William had relocated to Dover, New Hampshire; he joined, and was ordained a ruling elder in, the First (Congregational) Church. His duties as elder included not only assisting the pastor in the governance of the church and tending to the needs of the congregation, but also preaching and expounding on the scriptures. For many years, he officiated at religious services both in Dover, Exeter, and elsewhere. But it was at the Dover church that Elder William established his religious roots, and many generations of his Wentworth descendants continued to worship and baptize their children there.

Among Elder William's children was Ezekiel Wentworth, whose son, Benjamin, was John Wentworth Jr.'s grandfather. But Benjamin died before he could raise his own children to adulthood, and Benjamin's brother, Paul Wentworth, stepped in to adopt John Wentworth Sr., and to provide him with a Harvard education. John Sr. went on to similarly provide for his own son, John Jr., and to lead him into the cause of the Revolution.

Public service continued to flow through the Wentworths' blood. Both Ezekiel and six successive generations of his descendants served in the New Hampshire legislature. Another branch of the Wentworth family, descended from Ezekiel's brother, Samuel, produced Lieutenant Governor John Wentworth, then the highest executive of the colony; Governor Benning Wentworth, his son; and Governor John Wentworth, his nephew. While maintaining friendly relations with the revolutionists, it fell to the latter of these three royal governors to dissolve the New Hampshire General Assembly in 1774. Upon doing so, Governor Wentworth so notified the Assembly's Speaker, who was none other than John Wentworth Sr., a leader in the revolutionary cause. As the revolution unfolded, Governor Wentworth fled New Hampshire to become the governor of Nova Scotia.

John Wentworth Jr. was born in 1745 in Somersworth, New Hampshire (near Dover) to John Sr. and Joanna Gilman Wentworth. Joanna's own family had produced many notable figures, including her father and grandfather—respected judges. Notable also were her nephews, Nicholas Gilman—who went on to become a United States senator and signer of the United States Constitution; and John Taylor Gilman—who went on to become governor of New Hampshire. Wentworth likely attended the Somersworth (Congregational) Church, which was established in 1729. The growth of Somersworth and the distance to Dover had led a number of Dover parishioners, including Benjamin, Paul, and other Wentworths, to petition for the new parish. Ezekiel is known to have bequeathed funds to the Somersworth Church to be used for pious and charitable purposes, while Paul donated an acre of land. From its founding until his death in 1792, the Somersworth Church was led by Rev. James Pike, Wentworth's uncle; he was the husband of Joanna's sister, Sarah.

Upon graduating from Harvard in 1768, Wentworth studied law with Judge William Parker of Portsmouth, and then established his own law practice in Dover. In 1773, he was appointed by his namesake and distant cousin, then-Governor John Wentworth, as register of probate for Strafford County; he held that position until his death. Strafford County had been named for Wentworth's ancestor, Thomas, the first Earl of Strafford; prior to his beheading in 1641, Thomas had served as an advisor to King Charles I and as Lord Deputy of Ireland. Like his grandfather, the earlier Thomas Wentworth—who a century before had acquired the columns of the Monk Bretton priory for construction of the family church—he also served as the high sheriff of York.

Wentworth was also elected to the New Hampshire legislature in 1776, and to the Continental Congress in 1778, where he signed the Articles of Confederation that initially governed the emerging nation. He later succeeded his father on the state Council, and also served in the state Senate and on the New Hampshire Committee of Safety.

Wentworth was a member of the Congregational Church in Dover where his great-great-grandfather, Elder William, had served. In 1771, he married Margaret Frost of New Castle, who then joined him as a member of the Dover church; they raised and baptized their children there. Margaret's uncle, Judge George

Frost, also served in the Continental Congress and additionally served with Wentworth's father on the Court of Common Pleas. Wentworth's family worshipped in the Dover church under the ministry of Rev. Jeremy Belknap, who was himself a noted revolutionary and who later authored the voluminous *History of New Hampshire*. Through his mother, Rev. Belknap was related to Dr. Mather Byles, a loyalist yet celebrated Congregational minister; he was also descended from the famous Mather family of Congregational ministers and thus to the very Rev. John Cotton who earlier had defended Elder William's own former minister, Rev. John Wheelwright.

Wentworth passed into eternity in 1787 at the age of forty-two. He was buried in the Pine Hill Cemetery. But his legacy of public service and religious principle lived on in the lives of succeeding generations of Wentworths, including grandson John — who later served in Congress and as Mayor of Chicago — whose words (as expressed below) continued to reflect the religious conviction of Wentworth and his ancestors.

In His Own Words:

Description of John Wentworth Jr. (upon his death)[1]

[I]t was as a man that **his virtues shone forth pre-eminent. His benevolence was of the purest order**; he was **never wearied of well-doing**; and at this day, the aged speak of his character in terms of grateful remembrance. **He made his profession an instrument of doing good to his fellow-men**, and not as a stalking-horse on which he might ride to fame and wealth over the necks of the poor and the ignorant. Many anecdotes are related of the good natured address which he made use of in settling the disputes and difficulties between his neighbors, which might be referred to him in his professional capacity, and which, had he practised the arts of a pettifogger, he might have rendered sources of litigation and profit. When an account was placed in his hands for suit, he was in the habit of inquiring into the circumstances of the debtor, and if he found him unable to pay the demand, he would bring the parties together, and would effect a peaceable compromise between them, redounding more to the honor and profit of both debtor and creditor than if vigorous measures, better calculated to exasperate than reconcile, had been pursued. The name of this excellent young man deserves to be held by the citizens of New-Hampshire in affectionate and lasting remembrance.

Obituary of John Wentworth Jr.
New Hampshire Gazette, 1835[2]

As a lawyer, Mr. Wentworth was far above mediocrity, and as a statesman and lawgiver, he was superior to most of his contemporaries in the circle in which he moved; but **it was as a man that his virtues shone forth pre-eminent. His benevolence was of the purest order. He never wearied of well doing, and at this day the aged speak of his character in terms of grateful remembrance.**

Document Signed by Ancestor, Elder William Wentworth, Rev. John Wheelwright, and Others (in the formation of a government at Exeter, New Hampshire)
May 4, 1639[3]

Whereas it hath pleased the lord to move the heart of our Dread Soverayne Charles **by the grace of god**, King of England Scotland France & Ireland to grant licence & liberty to sundry of his subjects to plant themselves in the westerne partes of America: Wee his loyall subjects brethren of the church of Excetre, situate & lying upon the river of Pascataquacke, wth other inhabitants there, **considering wth ourselves the holy will of god & our owne necessity,** that we should not live wth out wholsome lawes & civil governement amongst us, of which we are altogether destitute: **doe in the name of christ, & in the sight of god, combine ourselves together, to erect & set up amongst us such governement as shall be to our best discerning agreeable to the will of god**: professing ourselves subjects of our Soverayne Lord, King Charles, according to the libertys of our English Colony of the Massachusits, & **binding ourselves solemnely by the grace & helpe of christ & in his name & feare, to submit ourselves to such godly & christian laws as are established in the Realme of England to our best knowledge: and to all other such lawes wch shall upon good grounds, be made & inacted amongst us according to god, y^t we may live quietly & peaceablely together in all godlyness & honesty.** Mo 5^t D 4^{tr} 1639

Oath of Ancestor, Elder William Wentworth (upon the formation of a government at Exeter, New Hampshire) May 4, 1639[4]

THE ELDERS OATH Y^e 4th DAY 5th M° 1639

You shall sweare by the great and dreadfull name of the high God, maker & Govr of heaven and earth and by the Lord Jesus Christ ye Prince of the Kings and Rulers of the earth that in his name and feare you will Rule and Governe this his people according to the righteous will of Gods Ministeringe Justice and Judgm^t upon the workers of iniquity and Ministering due incurridgm^t and Countinance to well doers — protecting of people so farre as in you by the helpe of [God] lyeth, from forren Annoyance and inward disturbance

that they may live a quiett and peacable life in all godlyness and honesty. Soe God bee helpful and Gratious to you and yo^{rs} in Christ Jesus.

Oath of Ancestor, Elder William Wentworth (as a citizen of the newly formed government at Exeter, New Hampshire) May 4, 1639[5]

THE OATH OF THE PEOPLE

Wee doe here sweare by the Great and dreadfull name of ye high God maker and Govern^r of Heaven & earth and by the Lord Jesus X^t ye King & Savio^r of his people that in his name & fear we will submitt o^{r}selves to be ruld & governed by, according to ye will & word of God and such holsome Laws & ordinances as shall be derived theire from by o^r honr^d Rulers and ye Lawfull assistance with the consent of ye people and y^t wee will be ready to assist them by the helpe of God in the administracon of Justice and p^{r}servacon of peace with o^r bodys and goods and best endeavo^{rs} according to God, soe God protect & save us and o^{rs} in Christ Jesus.

Excerpts of Will of Great-Uncle Paul Wentworth (in part providing bequests for John Wentworth Sr. and family) 1748[6]

In the name of God. Amen. The third day of February, one thousand seven hundred forty seven, eight, I, Paul Wentworth, of the Parish of Somersworth in the Province of New Hampshire, in New England, Esq., being much indisposed in body, but of perfect mind and memory (**thanks be given unto God**) and calling to mind the mortality of my body, and knowing that it is appointed for all men once to die, do make and ordain this my last will and testament: that is to say, **principally and first of all, I give and commend my soul into the hands of God that gave it, and my body I recommend to the earth to be buried in a decent Christian burial** at the discretion of my Executors **nothing doubting but at the general resurrection I shall receive the same again by the mighty power of God. And, as touching such worldly goods and estates wherewith it has pleased God to bless me in this life,** I give demise and dispose of the same in the following manner and form.

Item—**I give and bequeath to my Nephew John Wentworth, the son of my beloved brother Benjamin Wentworth**, deceased, all my homestead, that is to say, all the lands belonging to my homestead lying on both sides of the highway that passed from Salmon Falls to the Meeting House in the aforesaid parish, with all the buildings standing on said land as my dwelling house, barns and storehouse (excepting the Northwest corner Chamber in my dwelling house) with all the appurtenances priviledges and commodities belonging to my said homestead which contains about 120 acres of land to him, his heirs and assigns forever. . .

Item—**I give and bequeath 500 pounds old tenor for pious uses in the aforesaid parish of Somersworth forever — that is to say, I will that the said 500 pounds shall be taken care of by the minister of said parish and Deacons of the Church, in said parish for the time being, and that they improve the interest of said 500 pounds for pious uses in said parish as they shall judge most proper**, the principle not to be diminished at all, and at no time forever hereafter, which said 500 pounds is to be paid out of my outstanding debts, if there be enough of them, and if not to be made up out of my money.

Item — I give and bequeath 600 pounds old tenor to be improved by my executors that I shall hereafter name, for the bringing up of Paul Wentworth son to my said nephew John Wentworth to good learning **that he may be capable of serving God and his country**.

John Wentworth Sr.'s Call for General Congress (upon the dissolution of the New Hampshire Assembly) July 6, 1774[7]

Whereas the colonies in general upon this continent think it highly expedient and necessary, in the present critical and alarming situation of their public affairs, that DELEGATES should be appointed, by and in behalf of each, to Join a general CONGRESS, proposed to meet at Philadelphia, the first day of December next, to devise and consider what measures will be most advisable to be taken and pursued by all the colonies for the establishment of their RIGHTS AND LIBERTIES upon a Just and solid foundation, and for the restoration of union and harmony between the mother country and the colonies. And whereas the members of the late House of Representatives for this Province now met to deliberate on this subject, are unanimously of the opinion that it is expedient and necessary for this province to Join said CONGRESS for the above purpose, and recommend it to the towns in this province respectively to choose and empower one or more persons, in their behalf, to meet at Exeter on the 21st day of this instant, at ten of the o'clock in the forenoon, to Join in the choice of DELEGATES to the GENERAL CONGRESS. In order to effect the desired end it is necessary that each town, as soon as may be, contribute their proportion of the expense of sending: it is therefore desired that the same may be raised by subscription or otherwise, and if convenient sent by the person by your parish appointed: Your proportion of which is pounds lawful money.

The utility of which measure is so apparent we doubt not your ready compliance with this proposal.

By desire of the meeting,
JOHN WENTWORTH, *Chairman.*
Portsmouth, N. H., July 6, 1774.

P. S. Considering the distressing situation of our public affairs, Thursday, the 14th inst., is recommended to be kept as a day of fasting, humiliation, and prayer throughout this Province.

Address to the Inhabitants of the Province of New Hampshire, Adopted by Convention of Delegates, John Wentworth Sr., President 1775[8]

Brethren: — When we consider the unhappy condition to which you and your American brethren are reduced; when we reflect that for near ten months past you have been deprived of any share of your own government, and of those advantages which flow to society from legislative assemblies; when we view the lowering clouds, charged with ministerial vengeance, fast spreading over this extensive continent, ready to burst on the heads of its inhabitants, and to involve the whole British Empire in one common ruin, — at this alarming Juncture, **duty to Almighty God**, to our country, ourselves, and posterity, loudly demand our most strenuous exertions to avoid the impending danger.

[S]hould our enemies be successful, they will thereby rivet the chains of slavery upon us and our posterity. Thus surrounded with dangers and distresses on every side, **it behooves us to adopt and pursue such peaceful measures as under God will be most likely to prevent those dreadful calamities with which we are threatened**.

Firstly: Sensible that to point out with any degree of certainty **the methods by which you may shun the threatening evils would require more than human wisdom**, we can only recommend such measures as appear to us most likely to answer that desirable end, and best calculated to restore to you that peace and harmony so ardently wished for by every good and honest American. We therefore earnestly recommend:—

❊ ❊ ❊

Lastly, We earnestly entreat you at this time of tribulation and distress, when your enemies are urging you to despair, when every scene around you is full of gloom and horror, that, in imitation of your pious forefathers, with contrition of spirit and penitence of heart, you **implore the Divine Being, who alone is able to deliver you from your present unhappy and distressing situation**, to espouse your righteous cause, secure your liberties, and fix them on a firm and lasting basis; and we fervently beseech him to restore to you and your American brethren that peace and tranquillity so ardently sought for by every true Mend to liberty and mankind.

> By order of the Convention.
> JOHN WENTWORTH, *President*.

Letter from John Wentworth Sr. to the New Hampshire Committee of Safety
April 25, 1775[9]

My health is such, it is impracticable for me to be at Exeter this day... **I heartily wish the Divine direction and blessing may attend your consultations and determinations**; and, after assuring you that I am engaged in the same cause with you, am your sincere friend, and most obedient and humble servant,

JOHN WENTWORTH.

Address to the United States House of Representatives, by Representative John Wentworth, Grandson of John Wentworth Jr.
c. 1844[10]

We are poor, but, **thank God**, we are honest. Incorruptible, we suspect no man with British gold coming to buy us until the overt act. The young men of Illinois expect, in their day, to see her out of debt; and they are all bent on paying interest to some extent immediately.

We have a pride in having our state solvent once more, and paying every cent of her liabilities without any legal quibbles or dishonorable compromises. And a glorious consummation will that be for us all. For one, when it arrives, **I would say with the good man of old, "Lord, now lettest thou thy servant depart in peace, for mine eyes have seen our salvation." Sir, I would celebrate the day of such an event like a jubilee—ay, sir, next after the birth-day of our Savior**, and the day on which American Independence was declared, I would worship the day that redeems Illinois from bankruptcy and debt—the day of her credit restored and her honor regained.

What follows is a
summary of an article
from contemporary American life . . .

nearly 250 years after
John Wentworth Jr.
signed

the Articles of Confederation.

What Would John Wentworth Jr. Think?

TODD STARNES · Published February 8, 2018

Godless! Atheists complain about gospel music at MLK Day celebration

OPINION By Todd Starnes, | Fox News

The residents of Hobbs, New Mexico celebrated Martin Luther King Jr. Day with a march and program at Booker T. Washington Elementary School. It was advertised as "an opportunity to display hope and faith." But the Freedom From Religion Foundation objected because the program included "religious music performed by a gospel choir and numerous speakers that made reference to God and Jesus." According to the FFRF, "Officials are not permitted to lend credibility or prestige to religion by including religious messages in city events," and it urged city leaders to "cease including religious music and messages in official Hobbs events."

Has the FFRF forgotten that Dr. King was not only a civil rights leader, but a Baptist minister?

*https://www.foxnews.com/opinion/
godless-atheists-complain-about-gospel-music-at-mlk-day-celebration.*

William Whipple
(1730-1785)

Signer of the Declaration of Independence

Highest Office Attained:
Representative in Congress

Religious Affiliation:
Congregationalist

W illiam Whipple, the son of Captain William Whipple and Mary Cutt Whipple, was born in what is now Kittery Point, Maine in 1730. He was baptized in the First Congregational Church by its pastor, Rev. John Newmarch. Rev. Newmarch had been hired in 1694 to preach and teach school in Kittery Point, and he pastored there for some sixty years. Whipple attended the common schools in his hometown, and also was tutored by his mother's cousin, Robert Eliot Gerrish. Gerrish was a Harvard graduate descended from Captain William Gerrish, a puritan immigrant who left his native Bristol, England in 1639 and settled in Newbury, Massachusetts.

Whipple's maternal grandfather, Robert Cutt, was a ship-builder who hailed from a distinguished New Hampshire family. Robert's father, John Cutt, was the first president of New Hampshire, and his great-great-grandfather, Richard Cutt, was a member of the British Parliament in the 1650s.

Like his own father, Whipple was attracted to the sea, and at an early age found himself aboard one of his father's ships. By the age of twenty-one, he commanded a ship of his own, and quickly amassed a sufficient fortune to retire from the sea before the age of thirty. He then joined his brother in mercantile busi-ness pursuits in Portsmouth, New Hampshire.

Once in Portsmouth, Whipple found himself attracted to a maternal cousin, Mehitable Odiorne, daughter of Judge Jotham Odiorne and Mehitable Cutt Odiorne (Whipple's aunt). Rev. Samuel Langdon, later the president of Harvard College, was to officiate at their nuptials; but Mehitable left Whipple at the altar of the Old North (Congregational) Church of Portsmouth. Later, in 1767, Whipple married another cousin, Katharine Moffatt, daughter of Captain John Moffatt and Catherine Cutt Moffatt. Together, they had a son, William, who was baptized

at the Old North Church in 1772; he was buried in its cemetery not long after. Despite losing their own son, the Whipples
lovingly raised their niece and nephew, Mary and John Tufton
Moffatt, as their own.

Having suffered from the trade restrictions imposed by mother
England, Whipple became an early adherent to the patriot cause.
As revolutionary fervor grew, he was elected to the Committee of
Safety, the provincial convention, and the Executive Council of
New Hampshire. In 1775, he was chosen as a New Hampshire
delegate to the Continental Congress, along with Josiah Bartlett
and future New Hampshire Governor John Langdon. Langdon,
having wed Elizabeth Moffatt, was also a nephew (by marriage)
to Whipple. As a member of the Congress, Whipple voted for
and proudly signed the Declaration of Independence in 1776.

Although continuing in the Congress until 1779, Whipple
returned home to assume command of a New Hampshire militia
regiment. But before departing for battle, he entertained Rev.
Ezra Stiles—later the president of Yale College—of the Old
North Church, sharing with him a first draft of the Articles of
Confederation. He also freed his young slave, Prince, declaring,
"From this moment on you are a free man, Prince, hurry up now
and we will fight for our freedom together."

In 1777, then-Brigadier General Whipple commanded his
troops in critical battles, including the Battle of Saratoga, the
turning point of the revolution. Prince Whipple was at his side.
After escorting defeated British General John Burgoyne to the
authorities in Boston, Whipple regaled his friend, John Adams,
and Rev. Stiles with tales of battle.

In 1780, as the war was nearing its conclusion, Whipple
declined appointment to the Board of Admiralty, opting instead
to return home to Portsmouth; he then commenced service in
the New Hampshire legislature. He simultaneously served as the
tax collector for the state of New Hampshire and as a judge of
the New Hampshire Superior Court, a position he held until his
untimely death in 1785. Whipple was laid to rest near his infant
son, William, in the burial ground of the Old North Church.

In His Own Words:

Letter from William Whipple to His Brother-in-Law, Joshua Brackett
April 11, 1776[1]

> For my part, I see no alternative but freedom or slavery. **Providence has kindly offered us our choice; and shall we hesitate which to accept? I hope, not. God forbid that an American should be animated with so base a soul as not to embrace the former with eagerness!**

Letter from William Whipple to the President of New Hampshire, Meshech Weare
May 17, 1776[2]

> **May the Supreme Governour of the Universe Protect, & Defend us, Guide our Councils & Prosper our Arms**

Letter from William Whipple to His Brother-in-Law, Joshua Brackett
June 2, 1776[3]

> As every thing depends on this summer's campaign, every nerve should be exerted and **if we are successful, which by divine assistance I am in no doubt of**, our enemies will not be able to support the war another year.

Letter from William Whipple and Josiah Bartlett to the President of New Hampshire, Meshech Weare
June 4, 1776[4]

> We wrote you the 28th ultimo, since which Congress have resolved to send a further reinforcement into

Canada. Seven hundred and fifty men, including officers, will be required of our Colony to serve as Militia until the 1st of *December*, the officers to be commissioned by the Colony. It is absolutely necessary our posts should be supported in that country, for should the enemy get possession, we should certainly have a long and troublesome war on our hands; but **if we are successful, which by proper exertions and Divine assistance there is no doubt of, this campaign will place us out of the reach of their malice.** You will receive the resolution respecting this reinforcement from the President. The money mentioned in our last is yet gone forward, not having had an opportunity, but to leave in a few days.

Letter from William Whipple to His Brother-in-Law, Joshua Brackett
June 23, 1776[5]

What baseness are our Enemies not capable of, who wod wish to be connected with a people so destitute of every Vertue, God forbid it shod ever be the fate of America.

Letter from William Whipple to John Langdon
June 24, 1776[6]

May God unite our hearts in all things that tend to the well-being of the rising empire.

Letter from William Whipple to John Langdon
July 7, 1776[7]

General Howe has landed part of his army on Statten Island which you know was not in General Washington's power to prevent. However the Jersey and Pennsylvania militia with 3000 from Maryland are now on their march and will soon form a very formidable army on this side Hudson's River and General Washington has by this time got 20,000 men at York including the militia of York and Connecticut. **I cannot help flattering myself that all this, with the smiles of Providence, will enable us to give a good account of these fellows before the campaign is over.**

Letter from William Whipple to John Langdon November 7, 1776[8]

I by no means wod Discourage; my desire is to animate everyone to exert himself in the Glorious cause in which America is engaged, for my own part I have not a doubt of success, in the end, but my wish is to put a speedy end to Slaughter & devastation, which already is great, but must be still greater if the war continues, which nothing will prevent but the utmost exertions of the Friends to Liberty & Humanity, **such exertions, under the smile of Heaven, will restore peace to & establish Happiness in this Western World.**

Will of William Whipple June 21, 1751[9]

In the Name of God Amen. I William Whipple of Kittery in the County of York in the Province of the Massa : Bay Mariner being Sick & weak but of sound disposing Mind and Memory, and considering the Uncertainty of Life, and not knowing but that the time of my Departure out of this Life is near, Do make this my last Will & Testament. **And after humbly committing my Soul to God the Father of Spirits, hoping for his pardoning Mercy thrô the Merits & Mediation of Jesus Christ and my Body**

255

to a decent Interment according to the Discretion of my Executor herein after named believing in the Resurrection & hoping for eternal Life. My Worldly Estate I give & devise in the following Manner & Form, that is to Say, . . .

Item. Whereas **by the Providence of God** my Wife Mary Whipple is so indisposed in mind as to be incapable of Business, I give her One third part of my personal Estate but to remain in ye Hands of my Executor to be applied to her Use as he Shall judge proper and **if it Should please God** to restore her to her former Capacity then to be delivered to her.

What follows is a
summary of an article
from contemporary American life . . .

nearly 250 years after
William Whipple
signed

the Declaration of Independence.

What Would William Whipple Think?

OPINION · Published August 14, 2018

Todd Starnes: Air Force general is attacked by extremist group because he prays for others

OPINION By Todd Starnes, | Fox News

Brigadier General John Teichert serves his country as the wing commander at Edwards Air Force Base in California. But he also is a devout Christian whose faith compelled him to launch a personal website called, "Prayer at Lunchtime for the United States." The website encourages "Bible-believing Americans to take time to specifically pray for our nation at lunchtime every day."

That apparently was a bridge too far for the Military Religious Freedom Foundation, which contends that the website violates the Uniform Code of Military Justice. The MRFF demanded of then-Defense Secretary James Mattis that General Teichert be investigated, prosecuted, convicted and punished. According to the MRFF, General Teichert is a "fundamentalist Christian tyrant and religious extremist predator," and his "disgraceful, illegal and brazen promotion of his personal flavor of his weaponized version of Christianity represents one of the worst and most egregious cases MRFF has ever encountered in its 13 years of First Amendment civil rights advocacy." As a result, the MRFF says, "General Teichert should be doing time behind prison bars, not commanding a Wing wearing a General's stars."

https://www.foxnews.com/opinion/todd-starnes-air-force-general-is-attacked-by-extremist-group-because-he-prays-for-others.

Chapter Four:

Connecticut Signers

Andrew Adams
(1736-1797)

[Portrait Unavailable]

Signer of the Articles of Confederation

Highest Office Attained:
Representative in Congress; Chief Justice of Connecticut

Religious Affiliation:
Congregationalist

A ndrew Adams was born in Stratford, Connecticut in 1736. His father, Samuel Adams, was an accomplished attorney in town, as well as a Fairfield County judge. Samuel's mother, Abigail Oviatt Adams, traces her English ancestry to Sir John FitzAlan, the first Baron Arundel and the Lord Marshall of England in the 1300s; Sir John was himself descended from a long line of earls who preceded him in English nobility. Another branch of Anne's family leads to Sir Guy de Brienne, the first Baron of Bryan. Adams's mother, Mary Fairchild Adams, was descended from Thomas Fairchild and Robert Seabrook, who upon immigrating to America were among the early settlers of Stratford. Thomas served for many years as a deputy from Stratford to the General Court.

After graduating from Yale College in 1760, Adams studied law under his father; he then established his own law practice, initially in Stamford, Connecticut. He married Eunice Booth Adams, who would bear him several children. In 1772, he was named king's attorney for Litchfield County; soon thereafter, he moved to Litchfield, where he remained for the rest of his life. The family made its church home at the First Congregational Church; Adams served as a deacon. He also was a freemason; although non-denominational, freemasonry requires that its members hold a fundamental belief in a Supreme Being. Adams was member of St. Paul's Lodge in Litchfield; its first grand master was Ashbel Baldwin. Raised a strict Congregationalist in Litchfield, Baldwin later joined the Church of England and was ordained and named rector of Trinity (Episcopal) Church in New Haven; he later served a rector of Christ (Episcopal) Church in Stratford.

As relations with Britain soured, Adams joined Connecticut's Committee of Safety. He was also elected to the Connecticut House of Representatives in 1776. He served there until 1781, including as its Speaker. He also joined the Connecticut militia, achieving the rank of colonel and commanding the seventeeth Connecticut regiment during the ensuing war. This put him at odds with his brother, Dr. Samuel Adams. Dr. Adams, who had moved to what is now Arlington, Vermont, remained a loyalist. He was captured and imprisoned, but later escaped to Quebec. There, he joined the British army, forming an independent regiment known as Adams's Rangers. Serving with him were four of his sons.

In 1777, Adams was selected as a Connecticut delegate to the Continental Congress; the next year, upon returning from battle, he signed the Articles of Confederation. In 1789, Adams was appointed associate justice of the Connecticut Supreme Court. He advanced to the position of chief justice in 1793, and served in that position until his death in 1797. He was buried in the East Cemetery in Litchfield.

In His Own Words:

Letter from Andrew Adams to His Son, Andrew Adams Jr. (upon entering Yale College)[1]

Your standing in this world depends upon your mental ability rightly directed. Your acceptance of intellectual thought will produce the character you are to show throughout the remainder of your life. **I would have you ever maintain a most strict regard for truth, integrity and honor** all of which is not only compatible but necessary to the character of a gentleman. By this I do not mean a fawning complacence, but I do mean that **in all things you must have a strict regard for decency and decorum.**

Letter from Andrew Adams to Jonathan Trumbull Sr. September 5, 1778[2]

I sincerely pray that under your present heavy and grievious affliction you may be comforted with the consolations of God—which are neither few nor small, & that while you are deprived of such tender connections, and dear enjoyments in life, you may at the same time, rejoice in the God of your Salvation.

Inscription on Andrew Adams's Gravestone[3]

Having filled many distinguished offices with great ability and dignity, he was promoted to the highest judicial office in the State, which he held for several years, in which his eminent talents shone with uncommon lustre, and were exerted to the great advantage of the public and the honor of the High Court in which he presided. **He made an early profession of religion, and zealously sought to promote its true interests. He lived the Life and died the Death of a Christian.** His filial Piety and paternal tenderness are held in sweet Remembrance.

What follows is a
summary of an article
from contemporary American life . . .

nearly 250 years after
Andrew Adams
signed

the Articles of Confederation.

What Would Andrew Adams Think?

POLITICS 01/15/2016 04:53 pm ET | Updated Jan 18, 2016

Atheist Group Files Suit To Remove 'In God We Trust' From Currency

"The vast majority of nations manage to function without religious verbiage on their money," writes lawyer Michael Newdow.

 By Ryan Grenoble

A group of atheists filed suit in an Ohio federal court demanding that the United States remove its national motto, "In God We Trust," from all U.S. currency. They claim that it forces them to accept and share with others a message that violates their beliefs. Proponents of the change previously sued to remove the words "under God" from the Pledge of Allegiance.

https://www.huffpost.com/entry/in-god-we-trust-lawsuit_n_56994d-bae4b0778f46f94b28.

Titus Hosmer
(1736-1780)

Signer of the Articles of Confederation

Highest Office Attained:
Representative in Congress

Religious Affiliation:
Congregationalist

O ne of the most liberally educated and highly cultivated men of his time, Titus Hosmer was born in what is now West Hartford, Connecticut in 1736. The family belonged to the First (Congregational) Church, known as Center Church; Hosmer and his siblings were baptized there. Hosmer's great-grandfather, Stephen Hosmer Sr., was a deacon of that church. And in 1704, Hosmer's great-uncle, Rev. Stephen Hosmer, became the first minister of the First (Congregational) Church in East Haddam.

Another ancestor, Colonel Thomas Titus, had served as an officer in the army of Oliver Cromwell. Cromwell later became the Lord Protector of England; Cromwell's Protectorship was essentially a monarchy by another name, but one with a strict puritan and Protestant flair. After Cromwell died, the monarchy was returned to King Charles II. Colonel Titus then made his way to America.

Hosmer attended Yale College, graduating in 1757. He then studied law and established his law practice in Middletown, Connecticut. He wed Lydia Lord in 1761. She would bear him two sons. Son Stephen followed his father into the practice of law and became chief justice of the Connecticut Supreme Court; a noted Congregationalist minister, Rev. David Dudley Field, later described him as "a very skilful and acceptable leader in sacred music in the sanctuary of God," noting that he enjoyed his "large library, containing among other books, many on theology, which he loved to peruse." Son Hezekiah became a congressman from New York.

An accomplished writer of both verse and prose, Hosmer became one of the foremost attorneys in Connecticut. He held several local offices, and additionally served in the Connecticut legislature, including as Speaker of the House of Representatives. From that position, he worked to promote the interests of his emerging nation, advocating for the adoption of vigorous measures against Great Britain. In 1778, Hosmer was elected as a delegate to the Continental Congress, and affixed his signature to the Articles of Confederation. He later was appointed judge of the newly formed United States Maritime Court of Appeals. Dr. Noah Webster is said to have regarded him as one of the greatest men Connecticut ever produced. Hosmer died at the premature age of only forty-three; he was buried in the Mortimer Cemetery in Middletown.

In His Own Words:

Letter from Titus Hosmer to Silas Dean
May 22, 1775[1]

> **[T]he Scripture will tell the rest — tho' we have not so many Devils as Mary Magdalene had**; indeed the Devil of Avarice is all we have to complain of —

Letter from Jonathan Trumbull to Roger Sherman, Titus Hosmer, and Andrew Adams
August 25, 1778[2]

> I am exceedingly anxious to see our Confederation compleated. The four States, — how long must the others wait for them? if they are not like to comply soon, should we not confederate without them? . . .

> But they are gone, [lamenting that the French fleet had retired to Boston — rather than New London, Connecticut — to effect repairs] and with them are fled our fond hopes of success from this enterprise. This event will put a new aspect on our affairs. *The Lord reigneth is our hope; let it be our trust and confidence.*

Excerpts from: *An Elegy on the late Honorable Titus Hosmer,*
Esq., by **Joel Barlow**
1780[3]

TO MRS. LYDIA HOSMER, RELICT OF THE LATE HONORABLE TITUS HOSMER, ESQ THIS ELEGY IS INSCRIBED,

AS a Testimony of the Author's Veneration for **the many amiable Virtues which rendered her the Delight and Ornament of so worthy a Consort,** and still render her an Honor to a very numerous and respectable Acquaintance.

❊ ❊ ❊

He will, my friends — th' unbodied life above,

With every virtue brighten'd and refin'd,

That glow'd below, with patriotic love,

The love of happiness and human kind,

Will burn serener in a purer sky,

Where broader views and bolder thoughts unroll,

Where universal Being sills the eye,

And swells the unbounded wishes of the soul.

No tender thought by heaven's own breath inspir'd,

Which taught the gentle bosom here to glow,

Which the warm breast with patriot ardor fir'd,

Or stole the secret tear for silent woe,

No tender thought by heaven's own will approv'd,

Can e'er forsake the mansion first assign'd;

But reaches still the object once belov'd,

And lives immortal in th' immortal mind.

Fix'd in a brighter sphere, with surer aim,

Tho' greater scenes his growing views employ,

Yet Hosmer kindles with an Hosmer's flame,

And his dear country feeds his noblest joy.

Centennial Address, by Rev. David Dudley Field 1853[4]

Titus Hosmer . . . was, in one word, **a gentleman of correct moral habits**, a thorough scholar, a learned and eloquent lawyer, and a sound practical statesman; deeply versed in national law and universal history.

What follows is a
summary of an article
from contemporary American life . . .

nearly 250 years after
Titus Hosmer
signed

the Articles of Confederation.

What Would Titus Hosmer Think?

CONTROVERSIES · **Published** October 6, 2015 · **Last Update** December 20, 2015

Workers remove Ten Commandments monument from Oklahoma Capitol grounds

Under cover of darkness, the State of Oklahoma removed a six-foot-tall Ten Commandments monument from the grounds of the Oklahoma State Capitol. The Oklahoma Supreme Court had ruled that the monument violated the state constitution because public property was being used to support "any sect, church, denomination or system of religion." After the monument was erected in 2012, several groups petitioned for their own monuments. Among them was a New York satanic group seeking to erect a seven-foot-tall statue depicting Satan as Baphomet, a horned, bearded, winged, and goat-headed creature. Also competing for a monument was the Church of the Flying Spaghetti Monster.

https://www.foxnews.com/politics/workers-remove-ten-commandments-monument-from-oklahoma-capitol-grounds.

Samuel Huntington
(1731-1796)

*Signer of the Declaration of Independence and
the Articles of Confederation*

Highest Office Attained:
President of Congress; Governor of Connecticut

Religious Affiliation:
Congregationalist

O ne of ten children born into a puritan Connecticut family, Samuel Huntington was not educated in the ministry, but never found himself far from it. Three of his brothers studied theology at Yale College, including Rev. Joseph Huntington, the author of a posthumous work on universal salvation entitled, *Calvinism Improved, or the Gospel illustrated as a system, of real Grace, issuing in the salvation of all men.* As the eldest son, Huntington instead assisted his father on the family farm and, unable to share in the benefits of a public education, pursued reading and study on his own; eventually, his studies focused on the law. He read voraciously from the library of a local minister, Rev. Ebenezer Devotion; later, upon marrying Rev. Devotion's daughter, Martha, he became a part of the family. He also adopted two of his brother's (Rev. Joseph's) children.

In 1765, Huntington's blossoming legal career took him to the distinguished position of king's attorney for the colony of Connecticut. But after nine years, Samuel's burgeoning patriotism caused him to resign that post; he chose to forego the bright future associated with employment by the king, and instead devoted himself to public service in what became a new nation. In 1775, he was chosen to serve as a delegate to the Continental Congress, signing the Declaration of Independence on July 4, 1776.

On September 28, 1779, Samuel Huntington was elected the sixth president of the Continental Congress; it was during his term that he and others came to sign the Articles of Confederation, which for the first time designated the new nation as the United States of America. Some argue that this makes Samuel Huntington the first president of the United States.

Samuel Huntington continued his public service by becoming chief justice of the Connecticut Supreme Court in 1784. In 1786, he became the eighteenth governor of Connecticut, an office he held for ten years; during that time, Huntington publicly proclaimed Thanksgiving to the Almighty God, and called upon the people to offer prayer and public acknowledgement of their dependence on their Creator and their need for His mercy and forgiveness. Only upon his death was Huntington's seat in the house of the Lord vacant. His Christian character is said to have exemplified the ideal of the puritan magistrate dedicated to the betterment of society.

In His Own Words:

Address by Governor Samuel Huntington, Debates in the Several State Conventions on the Adoption of the Federal Constitution
1788[1]

> While the great body of freeholders are acquainted with the **duties which they owe to their God**, to themselves, and to men, they will remain free. But if ignorance and depravity should prevail, they will inevitably lead to slavery and ruin.

A Proclamation for a Day of Public Thanksgiving, by Governor Samuel Huntington
October 13, 1788[2]

By His Excellency
Samuel Huntington, Esquire
Governor and Commander in Chief,
in and over the State of Connecticut, in America.

A PROCLAMATION.

Considering the great and manifold favors, which it pleased Almighty God, the Father of Mercies, to bestow upon the inhabitants of this Land, and the people of this State in the course of the current year, which demand our sincere and grateful Acknowledgment:

I Have thought fit, by, and with the advice of the Council, and at the desire of the Representatives, in General Court assembled, to appoint, and do hereby appoint, Thursday the twenty-seventh day of November next, **to be religiously observed as a day of Public Thanksgiving throughout this State; earnestly exhorting ministers and people of all Denominations, with becoming devotion, to assemble for divine and social worship; and with grateful hearts, to acknowledge the divine goodness in the great and distinguishing Favors and blessings bestowed** upon these United States, and the people of this State in particular: **For the continuation of the inestimable privileges of the Gospel and means of Grace, the blessings of Peace, and for the general health enjoyed; the supplies of the fruits of the Earth**, notwithstanding the harvests are in some measure diminished; **and for all other innumerable favors and unmerited mercies conferred upon us from the fountain of all goodness:**

Also to offer up fervent supplication and prayer to Almighty GOD, the supreme Governor of the Universe, and ruler of the Kingdoms of Men, that it may graciously please him, to shower divine blessings upon the people of these Untied States; disposing them in a yet unexampled manner, to unite in voluntarily forming a salutary Constitution, which shall best fulfill the purposes of Civil Government, by securing the unalienable Rights of Individuals, and removing Oppression far from them, and in promoting the prosperity and permanent happiness of the Union: **Inspire all in civil Administration with wisdom and Integrity: Abundantly bless the inhabitants of this State: Succeed a preached Gospel and the means of Grace, and cause pure religion to flourish:** Grant us health in all our dwellings: Continue peace; make our land a quiet habitation and refuge for the oppressed; caused the Earth to yield her increase, and bless us in all our interests and concerns: Extend his mercies to all Mankind: Dispose the Nations of the Earth to universal peace, and put a period to the calamities of war; and **cause the world to be filled with the Knowledge and Glory of GOD.** And all servile Labor is forbidden on said day.

GIVEN at the Council Chamber at New-Haven, the Thirteenth day of October, in the Thirteenth Year of the independence of the United States of America, Annoque Domini, 1788.

SAMUEL HUNTINGTON.
By his Excellency's Command,
GEORGE WYLLYS Secretary

A Proclamation for a Day of Fasting, Humiliation, and Prayer,
by Governor Samuel Huntington
March 28, 1789[3]

BY HIS EXCELLENCY
SAMUEL HUNTINGTON, ESQUIRE

Governor and Commander in Chief of the State of
CONNECTICUT
A PROCLAMATION.

CONSIDERING the indispensable Duty of a People, to acknowledge the overruling Hand of Divine Providence, and their constant Dependence upon the Supreme Being, for all the Favor and Blessings they may enjoy, or hope to receive; and that notwithstanding the many Mercies and signal instances of Divine Favor conferred upon the Inhabitants of this Land, yet the Prevalence of Vice and Wickedness give us just Reason to fear the Divine Displeasure and Chastisement for our many Offenses, unless prevented by speedy Repentance and Reformation.

I have therefore thought fit by and with the advice of Council, to appoint, and do, hereby appoint WEDNESDAY the Twenty-Second Day of April next, **to be observed as a Day of FASTING, HUMILIATION, and PRAYER**, throughout this state; **earnestly exhorting Ministers and People of all Denominations to assemble for Divine Worship; that we may with becoming Humility, and united Hearts, confess and bewail our manifold Sins and Transgressions, and by Repentance and Reformation obtain Pardon and Forgiveness of all our Offenses, through the Merits and Mediation of JESUS CHRIST our only SAVIOR. Also, to offer up fervent Supplications to ALMIGHTY**

GOD the Father of Mercies, that he may bless the United States of America, gives Wisdom and Integrity to our National Council, direct their Proceedings at this important Crisis, in such Manner as shall best promote the Union, Prosperity and Happiness of the Nation:–**That it may graciously please Him to smile upon and bless the People of this State, inspire our Civil Rulers with Wisdom and Integrity becoming their Station: bless his Sacred Ambassadors, and cause pure and undefiled Religion to flourish**, grant us Health and Plenty; prosper us in all our lawful Employments, and crown the Year with his Goodness; succeed the Means of Education, **extend the peaceful Influence of the REDEEMER'S Kingdom, and dispose all Nations to live as Brethren in Peace and Amity, and fill the World with the Knowledge and Glory of GOD.**

And all servile Labour is forbidden on said Day.

GIVEN at Norwich, the 28th Day of March, in the thirteenth Year of the Independence of the United States of America, Annoque Domini 1789.

SAMUEL HUNTINGTON
By His Excellency's Command,
George Wyllys, Sec'ry

A Proclamation for a Day of Fasting, Prayer and Humiliation,
by Governor Samuel Huntington
March 9, 1791[4]

It becomes a people publicly to acknowledge the over-ruling hand of Divine Providence and their dependence upon the Supreme Being as their Creator and Merciful Preserver . . . and with becoming humility and sincere repentance to supplicate the pardon that we may obtain forgiveness through the merits and mediation of our Lord and Savior JESUS CHRIST.

What follows is a
summary of an article
from contemporary American life . . .

nearly 250 years after
Samuel Huntington
signed

the Declaration of Independence
and
the Articles of Confederation.

What Would Samuel Huntington Think?

TEXAS · Published July 1, 2019

Texas city takes down church's 'Jesus Welcomes You to Hawkins' sign overnight

 By Caleb Parke | Fox News

For four years, the thirteen hundred residents of Hawkins, Texas welcomed visitors with a sign that read, "Jesus Welcomes You to Hawkins." The Jesus Christ Open Altar Church erected the sign in 2015 in front of a local coffeehouse, on property the church claims to have bought from two funeral homes. But the Freedom from Religion Foundation complained. And the city proceeded to fight the church in court, claiming that it owned the property and that the funeral homes had no legal right to sell it. Church members stood guard over the welcome sign until, in the dead of night, city employees deep-six'ed it.

https://www.foxnews.com/us/city-texas-church-jesus-sign.

William Samuel Johnson (1727-1819)

Signer of the United States Constitution

Highest Office Attained:
United States Senator

Religious Affiliation:
Episcopalian

O ne of the most highly educated of the Founding Fathers, William Samuel Johnson was a true Christian statesman. He was the son of a respected Anglican clergyman, Rev. Samuel Johnson. Rev. Johnson, a convert from the dominant Congregationalism of puritan Connecticut, served as the first president of Kings College (later, Columbia College and Columbia University). Even on the eve of his birth, the younger Johnson was the subject of an October 14, 1727 entry in his father's private journal that foretold the importance his Christian faith would hold in his later public life: "This day, I am 31 years old, and this sevennight (Oct. 7) it hath pleased God of His goodness to give me the great blessing of a very likely son, for which, and in my wife's comfortable deliverance, I adore His goodness."

Under the tutelage of his father, including in the study of Hebrew, it appeared early on that Johnson might fulfill Rev. Johnson's wish that he follow his father into the ministry. Johnson acted as a catechist and reader for the church in Ripton, Connecticut; he received for his services an allowance from the Society for the Propagation of the Gospel in Foreign Parts. Ultimately, however, Johnson chose a career in the law, and became an accomplished attorney and justice of the Connecticut Supreme Court. He also served in both houses of the Connecticut state legislature, and acted as Connecticut's agent in England from 1767 to 1771.

Johnson found himself conflicted as independence approached. This was perhaps due to his experiences in England and his recognition of the superior advantages it held over the increasingly restless colonies; he also had close ties to English friends and the Church of England that he held so dear. Although he disagreed with many British policies, he came to oppose the more extreme elements of the movement for independence; he even refused to serve in the first Continental Congress to which he had been elected. He chose, instead, to work toward peace between Britain and the colonies. But his efforts to end the bloodshed through mediation fell into disfavor, and he was briefly arrested, on the order of Major General Oliver Wolcott; he was charged with communicating with the enemy.

Although he was never in the forefront of the movement toward independence, Johnson was instrumental to its success once it arrived. He again was elected to head Connecticut's delegation to the Continental Congress, whose charge was to revise the Articles of Confederation and render a federal Constitution. He served there from 1785 to 1787 as one of its most influential members; he advocated—on behalf of smaller states, such as Connecticut—for equal representation of the states. He also promoted the Connecticut Compromise—providing for proportional representation in the lower House of Representatives and equal state representation in the Senate. He was the first member selected to serve on the Committee of Style, where he served with James Madison, Alexander Hamilton, Gouverneur Morris, and Rufus King. He thus was instrumental in arranging—and crafting the style of—the United States Constitution to which he became a signatory.

Johnson was then chosen as the first United States senator from Connecticut; he held that position simultaneously with that of the first president of Columbia College—the predecessor of which his father had also headed. The importance to Johnson of his Christian faith, and the degree to which he felt it was fundamental to all of life's pursuits—including in the arena of government and the performance of civic duties—is perhaps no better evidenced than in Johnson's words to a Columbia College graduating class: "Your first great duties . . . are those you owe to Heaven, to your Creator and Redeemer." Far from favoring a severance of religion, biographers have described that Johnson "did not believe in any high intellectual culture separate from the spirit of sound morality and the principles of the Christian faith. A complete education, whether it related to the training of the character or of the intellect, involved, in his view, the use of religious motives and influences."[3] Upon his death in 1819, Johnson left behind in manuscript a book of prayers—a reflection upon his Christian character that no doubt would have made his father most proud.

In His Own Words:

Letter from William Samuel Johnson to His Father, Rev. Samuel Johnson (following an illness) February 6, 1768[1]

> [A]t present, **I thank God, I am very well, and under His protection** have great reason to hope for the continuance of my health, as the weather is now growing every day more and more favorable and spring will soon open upon us. . . . I will do all in my power to hasten my return, and **in God's good time hope for a happy meeting with you.**

Letter from William Samuel Johnson to His Father, Rev. Samuel Johnson September 12, 1769[2]

> Yet **thank God there are some burning and shining lights yet left in this dark age, by whom the sacred fire will still, I trust, be kept alive, and from whom it may catch and spread into a flame, whenever it shall please God that His Church shall be again bright as the sun in its glory,** and terrible as an army with banners, not indeed in the pomp an splendor of worldly power and prerogative, —to which some I fear are apt to apply such expression, —but **spiritually glorious; splendid by the purity of her faith and**

---

[3] See E. Edwards Bearsdsley, *Life and Times of William Samuel Johnson, LL.D.* (New York: Hurd and Houghton, 1876), 146, http://books.google.com/books?id=rdmfGCDg6YIC&printsec=titlepage#v=onepage&q&f=false.

institutions; bright by the piety, zeal, and ability of her ministers; glorious by her influence upon the hearts and lives of all her members, and terrible to all the powers of darkness by pushing her conquests into their remotest territories, and confounding their empire by converting their subjects, and **changing the children of Satan and slaves of darkness into the sons of God, and heirs of light and immortality.**

Letter from William Samuel Johnson to Robert Temple February 10, 1772[3]

For my part I have seen so much of the follies and villanies of the world, particularly the political part of it, where, as you justly remark, the practice is still the good of the public and the support of Government, while the real object is wealth, or power, or some other dirty selfish view, that **I am** heartily sick of politics and am **endeavoring** to forget all I have observed upon that subject; to erase from my mind every political idea as relative to the present conduct of affairs; and **to attend to my own duty only as a Christian, a man, and a member of society**. When iniquity abounds the love of many will wax cold. Iniquity does now abound; **let us take care that our Christianity (though put to the test as I doubt not yours has sufficiently been), be not in any degree shaken, and that our love for those things that are really good wax not cold.**

Address to Graduating Class, by William Samuel Johnson, President of Columbia College, c. 1787–1800[4]

You this day, gentlemen, assume new characters, enter into new relations, and consequently incur new duties. **You have, by the favor of Providence and** the attention of friends, received a public education, the purpose whereof hath been to qualify you the better to serve your Creator and your country. . . .

Your first great duties, you are sensible, are those you owe to Heaven, to your Creator and Redeemer. Let these be ever present to your minds, and exemplified in your lives and conduct. Imprint deep upon your minds the principles of piety towards God, and a reverence and fear of His holy name. The fear of God is the beginning of wisdom and its consummation is everlasting felicity. Possess yourselves of just and elevated notions of the Divine character, attributes, and administration, and of the end and dignity of your immortal nature as it stands related to Him. Reflect deeply and often upon those relations. Remember that it is in God you live and move and have your being, — that in the language of David He is about your bed and about your path and spieth out all your ways, — that there is not a thought in your hearts, nor a word upon your tongues, but lo ! he knoweth them altogether, and that he will one day call you to a strict account for all your conduct in this mortal life. Remember, too, that you are the redeemed of the Lord, that you are bought with a price, even the inestimable price of the precious blood of the Son of God. Adore Jehovah, therefore, as your God and your Judge. Love, fear, and serve Him as your Creator, Redeemer, and Sanctifier. Acquaint yourself with Him in His word and holy ordinances. Make Him your friend and protector and your felicity is secured both here and hereafter. And with respect to particular duties to Him, it is your happiness that you are well assured that he best serves his Maker, who does most good to his country and to mankind. . . .

As citizens, you are under every obligation, human and divine, to **exert every faculty that God has blessed you with**, and to **embrace every opportunity that He may furnish you with**, to promote, as far as possible, the peace, prosperity, and happiness of your country, and to devote all your talents and acquisitions, and even life itself, if need be, to its service : to awaken continually in your own bosoms, and to diffuse, as far as possible, around you every principle of public virtue and love of country that they may be drawn forth into action, to effectuate and accomplish that great and glorious and godlike design, the general happiness of civil society and the universal felicity of all mankind. . . .

Finally, gentlemen, in the elegant and expressive language of St. Paul, 'Whatsoever things are true, whatsoever things are honest, whatsoever things are just, whatsoever things are pure, whatsoever things are lovely, whatsoever things are of good report, if there by any virtue, and if there be any praise, think on these things' and do them, and the God of peace shall be with you, to whose most gracious protection I now commend you, humbly imploring Almighty Goodness that He will be your guardian and your guide, your protector and the rock of your defence, your Savior and your God.

What follows is a
summary of an article
from contemporary American life . . .

nearly 250 years after
William Samuel Johnson
signed

the United States Constitution.

What Would William Samuel Johnson Think?

LIFESTYLE · Published April 27, 2018

Alabama teacher says school told her to change shirt with 'just pray' on it

 By Kathleen Joyce, | Fox News

Chris Burrell, an Alabama teacher in the Mobile County Public School District, was sent home to change her shirt. Her offense? The T-shirt said, "just pray." Burrell explained that she "wasn't trying to promote religion, it was just my Monday feel-good shirt." In fact, Burrell wore the shirt to work because it reminded her of Aubreigh Nicholas, a local girl who had been diagnosed with an inoperable brain tumor. "Aubreigh's Army" had designed the shirt to raise money for Aubreigh's treatment.

The superintendent of the school district says that she is supportive of Aubreigh, but that "We have to be cognizant of everyone's beliefs or everyone's thoughts in a public school." Apparently, that requires that the shirt be banished from school premises.

https://www.foxnews.com/lifestyle/alabama-teacher-says-school-told-her-to-change-shirt-with-just-pray-on-it.

Roger Sherman
(1721-1793)

Signer of the Declaration of Independence, the
Articles of Confederation, and the United States Constitution

Highest Office Attained:
United States Senator

Religious Affiliation:
Congregationalist

B orn of a cobbler in Newton, Massachusetts, Roger Sherman was among the hardest working of our Founding Fathers. He hailed from an English family of clothiers, from which his great-grandfather, Captain John Sherman, emigrated to Watertown, Massachusetts around 1634. Although lacking formal legal training, Sherman became an accomplished lawyer and judge. But his passion proved to be politics and public service. Before the revolutionary war, he held positions in all three branches of Connecticut government—legislative, executive, and judicial. And as the birth of a new nation unfolded, his contributions multiplied.

But before all of that came to fruition, Sherman learned that the Sabbath began at sunset on Saturday and continued throughout the day on Sunday. As a youth, he worshipped at the pulpit of Rev. Samuel Dunbar of the First (Congregational) Parish in Stoughton, Massachusetts; the school he attended required its teachers to be "sound in the faith" and to catechize the students in the principles of Christian living. Sherman's upbringing instilled in him an unbending set of Christian values that guided him throughout his life.

After his father died in 1741, Sherman took into his charge his widowed mother, Mehetable Wellington Sherman, and his younger siblings; Mehetable's great-great-grandfather, Rev. Peter Wellington, had served as vicar of the Anglican parish in Luxulyan, in Cornwall, England. Together, the family followed Sherman's older brother, William, to New Milford, Connecticut. Sherman transferred his church membership to the New Milford (Congregational) Church. In New Milford, he became a surveyor, issued a series of almanacs that incorporated his own writings and astronomical observations, and was very active not only in the affairs of New Milford, but in the affairs of the church; he served as deacon; clerk of its newly-formed Ecclesiastical Society; and treasurer of its building committee. In 1749, Sherman married Elizabeth Hartwell, the daughter of Joseph Hartwell, a deacon of the church in Stoughton. In addition to surveying, Sherman operated a merchandising business with his brothers and studied law. In 1754, he was admitted to the bar and began a successful law practice; soon, he was chosen as a New Milford selectman; justice of the peace; and representative to the Connecticut General Assembly.

In 1760, Elizabeth died, and Sherman decided to move to New Haven, Connecticut. There, he operated a store, was elected as the city's first mayor, and again served in the General Assembly. He also joined the White Haven (Congregational) Church, pastored by Rev. Jonathan Edwards; Rev. Edwards was the son of his namesake, Rev. Jonathan Edwards, who was one of the leaders of the New Light movement within the church. And Sherman was a major financial contributor for the construction of a chapel on the grounds of Yale College (now, Yale University).

In 1763, Sherman wed Rebecca Prescott, the couple being joined in holy matrimony by Rebecca's grandfather, Rev. Benjamin Prescott; Rev. Prescott was the minister at the South (Congregational) Church in Danvers, Massachusetts. Rebecca would bear him eight children. In 1788, Sherman assisted White Haven Church in revising its creed, recording in his own handwriting its 1788 Confession of Faith. The following year, Sherman penned his own sermon, entitled, *A short sermon on the duty of self-examination preparatory to receiving the Lord's Supper, with an Appendix containing extracts from Richard Baxter's works*.

Although Sherman himself did not become a man of the cloth, two of his brothers — Rev. Nathaniel Sherman and Rev. Josiah Sherman — became Congregational ministers. And his immigrant great-grandfather's first cousin, Rev. John Sherman, was famous as one of the most renowned preachers in New England; he was also known as the best mathematician and astronomer in the colonies.

Sherman is one of only two persons—the other being Robert Morris—to have signed all three of founding documents of the United States of America—the Declaration of Independence, the Articles of Confederation, and the United States Constitution. And he is the only person to have also signed the Articles of Association (which preceded the Declaration). As the need for a declaration of independence became inevitable, Sherman was appointed—along with Thomas Jefferson, John Adams, Benjamin Franklin, and Robert Livingston—to a committee to draft what became the Declaration of Independence. He then served as Connecticut's representative on a committee of thirteen—one from each colony—charged with drawing up the Articles of Confederation.

While serving in the Continental Congress, Sherman dutifully purchased a Bible at the beginning of each session, read from it daily, and then gave it to one of his children when he returned home. During this time, Sherman also expressed concern that British authorities might expand the role of the Anglican church in Connecticut, where the Congregational Church was the established religion. His allegiance to his country and to his religious principles was so firm that fellow-Congregationalist John Adams came to describe Sherman as "an old Puritan, as honest as an angel and as firm in the cause of American Independence as Mount Atlas."

Following the Declaration, Sherman once again served in the Continental Congress as a delegate from Connecticut; he was instrumental in paving the way toward the adoption of the United States Constitution. His one hundred thirty-eight speeches at the Constitutional Convention of 1787 were surpassed only by Gouverneur Morris, James Wilson and James Madison. When the convention seemed at an impasse, Sherman seconded a motion from Benjamin Franklin to imbue the daily sessions with prayer. And with the delegates of small and large states seemingly deadlocked concerning the form that representation in Congress would take, Sherman forged the Connecticut Compromise—under which one house—the House of Representatives—would feature proportional representation and the other house—the Senate—would give each state equal representation. Sherman later was instrumental in securing Connecticut's ratification of the Constitution.

After the Constitution was ratified, Sherman continued serving in the House of Representatives, and then in the Senate. He passed away in 1793, and was buried in the Grove Street Cemetery in New Haven.

In His Own Words:

Letter from Roger Sherman to His Wife, Rebecca Sherman May 30, 1770[1]

This is your birth day. Mine was the 30th of last month. **May we so number our days as to apply our Hearts to wisdom: that is, true Religion. Psalm 90:12.**

Roger Sherman's "Confession of Faith" 1788[2]

I believe that there is one only living and true God, existing in three persons, the Father, the Son, and the Holy Ghost, the same in substance, equal in power and glory. That the Scriptures of the Old and New Testaments are a revelation from God, and a complete rule to direct us how we may glorify and enjoy Him. . . . That He made man at first perfectly holy; that the first man sinned, and as he was the public head of his posterity, they all became sinners in consequence of his first transgression, are wholly indisposed to that which is good and inclined to evil, and on account of sin are liable to all the miseries of this life, to death, and to the pains of hell forever. **I believe that God . . . did send His own Son to become man, die in the room and stead of sinners, and thus to lay a foundation for the offer of pardon and salvation to all mankind, so as all may**

be saved who are willing to accept the Gospel offer. . . . I believe a visible church to be a congregation of those who make a credible profession of their faith in Christ, and obedience to Him, joined by the bond of the covenant. . . . I believe that the sacraments of the New Testament are baptism and the Lord's Supper. . . . I believe that the souls of believers are at their death made perfectly holy, and immediately taken to glory: that at the end of this world there will be a resurrection of the dead, and a final judgment of all mankind, when the righteous shall be publicly acquitted by Christ the Judge and admitted to everlasting life and **glory**, and the wicked be sentenced to everlasting punishment.

Letter from Roger Sherman to His Son-in-Law, Simon Baldwin February 4, 1790[3]

Dr. Edwards. . . . I esteem him one of the best of preachers that I am acquainted with, sound in faith, and pious and diligent in his studies and attention to the duties of his office . . . .

Our Savior says "Wo to the world because of offences; but wo to that man by whom the offence cometh."

Letter from Roger Sherman to Samuel Hopkins June 28, 1790[4]

[I]t is the duty of all to acknowledge that the Divine Law which requires us to love God with all our heart and our neighbor as ourselves, on pain of eternal damnation, is Holy, just, and good. . . . The revealed law of God is the rule of our duty. . . .

God commands all men everywhere to repent. He also commands them to believe on the Lord Jesus Christ, and has assured us that all who do repent and believe shall be saved . . . . [G]od . . . has absolutely promised to bestow them on all these who are willing to accept them on the terms of the Gospel—that is, in a way of free grace through the atonement. "Ask and ye shall receive [John 16:24]. Whosoever will, let him come and take of the waters of life freely [Revelation 22:17]. Him that cometh unto me I will in no wise cast out" [John 6:37].

Letter from Roger Sherman to Samuel Hopkins October, 1790[5]

True Christians are assured that no temptation (or trial) shall happen to them but what they shall be enabled to bear; and that the grace of Christ shall be sufficient for them.

Inscription on Roger Sherman's Gravestone 1793[6]

IN MEMORY OF
THE HON. ROGER SHERMAN, ESQ.
MAYOR OF THE CITY OF NEW HAVEN
AND SENATOR OF THE UNITED STATES
HE WAS BORN AT NEWTOWN, IN
MASSACHUSETTS,
APRIL 19TH, 1721
AND DIED IN NEW HAVEN, JULY 23RD, A.D. 1793,
AGED LXXII.
Possessed of a strong, clear, penetrating mind,
and singular perseverance,
He became the self-taught scholar,
eminent for jurisprudence and policy.
He was nineteen years an assistant,

and twenty-three years a judge, of the superior court,
in high reputation.
He was a delegate in the first congress,
Signed the glorious act of Independence,
and many years displayed superior talents and ability
in the national legislature.
He was a member of the general convention,
approved the federal constitution,
and served his country, with fidelity and honor,
in the House of Representatives,
and in the Senate of the United States.
He was a man of approved integrity;
a cool, discerning Judge;
a prudent, sagacious politician;
a true, faithful, and firm, patriot.
**He ever adorned
the profession of Christianity
which he made in youth;
and, distinguished through life
for public usefulness,
died in the prospect
of a blessed immortality.**

**Excerpt from *The Globe* (regarding Roger Sherman)
August 15, 1837[7]**

**The volume which he consulted more than any
other was the Bible. It was his custom, at the
commencement of every session of Congress, to
purchase a copy of the Scriptures, to peruse it
daily, and to present it to one of his children on
his return.**

What follows is a
summary of an article
from contemporary American life . . .

nearly 250 years after
Roger Sherman
signed

the Declaration of Independence,
the Articles of Confederation,
and
the United States Constitution.

What Would Roger Sherman Think?

School District Threatens to Call Police over Bible Giveaway

Todd Starnes
Jul 10, 2018

Schoolchildren in La Harpe, Illinois need no longer be fearful of receiving a free Bible, thanks to the Freedom From Religion Foundation. The FFRF sprang into action when it learned that someone — it accused The Gideons, an international organization that provides free Bibles to, among others, hotels and schoolchildren — had distributed Bibles along a public roadway owned by the La Harpe Elementary School.

According to an attorney for the FFRF, "It is unconstitutional for public school districts to permit Gideons to distribute Bibles as part of the public school day" because "Public schools have a constitutional obligation to protect the rights of conscience of young and impressionable students." In response, the school district promised to call the police should anyone ever try to distribute Bibles again.

This wasn't then first time the FFRF threatened La Harpe Elementary. Its first offense? Distributing flyers to teachers at staff meetings that referred to Christmas and Easter: "Easter is the celebration of God's greatest gift — salvation through Jesus Christ"; "Easter blessings! May you feel Christ's Love in your Heart & be filled with his Peace & Joy this Easter Season"; even worse, they included adaptations of Bible passages like Isaiah 9:6 — "For to us a child is born, to us a son is given, and the government will be on his shoulders. And he will be called Wonderful Counselor, Mighty God, Everlasting Father, Prince of Peace."

https://www.toddstarnes.com/faith/school-district-threatens-to-call-police-over-bible-giveaway/.

William Williams
(1731-1811)

Signer of the Declaration of Independence

Highest Office Attained:
Representative in Congress

Religious Affiliation:
Congregationalist

T he son and grandson of Congregational pastors, William Williams nearly followed his forbears into the ministry. Instead, he became a successful merchant, local and state officeholder, and representative to the Continental Congress — where he affixed his name to the Declaration of Independence. Williams's father, Rev. Solomon Williams, DD, was the pastor of the First Congregational Church in Lebanon, Connecticut, for around fifty years. His grandfather and namesake, Rev. William Williams, had emigrated from England in 1637, settling in Roxbury, Connecticut. Both attended Harvard College, as did Williams himself, commencing at the age of sixteen. Upon graduating, Williams studied theology with his father, fully intending to also pursue a career in Christian ministry. But the French and Indian War intervened, and Williams's career pursuits were directed elsewhere. He remained, however, a devout Christian throughout his life, becoming a deacon in his church at an early age, and remaining in that position for the rest of his life.

Williams served for decades as town clerk of Lebanon and as a selectman, and served for forty-five years in the Connecticut Assembly, including as Speaker of its lower house. He later served as judge of the Windham County Court and as probate judge for the Windham district.

By June 1776, he was married to Mary Trumbull, daughter of Royal Governor Jonathan Trumbull. An outspoken advocate for independence, he was then appointed by the Connecticut Assembly as a delegate to the second Continental Congress; he replaced Oliver Wolcott, who had become ill. Williams was unable to participate in the debates leading up to the Declaration of Independence, or even in the vote for independence, as those events had already occurred by the time he arrived at the Congress. However, he was able to affix his signature to the Declaration, as well as to participate as a member of the committee that was instrumental in framing the Articles of Confederation. He also was a delegate to the Connecticut convention that ratified the United States Constitution; he voted in favor of ratification, but preferred language that, rather than barring any religious test for holding office, would have affirmatively required, as a condition of office, an explicit acknowledgement of God and His Providence.

In His Own Words:

Letter from William Williams to Joseph Trumbull (following a crushing defeat at the Battle of Brooklyn) September 13, 1776[1]

Our Affairs are truly in a critical Situation, but far I hope from desperate. **My trust & hope is in a merciful & just God, who with one Volition of his Will can change their appearance. I fear we shall be chastized for our Sins, but not forsaken I trust & firmly believe. But most certainly it becomes all to humble Themselves deeply before Him, repent of our Sins & most earnestly to supplicate his Favor.** He will be known in the Judgements he executes. He has a Controversie with His People, & will certainly accomplish his Design in it. We must bend or break.

No Means for our defence & Safety must be omitted & **may God grant Our Officers & Soldiers, great Wisdom, understanding, Courage & Resolution.**

Letter from William Williams to Jonathan Trumbull Sr. September 20, 1776[2]

These Events however, & signal advantage gained by our oppressors, & the Distress to which our Army & Country are & must be subjected in Consequence of them, are loud speaking Testimonies of the Displeasure & Anger of almighty God against a sinful People, louder than sevenfold Thunder. Is it possible that the most obdurate & stupid of the Children of America shod not hear & tremble? God has surely a Controversie with this People, & He is most certainly able to manage it & He will accomplish his Designs, & bring Us to Repentance & Reformation, or destroy Us. We must bend or break. The ways of his Providence are dark & deep but they are holy, wise, & just & altogether right, tho our feeble Understandings comprehend them not, & tho his Chastisements are severe & dreadful, They are dictated by unbounded Wisdom & Love. They have a meaning of awful & kind Import. Turn unto me for why will ye die O Sons of America. We have thought God was for Us & had given many & signal Instances of His Power & Mercy in our Favor, & had greatly frowned upon & disappointed our Enemies & verily it has been so, but have we repented & given Him the Glory? Verily no. His Hand seems to be turned & stretched out against Us, & strong is his Hand & high is his right Hand. He can & will accomplish all his Pleasure. It is God who has blunted the Weapons of our warfare, that has turned the Counsels of wise Men into Foolishness, that has thus far blasted & disappointed our Hopes, & made Us flee before our Enemies, & given them Possession of our Strong Holds. Trouble does not spring out of the dust nor rise out of the Ground. I have always thot this was a just & righteous Cause in which We are engaged. I remain unshaken in that firm persuasion, & that God wod sooner or later vindicate & support it, I believe so still, but I believe this People must first be brot to know & Acknowledge the righteousness of his Judgment, & their own exceeding Sinfulness

& Guilt, & be deeply humbled under his mighty hand, & look & cry to & trust in Him for all their Help & Salvation but in the Use & Exertion of all the Strength He has given Us. Surely We have seen enough to convince Us of all this, & then why are We not convinced, why is not every Soul humbled under the mighty hand of God, repenting & mourning For its Sins & putting away the evil of his Doings, & looking to Him that smites Us by humble, earnest & fervent Prayer & Supplication day & Night. Why are not the dear Children of God (surely there are many, tho the Scorn & Insult of our Enemies) beseiging the Throne of Grace, sighing & crying for their own Sins & back slidings & for all the abominations that are done in the Land, & saying spare, spare thy People O Lord & give not thine Heritage to Reproach. Let not the Vine which thy right Hand has planted here be rooted up & destroyed, let not thy Churches be wasted & devoured, let not virtue & the remains of Religion be torn down & trampled in the Dust, Let not thy Name be blasphemed, nor our insulting wicked Foes say where is your God, nor the profane world that there is no God that rules the world & regardeth the Right, that vindicateth the just & the righteous Cause. I know that God can vindicate his own Name & Honor without our Help, & out of the Stones raise up Children to Abraham, & it is amazing Folly & Madness to cry the Temple, the Temple of the Lord, & trust in that while We remain an incorrigible People. But Such Things are what God wod have Us learn & practice while his Judgments are abroad in the Land, & with such like Arguments fill our Mouths, & pour out our Souls before Him. Are any? Are not all? in N England especially, who have any Interest in Heaven, crying, beging & intreating for the out pouring of blessed Spirit of God upon the Land, tis a most grievous & distressing Consideration that God is pleased so to withhold the blessed Influences & operations thereof, without which We shall remain stupid forever. Therefore with redoubled fervency of ardent Prayer & Supplication, shod every Soul that has one Sparck of Heavenly Fire kindle it to a fervent Heat & expanded Blaze.

O New England, O my dear native Land, how does my Soul Love thee. **Be Instructed therefore lest Gods Soul depart from thee,** lest thou be like Corazin & Bethsaida in Condemnation as thou hast been in Privileges, lest He make thee as Admah & set thee as Zeboim. **Are the Ministers of the Gospel alive & awake & lifting up their Voices like a trumpet & sounding the Alarm of the Almightys Anger & Wrath ready to burst on the defenseless Heads of a guilty People? Are they warning the wicked of their infinite Danger, animating & arousing them to Consideration? Are they with ardent Zeal & Fervour animating & enlivening the languid Graces of the Godly, exciting & leading them to fervent Prayer, sighing & crying for their own Declensions & Luke warmness in Religion & for the Sins & Iniquities of the Land, praying, beging & intreating with unceasing & as it were resistless Importunity for the copious Effusions of the Blessed Spirit upon all orders & degrees of People & refusing to let God go, without an Answer of Peace, & in the midst of Wrath to remember Mercy, & not give up this his Heritage to Reproach nor blast the blooming Hopes & Prospects of this infant Country, the Asylum of Liberty & Relegion?**

Strange that Mankind shod need such alarming Providences to produce such an Effect. It is no

more than to act like reasonable Creatures, to possess a Spirit & Temper that will add a thousand fold sweetness & pleasure to all the Enjoyments of this World, to exchange the Slavery of the Devil, that accursed Enemy of our Souls, for the Service of God & the Liberty of his Children, to do justly, to love Mercy & walk humbly with our God, to answer the sole end of our Creation, to secure a Peace here infinitely better than the World can give, & an Eternity of Peace & Happiness in the World to come. But still more strange if possible, & astonishing is it that They Shod disregard the Voice of the most high, remain thoughtless & stupid under the dreadful Tokens of his Anger & the awful Judgments of his Hand, by Sickness & by the Sword of our unnatural & enraged Enemies threatening to depopulate the Land & drench the Plains with the Blood of its Inhabitants, leaving the weeping Widows, helpless Orphans & the all that survive the shocking Carnage & subsequent Masacre to drag out their Lives in Want, Wretchedness & miserable Bondage & all this aggravated with the certain Prospect of leaving this dreadful Curse intailed on all Posterity.

A thorough Repentance & Reformation, without all peradventure will appease the Anger of a holy & just God, avert these amazing Calamities, secure Liberty & Happiness to this & all succeeding Ages & eternal Felicity & Glory to all the Subjects of it. If such Considerations & Motives wont awaken a [] to serious Thoughfulness & Attention, I know n[ot] what will, but the Voice of the Arch Angel & the Trump[et] of God.

Letter from William Williams to Jonathan Trumbull Sr. July 5, 1777[3]

[W]e did not arrive here 'till Tuseday the 24th ulto, **thro the good Hand of God, in Health & Safety.** . . .

Our Sins are so great that We have reason to expect severe Correction. O that this People were wise, but there is no appearance of it. God will accomplish his own Designs & what He does is, & will be right & as You piously observe, "future Events are in the safe hand of the all wise & most merciful Director." The Enemy have left Jersey in Desolation & ruins where They had been & marked their way with merciless rage & Brutality. **May the God of Heaven look on & pity the Sufferings of his People & save Us from the further Effects of their Brutal Rage.** . . .

To their active zeal & exertions, it may in good measure (under God) be ascribed that the Enemy proceeded no further.

Letter from William Williams to Jonathan Trumbull Sr. August 2, 1777[4]

They are in the Hands of God almighty & all gracious, & in Him alone may we trust. . . . **For the Sake of all that's near & dear then, & let our Country men be roused this once & I hope all will be saved, & repent & God will certainly be on our Side. Let Them not fear nor be dismayened[.]**

Letter from William Williams to Jonathan Trumbull Sr. August 26, 1777[5]

But We know not what certainty what is before Us, & may be sanguine. **But this is certain N England has vast Occasion to bless & praise the Lord, for his wonderous Mercy in our Deliverance from the dreadful Scourge.** The distress had been beyond all discription had our Enemy invaded them in so critical a Moment. O that there was an heart in our Countrymen. **May God in infinite Mercy pour out his Spirit upon Us, I hope & trust is the earnest Cry of all that Love his Name.**

I am glad to See a Day of Fasting is appointed in Contt & Massa. May We no longer mock the Almighty with deceitfull Words from feigned Lips.

Letter from William Williams to Jonathan Trumbull Sr. September 13, 1777[6]

Thursday last was a day of most severe Conflict, & **it has pleased the holy God to suffer it end for that Time to our great disadvantage. . . .**

It is an awful Frown of divine Providence, but we are not at all humbled under it, a sad sign that more dreadful Evils await Us. We are indeed at a most critical & tremendous Crisis, a powerful Army, flushed with victory & animated by the strongest motives, Riches & Glory before them, no hope of Escape from Shame & Death but by Conquest, pursuing & at the Gates of this great City. Yet if we have a few Days & the People turn out & behave as They ought on such an Occasion, we might have yet great hope & to be sure, **I am far from Despairing, that God will yet save Us. Yet We have reason to**

tremble. Our amazing Sins totally unrepented of to all appearance, is the burden of my perpetual Fear, & apprehentions, but such Language is most exceedingly ungrateful & unattended to here. What can we then expect but God's Mercy is infinite & greater than our Sins. Yet does he usually save a People that wont be saved & fight against him Yet I must & cant but hope, but perhaps it is a false & illgrounded Hope. I must however entertain, till I know it is so.

The next News you receive from hence will be of vast importance, God grant in his infinite mercy, it may be happy. Shod They succeed, tho the blow must be terrible & the Wound deep. . . . What will become of us in such a Case, God only knows. . . . We are in the hands of an infinitely wise & great Being, who orders all Things well. O that every Soul was joining with you in ardent Supplications for the Reformation of this People & for the deliverance & Salvation of this Land.

Letter from William Williams to Jonathan Trumbull Sr. September 30, 1777[7]

I wish our Confidence was more placed & founded on the infinite Mercy & Goodness of God, & less on vain self Confidence & Sufficiency, but I hope God has great & merciful Designs for Us, notwithstandg. our infinite unworthiness. . . .

May God grant us Salvation for his own great Mercy & Name Sake & enable Us to Say not unto Us &c for I am sure we dont deserve it. I had but a faint Idea of the wickedness of the Country till I had traveled to this Country, seen & heard so much of & from the middle & southern parts. Well may we admire & adore the infinite Patience & long suffering of our God.

Letter from William Williams to Jonathan Trumbull Sr. October 2, 1777[8]

May the God of all Mercy appear for our help & Salvation, & the Glory be his only & forever.

Letter from William Williams to Jonathan Trumbull Sr. October 11, 1777[9]

There seems something very importantly remarkable in this Event, it is the hand of God, most conspicuously, we were not prepared for so great a Salvation. How happy shod we have thot our Selves had the Issue been according to the most promising Hopes, but we shod have ascribed it to our own Strength & Prowess & sacrificed to our own [. . .] &c & still I do not see that we are any more prepared to give Glory to the God of armys; how unnatural & shocking that We so much neglect & forget him in that Character, as well as in every other, & if We ever succeed against our Enemies, till we are generally brot to a deeper sense of our own Sinfulness & . . . of such Liberties & Privileges as no People ever before enjoyed it will be a most illustrious Instance of the Patience & Forbearance of the Almighty & all gracious God, & another Demonstration that He is indeed good to the Evil & unthankful & that his Mercy endureth forever but how unspeakably more happy & merciful wo'd be our deliverance & Salvation preceeded by or accompionied with sincere Repentance & Reformation & without it the Lords Controversie with Us will not be ended. . . .

Our Affairs are hastening to a most important Crisis. God in infinite mercy grant it may be happy.

Letter from William Williams to Jonathan Trumbull Sr. October 26, 1777[10]

What infinite reason have We to bless & extol the name of the Lord of Hosts the God of Armys, . . . tho We then tho't with good old Jacob, all these things are against Us. O, may the Mercies & Judgments of the Almighty, accomplish the great Design for which They are sent, our Repentance & Reformation.

I doubt not Congress will appoint a Day of Thansgiving on this great Occasion, thro out the Continent, & may God give Us Heart to celebrate it in a right & acceptable manner. . . .

Our officers there have deserved great Honor, & blessed be God, Who has inspired them with Courage & given Them so much Success.

Letter from William Williams to Mr. Babcock February 11, 1788[11]

When the clause in the 6th article, which provides that "no religious test should ever be required as a qualification to any office or trust, &c." came under consideration, I observed I should have chose that sentence and anything relating to a religious test, had been totally omitted rather than stand as it did, but still more wished something of the kind should have been inserted, but with a reverse sense, so far as to require an explicit acknowledgment of the being of a God, his perfections and his providence, and to have been prefixed to, and stand as, the

first introductory words of the Constitution, in
the following or similar terms, viz. We the people
of the United States, in a firm belief of the being
and perfections of the one living and true God, the
creator and supreme Governour of the world, in his
universal providence and the authority of his laws;
that he will require of all moral agents an account
of their conduct; that all rightful powers among
men are ordained of, and mediately derived from
God; therefore in a dependence on his blessing
and acknowledgment of his efficient protection
in establishing our Independence, whereby it
is become necessary to agree upon and settle a
Constitution of federal government for ourselves,
and in order to form a more perfect union &c., as it
is expressed in the present introduction, do ordain
&c., and instead of none, that no other religious test
should ever be required &c., and that supposing,
but not granting, this would be no security at all,
that it would make hypocrites, &c. yet this would
not be a sufficient reason against it; as it would be
a public declaration against, and disapprobation of
men, who did not, even with sincerity, make such
a profession, and they must be left to the searcher
of hearts; that it would however, be the voice of the
great body of the people, and an acknowledgment
proper and highly becoming them to express on
this great and only occasion, and according to
the course of Providence, one mean of obtaining
blessings from the most high. But that since it was
not, and so difficult and dubious to get inserted,
I would not wish to make it a capital objection;
that I had no more idea of a religious test, which
should restrain offices to any particular sect, class,
or denomination of men or Christians in the long
list of diversity, than to regulate their bestowments
by the stature or dress of the candidate, nor did

I believe one sensible catholic man in the state wished for such a limitation . . . .

I freely confess such a test and acknowledgment would have given me great additional satisfaction; and I conceive the arguments against it, on the score of hypocrisy, would apply with equal force against requiring an oath from any officer of the united or individual states; and with little abatement, to any oath in any case whatever; but divine and human wisdom, with universal experience, have approved and established them as useful, and a security to mankind.

I thought it was my duty to make the observations, in this behalf, which I did, and to bear my testimony for God; and that it was also my duty to say the Constitution, with this, and some other faults of another kind, was yet too wise and too necessary to be rejected.

What follows is a
summary of an article
from contemporary American life . . .

nearly 250 years after
William Williams
signed

the Declaration of Independence.

What Would William Williams Think?

Atheist Organization Attacks Governor Scott Walker for Bible Tweet

GARY DEMAR   MARCH 21, 2014

Wisconsin Governor Scott Walker had the audacity to post the following tweet on Twitter: "Philippians 4:13." That was it. He didn't even post the text of the scripture verse.

The Freedom From Religion Foundation was outraged, and sent Governor Walker a letter accusing him of a "misuse of gubernatorial and state of Wisconsin imprimatur." It warned, "As governor, you took an oath of office to uphold the entirely godless and secular United States Constitution."

Of course, the First Amendment to the United States Constitution provides for "the free exercise [of religion]," as well as "freedom of speech." And the Wisconsin Constitution expressly provides that "[t]he right of every person to worship Almighty God according to the dictates of conscience shall never be infringed." Hmmm . . . is an officeholder such as Governor Walker a "person"?

So, what was so offensive about the "Philippians 4:13" tweet? Well, the text of that passage reads, "I can do all things through Christ who strengthens me."

https://godfatherpolitics.com/atheist-organization-attacks-governor-scott-walker-bible-tweet/.

Oliver Wolcott
(1726-1797)

OLIVER WOLCOTT.

**Signer of the Declaration of Independence and
the Articles of Confederation**

Oliver Wolcott

Highest Office Attained:
Representative in Congress; Governor of Connecticut

Religious Affiliation:
Congregationalist

O liver Wolcott was a descendent of devout Puritans who emigrated to the American colonies to escape religious persecution; they honored their Creator through distinguished service both on the battlefield and in government. Sailing on the *Mary and John* in 1630, Wolcott's great-great-grandparents, Henry and Elizabeth Wolcott, were among the founders of Windsor, Connecticut and of its First (Congregational) Church. Henry was elected to the first legislature of the Connecticut colony, and also served for many years in the House of Magistrates.

Generations later, in 1726, Wolcott was born in Windsor, the youngest son of Roger Wolcott; Roger later would become the royal governor of the colony. Like his ancestors, Wolcott was a deeply-religious family man who lived a long life serving his Lord through service to his brethren. He served his country with honor, dignity and integrity inspired by his Christian faith. Wolcott attended Yale College and studied medicine, although he never practiced. Governor George Clinton of New York commissioned him a captain in the militia; he then raised a company of volunteers during the French and Indian War. He eventually rose to the rank of brigadier general of the Connecticut militia during the revolutionary war. In 1751, he became sheriff of Litchfield County, and he held that position for the next twenty years. He also studied law, was admitted to the bar, and served for twelve years as Litchfield's town counselor. He served on the Litchfield courts for several years, and was elected to the Connecticut General Assembly and the state Council.

In 1755, Wolcott wed Lorraine (Laura) Collins, who hailed from a family of Congregational ministers in Guilford, Connecticut. She would bear him five children, whom they raised in the Litchfield (Congregational) Church. As a declaration of independence increasingly appeared inevitable, Wolcott frequently penned letters to Laura that expressed his profound faith and trust in God; he called upon the Providence of the Almighty in protecting both his family and our emerging nation.

Wolcott served as a delegate to both the first and second Continental Congresses, and signed both the Declaration of Independence and the Articles of Confederation. He later served as lieutenant governor of Connecticut from 1786 to 1796, and as governor from 1796 to 1797—a position that his son, Oliver Wolcott Jr., later would also hold. While governor, Wolcott issued proclamations (excerpted and reproduced below) declaring "a Day of public THANKSGIVING and PRAYER to Almighty God" and "a Day of public Humiliation, FASTING and Prayer."

Upon his death on December 1, 1797, Wolcott was mourned by the citizens of Connecticut; he was remembered by those who knew him best as a devout and consistent Christian and an honorable and honest man. He was interred in the East Cemetery in Litchfield.

In His Own Words:

Letter from Oliver Wolcott to His Wife, Laura Wolcott April 10, 1776[1]

Merciful Providence still continues my Health to Me. Thro Various Scenes of Life God has Sustained me. May he ever be my unfailing Freind, May his Love cherish my Soul, May my Heart with Gratitude Acknowledge his Goodness and may my Desires be to him and to the Remembrance of his Name. Vanity by the Wisest of men has been inscribed on every Thing Mortal and no Experience has ever contradicted this Declaration. May We then turn our Eyes to the bright Objects above, and may God give us Strength to travel the upward Road. May the divine Redeemer conduct us to that Seat of Bliss which he himself

has prepared for his Freinds; at the Approach of which every Sorrow shall Vanish from the human heart, and endless scenes of Glory Open upon the enraptured Eye. There our Love to God and each other will grow stronger, and our Pleasures never be damp'd by the Fear of future Separation. How indifferent will it then be to us wheither We obtained Felicity by travailing the thorny or the agreable Paths of Life, wheither We arrived at our Rest by passing thro the envied and unfragrant Road of Greatness or Sustained Hardship and unmeritted Reproach in our Journey; **Gods Providence and Support thro the perilous perplexing Labyrinths of human Life, will then forever excite our Astonishment and Love.** May a Happiness be granted to those I most tenderly Love which shall continue and increase thro an endless Existence. Your Cares and Burdens must be Many and great, but **put your Trust in that God who has hitherto supported you and me, he will not fail to take Care of those who put their Trust in him. . . . It is most evident that this Land is under the Protection of the Almighty, and that We shall be Saved, not by our Wisdom nor by our might, but by the Lord of Host who is wonderfull in Councill and Almighty in all his Operations.**

Letter from Oliver Wolcott to His Wife, Laura Wolcott December 13, 1776[2]

I am Very Well, I think as much so as I have been at any time the year past. **A Favour for which may I possess the most gratefull Sentiments to that God who gives every Blessing. . . .** Wheither the Enemy will suceed in their cruel Designs against this City must be left to time to Discover. Congress have ordered the Genl to Defend it to the last extremity and **God grant that he may be successful in his**

exertions. Whatever Events may take Place the American Cause will be supported to the last; and **I trust in God that it will succeed. . . . The God Who governs the Universe and who holds Empires in his Hand Can with the least Effort of his Will grant us all that Security, Opulence and Power, which they have injoyed. . . . May the Almighty ever have you and them in His protection.**

Proclamation, by Governor Oliver Wolcott in Litchfield, Connecticut
March 17, 1797[3]

BY HIS EXCELLENCY
Oliver Wolcott, Esq.
GOVERNOR and COMMANDER in CHIEF of the
STATE of CONNECTICUT ,
A PROCLAMATION.

AS it peculiarly becomes a Christian People, at particular and stated Seasons, by Humiliation and Prayer, to pay their devout Homage to Almighty GOD; —

I HAVE thought proper to appoint, and do hereby appoint, FRIDAY, the Fourteenth Day of April next, to be observed as a **Day of public Humiliation , FASTING and Prayer,** throughout this State; recommending to all the People, in their solemn Assemblies, on that Day, **devoutly to acknowledge their Dependance on the Supreme Ruler of the Universe, and with sincere Repentance for our many Sins, humbly to implore, of a merciful God their Forgiveness and Remission, the gracious Aids of his Spirit, and the Blessings of his Providence.**

That he would continue to us and successive Generations, the Gospel of Peace and Salvation; — teach the Hearts of all Men to know its Truth and Excellence, and to obey its holy Precepts: — Succeed and Means of Education and Learning; bless our Youth, furnish their Minds with useful Knowledge, and enrich them with the christian Graces: — That he would smile on our Husbandry; give and preserve to us the goodly Fruits of the Earth: — Prosper our Commerce, restrain the arbitrary Enterprizes for extensively practiced upon it, and cause the Nations at War, to observe towards our Trade and Navigation, the Laws of Justice and good Faith; — save us from desolating Diseases; and grant that in all our lawful Business and Vocations, we may experience the Divine Care and Beneficence. And moreover, humbly to beseech the Throne of Grace, that the God of Wisdom would enlighten the public Councils of this State, thereby to increase the Means of social Improvement and Happiness among the People, and to confirm and perpetuate the public Order, Liberty and Tranquility.

That the United States may continue to be under the Superintendence and holy Protection of the Sovereign Arbiter of Nations: — That he would inspire all our Citizens with a Love of their Country, and each other; cement our Union; impart to all Departments of the Government Wisdom and Integrity, uprightly and ably to conduct the public Interests confided to their Care: — Still continue graciously to smile on our earnest and faithful Endeavours to preserve our Peace; — cause the Negociations with the French Republic to issue in the Acknowledgment and secure Establishment of our just Rights, and the Restoration of Amity and good Agreement between the two Countries.

And that it would please God to afford his gracious Aids to the President of the United States, in the Discharge of the arduous Duties on which he is entering; and that he may be enabled, by a wise and impartial Administration of them, to preserve that Confidence of the People in this Branch of our Government, by which it has been so eminently distinguished: — **That the Benedictions of Heaven may attend the late President of the United States, in his Retirement from his long, useful and disinterested Services to our Country.**

And that God, who is the Author of Peace and Lover of Concord, would restrain the Rage, and Pride of warring Nations, and cause them to submit to righteous and equitable Terms of Peace.

And that all those to whom the Ministration of the Gospel of Christ Jesus is committed, may be influenced by that Spirit which the Gospel is adapted to inspire; and that the Effect of their Ministration may be the Advancement of peaceful Kingdom of the Great Redeemer among Mankind.

All servile Labour on said Day is forbidden.

Given at Litchfield, this seventeenth Day of March, in the Year of our Lord one thousand seven hundred and ninety seven, and of the Independence of the United States of America the twenty-first.

OLIVER WOLCOTT.
By his Excellency's Command,
Samuel Wyllys, Secretary.

BY HIS EXCELLENCY

Oliver Wolcott, Efq.

GOVERNOR AND COMMANDER IN CHIEF OF THE STATE OF CONNECTICUT,

A PROCLAMATION.

AS it peculiarly becomes a Chriftian People, at particular and ftated Seafons, by Humiliation and Prayer, to pay their devout Homage to ALMIGHTY GOD;---

I HAVE thought proper to appoint,
and do hereby appoint FRIDAY, the *Fourteenth* Day of APRIL next, to be obferved as a Day of public HUMILIATION, *FASTING* and PRAYER, throughout this State; recommending to all the People, in their folemn Affemblies, on that Day, devoutly to acknowledge their Dependance on the *Supreme Ruler* of the Univerfe, and with fincere Repentance for our many Sins, humbly to implore, of a merciful GOD, their Forgivenefs and Remiffion, the gracious Aids of his Spirit, and the Bleffings of his Providence.

That he would continue to us and fucceffive Generations, the Gofpel of Peace and Salvation;---teach the Hearts of all Men to know its Truth and Excellence, and to obey its holy Precepts :---Succeed the Means of Education and Learning : blefs our Youth, furnifh their Minds with ufeful Knowledge, and enrich them with the chriftian Graces :---That he would fmile on our Hufbandry : give and preferve to us the goodly Fruits of the Earth ;---Profper our Commerce, reftrain the arbitrary Enterprizes fo extenfively practifed upon it, and caufe the Nations at War, to obferve towards our Trade and Navigation, the Laws of Juftice and good Faith ;---fave us from defolating Difeafes; and grant that in all our lawful Bufinefs and Vocations, we may experience the Divine Care and Beneficence. And moreover, humbly to befeech the Throne of Grace, that the God of Wifdom would enlighten the public Councils of this State, thereby to increafe the Means of focial Improvement and Happinefs among the People, and to confirm and perpetuate the public Order, Liberty and Tranquillity.

That the United States may continue to be under the Superintendence and holy Protection of the Sovereign Arbiter of Nations :---That he would infpire all our Citizens with a Love of their Country, and each other; cement our Union; impart to all Departments of the Government Wifdom and Integrity, uprightly and ably to conduct the public Interefts confided to their Care :---Still continue gracioufly to fmile on our earnell and faithful Endeavours to preferve our Peace;---caufe the Negociations with the French Republic to iffue in the Acknowledgement and fecure Eftablifhment of our juft Rights, and the Reftoration of Amity and good Agreement between the two Countries.

And that it would pleafe GOD to afford his gracious Aids to the *Prefident of the United States*, in the Difcharge of the arduous Duties on which he is entering ; and that he may be enabled, by a wife and impartial Adminiftration of them, to preferve that Confidence of the People in this Branch of our Government, by which it has been fo eminently diftinguifhed :---That the Benedictions of Heaven may attend the late Prefident of the United States, in his Retirement from his long, ufeful and difinterefted Services to our Country.

And that GOD, who is the Author of Peace and Lover of Concord, would reftrain the Rage and Pride of warring Nations, and caufe them to fubmit to righteous and equitable Terms of Peace.

And that all thofe to whom the Miniftration of the Gofpel of Chrift *Jefus* is committed, may be influenced by that Spirit which the Gofpel is adapted to infpire; and that the Effect of their Miniftration may be the Advancement of the peaceful Kingdom of the *Great Redeemer* among Mankind.

ALL SERVILE LABOUR ON SAID DAY IS FORBIDDEN.

GIVEN *at* Litchfield, *this* feventeenth *Day of* March, *in the Year of our* LORD *one thoufand feven hundred and* ninety feven, *and of the* Independence *of the United States of America the* twenty-firft.

By his Excellency's Command,   OLIVER WOLCOTT.
SAMUEL WYLLYS, *Secretary.*

***Proclamation*, by Governor Oliver Wolcott in Litchfield, Connecticut**
October 25, 1797[4]

I have therefore, with the Advice of the Council, and by the Desire of the House of Representatives, thought proper to appoint, and do hereby
appoint, THURSDAY the sixteenth day of November next to be observed as a **Day of public
THANKSGIVING and PRAYER to Almighty God,**
throughout this State;. . . .

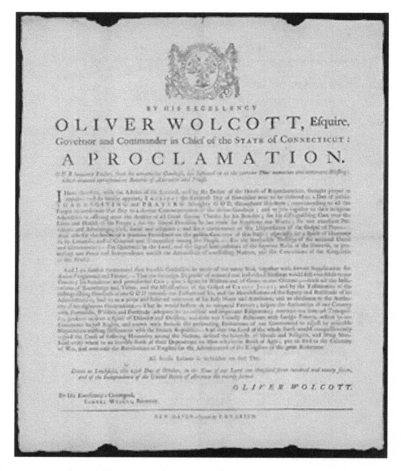

Statement by Oliver Wolcott at the Connecticut Convention to Ratify the United States Constitution
January 9, 1788[5]

The Constitution enjoins an oath upon all the officers of the United States. **This is a direct appeal to that God who is the avenger of perjury. Such an appeal to him is a full acknowledgment of his being and providence.**

What follows is a
summary of an article
from contemporary American life . . .

nearly 250 years after
Oliver Wolcott
signed

the Declaration of Independence
and
the Articles of Confederation.

What Would Oliver Wolcott Think?

Army says faith-based group can no longer put Bible verses on dog tags after complaint

By Caleb Parke | Fox News

For twenty years, Shields of Strength produced dog tags bearing Bible verses. Soldiers would sometimes wait in line for hours to get one. According to the organization's Kenny Vaughan, "Virtually every unit has contacted us and said, 'Would you make us a tag with our unit on it?' We've seen the fruit of the mission. Literally thousands of soldiers, airmen, marines, telling us with tears in their eyes how much it's meant to them, and many times the Gold Star families to be in possession of the dog tag they wore."

But the Military Religious Freedom Foundation complained. And the military branches then revoked or threatened the organization's license. Explained the Army's Trademark Licensing Program director, "You are not authorized to put biblical verses on your Army products. For example, Joshua 1:9. Please remove ALL biblical references from all of your Army products." Vaughan's response? "It's insane. It's incredibly selfish. All we do is provide a reminder of God's word. No one has to do this."

https://www.foxnews.com/faith-values/ army-bible-verse-dog-tags-complaint.

Chapter Five:
Rhode Island Signers

John Collins
(1717-1795)

[Portrait Unavailable]

Signer of the Articles of Confederation

Highest Office Attained:
Representative in Congress; Governor of Rhode Island

Religious Affiliation:
Protestant Christian

A s a son of Rhode Island—the bastion of religious freedom for all—it is perhaps fittingly difficult to describe John Collins as belonging to a particular religious denomination. His upbringing was decidedly Quaker; but he married a Congregationalist; and some of his children became Episcopalians.

Collins was born in 1717 to Samuel Collins Jr. and Elizabeth Thurston Collins; both hailed from longstanding Quaker families. Samuel's great-grandfather, Henry Collins, a starch maker, departed London with his family aboard the *Abigail* in 1635; he settled in Sagus (later, Lynn), Massachusetts. Formerly of London's parish church at Stepney, the Collins family initially attended the First (Congregational) Church, pastored by the puritan Rev. Samuel Whiting; after Rev. Whiting's arrival, the town was renamed "Lynn" in honor of Rev. Whiting's English hometown. In time, however, the Society of Religious Friends— the Quakers—developed a substantial following in Lynn; the Collins family was foremost among them. Indeed, Collins's grandfather, Samuel Collins Sr., hosted the first monthly meeting of the Lynn Quakers around 1690. Not long after, the witchcraft hysteria in the nearby town of Salem induced some of those who were persecuted to join the Quakers. But the persecution by the Puritans extended also to the Quakers; some Quakers found themselves jailed for failing to attend puritan religious services or for refusing to pay taxes to fund the Congregational church. After Samuel Sr.'s wife, Hannah, died in 1694, he married Rebecca Hussey; her father, Rev. John Hussey, was a Quaker minister in New Hampshire. Rev. Hussey was similarly fined, and he then departed for Pennsylvania. Rev. Hussey was descended from Christopher Hussey—a founder of Nantucket— and Rev. Stephen Bachiler—a notoriously non-conformist

English preacher whose religious views led him to flee initially to Holland and then to Massachusetts.

The Collins family largely remained in Lynn; this included a cousin, Rev. Micajah Collins, who later served as a Quaker minister and twenty-five-year teacher at the Friends school. But Collins's Quaker father left Lynn and settled in Newport, Rhode Island. There, he wed Elizabeth Thurston and was active in the Newport Meeting of the Society of Friends; the Meeting dutifully recorded the baptism of their children, including Collins in 1717. Not only were Elizabeth's paternal ancestors English Quakers, but her mother, Mary Easton Thurston, was descended from two Quaker governors of Rhode Island — her father, Governor John Easton, and her grandfather, Governor Nicholas Easton. And her maternal ancestry dates back to Quakers Peter and Lydia Hampton Gaunt; they, after leaving St. Bridget's parish in London, became early settlers of Sandwich, Massachusetts — the first town established on Cape Cod. Lydia's father was Rev. Thomas Hampton.

Collins established himself as a Newport businessman and merchant. He met a young Mary Avery of Boston, and they wed there in a ceremony believed to have been officiated by Rev. Jonathan Mayhew; Rev. Mayhew was the pastor of Boston's West (Congregational) Church and a fervent patriot whom Robert Treat Paine described as the father of civil and religious liberty in America. Rev. Mayhew laid an early foundation for American resistance by his publication in 1750 of his sermon entitled, *A Discourse concerning Unlimited Submission and Non-Resistance to the Higher Powers: With some Reflections on the Resistance made to King Charles I. And on the Anniversary of his Death: In which the Mysterious Doctrine of that Prince's Saintship and Martyrdom is Unriddled.*

Mary's parents had been wed at the Old South (Congregational) Church in Boston, Rev. Thomas Prince officiating. Her family included many men of the cloth. One was her grandfather, Rev. John Avery — who himself had two uncles in the ministry. Rev. Avery was the first — and for forty-four years — pastor of the Congregational church in the Cape Cod community of Truro, Massachusetts; he also served as the town's physician. Mary's uncle, Rev. Ephraim Avery, ministered in Brooklyn, Connecticut. And her great-uncle, Rev. Joseph Avery, pastored in Norton, Massachusetts. Known as "the Boston Merchant," Mary's father, John Avery Sr., was descended through his mother, Ruth Little Avery, from Richard Warren; Warren had immigrated in 1620 aboard the *Mayflower*. And Mary's brother, John Avery Jr., was an early revolutionary and one of the Loyal Nine—the forerunner to the Sons of Liberty—and participated in its incitement of mob protests in opposition to Britain's passage of the Stamp Act. He later served as the first secretary of the commonwealth of Massachusetts, having defeated his former boss, patriot Samuel Adams.

Collins was also an early supporter of the patriot cause. In 1766, he became one of the deed-holders to the "Liberty Tree lot" in Newport—and to its large Buttonwood tree that thereafter was known as the Tree of Liberty; it was held in trust "for the use of the Sons of Liberty" and as a "Monument of the Spirited and Noble Opposition made to the Stamp Act." In 1774, Collins was elected to the Rhode Island General Assembly and also served on Newport's Committee of Safety. In 1776, he was selected to report to General George Washington about the conditions in the state. He was then elected to the Continental Congress in 1778, and there became a signatory to the Articles of Confederation. In 1786, having earned the support of the rural farmers, he was elected governor of Rhode Island; he defeated the incumbent governor as a candidate of the Paper Money Party.

Collins's children appear to have taken divergent denominational paths. Daughter Mary Collins wed Dr. John Warren of Boston; he was a Congregationalist-turned-Episcopalian and grand master of the Massachusetts Grand Lodge (Antients) of freemasons. Their son, Dr. Jonathan Collins Warren, became a founder of *The New England Journal of Medicine and Surgery* and of Massachusetts General Hospital; he was also the first dean of the Harvard Medical School. Daughter Mary Collins wed Caleb Gardiner, a warden of Newport's Trinity (Episcopal) Church;

he was a second cousin of Rev. Gardiner Thurston of Newport's Second Baptist Church. And son John Avery Collins—who succeeded Collins as deed-holder to the Liberty Tree—turned to Rev. Thurston, who also was Collins's second cousin, to officiate at his nuptial ceremony. John Avery Collins's daughter, Mary, in turn was married in a Friends ceremony, while another daughter, Eliza, wed Rev. Joseph Covell, an Episcopalian minister. And the Covells' son, John Collins Covell—often mistakenly referred to as Collins's grandson, rather than his great-grandson—continued as a deacon in the Episcopal church and donated land for the building of St. Stephen's Episcopal Church in Romney, West Virginia; he also served as the church's first warden. For many years, John Collins Covell served as the principal of the Virginia School for the Deaf and Blind and of the West Virginia Schools for the Deaf and Blind.

During the revolution, the British used Rev. Gardiner Thurston's Second Baptist Church as a barracks during their occupation of Newport. It suffered significant ruin, as the occupiers used the church pews as firewood. During that time, Rev. Thurston was allowed to conduct his services at Trinity Church. Years later, however, Second Baptist hosted the debates over the ratification of the United States Constitution. Collins played a key role; although not initially a supporter of the Constitution— Rhode Island had failed to send any delegates to the 1787 constitutional convention—Governor Collins cast the deciding vote calling for a ratifying convention. At the resulting convention, held at the governor's kinsman's church, the vote to ratify initially failed; but it subsequently succeeded by a narrow 34-32 margin, and Rhode Island thus became the last of the thirteen colonies to officially join the union.

Collins continued as governor until 1790, when he lost his bid for reelection. He was subsequently elected to the first post-Constitution Congress, but declined to serve. He retired to his Brenton Neck farm, where he passed away in 1795.

In His Own Words:

Letter from John Collins to former Governor Samuel Ward
July 17, 1774[1]

It is the honest yeomen of the land We must finally depend on for the salvation of our Libertys. . . . **[The merchants'] Religion is trade and their God is gain and they that Expect men to sacrifice their God and their Religion for the Publick will Certainly be disappointed.**

Letter from Governor John Collins to the President of Congress
September 15, 1787[2]

As the freemen at large here have the power of electing delegates to represent them in the Congress, we could not consistently appoint delegates in a convention which might be the means of dissolving the Congress of the Union, and having a Congress without a confederation. . . . You will impute it, sir, to our being diffident of power, and an apprehension of dissolving **a compact which was framed by the wisdom of men who gloried in being instrumental in preserving the religious and civil rights of a multitude of people,** and an almost unbounded territory, that said requisition hath not been complied with; and fearing, when the compact should once be broke, we must all be lost in a common ruin.

An Act of the General Assembly of the State of Rhode Island and Providence Plantations, Signed by Governor John Collins
October 1787[3]

An Act to prevent the slave trade, and to encourage the abolition of slavery.

Whereas, **the trade to Africa for slaves**, and the transportation and selling of them into other countries, is **inconsistent with justice, and the principles of humanity, as well as the laws of nature**, and that more englighted and civilized sense of freedom which has of late prevailed . . . Be it enacted by this General Assembly, and by the authority thereof it is enacted, that no citizen of this state, or other person residing within the same, shall, for himself or any other person whatsoever, either as master, factor or owner of any vessel, directly or indirectly import or transport, buy or sell, or receive on board their vessel with intent to cause to be imported or transported from their native country, any of the natives or inhabitants of any state or kingdom in that part of the world called Africa, as slaves, or without their voluntary consent. . . .

What follows is a
summary of an article
from contemporary American life . . .

nearly 250 years after
John Collins
signed

the Articles of Confederation.

What Would John Collins Think?

Atheists Strong Arm Wrestling Team over Bible Verse

 Todd Starnes | Posted: Apr 22, 2014 9:17 AM   Share

For ten years, no one complained about the motto of the South High School wrestling team in Parkersburg, West Virginia: "I can do all things through Him that strengthens me." The motto appeared on the back of team shirts—but only if the students wished to wear them. There were no official uniforms and no one was required to wear the shirts, which were paid for by moms and dads. But that didn't matter to the Freedom From Religion Foundation; it claimed that the shirts were unconstitutional because the motto paraphrases a Bible verse—Philippians 4:13. For the time being, the school district is allowing the students to wear the shirts, so long as they belong to the students. But the motto has been scrubbed from the team's website. And the parents stand ready to sue if the school district caves to the FFRF on the shirts as well.

https://townhall.com/columnists/toddstarnes/2014/04/22/atheists-strong-arm-wrestling-team-over-bible-verse-n1827501.

William Ellery
(1727-1820)

Signer of the Declaration of Independence and
the Articles of Confederation

Highest Office Attained:
Representative in Congress; Chief Justice of Rhode Island

Religious Affiliation
Congregationalist

William Ellery, who became known as the "Congressman on Horseback," was born in Newport, Rhode Island in 1727; his parents were William Ellery Sr. and Elizabeth Almy Ellery. Ellery's father was a merchant who served as the deputy governor of the Rhode Island colony. His grandfather, Hon. Benjamin Ellery, immigrated from Gloucester, England, and served as a judge; as assistant Speaker of the Rhode Island House of Deputies; and as a member of the Newport town council. Ellery's mother was descended from William Almy and Audrey Barlow Almy, who immigrated to Lynn, Massachusetts aboard the *Abigail* in 1635; they later relocated to the Cape Cod community of Sandwich, and then to Portsmouth, Rhode Island. Portsmouth was situated on the northern end of the same island as Newport.

Another of Elizabeth's ancestors was Thomas Cornell, a friend of Rev. Roger Williams's; Rev. Williams was a puritan minister who fled religious persecution in England in 1631 and, favoring complete separation from the Church of England over a purification of it, was subsequently banished from Massachusetts. He then founded the Rhode Island colony as a bastion of religious liberty. Upon immigrating from England around 1636, Cornell and his wife, Rebecca Briggs Cornell, and their family established themselves initially in Boston; they counted among their friends and neighbors, Anne Hutchinson. Hutchinson was the Antinomian leader who, after settling in Massachusetts following the persecution of her own minister-father in England, found herself similarly accused of religious heresy and banished from Massachusetts. The Cornells also fled Massachusetts, seeking greater religious liberty. They first founded a settlement known as "Cornell's Neck" in what is now Westchester, New York. On the advice of Rev. Williams, they then settled in Rhode Island and helped found Portsmouth; they became part of the Portsmouth Quaker community.

The Ellerys were members of the Congregational church in Newport, originally pastored by Rev. Nathaniel Clap. When a split occurred in the church, Second Congregational was born, and Ellery's grandfather contributed a substantial sum for the building of a new church. Ellery was tutored by his Harvard-educated father, and then followed his father's footsteps to that very Cambridge institution; he excelled in Greek and Latin studies. Ellery joined the masons, a fraternal organization that, while not sectarian in nature, requires of its members a belief in a Supreme Being, and became a master mason of the Grand Lodge of Massachusetts—the oldest masonic lodge in the western hemisphere. He also met his future wife, a young Ann Remington. She was a daughter of Judge Jonathan Remington, and her ancestors included royal Massachusetts governors Thomas Dudley and Simon Bradstreet. Ann's sister, Martha, wed the learned Judge Edmund Trowbridge of Cambridge, Massachusetts; another sister, Mary, wed Rev. Benjamin Stevens of the Congregational Church in what is now Kittery Point, Maine.

Upon graduating from Harvard, Ellery returned to Newport; he worked alongside his father in his mercantile business, and also became a naval officer; a customs collector; and the clerk of the Rhode Island General Assembly. In 1750, he and Ann Remington were wed; together, they had seven children. One daughter, Lucy, later married William Channing, the attorney general of Rhode Island; their son, Rev. William Ellery Channing, became an eminent theologian and founder of Unitarianism. And another daughter, Elizabeth, later wed Francis Dana, a Massachusetts signer of the Articles of Confederation.

In 1764, Ellery and his pastor at Second Congregational, the esteemed Rev. Ezra Stiles—who later officiated at the wedding of Ellery's son, Benjamin—were approached by Baptist leaders about writing a college charter. This led to Ellery's role in incorporating and founding Rhode Island College (now,

Brown University). By the time Ann died that same year, revolu-tionary fervor was underway, and Ellery was in the forefront of the patriot movement. He became a leader of the Rhode Island Sons of Liberty, and upon Britain's passage of the Stamp Act in 1765, led the riotous protests that resulted. He also took up the study of law, and wed a distant cousin, Abigail Cary, with whom he had another twelve children. Abigail was descended from William Wanton, who had served as royal governor of the Rhode Island colony; upon the coupling, Abigail's maternal grandmother, Abigail Ellery Wanton—who was William Ellery Sr.'s sister—also became her aunt.

In 1776, when former Governor Samuel Ward passed away, Ellery was selected to take his place in the Continental Congress. He emphatically signed the Declaration of Independence, and later the Articles of Confederation that initially governed the new nation. He served in the Congress until 1786, became a strong abolitionist, and frequently returned home on horseback—thus earning his "Congressman on Horseback" moniker—to meet with his constituents. He briefly served as chief justice of the Rhode Island Superior (now, Supreme) Court. And in 1790, he was appointed by President George Washington to serve as the first collector of customs for the port of Newport; he would hold that position for the rest of his life. Ellery passed into eter-nity in 1820 at the age of ninety-two; over his many decades, he demonstrated his strong intellect, his unsurpassed work ethic, and his staunch religious convictions. He was initially interred at the Coggeshall Cemetery in Newport, and was later moved to its Common Burying Ground.

In His Own Words:

Letter from William Ellery Jr. to His Brother, Benjamin Ellery July 10, 1776[1]

The Events of War are uncertain. **God send the Victory.**

Letter from William Ellery Jr. to Nicholas Cooke
December 24, 1776[2]

> **I hope in God better Fortune will attend our future**
> **Operations.**

Letter from William Ellery Jr. to William Vernon
March 16, 1778[3]

> **With the Aid of Heaven we will crush the Serpents**
> **head next Summer, and force our Enemies to be**
> **at peace with Us!**

Letter from William Ellery Jr. (and Henry Marchant, as
Rhode Island Delegates to the Continental Congress) to
William Greene
June 27, 1778[4]

> We place no great Expectations from that Resolution,
> unless the Campaign should soon end successfully on
> Our Part in the Jerseys, **And which by the Blessing**
> **of God we have great Hopes of.**

Letter from William Ellery Jr. to His Brother,
Christopher Ellery
January 26, 1779[5]

> When the war will end I know not; but I hope it will
> not extend beyond this year at farthest. **It will end**
> **sooner if the divine Providence** should remove from
> British Councils that infatuation which hath so long
> prevailed in them; but **quos Deus vult perdere prius**
> **dementat.** [a common Latin quotation derived from
> Euripida, meaning, **"Those whom God wishes to**
> **destroy he first makes mad."**]

Letter from William Ellery Jr. (and John Collins, as Rhode Island Delegates to the Continental Congress) to William Greene May 8, 1779[6]

> We have reason to think that Great-Britain will strengthen her armies in America, and that they will exert themselves to the utmost of their power, this campaign. It behoves us therefore to guard ourselves. They have possessed themselves of Georgia, and aim at the possession of South Carolina. If they should obtain that, and add our State to their acquisitions, **which God in his infinite mercy, forbid**, the War would be protracted to a most ruinous length or we must be compelled to submit to a disadvantageous, dishonorable peace.

Letter from William Ellery Jr. (and Others, on Behalf of the Second Congregational Church of Newport) to John Adams May 26, 1783[7]

> **Conscious of your attachment to religious liberty, in which our Society is founded, and of your disposition and capacity to support that glorious cause**, as well as the civil liberties of mankind we have ventured to inclose that address to your patronage and care; and we request that you will be pleased to place it in the hands of such of the principal pastors of the Reformed as you shall think will be best disposed to circulate subscriptions and otherwise make collections **for the purpose of repairing our ministry and meeting house and towards a ministerial fund**. . . .
>
> We would only add here that the General Assembly of this State at a late Session repealed an old law which excluded Roman Catholics from the privileges of citizenship.

Letter from William Ellery Jr. to His Brother, Christopher Ellery
January, 1785[8]

> **Thank God**, I enjoy a pretty good state of health . . . .

Letter from William Ellery Jr. to His Grandson, Rev. William Ellery Channing
January, 1796[9]

> I have been a clerk of the court, a quack lawyer, a member of Congress, one of the lords of the admiralty, a judge, a loan officer, and finally a collector of the customs, and thus, not without many difficulties, but as honestly, **thank God**, as most men, I have got almost through the journey of a varied and sometimes anxious life.

Letter from William Ellery Jr. to His Grandson, Rev. William Ellery Channing
June 10, 1806[10]

> **There is but one correct system of Divinity, and that is contained in the Scriptures. What is not therein expressly declared or fairly to be inferred therefrom is human, and by consequence imperfect and incorrect.**

Inscription on William Ellery Jr.'s Gravestone[11]

> He was in the full possession of his powers to the close of his long life, rarely unfitted by disease for study, society, or official duty and **waiting for death with the hope of a Christian.**

What follows is a
summary of an article
from contemporary American life . . .

nearly 250 years after
William Ellery
signed

the Declaration of Independence
and
the Articles of Confederation.

What Would William Ellery Think?

Opinion: Attacks on Christian Homeschooling Are No Longer Subtle

 Charlotte Allen

May 8, 2021 Updated: May 10, 2021 A A F

Harvard Law School professor Elizabeth Bartholet believes there should be a "presumptive ban" on homeschooling, and that parents who choose to homeschool their children should have to prove that "their case is justified." Otherwise, they would be required to send their children to public schools.

Now the attacks are focusing on *Christian* homeschoolers. Said the *Huffington Post*, for example, "Language used in the [homeschooling textbooks] overlaps with the rhetoric of Christian nationalism, often with overtones of nativism, militarism, and racism." Added Yale sociology professor Philip Gorski, "Christian homeschooling was—and is— often—if not always—a major vector of White Christian Nationalism." Critics typically also can't resist sarcastically referring to the belief that the Bible is "sacred, absolute truth."

https://www.theepochtimes.com/attacks-on-christian-homeschooling-are-no-longer-subtle_3805174.html.

Stephen Hopkins
(1707-1785)

Signer of the Declaration of Independence

Highest Office Attained:
Representative in Congress; Governor of Rhode Island; Chief Justice of Rhode Island

Religious Affiliation:
Quaker

S tephen Hopkins was born in 1707 in the Cranston area of Providence, Rhode Island; he was the son of William Hopkins and Ruth Wilkinson Hopkins. The family moved to nearby Scituate when Hopkins was very young, and he was raised there on the family farm. Receiving little formal schooling, he was largely educated by his Quaker mother, and devoured books on Greek, Roman, and British history from his grandfather's library. Ruth's mother, Plain Wickendon Wilkerson, was the daughter of Rev. William Wickendon, one of the founders of Providence. He had followed Rev. Roger Williams there around 1737 after Rev. Williams himself fled religious persecution in Massachusetts; Rev. Williams then established the colony of Rhode Island as a place where all religious persuasions could flourish. Like Rev. Williams, Rev. Wickendon was a Baptist minister; Rev. Wickendon served as pastor of the First Baptist Church in Providence, which had been founded by Rev. Williams. In those early days, services were held in members' homes. Raised a Baptist, grandmother Plain married a Quaker, Samuel Wilkinson, and it was in the Quaker tradition that she raised Ruth; Ruth later imparted that same tradition to Hopkins. On his father's side, Hopkins was descended from his great-grandfather, Thomas Hopkins, who had also followed Rev. Williams to Providence. Thomas had sailed from England in 1635 with his cousin, Benedict Arnold — great-grandfather of his treasonous namesake who defected to the British during the war for independence — and was among the original settlers of that town. Cousin Benedict Arnold later became the first governor of the Rhode Island colony under the royal charter of 1663.

In 1726, Hopkins wed a fellow Quaker, Sarah Scott, who, like Hopkins, was then just nineteen years of age. Sarah's maternal grandfather, Joseph Jencks, had immigrated with his family at the age of two; he became the founder of Pawtucket, Rhode Island. Sarah's uncle, Joseph Jencks III, also served as governor of the colony. And her paternal grandfather, Richard Scott, is considered the first Quaker in Rhode Island and the first Quaker preacher in Providence. He and his wife, Katherine Marbury Scott, the first woman to convert to Quakerism in the New World, also followed Rev. Williams to Providence. So did Katherine's older sister, Anne Hutchinson, who, like the sisters' English father, Rev. Francis Marbury, was persecuted for her religious beliefs; like Rev. Williams, she too found herself banished from Massachusetts.

Hopkins was initially employed as a land surveyor, and became instrumental in establishing Rhode Island's present boundaries. But, by the age of twenty-three, he was also embarking on what became a long and storied career of public service. As Scituate was being formally separated from Providence, Hopkins served as the town moderator, and then as town clerk and as president of the town council. He was elected to the Rhode Island General Assembly in 1732, and served as its Speaker. In 1742, Hopkins moved to Providence; he established a mercantile and shipping business with his brother, Esek, and simultaneously served on the Rhode Island Superior Court—the highest court in the colony—including as its chief justice. He and Esek also partnered with the well-known Brown brothers of Providence in their mercantile business. They also joined together in establishing the Hope Furnace, which later manufactured cannon for use during the war for independence. Sarah passed away, however, in 1753, and Hopkins was left to care for their young family. Still, he found time to attend the Albany Congress in 1754; it was called in an effort to unite the colonies and to arrange an alliance with the natives in the face of a likely war with France. Although the effort proved to be unsuccessful, it resulted in a lasting friendship with Benjamin Franklin; Franklin later would become the only signer of the Declaration of Independence older than Hopkins.

The year 1755 was an eventful one for Hopkins. He married Anne Smith, great-granddaughter of another early Providence settler, John Smith; he was among those who fled with Rev. Williams from Massachusetts in 1636. Hopkins formalized his relationship with the Providence Meeting of the Society of Friends. And he was elected governor of Rhode Island, defeating the incumbent governor, William Greene. This was the first of many such elections occurring between 1755 and 1768; during those years, Hopkins and Samuel Ward—a Sabbatarian, or Seventh Day Baptist, from Newport—repeatedly opposed each other in the contest, frequently alternating victories. This personal rivalry was also a geographic one; Hopkins's base of support was the more northern and historically more rural and insular community of Providence, while Ward was backed by the more southern and historically more economically advanced area of Newport. But, during this time, the commercial viability of Providence came to equal or surpass that of Newport.

In 1764, Hopkins authored, under the pseudonym "P," *The Rights of the Colonies Examined*; in it, he extolled the virtues of liberty and presented an early critique of British policies toward the colonies. He also assisted in the founding of Rhode Island College (now, Brown University). Establishing a college in Rhode Island had long been a dream both of Baptist leaders and of Rev. Ezra Stiles; Rev. Stiles was then pastor of the Second Congregational Church in Newport, and later served as president of Yale College. The Baptists enlisted Rev. Stiles to draft a college charter. His original draft would have evenly divided control of the institution between the Baptists and the Congregationalists. As adopted, however, the charter gave the Baptists complete control, while still affording representation to the Congregationalists; the Quakers; and the Episcopalians. It also ensured that the teachings at the institution were not to be sectarian. Professorships were to be open to adherents of all Protestant denominations, as were all offices except the office of president; it was to be retained by a Baptist. In 1764, Hopkins—a Quaker—was chosen as the college's first chancellor, while Rev. James Manning—a Baptist minister—was named its first president. Over the next several years, Providence and Newport vied for the right to become the college's home; ultimately, this was a battle that Providence would win with the aid of Hopkins — and on the motion of Moses Brown, one of the Brown brothers who was then a member of the General Assembly.

The Brown brothers were sons of a Providence merchant, James Brown, who was himself descended from a long line of Baptist ministers. But, in 1774, Moses converted to Quakerism, perhaps under the influence of his mentor, Hopkins. This occasioned a split between Moses and his brothers over the issue of slavery; Moses adamantly opposed the institution, while his brothers were active in the slave trade. Similarly, while Hopkins's brother, Esek, was a ship captain in the Browns' fleet, Hopkins — although himself a slaveholder — became a fervent abolitionist. After returning to the Rhode Island General Assembly, Hopkins authored a bill to abolish slavery in the colony. Yet, Hopkins freed only some of his own slaves during his lifetime. This was despite strong pressure from the Quaker Meeting. Indeed, in 1773, the Quakers voted to disown Hopkins; they barred him from attending the business sessions of the Meeting, although he was allowed to continue worshipping at the Quaker meetinghouse.

By this time, Hopkins was again serving as chief justice of the Superior Court. When patriot rebels burned the British ship *Gaspee* as it was sailing up Narragansett Bay toward Providence, Hopkins was faced with an effort to bring those responsible to account. He instead opined that the actions of the commander of the *Gaspee* were probably illegal; he thus hindered any effort to take action against them.

In 1774, Hopkins and his political nemesis, Ward, were elected to represent Rhode Island in the Continental Congress; there, Hopkins became known for wearing his broad-rimmed Quaker hat while in the chamber. He served as chairman of the naval committee, and arranged for the appointment of his brother, Esek, as the navy's first admiral. During the difficult months leading up to the vote for independence, Hopkins provided some needed relief; John Adams later penned that

Hopkins "kept us all alive" with his wit and humor. In March of 1776, Ward died and was therefore unable to vote for or sign the Declaration of Independence. Hopkins did so proudly, notwithstanding the weakness of his handwriting as a result of the palsy from which he suffered; he proclaimed as he signed, "My hand trembles, my heart does not." Hopkins also served on committees that drafted the Articles of Confederation; but he chose to retire from the Congress in September of 1776, due to his failing health. He declined subsequent elections to Congress, although he continued to serve in the state legislature.

Over his lifetime of public service, Hopkins helped establish a public subscription library; founded the *Providence Gazette* and *Country Journal*; was a member of the American Philosophical Society of Newport; and helped erect a telescope in Providence to observe transit of Venus. Wife Ann passed away in 1782; Hopkins followed her into eternity three years later. He then rejoined both Sarah and Ann at the Old North Burial Ground in Providence.

In His Own Words:

Resolution of Stephen Hopkins (and Others) August 15, 1757[1]

> Whereas the British Colonies in America are invaded by a large Army of French and Indian enemies, who have already possessed themselves of Fort William Henry, and are now on their march to penetrate further into the country, and from whom we have nothing to expect should they succeed in their enterprise, but Death and Devastation. And as his Majestys principal Officers in the parts invaded, have in the most pressing and moving manner, called on all his Majesties faithful subjects for assistance to defend the Country.

Therefore, we whose names are underwritten, thinking it our duty to do everything in our power for the defence of our Libertys Families and Propertys are willing and agree to enter Voluntarily into the service of our Country, and go in a warlike manner against the Common enemy and hereby call upon and invite all our Neighbours who have familys and Propertys to Defend to Join with us in this undertaking, Promiseing to March as soon as we are Two Hundred and Fifty in Number, **recommending our selves and our Cause to the Favourable Protection of Almighty God.**

Proclamation, **by Governor Stephen Hopkins August 8, 1763**[2]

By the Honorable
STEPHEN HOPKINS, *Esq*;
Governor, Captain General and
Commander in Chief, in and over the
British **Colony of** *Rhode-Island*, **and** *Providence Plantations*, **in** *New-England*.

A PROCLAMATION.

The Burthens and Calamities of a cruel and expensive War, having been happily terminated by a just and glorious Peace, the King hath judged it proper, **that a** PUBLIC THANKSGIVING **to Almighty GOD, should be observed throughout all His colonies in** *America*; and hath accordingly signified His Royal Will and Pleasure,

THEREFORE, in obedience to the King's Command, and the Order of the General Assembly, made conformable thereto, **I DO hereby order, that** *Thursday* **the** *twenty-fifth* **Day of the present Month, be observed and kept as a Day of** PUBLIC

THANKSGIVING, **in and throughout their Colony; Calling upon and requiring all Christians, of every Denomination, to assemble themselves together on said Day, at the usual Places of their meeting for public Worship; and with Hearts filled with Gratitude, and Consciences void of Offense, to render sincere Thanks, and public Praise to Almighty GOD, for granting us all the Blessings of a safe and honorable Peace: And for the other innumerable Instances of His Goodness towards us.** And I DO also hereby strictly forbid and prohibit all servile Labor, and all Sports and Pastimes to be used or practiced on said Day, as all who offend herein shall answer their Contempt at their Peril.

GIVEN under my Hand and Seal at Arms, at Providence, the Eighth Day of August, in the Third Year of the Reign of our Sovereign Lord GEORGE the Third, by the Grace of GOD, King of Great-Britain, &c. Anno Dom. 1763,

STEP. HOPKINS

GOD Save the KING.

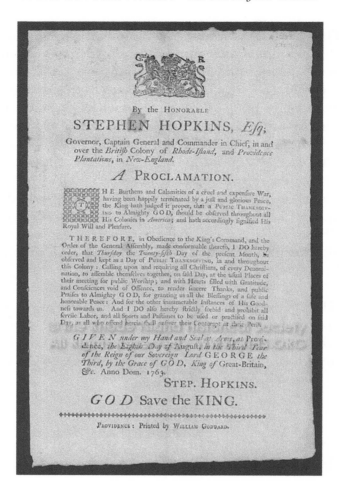

The Rights of the Colonies Examined, an Essay by Stephen Hopkins (under the pseudonym, "P") 1764[3]

From what hath been shown, it will appear beyond a doubt that the British subjects in America have equal rights with those in Britain; that they do not hold those rights as a privilege granted them, nor enjoy them as a grace and favor bestowed, but **possess them as an inherent, indefeasible right**, as they and their ancestors were freeborn subjects, justly and

naturally entitled to all their rights and advantages of the British constitution. . . .

We finally beg leave to assert that **the first planters of these colonies were pious Christians, were faithful subjects who, with a fortitude and perseverance little known and less considered, settled these wild countries, by GOD's goodness** and their own amazing labors, thereby added a most valuable dependence to the crown of Great Britain; were ever dutifully subservient to her interests; so taught their children that not one has been disaffected to this day, but all have honestly obeyed every royal command and cheerfully submitted to every constitutional law; have as little inclination as they have ability to throw off their dependency; have carefully avoided every offensive measure and every interdicted manufacture; have risked their lives as they have been ordered, and furnished their money when it has been called for; have never been troublesome or expensive to the mother country; have kept due order and supported a regular government; **have maintained peace and practiced Christianity**; and in all conditions, and in every relation, have demeaned themselves as loyal, as dutiful, and as faithful subjects ought; and that no kingdom or state hath, or ever had, colonies more quiet, more obedient, or more profitable than these have ever been.

May the same divine goodness that guided the first planters, protected the settlements, inspired Kings to be gracious, Parliaments to be tender, ever preserve, ever support our present gracious King; give great wisdom to his ministers and much understanding to his Parliaments; perpetuate the sovereignty of the British constitution, and the final dependency and happiness of all the colonies.

Manumission of Slave Saint Jago, by Stephen Hopkins October 28, 1772[4]

Know all men by these presents that, I Stephen Hopkins of Providence in the County of Providence Esquire, taking into Consideration the State and Circumstances of a certain Negro Man Named Saint Jago, who hath lived with me in the Quality of a Servant, or Slave, from his infancy till now; that he is about Thirty Three years old. And calling to mind that, he has always been a very Honest and faithful servant, and that he is duly qualified to provide for, and take care of himself, in a State of Freedom. **But, principally, and most of all finding, that the merciful and beneficent goodness of Almighty God; by the blessed Gospel of Jesus Christ our Lord: hath by the blessed Spirit taught all, who honestly obey its Divine Dictates, that, the keeping any of his rational Creatures in Bondage, who are capable of taking care of, and providing for themselves in a State of Freedom: is, altogather inconsistent with his Holy and Righteous Will.** For these reasons; the last of which is only prevalent, I the said Stephen Hopkins do, Manumit, set Free, and discharge, the said Saint Jago: and by these presents do, freely, fully, and absolutely, for my self, my Heirs, Executors, Administrators, and assigns, manumit, set free, and discharge, him the said Saint Jago: from every kind of Bondage, Servitude, or dependance what-soever. In Witness whereof, I have unto set my Hand and Seal, the 28.th Day of the Tenth Month called October Anno Dom 1772.

Letter from Stephen Hopkins (and Others) to Samuel Adams
December 25, 1772[5]

We doubt not you have before this heard of the difficulties this Colony labors under, on account of the destruction of the Gaspee, they being such as becomes the attention of the Colonies in general (though immediately to be executed on this only). As they affect in the tenderest point the liberties, lives, and properties of all America, we are induced to address you upon the occasion, whom we consider as a principal in the assertion and defence of **those rightful and natural blessings** . . .

Letter from Stephen Hopkins to His Daughter-in-Law, Ruth Hopkins
November 15, 1775[6]

I am in very good Health as your Mother also is wishing we might return to you. **When that will be Heaven only Knows.**

Letter from Stephen Hopkins to His Daughter-in-Law, Ruth Hopkins
December 9, 1775[7]

[T]he Season of the year is now So far advanced that I think you must not have a great Prospect of Seeing us again before Spring and **then I hope Heaven will permit us to Meet Again.**

What follows is a
summary of an article
from contemporary American life . . .

nearly 250 years after
Stephen Hopkins
signed

the Declaration of Independence.

What Would Stephen Hopkins Think?

TODD STARNES · Published September 15, 2014 · Last Update May 7, 2015

Attorney: University broke law by banning crosses on football helmets

OPINION By Todd Starnes, | Fox News

The Arkansas State University football team suffered a dual tragedy when teammate Markel Owens was killed during a home invasion and equipment manager Barry Weyer was lost in an automobile accident. In honor of their fallen friends, team members took to the field, their helmets sporting a small memorial decal. The problem? The decal portrayed a small white cross on the red stripe that reached to the back of the helmet. This drew the ire of the Freedom From Religion Foundation, which demanded that the team find another way to honor Owens and Weyer, like wearing a black armband that was "free from religion imagery."

Fearing a lawsuit, the university quickly capitulated, ordering the team to either remove the decal or cut off the bottom of the cross to turn it into a "plus sign." An attorney for an unnamed student responded that the out-of-town atheists from the FFRF have a "lengthy track record of bullying and intimidating schools across the country into driving any apparent religious reference from public sight."

https://www.foxnews.com/opinion/ attorney-university-broke-law-by-banning-crosses-on-football-helmets.

Henry Marchant
(1741-1796)

Signer of the Articles of Confederation

Highest Office Attained:
Representative in Congress; United States District Judge

Religious Affiliation:
Congregationalist

Although a Congregationalist, Henry Marchant embodied a diversity of religious influences—his Rhode Island homeland having been founded as a bastion of religious liberty that attracted a wide array of those seeking religious freedom. Marchant was born in 1741 to Huxford Marchant. Huxford's paternal great-great-grandfather, Captain John Marchant, had immigrated from Somerset, England in the early 1600s; he settled in the Cape Cod community of Yarmouth, Massachusetts. Huxford's father, John Marchant, relocated to the Edgartown area of Martha's Vineyard, and it was there that he met and married Hepsibah Huxford. Hepsibah died when their son, Huxford, was only nine years old, but through his given name he carried on her "Huxford" family name. Huxford later wed another Edgartown native, Sarah Butler; the Marchant and Butler families had earlier been joined by the wedding of Huxford's sister, Thankful Marchant, to Sarah's uncle, Nicholas Butler Sr.

Not long after Marchant was born to Huxford and Sarah, the young family moved from their Martha's Vineyard home; they settled in Newport, Rhode Island. But the fate that had befallen Marchant's father as a youth was even crueler to Marchant; his mother, Sarah, died when Marchant was only four years of age. Huxford, a merchant captain in the employ of Newport's Henry Collins, then wed Isabel Ward. But fate would again strike; Huxford was lost at sea while voyaging to the West Indies, and eight-year-old Marchant was left in the care of his step-mother, Isabel. Isabel was fortunate to have had the strong support of her family in caring for young Marchant. She was the daughter of Richard Ward, who had just completed his service as the governor of the Rhode Island colony—a position that Isabel's brother, Samuel Ward, would also later hold. And

Collins not only had employed Huxford, but as Richard's half-brother, he was also Isabel's uncle; their mother, Amey Billings Ward Collins, had wed Collins's father, Arnold Collins, after Richard's father passed away.

Isabel's paternal great-grandfather, John Ward, had the distinction of having served in puritan Oliver Cromwell's army during the English civil war. Following the war and the execution of King Charles I, Cromwell established the Protectorate; it was effectively a monarchy by another name, with Cromwell serving as Lord Protector. His reign was marked by strict religious and social laws, along radical Protestant lines. Following Cromwell's death in 1658, and the unsuccessful effort of his son to succeed him, Parliament offered the monarchy back to King Charles II, in return for promises of religious toleration and general amnesty. The restoration of the monarchy saw Cromwell's body exhumed in 1661, hung, decapitated, and his head displayed for the next twenty years outside Westminster Hall. After Cromwell's death, John and his son, Thomas—a Baptist—came to America.

The Baptist tradition is one that ran deep on both sides of Isabel's family. Her mother, Mary Tillinghast Ward, was the granddaughter—on her father's side—of Rev. Pardon Tillinghast; Rev. Tillinghast was an English immigrant who had settled in Providence, Rhode Island. He served as pastor of the First Baptist Church, personally funding the building of its first meeting house. He also authored a paper in 1689 entitled, *Water-Baptism Plainly Proved by Scripture to Be a Gospel Precept*. His church, the first Baptist church in the New World, had been founded in 1638 by Rev. Roger Williams, a puritan minister who had fled religious persecution in England in 1631. Favoring complete separation from the Church of England over a purification of it, he was subsequently banished from Massachusetts. Rev. Williams then settled in Providence and founded the Rhode Island colony as a bastion of religious freedom for all— one that, unlike the other colonies, had no established church or religious requirements. Rev. Tillinghast not only came to pastor the church founded by Rev. Williams, but his son, John

Tillinghast—Isabel's grandfather—married Isabel Sayles, the granddaughter of none other than Rev. Williams. Marchant's step-mother, Isabel Ward, was therefore both the daughter and the sister of governors of Rhode Island; she was also both the great-granddaughter of Rev. Pardon Tillinghast and the great-great-granddaughter of Rev. Roger Williams, the founder of Rhode Island.

Isabel's parents had been wed in 1709 by Rev. James Honeyman in Newport's Trinity (Episcopal) Church. Rev. Honeyman was a native of the Fife region of Scotland; he arrived in Boston in 1704 as a missionary for the Society for the Propagation of the Gospel. He then settled in Newport, where he served as rector of Trinity Church for forty-six years. Known as the founder of the Episcopal Church in Rhode Island, Rev. Honeyman—whose son, James, served as attorney general of Rhode Island—was descended from a long line of pastors dating back to Rev. Andrew Honyman. This Rev. Honyman was the Lord Bishop of Orkney and Zetland, and he later married into the Scottish royal family of Stewarts (or Stuarts). Although devoutly Episcopalian, Rev. Honeyman was known to embrace all sincere followers of Christ, and many Quakers and Baptists came to love his church.

Indeed, generations of the Ward family were known to have been Sabbatarians, or Seventh Day Baptists—whose beliefs are in many respects similar to those of traditional Baptists, but call for worshipping on the seventh day of the week, rather than the first day. At the time of her death in 1769, Isabel's mother is said to have been a Sabbatarian for fifty-five years. Isabel's father also attended Sabbatarian services and was formally baptized in the Sabbatarian church in 1753. Her step-father, Arnold Collins, was a trustee of the Sabbatarian church. And her brother, Governor Samuel Ward, was also a Sabbatarian who made a formal confession of faith to the Sabbatarian church in 1769. Samuel also served as chief justice of Rhode Island and in the Continental Congress—after resigning as governor in protest of the Stamp Act—and he nominated George Washington as general of the revolutionary army. He also co-founded Rhode

Island College (now, Brown University). Samuel served as one of its four Sabbatarian—out of seven total—original trustees, hiring Sabbatarian Rev. James Manning as the college's first president. Samuel died of smallpox in March 1776, shortly before the signing of the Declaration of Independence; William Ellery Jr. assumed his place in the Continental Congress—thus becoming a signer of that founding document in Samuel's stead. Samuel's great-granddaughter, Julia Ward Howe, later wrote *The Battle Hymn of the Republic*.

The misfortune of Marchant's early loss of his parents therefore had a silver lining; the well-established Wards, with the aid of Henry Collins, were able not only to instill in him religious values that guided him throughout his life, but to plant him on a solid educational footing. They afforded him the best schooling available in Newport, and then sent him to the College of Philadelphia (later, the University of Pennsylvania). Graduating in 1762, he studied law in Cambridge with Judge Edmund Trowbridge, who was then serving as attorney general of Massachusetts. One of the most eminent attorneys of his time, Judge Trowbridge received Marchant on the recommendation of Newport's William Ellery Sr., whose son, William Ellery, Jr.—a brother-in-law by marriage of Judge Trowbridge—later joined Marchant in signing the Articles of Confederation. Also joining them in that signing was Francis Dana, Judge Trowbridge's nephew; Dana was also married to Ellery, Jr.'s daughter. Judge Trowbridge was a member of the First Congregational Church in Cambridge, while Marchant—along with the Ellerys—belonged to the esteemed Rev. Ezra Stiles's Second Congregational Church in Newport.

In 1765, Marchant wed Rebecca Cooke, daughter of Silas Cooke and Rebeckah Wood Cooke. Rev. Marmaduke Brown officiated at Trinity Church, the same venue where Isabel's parents had wed. Silas also was a member and vestryman at Trinity. However, Rebeckah was from a Quaker family; her parents were Peleg Wood and Rebecca Coggeshall Wood. And Silas and Rebeckah had themselves been married in a Quaker ceremony in 1734.

Upon returning to Newport, Marchant was admitted to the bar and began practicing law. His community contributions included serving as an officer of the Redwood Library and Athenaeum, which had been founded by Abraham Redwood. Redwood's wife, Martha Coggeshall Redwood, was a distant Quaker cousin of Rebecca's mother. Their common great-grandfather, John Coggeshall, hailed from the town of Coggeshall in Essex, England; he had emigrated to America aboard the same ship that carried Rev. Williams there in 1631. Settling first in Massachusetts and, like Rev. Williams, having been banished for reasons of religion, Coggeshall reconnected with Rev. Williams in Rhode Island; he helped found the settlement that became Newport, and became the first president of the combined government of Providence, Portsmouth, Newport and Warwick. Redwood's library was supported by a literary and philosophical society that counted among its members Thomas Ward; Henry Collins—who donated the land for the library; and James Honeyman Jr. The founding officers of the library included Thomas Ward, Collins, and Rev. Honeyman; and members of the Tillinghast and Ellery families also came to serve as officers of the institution. Rev. Stiles served for many years as its librarian; indeed, it was the classical and theological works housed in the library that had served as a primary inducement for Rev. Stiles to have made his home in Newport.

But for Marchant, public service soon beckoned. In 1771, he was appointed attorney general of Rhode Island; by then, he well known as a staunch supporter of the patriot movement. So too were the members of Second Congregational generally. They demonstrated this as early as 1765, when, ignoring the advice of their pastor, Rev. Stiles—later, the president of Yale College—they hung effigies of local tax officials, incited a riot, and ransacked the officials' homes. Ellery Jr. was among the instigators. During the later war for independence, British troops reciprocated not only by occupying Newport, but by using the church as their living quarters; building a chimney in the church sanctuary; and destroying the church pews.

Marchant soon embarked for London; the Rhode Island Assembly had chosen him to act as its co-agent in negotiating for monies claimed to be owed by the motherland. As he departed, his well-wishers included Rev. Stiles and Ellery Jr., as well as Bostonians Samuel Adams, Dana, and Governor Thomas Hutchinson. Marchant recorded his experiences in his *Journell of Voyage from Newport in the Colony of Rhode Island &c to London, Travels thro' many Parts of England & Scotland—begun July 8th 1771—*. He took with him letters of introduction to prominent business, legal, and governmental leaders; and Rev. Stiles paved the way for him to also meet with prominent dissenting (from the Anglican church) clergymen. He also was able to renew an acquaintance from his days in Philadelphia—Benjamin Franklin. Franklin, who was then representing several colonies in England; facilitated Marchant's engagements there, including in an extensive visit to Scotland. Marchant frequently met with Rev. Richard Price—a Welsh-born Presbyterian minister who became a vigorous defender of the American revolution—and other clergyman at their New York Coffee House gathering place; he was later able to introduce Rev. Price to Rev. Stiles.

In June 1772, Rhode Islanders burned the British schooner *Gaspee* in Narragansett Bay, effectively ending any hope that Marchant's mission to London could be successful. So, to Newport he returned. He continued his service as attorney general. He secured a donation to the Redwood Library from author Catherine Macaulay, whom he had befriended while in London; she presented the library with her six-volume *History of England*. As relations with Britain escalated into war, Marchant acquired an estate in Narragansett; he correctly anticipated that Newport would soon be occupied by British troops. The Marchants remained there throughout the war. Rebecca's father, Silas, remained in Newport; although described by Rev. Stiles as a Tory, he suffered severe losses at the hands of the British.

In 1777, Marchant was elected to the Continental Congress, where he signed the Articles of Confederation. Following his service in the Congress, he returned to his farm in Narragansett; he remained there for the next several years. He and Ellery

Jr. were among those from Second Congregational who petitioned John Adams—who then was on a diplomatic mission
to France—for his assistance in securing financial aid from the
reformed churches of France, to help rebuild the church and its
ministry in the aftermath of the war. Marchant then returned to
Newport. He was promptly elected to the Rhode Island General
Assembly. He was also a member of the Rhode Island constitutional convention that ratified the United States Constitution.
In 1790, President George Washington appointed Marchant
to the United States District Court for the District of Rhode
Island, a position he continued to hold when he passed away in
1796. Marchant was buried in the Common Burying Ground
in Newport.

In His Own Words:

**Letter from Henry Marchant to Rev. Richard Price
November 21, 1771[1]**

> **If there is any Thing worth living and dying for, I
> think it is civil and religious Liberty.**

**Journal Entry by Henry Marchant
December 20, 1771[2]**

> Those young Gentlemen were both Undergraduates
> at cambridge University. And by their Account of the
> Drinking & Riots of the collegians, One would be led
> to think **very little Learning, Religion or Morals
> were to be obtained at ye Universities**.

**Journal Entry by Henry Marchant
(regarding church service at King's Chapel)
c. January 1772[3]**

> The Chanting was excellent by Men & Boys
> accompanied with the Organ. So was the Anthem and

Christmas Hymn Sung—**The Archbishop of York preached a Sermon in which he insisted much upon the Necessity of Revelation & Obedience thereto.** The Bishop of London Read the Communion Service. And the Bishop of Winchester gave his Attendance.

Journal Entry by Henry Marchant (regarding church service at Magdaline Chapel) January 12, 1772[4]

In the Evening went to Magdaline Chapel and heard the Revd. Dr. Dodd preach from Romans 2d.—28th & 29th. He is an elegant pretty Preacher . . .—I was extremely charmed with the Hymns & Psalms sung by those once unhappy Women. I can hardly call them so now—The Organ was played upon by One of the Magdalene Subjects. **An Idea struck me very sensibly while There:—and I contemplated much upon it—That the Emancipation from Vice into Virtue and the Praises of Mortals thereon in such a Publick Manner was a most glorious Display of divine Power**—And was in some Degree making **[] subservient to the divine Glory**[.] as it most certainly raises our Ideas of his divine Love we [] more conspicuously.

Letter from Henry Marchant to Francis Dana January 1773[5]

It is a pity that both We and They at home were not better employed and **that our Study & Efforts were not exerted to make us all better and happier Men Subjects and Christians**. This Crysis of American Independence (if such a Crysis is to take place) is hastened on by every Measure of Administration. They seem to be infatuated and charmed on to Destruction of the greatest and most noble Kingdom upon Earth. **Heaven only knows where their Evils will end.**

Letter from Henry Marchant to Nicholas Cooke
September 3, 1777[6]

We might expect soon by the Blessing of God to establish the Peace and Happiness of the States.

Letter from Henry Marchant to His Daughter, Sarah Marchant
September 9, 1777[7]

It is no small Pleasure to find a growing and improving Correspondent in my Daughter Sally. Go on my Dear thus improving, and **add daily one Virtue to another. And may God grant that his Grace may really affect your Heart with suitable Impressions of His Goodness. Remember that God made You, that God keeps you alive, and preserves you from all Harm, and gives You all the Powers and the Capacity whereby you are able to read of Him, and of Jesus Christ your Saviour and Redeemer, and to do every other needful Business of Life. And while you look around you and see the great Priveleges and Advantages you have above what other Children have, of learning to read and write, of being taught the meaning of the Great Truths of the Bible, you must remember not to be proud on that Account, but to bless God, and be thankful and endeavour in your turn to assist others with the knowledge you may gain. And be kind and good to all poor People, and poor Children that have not your Opportunity, especially in a kind and tender Manner assist your Sister and Brother. . . . Let us all be thankful to God for giving us such a Plenty of the Fruits of the Earth.**

Letter from Henry Marchant to His Children
(Sally, Betsy, and Billy Marchant)
July 20, 1778[8]

[G]o on my dear Children and **strive to excell in all useful Knowledge, especially such as relates to God and that other World, where we are all to go. To them that behave well in this World, the next will be a World of Happiness indeed — but to such as do ill here, it will be a world of everlasting Torment. God grant that when we have all left this World, we may not be parted from each other in the World to come; but that all, Father and Mother, Brother and Sisters, may meet together, never to part again, but live a whole Eternity with God and Christ — with Abraham, Isaac & Jacob, and all other good Men & Women and Children who have gone there before us. Remember that God hates a Lye, and every thing that is dishonest — and that you must always be chearful and willing to do your Duty to God and Man, and to your Parents and to love one another and all good People, and that you must try to perswade naughty Children to behave better and to quit all their wicked words and ways, if they would ever expect to be happy.** . . .

Miss Sally has been very industrious to have read the Books She mentions twice over. **I rejoice that She does not forget her Bible — her Catechism & Prayers.** . . .

And the King of France has also sent us a great many large Ships, to assist in taking the British Ships & People, and to drive them away from **this good Land which Heaven gave to Our Fore-Fathers**, and to us their Children, and which the King of England and his wicked People have been endeavouring to take from Us—And **I hope by the Blessing of God that We shall by & by have Peace thro' all this Country, and that you may live to grow up and enjoy it with Thankfulness to God, and never forget what great Things the Lord hath done for You.** Was it not for this Hope my Dear Children, I could never consent to leave you & your good Mamma so long year after year. **Hoping we may soon meet & praise God for his great Goodness to Us all**, I remain Your affectionate Father, Henry Marchant

Letter from Henry Marchant to William Greene August 3, 1778[9]

My Countrymen of Rhode Island step forth-and maintain that Rank you so worthily hold amongst the American brave Sons of Freedom. Every Moment swells with important Events. **One glorious Effort— and this fall by the Blessing of God settles the United States in Safety and Honor, and brings a Harvest of lasting Blessings to Posterity.**

Letter from Henry Marchant to the Rhode Island Assembly August 11, 1778[10]

By this Day, perhaps at this Moment, We are reaping the Blessings arising, from a Treaty with so powerful an ally [France]. **I think the Connection brought about by the Hand of Heaven, and that therefore, it promises to be as lasting as it is mutually beneficial, generous and noble.**

Letter from Henry Marchant to Robert Treat Paine September 19, 1778[11]

I entirely agree with you Sir, that we have had & still have more to fear from **the Decay of publick &**

private Virtue, than from the Arms of Britain, With any possible Aids she might procure. **This is an Evil that not only Congress, but every Legislature, ought immediately with Might & Main to pay their Attention to.**

America would have had Peace before this Day had she deserved it; and **I wish to God she was as ready for the Blessing, as Heaven is to grant it. It is to Miracles we are to ascribe Our present Situation** . . . .

I lament Sir the Failure of the Expedition agt. Rhode Island. I rejoice however that the Arms of America far from being sullied, have reaped Glory & Honor in the Attempt. **I resolve the Misfortune into the just Providence of God. Again I say Heaven knows we were not under proper Habits and Temper of Mind to receive the fulfillment of the Blessings, which yet I trust are reserved for this Land.**

Letter from Henry Marchant to General Horatio Gates August 24, 1779[12]

[Y]our Post must still be committed to Our own internal Exertions, as has been for most of the Time the Case, To your superior Generalship, and **what is most to be relyed upon — The Care of Heaven.** . . . I pray **God** his Miracles may not cease.

Letter from Henry Marchant (and Others, on Behalf of the Second Congregational Church of Newport) to John Adams May 26, 1783[13]

Conscious of your attachment to religious liberty, in which our Society is founded, and of your disposition and capacity to support that glorious

cause, as well as the civil liberties of mankind we have ventured to inclose that address to your patronage and care; and we request that you will be pleased to place it in the hands of such of the principal pastors of the Reformed as you shall think will be best disposed to circulate subscriptions and otherwise make collections **for the purpose of repairing our ministry and meeting house and towards a ministerial fund**. . . .

We would only add here that the General Assembly of this State at a late Session repealed an old law which excluded Roman Catholics from the privileges of citizenship.

What follows is a
summary of an article
from contemporary American life . . .

nearly 250 years after
Henry Marchant
signed

the Articles of Confederation.

What Would Henry Marchant Think?

TODD STARNES · Published April 14, 2016 · Last Update April 15, 2016

High school wants to shut down off-campus 'Jesus Lunch'

OPINION By Todd Starnes, | Fox News

Middleton High School in Middleton, Wisconsin allows its students to eat lunch off-campus, even to delight in the culinary cuisine at McDonald's or Taco Bell. But when the kids began meeting with their parents at a local park for a weekly home-cooked meal, school officials sprang into action to protect them. Why? Because the popular lunch event— known as the "Jesus Lunch"—included not only plump juicy chicken breasts, but a Christian-themed inspirational message. Said one mom, "[w]e show up every week just to show the love of Jesus. Our mission statement for Jesus Lunch is 'food for the body, nutrition for the soul.'"

But Superintendent Donald Johnson and Principal Stephen Plank demanded an end to the lunches, which they called "divisive." "We believe that religious or political events do not have a place in our school or on our campus, except when sponsored by a student group in accordance with our rules, which require prior approval," they said. They also claimed that they needed to approve any food that is served to the students and that the public park was effectively school property because the school leased it (even though the moms had rented the park pavilion from the city). Guess the moms better leave the brownies at home, at least so long as they are tainted with Christian virtue.

https://www.foxnews.com/opinion/ high-school-wants-to-shut-down-off-campus-jesus-lunch.

Chapter Six:

New York Signers

James Duane
(1733-1797)

Signer of the Articles of Confederation

Highest Office Attained:
Representative in Congress; Mayor of New York City; United States District Judge

Religious Affiliation:
Episcopalian

O f Irish and Dutch ancestry, James Duane was born in New York City in 1733. His father, Anthony Duane, was an Irish Protestant who was born in County Galway, Ireland in 1679. By the age of nineteen, Anthony was an officer in the royal navy, and in that role embarked for America in 1698. He met and married Althea Ketaltas, the daughter of a Dutch merchant, Abraham Keteltas, a New York City alderman. Althea's half-brother was Rev. Abraham Keteltas; he was born of Abraham's marriage to Janneke Jacobs Keteltas, following the death of Althea's mother, Annette Koeck Keteltas. Rev. Keteltas filled the pulpit in both French and Dutch churches in Jamaica and Long Island, New York, and in Presbyterian churches in Elizabethtown, New Jersey, as well as in Massachusetts and Connecticut. A fervent revolutionary, Rev. Keteltas was more readily inclined toward separation from Great Britain than initially was Duane, given the Duane family's closer ties to the motherland.

At the age of three, Duane's mother, Althea, passed away. But the Dutch influence upon him continued; in 1741, his father married Margaret Riker (or Rycken), whose family was active in the Dutch Reformed Church. By the age of fourteen, Anthony also had passed, and Duane found himself under the guardianship of Robert Livingston, the third lord of Livingston Manor. Livingston's brother, Philip, later signed the Declaration of Independence; another brother, William, signed the United States Constitution. Duane then went to live with the Livingston family at the manor, located south of Albany, New York. He completed his education under the watchful eye of the Livingstons, also longstanding members of the Dutch Reformed Church. During this time, Duane's eye was also watchful, as he fell in love with — and later wed — Livingston's daughter, Maria (Polly) Livingston. Polly's maternal ancestry dates back to Governor Rip Van Dam, who was raised in the Dutch Church of Albany and who served as interim acting governor of the province of New York in the early 1730s.

Duane then studied law under an esteemed Episcopalian lawyer and Livingston friend, James Alexander, formerly the attorney general of New York — a position that Duane would himself later hold. Admitted to the New York bar in 1754, Duane became one of New York's leading lawyers in the days leading up to the revolution. Among his clients was Trinity (Episcopal) Church, where he served as a warden and vestryman. In 1774, Duane was elected to the Continental Congress; he served there until 1783. Had he not been in New York drafting the New York state constitution at the time that independence was declared in Philadelphia in 1776, his name likely would be affixed to the Declaration of Independence. But he did sign the Articles of Confederation under which the new nation operated during its early years. Duane later served in the New York state Senate and as the first mayor of New York City; he worked tirelessly to rebuild what was then the new nation's capital following the ravages of war. He also served as a delegate to the New York state convention that ratified the United States Constitution; he moved that the convention be opened every day with prayer. He was a founder of the New York Manumission Society, whose mission was the abolition of slavery. In 1789, President George Washington appointed him the first United States District Judge for the District of New York.

As Duane's career brought him greater wealth, he added to the landholdings that his father had acquired in what is now known as Duanesburg, New York, near Schenectady. There, Duane founded — and paid for the building of — Christ (Episcopal) Church. Upon his death in 1797, Duane was fittingly interred under Christ Church in Duanesburg.

In His Own Words:

James Duane's Notes for a Speech in Congress
May 23, 1775[1]

> **May that gracious being upon whom we depend inspire our councils with wisdom and bless our efforts with success! and speedily restore US to that Peace and harmony with Great Britain on principles of liberty and mutual advantage — which is the ultimate wish of every virtuous patriot. . . .**

> Let this be ever considered as a family quarrel, unnatural, disgraceful and ruinous into which we are innocently plunged by intolerable oppression, and which we are sincerely disposed to appease and reconcile, **whenever the good providence of God shall put it in our power, consistent with the preservation of our just rights.**

Letter from James Duane to Robert Livingston
June 7, 1775[2]

> Your kind favour of the 23d May gave me very great pleasure as it communicated the agreeable Intelligence of the safe Arrival and Health of my dearest Polly and our Children. It was with painful Anxiety that I found myself under an indispensible Obligation to leave her when she was very feeble and not yet recovered from a severe Indisposition. **May the good Providence of God preserve her and you and all we love under his gracious Protection. . . .**

> We contend in a good Cause, and if we continue firm & united among ourselves, If by a wise and temporate Conduct we manifest to the World a desire of Reconciliation and reunion with the parent

State, on Terms consistent with our Safety and the Interest and Happiness of the whole Empire, **We may hope with the Blessings of Heaven that our virtuous Struggles will be rewarded with Success.**

Letter from James Duane to George Clinton
October 3, 1777[3]

We cannot be sufficiently thankful to the Supreme Being for rescuing our bleeding Country from the Calamities of an Indian war which threatned our western frontier with ruin and desolation. That under Heaven it was saved by the valor and good Conduct of our own Countrymen is an additional Satisfaction. Every mouth is full of the Praises of Herkemer, Gansevoort, & Willet. The Victory acquird by General Starke was as seasonable, as glorious, and is the more eminently distinguished as it was gaind by Militia over veteran and experiencd Troops; and tho' nothing decisive has taken place between the grand armies under General Gates and General Burgoine, the late gallant Behaviour of the left wing of our Army, with the Embarrassments which surround the British Troops & the Superiority of our Forces, **give us the highest reason to look up to divine Providence for a Happy issue of the Campaign in that Quarter. God graciously grant the full scope of your wishes, "that it may conduce to render the present Campaign decisive."**

Letter from James Duane to John McKesson
November 22, 1777[4]

That God in whom we trust, will, I hope, inspire us with vigour and fortitude, and enable us to put a speedy termination to these trying calamities.

Letter from James Duane to His Wife, Maria (Polly) Duane January 14, 1779[5]

My dearest Polly

I now sit down to answer your kind Letter of the 26th of December, & in the first place **I express my gratitude to Heaven that you & our dear Children continue in Health.** . . . If there shoud be peace & safety in that Quarter it woud be my firm wish: **God who rules over all only knows whether this Happiness is so near. . . . We ought to be thankful** that we have less Reason than most of our Acquaintance to be uneasy. Our Lands will rise in Value And (your) our kind Father can & will assist Us: Besides which I have a profession which **with Gods blessing will without any other Aid support us.**

Letter from James Duane to His Wife, Maria (Polly) Duane March 29, 1779[6]

I do not know when I enjoyd better Health for which I cannot be sufficiently grateful to the Almighty. May he graciously dispense the same Blessing to you, our dearest Children & Friends! Make my Duty, Compliments & Blessing Acceptable to them all in their respective Relations.

Letter from James Duane to His Wife, Maria (Polly) Duane July 21, 1779[7]

I flatter myself we shall have a glorious Campaign in every Quarter And that the Almighty Being who has hitherto so manifestly protected us will soon bring this War to a Safe & honourable Conclusion.

Letter from James Duane to George Washington
October 12, 1782[8]

I know there are some who yielding to the Impulse of Just Indignation at the enormous Cruelties of the Enemy, wish for Victims to the Manes of our murderd Friends. There are others who think that our national Glory will be tarnished by a Clemency inconsistent with former menaces of Retaliation. Altho' the Change of Circumstances obviously requires a Change of Measures corresponding to the Nature of Retaliation, I censure Neither. **Whatever may be the Desire of others, it is mine that this war may be concluded, as it has hitherto been conducted by us, with the Humanity which a benevolent Religion, civilized manners, and true military Honour inspire; This is a Conduct worthy of the Patrons of Liberty; It is a Conduct which will give this Infant Republick a distinguished Rank among refined and civilized Nations; and recommend her to to the Favour and Protection of Heaven.**

Letter from James Duane to His Wife, Maria (Polly) Duane
October 6, 1783[9]

I bless God that I continue in Health as it is my earnest prayer that you, our dear Children and Friends enjoy the same Happiness.

Letter from James Duane to George Washington
April 8, 1794[10]

Permit me to assure you that amongst a People so eminently benefited by your military atcheivements, and civil administration, **there is no man who prays with more sincerity, and ardor, that you may uninteruptedly, enjoy every honor and every** blessing which an indulgent heaven can bestow, than him who is—with the utmost attachment respect and esteem Sir your most obliged most faithful and most obedient Servant.

Inscription at the Burial Place of James Duane, Christ Church, Duanesburg, New York[11]

To the Honour of CHRIST
and to the welfare of the People
of Duanesburgh: **this Church was erected
by the Honourable JAMES DUANE Esquire;
whose Remains here rest, untill that day, which shall give
to the Patriot, the Man of Virtue, and the Christian, the
Plaudit of a GOD!**
Eminent at the Bar, enlightened and impartial as a Judge;
to the knowledge of a Statesman,
the manners of a Gentleman were joind;
and all the domestic Virtues, the social affections were
his. Planted in the Wilderness by his hand, people of
Duanesburgh! you were his Children; **imitate his Virtues.
Adore the Deity. love your Country. love one another.**
To the Memory
of her dear departed friend;
his Widowed Partner,
has erected this Monument,
due to his Worth, to her affection,
and her Grief.

Born Feb.ry 6th, 1732
Died Feb.ry 4th, 1797

To the Honour of CHRIST
and to the welfare of the People
of Duanesburgh this Church was erected
by the Honourable JAMES DUANE Esquire
whose Remains here rest untill that day which shall
give to the Patriot, the Man of Virtue and the Christian
the Plaudit of a GOD!
Eminent at the Bar, enlightened and impartial as a Judge
to the knowledge of a Statesman
the manners of a Gentleman were joind
and all the domestic Virtues, the social affections were his.
Planted in the Wilderness by his hand, people of Duanesburgh!
you were his Children; imitate his Virtues.
Adore the Deity, love your Country, love one another.
To the Memory
of her dear departed friend
his Widowed Partner
has erected this Monument,
due his Worth, to her affection
and her Grief.

Born Feb.ʸ 6.ᵗʰ 1732   Died Feb.ʸ 1.ˢᵗ 1797

What follows is a
summary of an article
from contemporary American life . . .

nearly 250 years after
James Duane
signed

the Articles of Confederation.

What Would James Duane Think?

FAITH · Published October 20, 2016

Faith-based film 'I'm Not Ashamed' slammed by atheists

By | Fox News

ALL NEW S
STREAMIN

Rachel Scott was the first victim killed in the massacre at Denver's Columbine High School on April 20, 1999. According to Richard Costaldo, an eyewitness who was with Scott at the time, the killers opened fire after she affirmed that she believed in God.

PureFlix's faith-based film, "I'm Not Ashamed," commemorates Rachel's God-centered life, including the following dialogue based on Costaldo's first-hand account, after which Harris opened fire, killing Scott:

Eric Harris [Killer]: Do you still believe in God?
Scott: You know I do.
Harris: Then go be with him.

Atheist groups are outraged. Apparently, they believe the account is fictitious because it isn't included in the police reports of that day. YouTube blocked the film's trailer for eleven months.

*https://www.foxnews.com/entertainment/
faith-based-film-im-not-ashamed-slammed-by-atheists.*

William Duer
(1747-1799)

Signer of the Articles of Confederation

Highest Office Attained:
Representative in Congress

Religious Affiliation:
Episcopalian

William Duer was born in Devon, England in 1747, the son of John Duer and Frances Frye Duer. It was there that he was baptized in the Anglican church. His older brother, Rev. Rowland Duer, later would serve as the chaplain to the Bishop of Lincoln.

Duer's father was a planter who had inherited an estate in Antigua, in the West Indies, but he also maintained a villa in England. Duer was educated at the prestigious Eton School and then was commissioned as an ensign in the British army. Named an aide-de-camp to Lord Robert Clive, he accompanied Clive to India in 1764 when Clive returned there as governor of Bengal. The climate was not to Duer's liking, however, and he soon returned to England; upon his father's death later that year, he inherited a share of the family's Antigua plantation. So, to the West Indies ventured Duer.

By 1768, Duer had made his way to New York, encouraged by a trading partner, future General and United States Senator Philip Schuyler. He acquired thirteen hundred acres of land at Fort Miller, about forty miles north of Albany. And he began the mercantile pursuits that would, for a time, make him a wealthy man. His business interests included sawmills from which he supplied the royal navy with timber needed for the masts and booms of its ships.

In 1775, Duer became a member of the Provincial Congress. After independence was declared in 1776, he helped draft the New York state constitution and served in the New York state Senate. He also served as a judge of the Court of Common Pleas. He was elected to the Continental Congress in 1778, and there became signatory to the Articles of Confederation that initially governed the fledgling new nation.

By then, Duer was courting a young Catherine Alexander, daughter of Major General William Alexander; he was a confidante of General George Washington and one of his foremost generals during the revolutionary war. Alexander claimed to be the rightful heir to the Scottish earldom of Sterling; although he was unable to persuade the English crown to recognize that distinction, he nonetheless carried the title of Lord Sterling throughout his life. Alexander's wife was the former Sarah Livingston, daughter of Philip Livingston, the second lord of Livingston Manor; she was the sister of Philip Livingston Jr.—signer of the Declaration of Independence—and William Livingston—governor of New York and signer of the United States Constitution. And she was a cousin to Robert Livingston—another member of the Continental Congress who later administered the oath of office to President George Washington.

In 1779, then-General Washington gave Alexander leave to return to his estate in Basking Ridge, New Jersey; the occasion was the wedding of young Catherine, known as Lady Kitty, to Duer. By some accounts, Washington himself gave Lady Kitty away at the ceremony. By this marriage, Duer extended his familial relationships not only to the Alexanders, but to the Livingstons, the Schuylers, and to Alexander Hamilton and John Jay. The couple initially settled in Fishkill, New York, but the first two children born of the union were baptized at the Reformed Dutch Church in Rhinebeck, New York; Robert Livingston worshipped there in pew sixty-three. By 1782, Duer had leased the parsonage of the Albany Dutch church, where the Livingstons and Schuylers had been fixtures for generations. Duer and his young, growing family remained there for the next two years.

Following the war, Duer relocated to New York City. He expanded his business pursuits, assisted in the formation of the Bank of New York, was elected to the New York state Assembly, and ultimately became Alexander Hamilton's assistant secretary at the new United States Department of Treasury. The Duers also worshipped at Trinity (Episcopal) Church in New York, and Duer served the church as a trustee.

But Duer also transgressed into a lifelong pursuit of personal, financial gain. That pursuit ultimately led to his extraordinary speculation in land and government bonds, often with borrowed money; and he became unable to repay his creditors. The financial panic of 1792, and the near-collapse of the young nation's banking system, were catastrophes averted only by the steady hand of Hamilton himself. Duer, though, soon found himself ensconced in debtor's prison, partly to secure his own safety; there, he would spend virtually the rest of his life.

In 1799, Duer fell ill and was released on parole. He died in May of that year. Lady Kitty then married merchant William Neilson, and together they raised the Duer children and others of their own. Son William Alexander Duer became president of Columbia University. Grandson William Duer later served in the United States House of Representatives.

By some accounts, Duer was initially buried in a family vault at St. Thomas (Episopal) Church, but Trinity Church also claims his interment. Later, he was reinterred at Grace (Episcopal) Church in Jamaica, New York, where a great-grandson, Rev. Beverly Robinson Belts, spent his pastoral retirement years. Following her death in 1826, Lady Kitty rejoined him there.

In His Own Words:

Letter from William Duer to the New York Convention April 17, 1777[1]

> **Would to Heaven that the Spirit and activity which has of late animated the Councils of the State of New York would diffuse itself throughout the other States!**

Letter from William Duer to Robert R. Livingston May 28, 1777[2]

> **Like an old Sinner who has deferr'd Repentance,** I should almost be afraid to write to you after so long

a Silence, if I did not trust that your Lenity would be a powerful Advocate in my favor, more particularly when I can with Truth assure you that my attention has been so engross'd in defeating the Designs of a Mischevious Combination, and in cultivating the Friendship of the Members from the Southern States that I have had little or no Time to write to you as fully as I have wishd.

Letter from William Duer to Philip Schuyler
July 29, 1777[3]

May heaven preserve you, and may I shortly see you crowned with Laurels, or may I have an opportunity (should fate decide for the worse) **to rescue your memory from the cruel assasinations of wicked men**, who are endeavoring by every artifice in their power to raise the popular clamor against you, and your friends, in order to divert the public attention from the true source of our misfortunes in your quarter.

Letter from William Duer to Francis Lightfoot Lee[4]
February 14, 1778[4]

God bless you, and Yours!

Letter from William Duer to Robert Morris
March 5, 1778[5]

God bless you and your Family to whom I beg to be particularly remembered.

Letter from William Duer to Robert R. Livingston
March 10, 1778[6]

God bless you my dear Freind, and all your Connections . . . .

What follows is a
summary of an article
from contemporary American life . . .

nearly 250 years after
William Duer
signed

the Articles of Confederation.

What Would William Duer Think?

TODD STARNES · Published July 29, 2016

Newspaper rejects ad over the word "Christian"

Lois McGinnis operates a bookstore in Knoxville, Tennessee. After deciding to close a second location of the store, she placed an ad in the classified section of the local newspaper, the *Knoxville News Sentinel*:

> Store closing sale — Cedar Springs Christian Store — Clinton Highway location — All merchandise, fixtures, slat walls must go. Sale through August 13, phone 865.947.XXXX.

But the ad never appeared. When McGinnis inquired with the *News Sentinel* about the omission, she was told that the ad was rejected because it contained an "offensive word." The offensive word? "Christian."

So McGinnis posted the following on Facebook: "Do you find the word 'Christian' offensive?" Apparently, the people of Knoxville didn't, as they let the *News Sentinel* know what they thought. The paper then apologized "for any misunderstanding about the *News Sentinel* stance on Christianity." It said, "We had a system failure, which resulted in a classified ad for Cedar Springs getting hung up in our front end system."

https://www.foxnews.com/opinion/newspaper-rejects-ad-over-the-word-christian.

William Floyd
(1734-1821)

Signer of the Declaration of Independence

Highest Office Attained:
Representative in Congress

Religious Affiliation:
Presbyterian

P resbyterian William Floyd was born in Brookhaven (now, Mastic), Long Island, New York in 1734. His father, Nicoll Floyd, was descended from Sir John Floyd, a Welshman knighted by Queen Elizabeth I—daughter of King Henry VIII and Anne Boleyn—in 1586. Sir John's son, Richard—Floyd's great-grandfather—crossed the ocean in 1654, and was among the founders of nearby Setauket, Long Island. Later, Richard's son, Richard II, acquired over forty-four hundred acres of land and established the family estate later inherited by Floyd's father, Nicoll.

From his mother, Margaret Floyd, Nicoll acquired his given name, as Margaret was descended from a distinguished line bearing the Nicoll surname. Her father, Captain Matthias Nicoll Jr., left his native Devon, England in 1664; he became secretary of the new province of New York, and established a two-thousand-acre plantation in present-day Plandome Manor, Long Island. He served in numerous positions of public service, including as the chief justice of New York and the sixth mayor of New York City. Captain Nicoll's father of the same name, Rev. Matthias Nicoll, was a priest of the established Church of England; he briefly served as rector of Mells and thereafter ministered in Islip and Plymouth. Plymouth's St. Andrew's (Anglican) Church was where Rev. Nicoll's children, including a young Matthias Jr., were baptized. Also serving the Church of England as a priest in his own right was Rev. Matthias's brother, Rev. Ferdinando Nicoll (or Nicolls), who served as temporary vicar of Twickenham and as rector of Exeter; as a protegé of the charismatic Rev. John White, he espoused a more puritan version of Anglicanism. These reverend brothers were sixth-generation descendants of John Nicoll, who proudly displayed the family's coat of arms at the Church of St. Nicholas (Anglican) in Islip; he was buried in that parish's graveyard in 1467.

Floyd's mother, Tabitha Smith Floyd, hailed from Smithtown, Long Island, a village founded by her great-grandfather, Richard Smith, a Quaker — indeed, the first Quaker on Long Island — who immigrated from England in the 1630s. But it was Tabitha who gave young Floyd his Presbyterian roots. Tabitha's paternal grandmother, Sarah Brewster Smith, was the daughter of Rev. Nathaniel Brewster. Although a native of Bristol, England whose parents were married there in Christ (Anglican) Church in 1624, Rev. Brewster was numbered among the first graduating class at Harvard College. Upon entering the priesthood, Rev. Brewster ministered in England, and was sent to Ireland by Oliver Cromwell — then the puritan Lord Protector who ruled England in the aftermath of the English civil war and the execution of King Charles I. After later coming to America, Rev. Brewster settled with his family in Sektauket in 1665. He served for twenty-five years as the first minister of what was then known as the First Presbyterian Church (now, Setauket Presbyterian Church).

Floyd received little formal education growing up in Brookhaven, and, by the time he reached the age of twenty-one, had lost both of his parents within just a few months of each other. It fell to Floyd to manage the family farming operations. He was soon joined in that endeavor by Hannah Jones of Southampton, Long Island, whom he wed in 1760 and who bore him three children. Indeed, farming proved to be Floyd's life passion, although public service soon also beckoned. He served in local politics, and was elected to the Provincial Assembly. In the early 1770s, he received a commission as a colonel in the Suffolk County militia, a title previously held by his paternal grandfather and great-grandfather. In 1774, he was elected to the Continental Congress, where he advanced the cause of liberty by signing the Declaration of Independence.

During all of this time, Floyd was a faithful member of the South Haven Presbyterian Church in Brookhaven; its minister during the revolutionary years, Rev. David "Priest" Rose, offered sermons that aroused the patriotism of its members to the point of personal sacrifice. Indeed, Floyd and his family were among those who suffered the severe consequences of the bold effort to secure liberty, and of Floyd's role in it; the British overran the entirety of Long Island, taking possession of his family farm and pillaging its crops and livestock, all while Floyd was still with the Congress in Philadelphia. Hannah and their young family escaped, fleeing to Connecticut; the family had many friends and relatives there, and Floyd's father, Nicoll, had once loaned money to its governor, Jonathan Trumbull. Floyd continued his service in the Congress, as well as in the New York state Senate, and was promoted to major general in the militia. But the stress was too much for Hannah, and she passed away in 1781, at the age of forty-one. She was laid to rest in Mortimer Cemetery in Middletown, Connecticut.

Floyd returned to the family estate in 1783, but little beyond devastation remained. That same year, he married Joanna Strong of the very village of Setauket that Floyd's paternal great-grandfather, Richard Floyd I, had founded, and where his maternal great-great-grandfather, Rev. Brewster, had ministered. He helped formally incorporate his longstanding South Haven Presbyterian Church, and assisted in selecting its officers, including his son, Nicoll, as a trustee.

Anxious to return to farming, Floyd acquired a tract of land along the Mohawk River, in the frontier that is now Westernville, New York. There, he and Joanna began anew, and would raise two more children in the Westernville Presbyterian Church. Although son Nicoll declined Floyd's request to move to Westernville, Nicoll's son, William, did join him there and ultimately inherited from Floyd a new family estate that future generations of Floyds would call home.

In 1789, Floyd was elected to the first Congress established under the new United States Constitution; he served there until 1791. In 1792, he served as a presidential elector—as he also did on three subsequent occasions—casting his ballot for President George Washington. He was unsuccessful as a candidate for

New York lieutenant governor in 1795, losing to John Jay, but returned to the state Senate in 1808.

In 1821, William Floyd passed away at the age of eighty-seven. He was buried in the graveyard of the Westernville Presbyterian Church; he was later joined there by Joanna, as well as by his first wife, Hannah.

In His Own Words:

Letter to the Inhabitants of Quebec, Approved by the Continental Congress (including William Floyd) October 26, 1774[1]

When the fortune of war, after a gallant and glorious resistance, had incorporated you with the body of English subjects, we rejoiced in the truly valuable addition, both on our own and your account; expecting, as courage and generosity are naturally united, our brave enemies would become our hearty friends, and **that the Divine Being would bless to you the dispensations of his over-ruling providence**, by securing to you and your latest posterity the inestimable advantages of a free English constitution of government, which it is the privilege of all English subjects to enjoy. . . .

These are the rights you are entitled to and ought at this moment in perfection, to exercise. And what is offered to you by the late Act of Parliament in their place? Liberty of conscience in your religion? No. **God gave it to you; and the temporal powers with which you have been and are connected, firmly stipulated for your enjoyment of it. If laws, divine and human, could secure it against the despotic caprices of wicked men, it was secured before.** . . .

"**Seize the opportunity presented to you by Providence itself.** You have been conquered into liberty, if you act as you ought. **This work is not of man.** You are a small people, compared to those who with open arms invite you into a fellowship. A moment's reflection should convince you which will be most for your interest and happiness, to have all the rest of North-America your unalterable friends, or your inveterate enemies. The injuries of Boston have roused and associated every colony, from Nova-Scotia to Georgia. Your province is the only link wanting, to compleat the bright and strong chain of union. Nature has joined your country to theirs. Do you join your political interests. For their own sakes, they never will desert or betray you. Be assured, that the happiness of a people inevitably depends on their liberty, and their spirit to assert it. The value and extent of the advantages tendered to you are immense. **Heaven grant you may not discover them to be blessings after they have bid you an eternal adieu.**" . . .

That Almighty God may incline your minds to approve our equitable and necessary measures, to add yourselves to us, to put your fate, whenever you suffer injuries which you are determined to oppose, not on the small influence of your single province, but on the consolidated powers of North-America, and may grant to our joint exertions an event as happy as our cause is just, **is the fervent prayer of us, your sincere and affectionate friends and fellow-subjects.**

Petition to King George III, Signed by William Floyd and Other Members of the Continental Congress October 26, 1774[2]

We ask but for peace, liberty, and safety. . . . [W]e present this petition only to obtain redress of grievances and relief from fears and jealousies occasioned by the system of statutes and regulations adopted since the close of the late war . . . .

Permit us then, most gracious sovereign, in the name of all your faithful people in America, with the utmost humility to implore you, **for the honour of Almighty God, whose pure religion our enemies are undermining**; for your glory, which can be advanced only by rendering your subjects happy and keeping them united; for the interests of your family depending on an adherence to the principles that enthroned it; for the safety and welfare of your kingdoms and dominions threatened with almost unavoidable dangers and distresses; that your majesty, as the loving father of your whole people, connected by the same bands of law, loyalty, faith and blood, though dwelling in various countries, will not suffer the transcendant relation formed by these ties to be farther violated, in uncertain expectation of effects, that, if attained, never can compensate for the calamities, through which they must be gained. We therefore most earnestly beseech your majesty, that your royal authority and interposition may be used for our relief; and that a gracious answer may be given to this petition.

Letter from William Floyd to George Clinton
December 21, 1779[3]

God only knows what will become of us next Campaign.

Letter from William Floyd to George Clinton
January 28, 1780[4]

The Embarkation of General Clinton's troops at New York with himself, and it is Said Cornwallace, left the hook two Days before the violent Storm. But we have not heard of them Since; Though **We hope providence has Disposed of them to our Advantage.**

Resolution Adopted by Continental Congress
(including William Floyd)
September 25, 1789[5]

Resolved, That a Joint Committee of both Houses be directed to wait upon the President of the United States, to request that he would **recommend to the People of the United States, a day of public thanksgiving and prayer, to be observed, by acknowledging, with grateful hearts, the many signal favors of Almighty God**, especially by affording them an opportunity peaceably to establish a Constitution of Government for their safety and happiness.

What follows is a
summary of an article
from contemporary American life . . .

nearly 250 years after
William Floyd
signed

the Declaration of Independence.

What Would William Floyd Think?

Christian Farm Family's State Training Contract Canceled for Prayers, God

Social welfare program exposes low income individuals to horticulture

By Tom Gantert 🐦 | July 12, 2017

For three years, the Gothard family of Lake City, Michigan shared with low-income women their knowledge of farming methods, under a contract with the State of Michigan. According to Robert Gothard, "we talked every aspect of growing."

But the state soon discovered a problem. As it turned out, the Gothards' "3rdDayFarm" was named after the biblical account in Genesis 1:9 that on the "third day," "God said, 'Let the waters under the heavens be gathered together into one place, and let the dry land appear'; and it was so." Worse still, the Gothards' curriculum mentioned God, and its instructors began the day with a prayer.

So, the Michigan Department of Health and Human Services promptly terminated its contract with the Gothards "because the Farm refused [to] exclude prayer and religion as part of their training for low-income women on how to grow nutritious foods." And the Gothard family said that it was then inspected, threatened with a shut-down, required to pay for a meat-storing license, and asked for passwords for all personal email and social media accounts.

https://www.michigancapitolconfidential.com/christian-farm-familys-state-training-contract-canceled-for-prayers-god.

Alexander Hamilton (1755-1804)

Signer of the United States Constitution

Highest Office Attained:
Secretary of the Treasury

Religious Affiliation:
Presbyterian; Episcopalian

L ike all of us, Alexander Hamilton was a man with personal foibles, and he did not always outwardly display his religiosity. But he had a deep and abiding faith in God that guided him as he rose from hard-scrabble beginnings to become one of our nation's greatest Founding Fathers.

Born on the island of Nevis in the British West Indies, Hamilton's childhood was filled with misfortune. Indeed, life for young Hamilton was anything but a Caribbean paradise. His mother, Rachelle Faucette, was born on Nevis in 1729. Her father, John Faucette, was a French Huguenot physician who had emigrated to the West Indies after King Louis XIV revoked the Edict of Nantes—which had protected French Protestants from religious persecution—in 1685. There, in St. George's parish (called Gingerland), he wed a British woman, Mary Uppington. Together, they had seven children, Rachel among the youngest, and lived on a small sugar plantation. The Faucette marriage, however, was fraught with discord, perhaps exacerbated by the deaths of five of their children—all but Rachel and her much older sister, Ann. In 1740, the Faucettes agreed to legally separate; Mary and young Rachel started their lives anew on St. Croix, a nearby Danish isle to which Ann and her well-to-do planter husband, James Lytton, had previously migrated.

It was there that Rachel met a much older Johann Michael Lavien, a merchant who aspired to higher status as a planter. Against her own inclination, Rachel acceded to the desires of her mother and wed Lavien at the age of sixteen. She gave birth the following year to her one legitimate son, Peter; but her marriage proved to be one of no greater bliss than was her mother's. Around 1750, Rachel abandoned the home. This act soon led to her being housed in the local jail, as Lavien seized upon a Danish law that allowed a husband to jail his wife if she was twice found guilty of adultery and no longer resided with him. Upon her release, Rachel's indomitable spirit did not permit her to resubmit to Lavien, as perhaps he had expected her to do; instead, she followed the trail blazed by her mother in fleeing her unhappy marriage.

Abandoning the benefits of a legal separation, Rachel and her mother fled to St. Kitts, leaving behind not only Lavien but son Peter as well. And, although Lavien attained for himself a divorce from Rachel, he prevented her from obtaining one; this forever relegated her future children's status—including that of Hamilton—to that of illegitimacy.

Meanwhile, James Hamilton had made his way to St. Kitts, emigrating from the Stevenston Parish of Ayrshire, Scotland, southwest of Glasgow. Raised in the family estate at Kerelaw Castle, James was the son of another Alexander Hamilton, the fourteenth laird of Grange in the Cambuskeith line of Hamiltons. But despite his high-brow pedigree and family wealth, James— as the fourth of eleven children—faced little prospect of an inherited future. Despite his general lack of ambition and work ethic, James determined, as did many young aristocrats of his day, to seek a seemingly easy (yet evasive) fortune in the sugar islands of the West Indies. There, he met Rachel, who, like James, had suffered a precipitous decline in social standing and faced an uncertain economic future.

Rachel had inherited from her father a waterfront property on the main street in Charlestown, the capital of Nevis. And it was there that Hamilton was born to Rachel and James, her common-law husband. While surrounded by natural beauty, the young family was quickly exposed to the dregs of society; the British had colonized the island with what the minister of a local Anglican church once described as "whole shiploads of pickpockets, whores, rogues, vagrants, thieves, sodomites, and other filth and cutthroats of society." They were joined by slaves whom he described as "inclined to "laziness, stealing, stubbornness, murmuring, treachery, lying, drunkenness and the like."

Hamilton's illegitimate birth precluded him from receiving Anglican instruction. So, his early education consisted of individual tutoring and schooling from a local Jewish woman, from whom he learned to recite the Ten Commandments in Hebrew. Not long after the family relocated to the very St. Croix from which Rachel had earlier made her escape, James abandoned his family, finding himself unable to provide the necessary support. Ever resilient, Rachel took up residence, along with Hamilton and his older brother, James, in an upper flat on Company Street in Christiansted, near St. John's Anglican church and school; she operated a store on the floor below, selling foodstuffs to the local planters. She acquired most of her merchandise from Nicholas Cruger and David Beekman, the local representatives of a New York export-import business.

In 1767, Rachel and Hamilton both succumbed to a raging fever. Although Hamilton survived, Rachel, all of thirty-eight years of age, did not. She was denied a burial at the nearby Anglican church, likely because of her marital status and two illegitimate births—this may explain Hamilton's later ambivalence, notwithstanding his fervent religious beliefs, toward regular church attendance. She was instead laid to rest beneath a mahogany grove on her sister's Lytton estate, fittingly called, The Grange. Hamilton, not yet a teenager, and James then found themselves in the guardianship of their cousin, Peter Lytton. But he too soon left them, the victim of an apparent suicide. And they not only inherited nothing from him, but were also disinherited from their mother, Rachel, whose only legitimate heir was determined to be her first-born son, Peter Lavien.

Hamilton next found himself in the home of Thomas Stevens, a merchant, and his wife, Ann; Hamilton soon became lifelong friends with their son, Edward. Hamilton also was by then clerking with the Beekman and Cruger mercantile firm from which Rachel previously had purchased her wares. There, Hamilton quickly demonstrated his business prowess; while still a teenager, he was entrusted with the management of the firm while its principals were an ocean away.

The year 1772 brought with it a fearsome hurricane. Hamilton by then had begun dabbling in poetry, some of a decidedly religious bent; he penned a poetic letter to his father, detailing the horror of the experience and depicting the wrath of the hurricane as a divine rebuke of human vanity and pomposity. He shared the letter with a newly-acquired mentor, Rev. Hugh Knox; Rev. Knox was a local Presbyterian minister who had taken Hamilton under his wing, and who encouraged his writing and prodded him toward scholarship. Rev. Knox, also of Scottish ancestry, had studied divinity at the College of New Jersey (later, Princeton University) under its president, Rev. Aaron Burr Sr. — father of Hamilton's later nemesis of the same name — and had been sent to the West Indies to propagate the gospel there. A self-taught physician and apothecary, Rev. Knox doubled as a part-time journalist who occasionally filled in for the editor of *The Royal Danish American Gazette*; he persuaded Hamilton to publish the letter, just as he had earlier published some of his poems.

The publication of the letter changed Hamilton's life. It captured the attention of the area's business leaders and even the island's governor, who saw great promise in the aspiring author. A subscription fund was soon established, sponsored chiefly by Rev. Knox; it was supported generously by Cruger and his partners, by Stevens, and by a first cousin, Ann Lytton Venton — the daughter of Rachel's sister, Ann. And soon, buoyed by the beneficence of these benefactors, Hamilton set sail for the educational pursuits available only on the North American mainland, never to return to the West Indies. Before departing, Hamilton inked an unsigned hymn for publication in the *Gazette* entitled, *The Soul Ascending into Bliss*; it was a work later cherished by Hamilton's wife as reflecting Hamilton's religious devotion.

Before arriving in Boston following a three-week journey, Hamilton's ship caught fire. But the charred vessel limped safely into the harbor. Hamilton immediately traveled to New York to pick up his allowance from the subscription fund, which was managed by Cruger's firm, then known as Kortright and Company. He knew no one on the continent, save Edward Stevens. Rev. Knox sent with him, however, letters of introduction, including to two of New York's most eminent Presbyterian clergymen, Dr. John Rodgers — Knox's former mentor — and

Rev. John M. Mason. Rev. Knox also facilitated Hamilton's preparatory education at the Elizabethtown Academy in Elizabethtown (now, Elizabeth), New Jersey, headed by Francis Barber; there, Hamilton received the requisite pre-college training in Latin, Greek, and advanced mathematics. He resided with William Livingston—later, the first governor of the state of New Jersey; and he was a regular guest of Elias Boudinot—also a descendant of French Huguenots—later, the president of the Continental Congress.

Within six months, Hamilton was prepared to enter college. With Livingston's introduction, he secured an interview with the renowned Presbyterian, Rev. John Witherspoon, president of the College of New Jersey—and, later, a signer of the Declaration of Independence. Of Rev. Witherspoon, the brash and driven Hamilton had one request: to pursue an accelerated course of study limited only by the reach of his own exertions. When that request could not be honored, Hamilton opted instead for King's College (later, Columbia University), headed by the loyalist Dr. Myles Cooper. In doing so, he perhaps unwittingly transported himself away from a decidedly pro-resistance Presbyterian environment—where, in Rev. Witherspoon's words, "the spirit of liberty" ran "high and strong"—to the decidedly pro-British environment of an Anglican college. But he also thrust himself out of the insular community of Princeton and into the hotbed of New York, where his political thinking could fully develop in the midst of the unfolding patriotic drama.

While a student at King's College, Hamilton happily participated in the required religious activities; this included chapel before breakfast, evening prayers, and two Sunday church services. But even in that environment, his friends were struck by his pervasive religious nature; he exhibited not only strong attention to public worship and a habit of kneeled prayer, but prodigious studies of religious writings, fervent and eloquent prayers, and zealous beliefs in fundamental Christian doctrine.

Although Hamilton initially aspired to be a doctor, other interests and events soon directed him elsewhere. He helped form a debating club, of which he became the undisputed star.

He wrote political essays that, over time, evolved from loyalist in viewpoint to avowedly anti-British; he used the debating club to hone and preview his essays. And he earned the ire of Dr. Cooper when, at a gathering of the Sons of Liberty on the grassy Common near King's College, a youthful, nineteen-year-old Hamilton transfixed the audience with an impromptu oration endorsing the Boston Tea Party, calling for colonial unity against unfair taxation, and favoring a boycott of British goods.

Within approximately two years, Hamilton had qualified for a bachelor's degree and had begun preliminary legal studies. But he never formally graduated, because of the outbreak of the revolution. By April 1776, King's College was commandeered by patriot rebels, and its facilities were used as a military hospital.

Hamilton too picked up a musket and joined the militia. He proved an adept soldier, quickly advanced up the ranks, and participated in such conflicts as the Battle of Long Island. Having gained a stellar military reputation, he was introduced to General George Washington, who made Hamilton his aide-de-camp and personal secretary, with the rank of lieutenant colonel. Hamilton remained in that position for four years, but longed for the battlefield; ultimately, he resigned from Washington's staff on less than amicable terms, but later earned laurels for his battlefield service at Monmouth and Yorktown.

His service to General Washington engendered a relationship not only with the future, first President of the United States, but with the future Mrs. Hamilton, Elizabeth Schuyler. Elizabeth was the daughter of General Philip Schuyler and Catherine Van Rensselaer; Hamilton had met them while on a mission to Albany, New York. The Schuylers and Van Rensselaers were among the most wealthy and prominent of New York families, and were related as well to the Livingstons. Hamilton and Elizabeth were wed in 1780 at the Schuyler family mansion by Rev. Eliardus Westerlo, pastor of the Albany Dutch Church; the Schuylers were longtime members of the church. Together, they would have eight children.

Following the war, Hamilton was elected to the Congress of the Confederation, but resigned and established a highly successful law practice in New York. Yet, to public service he would soon return. He served in the New York legislature and, in 1787, was chosen as a New York delegate to the Constitutional Convention. Hamilton had called for the convention to strengthen the Articles of Confederation under which the fledgling new nation was operating. Hamilton then became a signatory to the United States Constitution that emerged from that convention; even more importantly, he became perhaps the most important force in securing its ratification. The case for ratification was made in a series of essays under the collective title, *The Federalist*—later known as *The Federalist Papers*. Hamilton wrote fifty-one of the eighty-five essays; the others were written by James Madison and John Jay. Together, they turned the tide of opposition, paving the way for ratification. Hamilton also helped found and lead the Federalist political party.

Upon Washington's election as president, Hamilton was named the first secretary of the treasury; there, he employed the economic acumen he first demonstrated as a young clerk back on St Croix. Hamilton believed in a strong, central government and established the first national bank and the national monetary system. He served in that position until 1795, when he resigned in the aftermath of a sordid affair with Maria Reynolds and his payment of hush money to her husband. Hamilton returned to the practice of law, but continued his involvement in public affairs, including as an informal adviser to President Washington.

Upon Washington's retirement, Hamilton conceived a scheme, under the electoral system then in place; he hoped to swing the presidential election of 1796 to fellow-Federalist Thomas Pinckney, rather than to John Adams—also a Federalist—or Thomas Jefferson—the leader of the opposition Democratic-Republican Party. The scheme backfired, however, as Adams was elected president and Jefferson was elected vice-president. Hamilton nonetheless served for two years under Adams as commanding general of the United States army. In that position, he asked Congress to hire a chaplain for each brigade to enable them to worship.

In 1800, Hamilton tried again, this time scheming to elect Charles Cotesworth Pinckney—Thomas's brother—as president, and to relegate Adams to the position of vice-president. But, again, the scheme failed; Hamilton's efforts served to damage Adams's reputation, and the election instead resulted in a tie between the two Democratic-Republican candidates, Jefferson and Aaron Burr Jr. Hamilton then used his influence to help swing the election from Burr, his former courtroom rival, in favor of Jefferson, notwithstanding their past, political differences.

Once again, Hamilton returned to the practice of law, and soon established the *New York Evening Post*, from which he was able to launch attacks on the Jefferson administration. One of his disagreements with Jefferson was what he saw as an embrace of the French Revolution—in which the French monarchy was replaced by a republic—notwithstanding what Hamilton perceived as a move away not only from the established Catholic church but toward atheism. The French Revolution served to reinvigorate Hamilton's youthful religiosity, as Hamilton believed that all law and morality was based in religion, and that, without it, the world would be a hellish place.

In 1801, tragedy again struck, as Hamilton's oldest son, Philip, was killed in a duel; he died defending his father's honor against attacks by a New York lawyer, George Eacker. That fateful experience likely further contributed to a resurgence of Hamilton's earlier religious fervor; he was known thereafter to pray daily and to scribble notes in the margins of the family Bible. It also likely contributed to Hamilton's own death just a few years later.

In 1802, Hamilton and Eliza purchased a country home they fittingly called, in tribute to his father's lineage, The Grange. On Sunday mornings, they would gather in the garden and sing hymns, and Hamilton would read aloud from the Bible to the family. He spoke of building a chapel on the property. He also insisted that his children attend Sunday church services, and while he likely did not as faithfully attend, Eliza surely did; the family rented pew ninety-two at Trinity (Episcopal)

Church in New York. A number of the Hamilton children had been baptized there, and Hamilton performed free legal work for the church. Hamilton also proposed at this time the creation of the Christian Constitutional Society; its mission would be twofold: (1) to support the Christian religion; and (2) to support the Constitution of the United States. And Eliza, ever the devout Christian, served as a member of the multi-denominational Society for the Relief of Poor Widows with Small Children, founded by a devout, Presbyterian, Scottish widow, Isabella Graham.

In 1804, President Jefferson ran for reelection, but decided to remove Vice President Burr from his ticket. Burr instead ran for governor of New York. Hamilton once again opposed his election, and Burr once again lost. His antipathy toward Hamilton reaching the boiling point, Burr challenged Hamilton, in what was then an all-too-common practice, to a duel. Hamilton accepted, but having lost his own son to a duel just three years prior, resolved not to fire a fatal shot. On July 4, 1804, he penned a letter to his beloved Eliza, to be delivered to her only posthumously, imploring her of the consolations of religion. On the following Sunday morning, Hamilton, Eliza, and their children strolled along the grounds of The Grange. Later, he read with them the morning's Episcopal service, and then gathered with them under the stars shining from heaven above. He penned a final letter to Eliza on July 10, 1804, charging her to remember that she was a Christian and that the will of a merciful God was good. The next day, shots rang out. Hamilton's pistol fired harmlessly into the air, but Burr's inflicted a mortal injury.

On his deathbed, Hamilton sought out former loyalist Rev. Benjamin Moore to administer holy communion. Rev. Moore was rector of Trinity Church and Episcopal Bishop of New York — and acting president of King's College before it was shut down by the revolution. But, despising the practice of dueling and considering Hamilton to have been an insufficiently regular churchgoer, Rev. Moore initially declined the request. Hamilton turned to an old friend, Rev. Mason of the Associate Reformed (Presbyterian) Church of New York; he was one of the first

acquaintances Hamilton had made upon arriving in New York
by way of Rev. Knox's introductory letter. But Rev. Mason also
demurred, noting that his church did not administer communion
privately under any circumstances, and that it is not a requirement of salvation. The ensuing deathbed conversation between
Hamilton and Rev. Mason confirmed Hamilton's abiding faith,
his acknowledgment of his sins, and his "tender reliance on the
mercy of the Almighty, through the merits of the Lord Jesus
Christ." He was, he said, reconciled to God, held no malice
toward Burr, and was dying in peace.

At two o'clock p.m. on July 12, 1804, thirty-one hours after
the fatal shot was fired, and shortly after Rev. Moore rethought
his position and returned to administer communion, Hamilton,
one of America's greatest statesmen, passed into heaven. He
was eulogized at Trinity Church by his friend, Rev. Eliphalet
Nott of Albany's Presbyterian Church—to the building of which
Hamilton had contributed—in an eloquent appeal denouncing
the practice of dueling, and was buried in the Trinity Church
graveyard. Fifty years later, Eliza rejoined him there.

In His Own Words:

**Letter from Alexander Hamilton to His Father, James
Hamilton, as Reprinted in *The Royal Danish American Gazette*
September 6, 1772**[1]

> I take up my pen just to give you an imperfect account
> of one of the most dreadful Hurricanes that memory
> or any records whatever can trace, which happened
> here on the 31st ultimo at night. . . .

> My reflections and feelings on this frightful and
> melancholy occasion, are set forth in the following
> self-discourse.

> Where now, oh! vile worm, is all thy boasted fortitude
> and resolution? What is become of thine arrogance

and self sufficiency? Why dost thou tremble and stand aghast? How humble, how helpless, how contemptible you now appear. And for why? The jarring of elements—the discord of clouds? Oh! impotent presumptuous fool! **how durst thou offend that Omnipotence, whose nod alone were sufficient to quell the destruction that hovers over thee, or crush thee into atoms? See thy wretched helpless state, and learn to know thyself. Learn to know thy best support. Despise thyself, and adore thy God.** How sweet, how unutterably sweet were now, the voice of an approving conscience; Then couldst thou say, hence ye idle alarms, why do I shrink? What have I to fear? A pleasing calm suspense! A short repose from calamity to end in eternal bliss? Let the Earth rend. Let the planets forsake their course. Let the Sun be extinguished and the Heavens burst asunder. Yet what have I to dread? **My staff can never be broken—in Omnip[o]tence I trusted.**

He who gave the winds to blow, and the lightnings to rage—even him have I always loved and served. His precepts have I observed. His commandments have I obeyed — and his perfections have I adored. He will snatch me from ruin. He will exalt me to the fellowship of Angels and Seraphs, and to the fullness of never ending joys.

But alas! how different, how deplorable, how gloomy the prospect! Death comes rushing on in triumph veiled in a mantle of tenfold darkness. His unrelenting scythe, pointed, and ready for the stroke. On his right hand sits destruction, hurling the winds and belching forth flames: Calamity on his left threatening famine disease and distress of all kinds. And Oh! thou wretch, look still a little further; see the gulph of eternal misery open. There mayest thou shortly plunge — the just reward of thy vileness. Alas! whither canst thou fly? Where hide thyself? **Thou canst not call upon thy God; thy life has been a continual warfare with him.**

Hark — ruin and confusion on every side. 'Tis thy turn next; but one short moment, even now, Oh Lord help. Jesus be merciful!

Thus did I reflect, and thus at every gust of the wind, did I conclude, 'till it pleased the Almighty to allay it. Nor did my emotions proceed either from the suggestions of too much natural fear, or a conscience over-burthened with crimes of an uncommon cast. I thank God, this was not the case. The scenes of horror exhibited around us, naturally awakened such ideas in every thinking breast, and aggravated the deformity of every failing of our lives. It were a lamentable insensibility indeed, not to have had such feelings, and I think inconsistent with human nature.

Our distressed, helpless condition taught us humility and contempt of ourselves. The horrors of the night, the prospect of an immediate, cruel death — or, as one may say, of being crushed by the Almighty in his anger — filled us with terror. And every thing that had tended to weaken our interest with him, upbraided us in the strongest colours, with our baseness and folly. That which, in a calm unruffled temper, we call a natural cause, seemed then like the correction of the Deity. Our imagination represented him as an incensed master, executing vengeance on the crimes of his servants. The father and benefactor were forgot, and in that view, a consciousness of our guilt filled us with despair.

But see, the Lord relents. He hears our prayer. The Lightning ceases. The winds are appeased. The warring elements are reconciled and all things promise peace. The darkness is dispell'd and drooping nature revives at the approaching dawn. Look back Oh! my soul, look back and tremble. Rejoice at thy deliverance, and humble thyself in the presence of thy deliverer.

Yet hold, Oh vain mortal! Check thy ill timed joy. Art thou so selfish to exult because thy lot is happy in a season of universal woe? Hast thou no feelings for the miseries of thy fellow-creatures? And art thou incapable of the soft pangs of sympathetic sorrow? Look around thee and shudder at the view. See desolation and ruin where'er thou turnest thine eye! See thy fellow-creatures pale and lifeless; their bodies mangled, their souls snatched into eternity, unexpecting. Alas! perhaps unprepared! Hark the bitter groans of distress. See sickness and infirmities exposed to the inclemencies of wind and water! See tender infancy pinched with hunger and hanging on the mothers knee for food! See the unhappy mothers anxiety. Her poverty denies relief, her breast heaves with pangs of maternal pity, her heart is bursting, the tears gush down her cheeks. Oh sights of woe! Oh distress unspeakable! My heart bleeds, but I have no power to solace! O ye, who revel in affluence, see the afflictions of humanity and bestow your superfluity to ease them. Say not, we have suffered also, and thence withold your compassion. What are you[r] sufferings compared to those? Ye have still more than enough left. Act wisely. **Succour the miserable and lay up a treasure in Heaven.**

The Soul Ascending into Bliss, a Poem by Alexander Hamilton
October 17, 1772[2]

> AH! whither, whither, am I flown,
> A wandering guest in worlds unknown?
> What is that I see and hear?
> What heav'nly music fills mine ear?
> Etherial glories shine around;
> More than Arabias sweets abound.
> Hark! hark! a voice from yonder sky,
> Methinks I hear my Saviour cry,
> Come gentle spirit come away,
> Come to thy Lord without delay;
> For thee the gates of bliss unbar'd
> Thy constant virtue to reward.
> I come oh Lord! I mount, I fly,
> On rapid wings I cleave the sky;
> Stretch out thine arm and aid my flight;
> For oh! I long to gain that height,
> Where all celestial beings sing
> Eternal praises to their King.
> O Lamb of God! thrice gracious Lord
> Now, now I feel how true thy word;
> Translated to this happy place,
> This blessed vision of thy face;
> My soul shall all thy steps attend
> In songs of triumph without end.

The Farmer Refuted, an Essay by Alexander Hamilton
February 23, 1775[3]

There is so strong a similitude between your political principles and those maintained by Mr. Hobbs, that, in judging from them, a person might very easily *mistake* you for a disciple of his. His opinion was, exactly, coincident with yours, relative to man in a state of nature. He held, as you do, that he was, then, perfectly free from all restraint of *law* and *government*. Moral obligation, according to him, is derived from the introduction of civil society; and there is no virtue, but what is purely artificial, the mere contrivance of politicians, for the maintenance of social intercourse. But the reason he run into this absurd and impious doctrine, was, that **he disbelieved the existence of an intelligent superintending principle, who is the governor, and will be the final judge of the universe.**

As you, sometimes, swear *by him that made you*, I conclude, your sentiment does not correspond with his, in that which is the basis of the doctrine, you both agree in; and this makes it impossible to imagine whence this congruity between you arises. **To grant, that there is a supreme intelligence, who rules the world, and has established laws to regulate the actions of his creatures; and, still, to assert, that man, in a state of nature, may be considered as perfectly free from all restraints of *law* and *government*, appear to a common understanding, altogether irreconcileable.**

Good and wise men, in all ages, have embraced a very dissimilar theory. They have supposed, that the deity, from the relations, we stand in, to himself and to each other, has constituted an eternal and immutable law, which is, indispensibly, obligatory upon all mankind, prior to any human institution whatever.

This is what is called the law of nature, "which, being coeval with mankind, and dictated by God himself, is, of course, superior in obligation to any other. It is binding over all the globe, in all countries, and at all times. No human laws are of any validity, if contrary to this; and such of them

as are valid, derive all their authority, mediately, or immediately, from this original." Blackstone. Upon this law, depend the natural rights of mankind, the supreme being gave existence to man, together with the means of preserving and beatifying that existence. He endowed him with rational faculties, by the help of which, to discern and pursue such things, as were consistent with his duty and interest, and invested him with an inviolable right to personal liberty, and personal safety.

Hence, in a state of nature, no man had any *moral* power to deprive another of his life, limbs, property or liberty; nor the least authority to command, or exact obedience from him; except that which arose from the ties of consanguinity.

Hence also, the origin of all civil government, justly established, must be a voluntary compact, between the rulers and the ruled; and must be liable to such limitations, as are necessary for the security of the *absolute rights* of the latter; for what original title can any man or set of men have, to govern others, except their own consent? To usurp dominion over a people, in their own despite, or to grasp at a more extensive power than they are willing to entrust, is to violate that law of nature, which gives every man a right to his personal liberty; and can, therefore, confer no obligation to obedience.

"The principal aim of society is to protect individuals, in the enjoyment of those absolute rights, which were vested in them by the immutable laws of nature; but which could not be preserved, in peace, without that mutual assistance, and intercourse, which is gained by the institution of friendly and social communities. Hence it follows, that the first and primary end of human laws, is to maintain and regulate these *absolute rights* of individuals." Blackstone. . . .

The fundamental source of all your errors, sophisms and false reasonings is a total ignorance of the natural rights of mankind. Were you once to become acquainted with these, you could never entertain a thought, that all men are not, by nature, entitled to a parity of privileges. You would be convinced, that natural liberty is a gift of the beneficent Creator to the whole human race, and that civil liberty is founded in that; and cannot be wrested from any people, without the most manifest violation of justice. *Civil liberty, is only natural liberty, modified and secured by the sanctions of civil society.* It is not a thing, in its own nature, precarious and dependent on human will and caprice; but is conformable to the constitution of man, as well as necessary to the *well-being* of society.

Upon this principle, colonists as well as other men, have a right to civil liberty: For, if it be conducive to the happiness of society (and reason and experience testify that it is) it is evident, that every society, of whatsoever kind, has an absolute and perfect right to it, which can never be withheld without cruelty and injustice. . . .

The sacred rights of mankind are not to be rummaged for, among old parchments, or musty records. They are written, as with a sun beam, in the whole *volume* of human nature, by the hand of the divinity itself; and can never be erased or obscured by mortal power.

Letter from Alexander Hamilton to His Wife, Elizabeth Schuyler Hamilton
August 8, 1780[4]

> Adieu My Dear lovely amiable girl. **Heaven preserve you and shower its choicest blessings upon you.**

Letter from Alexander Hamilton to His Wife, Elizabeth Schuyler Hamilton
September 1781[5]

> **I sink at the perspective of your distress, and I look to heaven to be your guardian and supporter.**

Letter from Alexander Hamilton to His Wife, Elizabeth Schuyler Hamilton
September 1781[6]

> How chequered is human life! How precarious is happiness! How easily do we often part with it for a shadow! These are the reflections that frequently intrude themselves upon me, with a painful application. I am going to do my duty. Our operations will be so conducted, as to economize the lives of men. **Exert your fortitude and rely upon heaven.**

Letter from Alexander Hamilton to Mr. Childs
October 17, 1787[7]

> [W]hether the New Constitution, if adopted, will prove adequate to such desirable ends, time, the mother of events, will show. For my own part, I sincerely esteem it a system which without the finger of *God*, never could have been suggested and agreed upon by such a diversity of interests.

The Vindication No I, an Essay by Alexander Hamilton May-August, 1792[8]

There is yet another class of opponents to the Government & its administration, who are of too much consequence not to be mentioned, a sect of political Doctors — a kind of *Popes* in Government — standards of political orthodoxy who brand with heresy all opinions but their own — men of sublimated imaginations and weak judgments pretenders to profound knowlege, yet ignorant of the most useful of all sciences, the science of human nature — men who dignify themselves with the appellation of Philosophers, yet are destitute of the first elements of true philosophy — Lovers of paradoxes, men who maintain expressly that Religion is not necessary to Society, and very nearly that Government itself is a nuisance, that Priests and Clergymen of all descriptions are worse than useless. . . .

People of America can ye be deceived by Arts like these? Will ye suffer yourselves to be cheated out of your confidence in men who deserve it most? Will ye be the dupes of hypocritical pretenders?

Think for yourselves. Look around you, consult your own experience. If any of you have doubts, listen calmly and dispassionately to the arguments and facts which in the course of the following numbers shall be opposed to the suggestions which would persuade you that the administration of your government has been in the aggregate weak or wicked or both!

Viewʃ on the French Revolution, an Essay by Alexander Hamilton 1794[9]

Facts, numerous and unequivocal, demonstrate that the present aera is among the most extraordinary, which have occurred in the history of human affairs. Opinions, for a long time, have been gradually gaining ground, which **threaten the foundations of Religion, Morality and Society. An attack was first made upon the Christian Revelation; for which natural Religion was offered as the substitute. The Gospel was to be discarded as a gross imposture; but the being and attributes of a God, the obligations of piety, even the doctrine of a future state of rewards and punishments were to be retained and cherished.**

In proportion as success has appeared to attend the plan, a bolder project has been unfolded. The very existence of a Deity has been questionned, and in some instances denied. The duty of piety has been ridiculed, the perishable nature of man asserted and his hopes bounded to the short span of his earthly state. Death has been proclaimed an Eternal Sleep—"the dogma of the *immortality* of the soul a *cheat* invented to torment the living for the benefit of the dead." **Irreligion, no longer confined to the closets of conceiled sophists, nor to the haunts of wealthy riot, has more or less displayed its hideous front among all classes. . . .**

A league has at length been cemented between the apostles and disciples of irreligion and of anarchy. Religion and Government have both been stigmatised as abuses; as unwarrantable restraints upon the freedom of man; as causes of the corruption of his nature, intrinsically good; as

sources of an artificial and false morality, which tyrannically robs him of the enjoyments for which his passions fit him; and as cloggs upon his progress to the perfection for which he was destined.

As a corollary from these premisses, it is a favourite tenet of the sect that religious opinion of any sort is unnecessary to Society; that the maxims of a genuine morality and the authority of the Magistracy and the laws are a sufficient and ought to be the only security for civil rights and private happiness. . . .

The practical developement of this pernicious system has been seen in France. It **has served as an engine to subvert all her antient institutions civil and religious**, with all the checks that served to mitigate the rigour of authority; it has hurried her headlong through a rapid succession of dreadful revolutions, which have laid waste property, made havoc among the arts, overthrow cities, desolated provinces, unpeopled regions, crimsonned her soil with blood and deluged it in crime poverty and wretchedness; and all this as yet for no better purpose than to erect on the ruins of former things a despotism unlimited and uncontrouled; leaving to a deluded, an abused, a plundered, a scourged and an oppressed people not even the shadow of liberty, to console them for a long train of substantial misfortunes, of bitter sufferings.

Draft of President George Washington's Farewell Address, Written by Alexander Hamilton
July 30, 1796[10]

To all those dispositions which promote political prosperity, **Religion and Morality are essential props.** In vain does that man claim the praise of patriotism who labours to subvert or undermine **these great pillars of human happiness these firmest foundations of the duties of men and citizens.** . . . **Tis essentially true that virtue or morality is a main & necessary spring of popular or republican Governments.**

Stand No. III, **an Essay by Alexander Hamilton under the pseudonym, "Titus Manlius"**
April 7, 1798[11]

In reviewing the disgusting spectacle of the French revolution, it is difficult to avert the eye entirely from those features of it which betray a plan to disorganize the human mind itself, as well as to **undermine the venerable pillars that support the edifice of civilized society. The attempt by the rulers of a nation to destroy all religious opinion, and to pervert a whole people to Atheism, is a phenomenon of profligacy reserved to consummate the infamy of the unprincipled reformers of France. The proofs of this terrible design are numerous and convincing.**

The animosity to the Christian system is demonstrated by the single fact of the ridiculous and impolitic establishment of the decades, with the evident object of supplanting the Christian Sabbath. The inscription by public authority on the tombs of the deceased, affirming death to be an eternal sleep, witness the desire to discredit the belief of the immortality of the soul. The open profession of Atheism in the Convention, received with acclamations; the honorable mention on its journals of a book professing to prove the *nothingness* of all religion; the institution of a festival to offer public worship to a courtezan

decorated with the pompous [title] of "Goddess of Reason;" the congratulatory reception of impious children appearing in the hall of the Convention to lisp blasphemy against the King of Kings; are among the dreadful proofs of a conspiracy to establish Atheism on the ruins of Christianity—to deprive mankind of its best consolations and most animating hopes—and to make a gloomy desert of the universe. . . .

Equal pains have been taken to deprave the morals as to extinguish the religion of the country, if indeed morality in a community can be separated from religion. . . .

The pious and the moral weep over these scenes as a sepulchre destined to entomb all they revere and esteem. The politician, who loves liberty, sees them with regret as a gulph that may swallow up the liberty to which he is devoted. He knows that morality overthrown (and morality *must* fall with religion) the terrors of despotism can alone curb the impetuous passions of man, and confine him within the bounds of social duty.

Letter from Alexander Hamilton to George Washington
October 21, 1799[12]

My trust in Providence which has so often interposed in our favour, is my only consolation.

Address by Alexander Hamilton to the Electors of the State of New York
March 21, 1801[13]

In vain are you told that you owe your prosperity to your own industry and to the blessings of

Providence. To the latter doubtless you are primarily indebted. You owe to it among other benefits the constitution you enjoy and the wise administration of it, by virtuous men as its instruments.

**Letter from Alexander Hamilton to James Bayard
April 16-21, 1802**[14]

In my opinion the present Constitution is the standard to which we are to cling. Under its banners, *bona fide* must we combat our political foes — rejecting all changes but through the channel itself provides for amendments. By these general views of the subject have my reflections been guided. I now offer you the outline of the plan which they have suggested. Let an Association be formed to be denominated, "The Christian Constitutional Society." Its objects to be

1st The support of the Christian Religion.

2nd The support of the Constitution of the United States.

**Letter from Alexander Hamilton to Unknown Friend
April 13, 1804**[15]

Arraign not the dispensations of Providence — they must be founded in wisdom and goodness; and when they do not suit us, it must be because there is some fault in ourselves, which deserves chastisement, or because there is a kind intent to correct in us some vice or failing, of which, perhaps, we may not be conscious; or because the general plan requires that we should suffer partial ill.

Statement by Alexander Hamilton to Unknown Friend, Undated[16]

I have examined carefully the evidence of the Christian religion, and if I was sitting as a juror upon its authenticity, I should rather abruptly give my verdict in its favor.

Statement by Alexander Hamilton to His Wife, Elizabeth Schuyler Hamilton, Undated[17]

I have studied [Christianity] and I can prove its truth as clearly as any proposition ever submitted to the mind of man.

Letter from Alexander Hamilton to His Wife, Elizabeth Schuyler Hamilton
July 4, 1804[18]

This letter, my very dear Eliza, will not be delivered to you, unless I shall first have terminated my earthly career; **to begin, as I humbly hope from redeeming grace and divine mercy, a happy immortality**.

If it had been possible for me to have avoided the interview, my love for you and my precious children would have been alone a decisive motive. But it was not possible, without sacrifices which would have rendered me unworthy of your esteem. I need not tell you of the pangs I feel, from the idea of quitting you and exposing you to the anguish which I know you would feel. Nor could I dwell on the topic lest it should unman me.

The consolations of Religion, my beloved, can alone support you; and these you have a right to enjoy. Fly to the bosom of your God and be

comforted. With my last idea; I shall cherish the sweet hope of meeting you in a better world.

Adieu best of wives and best of Women. Embrace all my darling Children for me.

Letter from Alexander Hamilton to His Wife, Elizabeth Schuyler Hamilton
July 10, 1804[19]

The Scruples of a Christian have determined me to expose my own life to any extent rather than subject my self to the guilt of taking the life of another. This must increase my hazards & redoubles my pangs for you. But you had rather I should die innocent than live guilty. **Heaven can preserve me and I humbly hope will but in the contrary event, I charge you to remember that you are a Christian. God's Will be done. The will of a merciful God must be good.**

Once more Adieu My Darling darling Wife

Deathbed Statement by Alexander Hamilton to Rev. John M. Mason
July 11, 1804[20]

I am a sinner; I look to his mercy. . . . I have a tender reliance on the mercy of the Almighty, through the merits of the Lord Jesus Christ.

What follows is a
summary of an article
from contemporary American life . . .

nearly 250 years after
Alexander Hamilton
signed

the United States Constitution.

What Would Alexander Hamilton Think?

CHRISTIANITY · **Published** February 5, 2017

Town takes stand after mayor forced to remove Christian flag

Veterans Memorial Park in Rienzi, Mississippi had long displayed a flag—white, with a blue upper left corner adorned by a red cross—the Christian flag. But when the Freedom From Religion Foundation threatened a $500,000 lawsuit, the mayor took the flag down, saying, "I never dreamed that something like this would have happened in a town this small, but it happened."

Outraged town residents—including a parade of bikers proudly displaying their own Christian flags—gathered at the memorial and returned the Christian flag to its flagpole. Said one, "I'm telling you folks I'm no preacher. But it's going to get worse; can I get an Amen? It's going to get worse, but we cannot bow down. We can't lay down if we stand up till our death, that's what we need to do. There just comes a point in time when you've got to be politically incorrect and take a stand." Said another, "As a proud American, but No. 1 as a proud Christian, I came today to stand up for the Lord and stand up for our freedom."

https://www.foxnews.com/us/town-takes-stand-after-mayor-forced-to-remove-christian-flag.

Francis Lewis
(1713-1802)

Signer of the Declaration of Independence and
the Articles of Confederation

Highest Office Attained:
Representative in Congress

Religious Affiliation:
Episcopalian

Although he opted to spend his life in commerce and public service, Francis Lewis bore a pedigree from which he seemed destined for the Episcopal ministry. He was born in 1713 in Llandaff, Cardiff, Wales, the son of Rev. Francis Lewis and Amy Pettingal Lewis. Rev. Lewis was the rector of the local parish of the established church, and Amy—his cousin—was the daughter of Rev. Francis Pettingal, also an Episcopal clergyman. Lewis's maternal great-aunt—the sister of Rev. Pettingal—was Anne Pettingal Lewis; she had married Morgan Lewis—Rev. Lewis's father—and she was therefore also Francis Lewis's paternal grandmother. Anne's and Rev. Pettingal's father—who was both Lewis's paternal great-grandfather and his maternal great-great-grandfather—was also a minister, also named Rev. Francis Pettingal; he served as vicar of St. Woollos in Wales. Another of Anne's brothers, Rev. John Pettingal, also became an Episcopal cleric who served as a prebendary of St. Paul's in London.

Lewis was orphaned at about the age of five, and was raised by a maternal relative; this likely was Anne's sister, Mary Pettingal—who later bequeathed a portion of her estate to Lewis. She taught him the ancient language of Wales known as Cymraeg; as a child, Lewis also spent time visiting family relation in Scotland, where he learned the Gaelic dialect. The Pettingals later sent Lewis to London, where he was schooled at Westminster and then took a job with a London merchant.

At the age of twenty-one, Lewis embarked for America. Having converted his inheritance into merchandise, he established mercantile houses in both New York and Philadelphia. He formed a business partnership with Edward Annesley, a fellow Welshman who was descended from an ancient family headed by the Earl of Anglesey. In 1745, Lewis wed Edward's younger sister, Elizabeth Annesley.

Lewis's business interests led to frequent travels around the world. During the French and Indian War, his business supplied uniforms to the British. In 1756, while at Fort Oswego tending to his business affairs, the fort was attacked by French forces and their native allies. British commanding Colonel Mersey was killed while standing aside Lewis, and Lewis was taken into captivity. Held prisoner for seven years, he was released in a prisoner exchange in 1763; the British government granted him five thousand acres of land in New York as compensation. After reestablishing himself in business and acquiring a substantial fortune, Lewis retired and turned his attention toward public service.

In 1765, Lewis attended the Stamp Act Congress and became a founding member of the Sons of Liberty. On the eve of the revolution, he attended the New York provincial convention and helped set up the colony's new government. In 1775, he moved his family to an estate he had acquired in Whitestone, New York, on Long Island. And he was elected to the Continental Congress, where he affixed his name to the Declaration of Independence. He also signed the Articles of Confederation in 1778.

Now a marked man with a price on his head, Lewis paid dearly for his acts of insurrection. Not content merely to pillage and destroy Lewis's Whitestone estate, the British saw fit also to take Elizabeth captive. Thrown into prison and treated harshly, she never fully recovered. She was released in a prisoner exchange after General George Washington ordered the arrest of Mrs. Barren, the wife of the British paymaster-general, and Mrs. Kempe, the wife of the attorney general of Pennsylvania. But Elizabeth's health was seriously impaired by her treatment at the hands of the British. She also had to confront the approaching death of her servant who had fallen ill and who, as a Roman Catholic, did not wish to die without being administered last rites. Because New York was under martial law and no priest was available, Elizabeth sent a messenger to Philadelphia; he located and smuggled a priest through

British lines to administer the last rights before the servant's passing. Elizabeth's own death, with Lewis beside her, would follow in 1779.

Though his dear Elizabeth was now gone, they had together raised three children to adulthood. Son Morgan Lewis, who befriended a young James Madison while a student at the College of New Jersey (now, Princeton University), was active in the revolutionary war; he later became governor of New York and helped found New York University. Against her father's wishes, daughter Ann had secretly wed Captain George Robertson of the British royal navy; he had been sent to the American colonies to help quell the brewing rebellion. He and Ann then set sail for England, never to return. Their daughter, Marianne Robertson, married Rev. John Bird Sumner, Archbishop of Canterbury; another daughter, Louisa Lewis Robertson, married Rev. John Mathias Turner, Bishop of Calcutta.

Lewis too continued to demonstrate his family's longstanding religious commitment. From 1784 to 1786, he served as a vestryman of Trinity (Episcopal) Church in New York. Indeed, at a time when the loyalist and patriot factions of the church were vying for control, Lewis was among those who wrested control from the then-loyalist rector; they secured an ordinance from the state of New York that formally vested the estate of Trinity Church in the hands of nine trustees—of whom one was Lewis.

Francis Lewis passed away on December 12, 1782, in his ninetieth year. He was buried alongside Elizabeth in the Trinity Churchyard.

In His Own Words:

The Petition of James Duane, R. R. Livingston, and Francis Lewis, and Others to the Council for the Temporary Government of the State
1783[1]

To the Honorable the Council appointed by the Act of the Legislature for the temporary government of the Southern District of this State etc. —

The Petition of the Subscribers humbly sheweth: —

That your Petitioners are by Education and Principle attached to the Mode of religious Worship used in the Episcopal Church commonly known and distinguished by the Name of the Church of England. That they formed a Part of that Church in this City, and were as such entitled to a Participation in the Rights and Property held for the benefit of the Said Congregation by the Corporation of Trinity Church. That your Petitioners attached to the cause of Freedom and conceiving that Personal Interests could not in any case be placed in Competition with their duty as Citizens, for the most part left their native Homes, and relinquished their Property and their occupations, and went into voluntary Exile, that they might as good Citizens, according to their respective Abilities, promote the Interest of their Country.

That your Petitioners think it unnecessary to recapitulate the hardships they suffered during their Exile, the Distresses to which many of their Families have been reduced; the Hazards to which they have been Exposed; their loss of Property; and the more affecting Loss of brave and worthy Relations and Connections that have fallen in the Field, or died in the Prisons of their Vindictive Enemy. They numbered Private losses among the Hazards they were to run; and they submit to those they have sustained. But while your Petitioners acquiesce in these, they **cannot consent that Rights to which they are entitled as Members of a Religious Community, should be wrested** from them, while they were endeavoring to establish the Civil and Religious Privileges of every Citizen of the State; more especially that they should be surrendered to Persons who have preferred their own Interest to that of their Country; and by their Submission to, in some sort encouraged the Attempt of Britain to Establish her Oppression.

Your Petitioners therefore humbly looking up to this Council for Relief, beg Leave to Shew to your Honors, that a Number of Persons were elected under the Influence of the British Government to places in the Corporation, while your Petitioners and others entitled to vote at such elections were, by an armed Force Prevented from Exercising such Right and others of your Petitioners who were unavoidably detained within the British Lines, and whose Attachment to the Independence of this State was avowed, were deterred by Threats and other Means from the free Enjoyment of their Religious Privileges.

That the Persons so elected calling themselves the Church-wardens and Vestrymen of Trinity Church have not only possessed themselves of the Estate of the Church, but in open Defiance of the Authority of this State, and in direct contempt of its Laws placed at the Head of the said Corporation, as Rector of the said Church, a Man since attainted

441

for Treasons before that appointment committed, and caused him to be inducted into the said Church by Mr. Tryon, the pretended Governor of the State, even after His Excellency, the present Governor, was in the full exercise of his Office.

That in Pursuance of the same System, and with Design to keep your Petitioners and Others, well attached to the Independence of the State, from a share in the Government of the said Church, the said persons calling themselves the Church-wardens, and Vestrymen, after the said Rector had left the State to avoid the Penalties of the Law, did, a few Days before the Evacuation of this City, unnecessarily and merely to prevent your Petitioners from being consulted in the Choice, proceed to choose the Reverend Benjamin Moore, Rector of the said Church, tho' it was well known that the choice would be disagreeable to your Petitioners; the said Benjamin Moore having upon every occasion evinced a most decided attachment to the British Government, and an utter aversion to that of the State, as far as his Situation would admit. **So that your Petitioners, without the Aid of your Honors, find themselves reduced to the disagreeable Necessity, either of abandoning the mode of worship in which they have been Educated,** and of yielding up their rights in the Corporation, or of joining in Prayer with one whose Political Principles they detest, and whose Prayers for the Success of the British Army all good Citizens must, with Hearts overflowing with Gratitude, on every Solemn Occasion, thank the Supreme Governor of the Universe for having rejected.

Your Petitioners omit at this time any observations upon the Inconsistency of some Parts of the Charter of Trinity Church with the Constitution of this State, as they humbly hope to obtain from the Legislature a Renewal thereof, with such alterations as may consist therewith.

For the same Reason, your Petitioners do not think it proper to observe upon any non-user or mis-user thereof, by any Persons who have assumed to act as Members of the said Corporation, other than, that the Persons who at Present call themselves Church-wardens and Vestry-men, or the greater Part of them, are disqualified by a Law of this State from holding any Place within this State, or Voting at Elections; and that **your Petitioners are now by an armed Force withheld from the free Exercise of their Rights.** That **sound Policy concurring with the Justice due to your Petitioners directs that a new Election be held by Persons qualified by Law to elect out of Persons Members of the Congregation of the said Church eligible by Law, and that they be vested with all the Powers heretofore granted by Charter to the Corporation of Trinity Church, till the Legislature can declare their Sense thereon**, in like manner as it has pleased this honorable Council to direct in the case of the Corporation of this City.

Your Petitioners beg leave further to assure your Honors, that in presenting their humble Petition, they are **influenced by no other Motives than those that affect them merely as Members of the Congregation of the episcopal Church**, being well persuaded that without Interposition of your Honors, the flagrant Violation of the Rights of your Petitioners, and the Early attempt at Power, by Persons who ought to deem themselves too happy in the Protection of Government, will greatly endanger the Peace of this City, and excite Tumults which it is the Earnest Wish of your Petitioners as Members of this Committee to prevent.

Your Petitioners therefore pray, that this honored Council would be pleased to take their Case Into Consideration, and grant them such Relief in the Premises as to your Honors shall seem Meet.

And your Petitioners as in Duty bound shall ever Pray etc.

Letter from Francis Lewis and Others to Rev. Benjamin Moore, Rector of Trinity Church
February 5, 1784[2]

Reverend Sir,
The Reverend Mr. Provoost has been pleased in compliance with our Invitation, to take the charge of the Episcopal Churches in this City, and we have delivered him the Keys.
We by no means wish to abridge your usefulness in a Congregation where you have many friends. The object of this Letter is only to apprize you that Mr. Provoost in future will have the direction in the same manner as it was exercised by former Rectors.

We are Reverend Sir
Your most humble Servts.

What follows is a
summary of an article
from contemporary American life . . .

nearly 250 years after
Francis Lewis
signed

the Declaration of Independence
and
the Articles of Confederation.

What Would Francis Lewis Think?

TODD STARNES · Published February 27, 2017

Town hall agitators explode at the name of Jesus

When United States Senator Bill Cassady returned home to hold a town hall meeting in Metairie, Louisiana, the secular protestors were ready. The Louisiana state chaplain, Michael Sprague, and an unidentified Vietnam War veteran began the event with an invocation and the Pledge of Allegiance. They had barely begun when the invectives were unleashed: "Pray on your own time. This is our time." "Amen. Let's get on with it." "Separation of church and state." Said Chaplain Sprague, "I've never been shouted down throughout a time of prayer like that. I've never been in a situation like that. It's sad there wasn't honor and respect for God." Lamented Senator Cassady, "Wow, they booed the name of Jesus." And the veteran once again faced combat as crowd members responded to his call for the Pledge by sitting on their hands — rather than putting them on their hearts — turning their backs, and shouting.

https://www.foxnews.com/opinion/ town-hall-agitators-explode-at-the-name-of-jesus.

Philip Livingston
(1716-1778)

Signer of the Declaration of Independence

Highest Office Attained:
Representative in Congress

Religious Affiliation:
Dutch Reformed

Philip Livingston was a lifelong member of the Dutch Reformed Church, although his paternal ancestry is steeped in the annals of Scottish Presbyterianism. His great-great-great-grandfather, Rev. Alexander Livingston, became the first rector of Monyabroch (now, Kilsyth) after the legal establishment of the reformed doctrines in Scotland in the 1500s. He was succeeded in that position by his son, Rev. William Livingston; but Rev. William ultimately was deposed from that position after opposing the restoration of the Episcopacy in Scotland and refusing to submit to the canons and ceremonies of the Church of England.

Rev. William found a new church in Lanark, Ireland; together with his son, Rev. John Livingston, the Earl of Linlithgow, he continued to resist conformity. Both of these Presbyterian reverends were periodically suspended from the ministry, both in Ireland and in Scotland; yet, Rev. John became one of the most revered names in all of Scottish ecclesiastical history. After Rev. John attempted unsuccessfully to make passage to America in pursuit of its religious freedoms, his father officiated at his wedding in 1635 to Janet Fleming. The ceremony was held at St. Cuthbert's Church—then known as West Kirk. One of the sites of the resistance to the Episcopacy, it stood at the foot of the Castle of Edinburgh. Following the nuptials, the newly-married couple fled back to Ireland amid reports that the bridegroom's arrest was imminent. After another failed attempt to emigrate to America, he took exile in 1663 in Rotterdam, The Netherlands; he was welcomed by a colony of fellow Scots who had similarly sought refuge there. He was later joined by his wife, Janet, and young family—including nine-year-old Robert Livingston, the signer's grandfather.

Ten years later, Robert Livingston made the journey that had twice failed his father, sailing with Captain John Phillips aboard the *Catherine of Charlestown*. He settled in Albany, New York; there, he put his knowledge of the Dutch language to good use and quickly became a successful landowner, businessman, and holder of a number of important, local public offices. He wed Alida Schuyler, whose family was one of the wealthiest and most longstanding in all of New York. The nuptials were held in the Dutch Reformed Church in Albany, Rev. Gideon Schaats officiating. Alida—who took her mother's surname— was the daughter of Dutch Reformed immigrants, Col. Philip Pieterse and Margarietje Grijt Schuyler; she was widowed from Amsterdam-born Rev. Nicholas Van Rensselaer, a scion of a similarly established and prosperous family, for whom Robert had worked as an accountant. Rev. Van Rensselaer had pastored under Rev. Schaats at the Dutch church in Albany, but his ties to England and the Anglican Church led him never to be fully accepted by that church.

Robert and Alida were faithful members of Albany's Dutch Reformed Church, as were the Schuylers, including Alida's brother, Pieter Schuyler. After he and Robert secured from the governor a municipal charter, Pieter served as the first mayor of Albany; Robert served as its first town clerk. The Livingstons baptized their children in that church, and one of them, son Philip (Philip Sr.), became the father of the signer. While a fixture in Albany society and civic affairs, Robert developed a far-reaching business empire, amassed great wealth, and acquired significant property about forty miles south of Albany; there, he built what became Livingston Manor. He secured a grant from the governor proposing to erect a church under the direction of the Reformed Church of Holland. He then built, at the manor— largely with his own funds—a church that later became known as the Reformed Church of Linlithgo. He served as a founding elder, as did his son, Gilbert Livingston. Beneath the church, Robert constructed a burial vault, in which he and Alida were interred following their deaths.

Upon the deaths of Robert and Alida, Philip Sr. took charge of his father's business affairs; he also assumed many of the same local offices in Albany, and became the second lord of Livingston Manor. He married Catharina Van Brugh, daughter of Albany mayor Pieter Van Brugh and Sarah Hendrickse Cuyler Van Brugh; together, they had twelve children, including signer Philip Livingston and his brother, William Livingston—a signer of the United States Constitution. They were raised in the Dutch Reformed Church in Albany, with the assistance of their maternal grandmother, Sarah.

Philip Livingston the signer was born in 1716 in Albany. He was raised at Livingston Manor, although he never became "lord" of the manor. That title—and much of the associated wealth—instead went to his older brother, Robert. But Livingston, after graduating from Yale College in 1737, became very successful in his own right.

In 1740, he married Christina Ten Broeck, who hailed from another respected and well-to-do Albany family, at the Albany Dutch Church. Her father, Dirck Wesselsen Ten Broeck, was the twenty-eighth mayor of Albany; his grandfather, Dirck Wesselje Ten Broeck, served as the city's fourth mayor, the very position that was first held by Pieter Schuyler, brother of Livingston's grandmother, Alida. Both families were fixtures in the Albany Dutch Church, where Dirck Sr. had served as a deacon; Livingston and Christina's first three children were baptized there.

Livingston and his young family then moved to New York City, where Livingston established a thriving import business that allowed him to acquire a substantial fortune. They maintained a townhouse in Manhattan, and later also acquired a country home in Brooklyn Heights and a third residence in Esopus (later, Kingston), New York. They attended the Reformed Dutch Church of New Amsterdam and New York, where Livingston and Christina's youngest six children were baptized; Livingston served as a church elder and deacon.

Described as a firm believer in the great truths of Christianity and a sincere and humble follower of the divine Redeemer,

Livingston also became an influential political figure. In 1754, he became a New York City alderman, and he subsequently served in the Provincial Assembly, including as its president. In 1774, he was selected to simultaneously serve as a representative to the Continental Congress. As conditions with Great Britain worsened, Livingston was among the signatories to the Olive Branch Petition, which made a final effort to reach conciliation with the motherland. When that effort failed, Livingston became an adamant proponent of independence. Although he was not present in Congress when independence was declared, he proudly returned to formally sign the Declaration of Independence that he had participated in drafting.

Livingston paid a significant financial price for his participation in the American rebellion. Not only did he personally help finance the fledgling patriot army, but the British confiscated his business interests and seized his Manhattan and Brooklyn Heights homes. They used the former as a barracks and the latter as a royal navy hospital; the Brooklyn Heights home was where General George Washington—in whose guard Livingston's son, Henry, served—had earlier convened his council of war following a defeat at the Battle of Long Island. Livingston and his family then fled to Kingston, a city that the British later burned to the ground. He continued to serve in the post-Declaration Congress, and simultaneously was elected as a state senator under the newly adopted constitution of the state of New York.

Livingston's Dutch Reformed roots were further strengthened by the nuptials of his children. In 1775, daughter Sarah wed her second cousin (a grandson of Gilbert), the celebrated Rev. John Henry Livingston; he was known as the father of the Dutch Reformed Church in America. This Rev. Livingston was at that time the minister at the family's own Reformed Dutch Church of New Amsterdam and New York; he pastored there from 1770 to 1820, except for a brief period of interruption while the British occupied New York City during the revolution; during that time, the newlyweds accompanied Livingston and his family to Kingston. Rev. Livingston then accepted an invitation to preach at the Albany Dutch Church—together with its pastor, Rev. Eliardus Westerlo—and, later, at the Livingston Manor church. He also served as the chaplain of the Provincial Congress, and, beginning in 1810, served as president of Queen's College (now, Rutgers University); it was chartered in 1776, with Livingston's assistance, by Benjamin Franklin's son, William Franklin, as a Dutch Reformed institution of higher education.

Meanwhile, just months before Sarah's wedding, another daughter, Catharine, married Rev. Westerlo of the Dutch Reformed Church of Albany, the very site of her baptism. She was widowed from Stephen Van Rensselaer II, the great-grandson of Jeremias Kiliaen Van Rensselaer; Jeremias was the brother of the very Rev. Nicholas Van Rensselaer who had ministered at the Dutch Reformed Church of Albany and from whom Livingston's grandmother, Alida, was widowed before marrying Livingston's father, Robert. Catharine remained the first lady of that church, which had been so formative in the lives of the Livingstons, until Rev. Westerlo's death in 1790.

Livingston's community activities and philanthropy extended to—and well beyond—his Dutch Reformed church. Together with Zacharias Hoffman, a distant cousin by marriage to Livingston's wife, Christina, Livingston donated land for the Dutch Reformed Church in Red Hook, New York. He also established a professorship of divinity at his Yale alma mater. And he was one of the founders of King's College—an Episcopalian institution now known as Columbia University—which his brother, William, had staunchly opposed. He was also one of the builders of the first meeting houses for the Methodist Society in America; was a founder of the New York Society Library and of the New York Chamber of Commerce; was one of the first governors of the New York Hospital; and was the founder and first president of St. Andrew's Society. The society was New York's first benevolent organization and initially was founded to assist natives of Scotland and their Presbyterian descendants who might be in want or distress.

In 1778, while the Congress of the new nation was assembled in York, Pennsylvania, Livingston fell ill with dropsy (edema). He succumbed to the illness at the age of sixty-two, and was initially buried at the German Reformed Church (later, the Zion Reformed Church, and now the Zion United Church of Christ) in York. It was there, in 1777, that the Congress had met to celebrate the first Thanksgiving Day proclaimed by Congress. The pastor of that church, Rev. John Daniel Wagner, officiated at the ceremony. Later, to accommodate the need for a church addition, Livingston's remains were relocated to the Prospect Hill Cemetery in York. Christina spent her remaining years in Albany with her daughters and grandchildren; upon her passing in 1801, she was buried in the cemetery of the Albany Dutch Church.

In His Own Words:

**Last Will and Testament of Philip Livingston
May 18, 1778[1]**

> **In the Name of God Amen . . .**
>
> **First, I do resign my soul to the great most mighty and most merciful God who gave it in Hopes thro Mercy alone by the Merits of Jesus Christ to have a joyful Resurrection to Life eternal and my body I commit to the Earth . . . .**

**Valedictory Letter by Philip Livingston to Friends in Albany (as his death approached)
1778[2]**

> [R]emain firm in the cause of Liberty — **trust in God for deliverance.**

What follows is a
summary of an article
from contemporary American life . . .

nearly 250 years after
Philip Livingston
signed

the Declaration of Independence.

What Would Philip Livingston Think?

TODD STARNES · Published August 24, 2016

Good Lord! Cop says Red Cross told him not to pray with flood victims

OPINION By Todd Starnes, | Fox News

When Louisiana flood victims were in need, the Red Cross stepped in to help. Or did it? According to Clay Higgins, a law enforcement officer in Lafayette, Louisiana, he stopped by a Red Cross shelter to thank volunteers and to offer prayers and encouragement to those in need.

But the Red Cross had a problem with the Bible he was carrying and with the prayers he shared with flood evacuees. According to Higgins, a Red Cross supervisor asked him to leave, noting that the Red Cross does not allow spiritual counseling in its shelters or religious interaction with shelter residents. One flood victim approached Higgins during that conversation, asking him to pray. But Higgins was only allowed to do so outside the Red Cross shelter. Said Higgins, "Christian compassion was not welcomed there in the manner I had provided."

Meanwhile, four families left another Red Cross shelter in Albany, Louisiana after being told that they could not pray or read their Bibles at their cots. They sought aid from a pastor in town, who recounted that "[a] Red Cross worker told them they could not pray or read their Bible in public." After traveling to the shelter in question, the pastor said that he "hadn't even made it in the door" when others informed him that "the Red Cross workers told them they could not pray or read Bibles. I told them to go to their cot and pray and read. I told them they're on church property and they could read a Bible on church property."

https://www.foxnews.com/opinion/ good-lord-cop-says-red-cross-told-him-not-to-pray-with-flood-victims.

Gouverneur Morris
(1752-1816)

*Signer of the Articles of Confederation and
the United States Constitution*[4]

---

[4] Gouverneur Morris represented New York when signing the Articles of
Confederation; he represented Pennsylvania when signing the United
States Constitution.

Highest Office Attained:
United States Senator; Minister to France;
Minister to Great Britain

Religious Affiliation:
Episcopalian

Gouverneur Morris, the "Penman of the Constitution," was born in 1752 at Morrisania, the family manor established in 1697 by Morris's grandfather, Lewis Morris. Morris was descended from his Welsh great-grandfather, Richard Morris, a distinguished officer under Oliver Cromwell's command during the English civil war of 1648. Cromwell, a member of Parliament who had become commander of the parliamentary army, was an outspoken critic of royal policies and, as a puritan convert, of the established Anglican church. Following the civil war, he established the Protectorate, effectively a monarchy by another name, with himself as Lord Protector. His reign was marked by strict religious and social laws, along radical Protestant lines. Following Cromwell's death in 1658, and the unsuccessful effort of his son to succeed him, Parliament offered the monarchy back to King Charles II, in return for promises of religious toleration and general amnesty. The restoration of the monarchy saw Cromwell's body exhumed in 1661, hung, decapitated, and his head displayed for the next twenty years outside Westminster Hall.

Following the Restoration, Richard Morris departed England for Barbados. There, he met Sarah Pole, and they were married in 1669 at St. Michael's (Episcopal) Church in Bridgetown, Barbados. In 1670, the couple emigrated to New York, where Richard and his brother, Colonel Lewis Morris, purchased from Jonas Broncks a large parcel of land in what is now the South Bronx area of New York City. By 1673, both Richard and Sarah had died, leaving their infant son, Lewis Morris — Morris's grandfather — in the care of his uncle, Colonel Morris.

Although orphaned at an early age, Lewis Morris — Morris's grandfather — was a man of great promise and accomplishment.

Largely self-educated, having objected to his uncle's choice of a pious Quaker as his tutor, he learned to read Latin, Hebrew, Arabic, and German; he also demonstrated wide-ranging interests in politics, law, history, science, and religion. But his home-life was difficult; at the age of seventeen, he left home, first for Bermuda and then for Jamaica. He soon returned and made amends with his uncle, who then facilitated young Lewis's marriage to Scottish-born Isabella Graham, the daughter of the New York attorney general, James Graham. When Colonel Morris died in 1691, the nephew found that he was not the sole executor of his uncle's will; but after contesting the will, he ultimately prevailed to inherit the family estate, which by then numbered several thousand acres. In 1697, he acquired from Royal Governor Benjamin Fletcher of provincial New York a patent for the estate that then became known as the Manor of Morrisania. That nephew, grandfather Lewis, the first lord of the manor, went on to become the chief justice of New York and, having successfully advocated with the British crown for the separation of New Jersey from New York, the first governor of New Jersey. He was also a devout Christian and an active churchman; upon the granting of a charter for Trinity (Episcopal) Church in New York in 1697, and in order to further the Lord's work, he secured the largest and best logs that he could and donated the timber for the building of the church. So pleased were church leaders with the generous gift that they granted to the Morris family—which came to include eight children—the highest compliment that the social code of the day allowed: a square pew in the church. Grandfather Lewis also served from 1697 to 1700 as a vestryman of Trinity Church and encouraged the missionary efforts of the Society for the Propagation of the Gospel.

Upon grandfather Lewis's death in 1746, his son, Lewis—Morris's father—inherited the Manor of Morrisania. This Lewis served as a judge of the Vice-Admiralty Court of New York for many years, and married Tryntje (a/k/a Katrijntje or Catherine) Staats, the daughter of Dr. Samuel and Johanna Staats of Albany. Tryntje's grandfather, Dr. Major Abraham Staats, had emigrated with his wife, Tryntje Wessels Staats, from Amsterdam, The Netherlands in 1642; he became a prominent member of Albany society and an officer and member of the Albany Dutch Church. Tryntje Staats Morris bore several children—including Morris's brother, Lewis, a signer of the Declaration of Independence— before her death in 1730. Morris's father later married his niece, Sarah Gouverneur (whose mother, Sarah, was Tryntje's sister); she bore him additional children, including Morris, later a signer of the Articles of Confederation and the United States Constitution. Sarah hailed from the French Huguenot family of Governeurs who fled religious persecution in France in the 1590s, initially settling in The Netherlands and then immigrating to New York in 1663.

Showing educational promise at an early age, Morris was educated by private tutors and enrolled in a boarding school run by Rev. Pierre Stouppe in New Rochelle, some eighteen miles from home. New Rochelle had been founded by French Huguenots, and Rev. Stouppe was pastor of New Rochelle's Trinity Church; during Rev. Stouppe's pastorship, it formally came to adopt the Episcopalian traditions. Rev. Stouppe was the son (or other close relative) of Rev. M. Stouppe, pastor of the French Protestant church in London; he was sent into service in Geneva, Switzerland by the same Oliver Cromwell under whom Richard Morris had served. In New Rochelle, Morris was schooled in the classics and learned to speak French, as it was then regularly spoken at New Rochelle's Trinity Church.

At the age of twelve, Morris entered King's College, an Anglican institution now known as Columbia University. Said to have favored Latin and mathematics in his studies, Morris graduated at the age of sixteen; he then commenced the study of law with the esteemed William Smith, author of *The History of the Province of New-York*. Later the chief justice of New York, Smith introduced Morris to such patriots as John Jay and Alexander Hamilton. Morris was admitted to the bar in 1771, at the age of twenty-one, and also received a master's degree from King's College. By 1775, politics was beckoning, and he was elected to New York's Provincial Congress. The following year, as his

brother, Lewis, was signing the Declaration of Independence —
on instructions from the Provincial Congress on which Morris
served — Morris joined the militia; he did so notwithstanding a
disfiguring injury he had suffered when, at the age of fourteen,
scalding water was spilled on his right arm and side. He also
helped draft the first constitution of New York, advocating for
its protection of religious freedoms. In 1777, Morris was elected
to the New York state legislature and served on the New York
Council of Safety; the following year, at the youthful age of twen-
ty-six, he took the place of his brother, Lewis, in the Continental
Congress, where he signed the Articles of Confederation as a
representative from New York.

The then-ongoing war for independence split the Morris
family. While Morris and his brother, Lewis, sided with the
patriots, and Morris himself spent the winter of 1777-1778 with
General George Washington at Valley Forge, another half-
brother, Staats Morris, served as a general in the British army.
Morris's mother also remained a loyalist, and his loyalist sister,
Catherine, took refuge in England. Another sister, Isabella, and
her loyalist husband, Isaac Wilkins, departed for England and
Nova Scotia; they later returned, and Wilkins was ordained an
Anglican minister, serving as rector of St. Peter's (Episcopal)
Church in the Bronx for thirty years.

In 1779, with Morrisania under the control of the British,
Morris relocated to Philadelphia; he resumed the practice of law,
and then served as the principal assistant to another (although
unrelated) Morris, Robert Morris, the superintendent of finance
for the United States. In that capacity, Morris introduced the
concept of decimal coinage and conceived the word, "cent."
During that time, Morris is said to have been thrown from a
carriage, suffering his second debilitating injury—this time
to his leg, requiring its amputation. Morris thereafter wore a
wooden leg.

In 1787, Morris represented his adopted state of Pennsylvania
at the Constitutional Convention. He was among the leaders
of the convention, speaking more times (one hundred seven-
ty-three) than any other delegate. He was named the chair of the

Committee of Style and Arrangement, and is the principal author of the United States Constitution. In particular, he is credited with drafting the nationally unifying language of the Preamble: "We the People of the United States"—rather than of the separately-identified, individual states. Although clearly a supporter of the Constitution he did so much to author, Morris declined Alexander Hamilton's request to help write *The Federalist Papers* (which were designed to secure its ratification by the states).

Morris then returned to New York, having acquired the family's Morrisania estate. While visiting Virginia in 1788, he met a much younger Anne ("Nancy") Cary Randolph, whom he would later wed. Said to be a direct descendent of Pocahantas, Anne was close friends as a child with her third cousin, Martha Jefferson. Martha was Thomas Jefferson's daughter, and she would later marry Anne's brother, Thomas Randolph. But Morris's and Anne's romance did not kindle at that time, as Morris embarked on a business trip to Europe with Robert Morris in 1789. There, he witnessed the beginnings of the French Revolution, which, despite his earlier advocacy of a strong national government, led him to fear the excesses of governmental power. He remained in Europe, by appointment of President George Washington, first as Minister to England, and then as Minister to France, succeeding Jefferson. After returning to the United States in 1799, Morris was elected to the United States Senate, but he left the Senate in 1803 after losing his re-election bid. He then returned to Morrisania. In 1804, he helped found the New York Historical Society (which he later served as its president) and also delivered a eulogy for Alexander Hamilton at New York's Trinity Church. An early advocate of the Erie Canal, Morris served as its founding chairman, and as a member of the Erie Canal Commission from 1810 to 1816. He so opposed the war of 1812 that he promoted the idea that New York and the New England states secede from the union to whose formation Morris had so significantly contributed.

In April 1809, Morris hired a housekeeper for his Morrisania estate—none other than the Anne Cary Randolph he had met more than twenty years earlier in Virginia. On Christmas day of that year, Morris shed his bachelor lifestyle at the age of fifty-seven, as he and Anne were married. In 1813, Anne would bear him a son, Gouverneur Morris Jr., although Morris would only live to see him reach the age of three. Morris died in 1816, in the same room at Morrisania in which he was born, having suffered an infection after attempting to clear a blocked urethra using a whalebone. Anne would live until 1837, and both she and Morris were interred at Morrisania at the St. Ann's (Episcopal) Church that Gouverneur Jr. built there in her honor in 1741.

In His Own Words:

Letter from Gouverneur Morris to John Jay
February 1, 1778[1]

> The Continental Congress & Currency have both depreciated but **in the Hands of the almighty Architect of Empires** the Stone which the Builders have rejected may easily become Head of the Corner.

Letter from Gouverneur Morris to His Mother, Sarah Morris
April 16, 1778[2]

> Content with what I have and what I am **I look forward serenely to the Course of Events confident that supreme Wisdom & Justice will provide for the Happiness of his Creatures.** It gives me Pain that I am seperated from those I love but comparing this with what thousands suffer I dare not repine. **Let me earnestly recommend to you so much of either Religion or Philosophy as to bear inevitable Evils with Resignation.** . . . Whenever the present Storm subsides I shall rush with Eagerness into the Bosom of private Life but while it continues and while my Country calls for the Exertion of **that little Share of Abilities which it hath pleased God to bestow on me** I hold it my indispensible Duty to give myself to

her. I know that for such Sentiments I am called a Rebel and that such Sentiments are not fashionable among the Folks you see. It is possible (tho I hope not) that your maternal Tenderness may lead you to wish that I would resign these Sentiments. But that is impossible and therefore for the present I cannot see you. Let me however intreat that you be not concerned on my Account. I shall again see you. Perhaps the Time is not far off. I am much distressed for Wilkins. . . . I hope it may be in my Power to return his Attention by the Protection of a Parent. **God forbid he should need it or any of them.**

Letter from Gouverneur Morris to General George Washington
May 21, 1778[3]

Had our Saviour addressed a chapter to the rulers of mankind, as he did many to the subjects, I am persuaded his good sense would have dictated this text; *Be not wise overmuch*.

Letter from Gouverneur Morris to Anthony Wayne
May 21, 1778[4]

Your good Morals in the Army give me sincere Pleasure as it hath long been my fixed Opinion that Virtue and Religion are the great sources of human Happiness. More especially is it necessary in your Profession firmly to rely upon the God of Battles, for his Guardianship and Protection in the dreadful Hour of Trial. But of all these Things you will and I hope in the merciful Lord you have been made fully acquainted by that pious young Man Friend Hutchinson.

Letter from Gouverneur Morris to George Clinton
September 6, 1778[5]

I am of no Party but that of my Country and as I always have, so I trust I always shall, consult her Interests **according to that measure of abilities which it hath pleased Heaven to dispense to me**.

Diary Entry by Gouverneur Morris
April 17, 1789[6]

It would indeed be ridiculous for those to believe in man who affect not to believe in God.

Diary Entry by Gouverneur Morris
February 28, 1790[7]

After supper the conversation is accidentally turned to religion, and a gentleman present observes that in all countries there is an established religion. I assure him that there is none in America. We are led too far on this head, for this country is too ignorant as yet to understand the true principles of human policy with respect to religion, and too bigoted, so that truths almost universally acknowledged appear almost like atheism. At least such is my conjecture, from the countenances of the company, when **I tell them that God is sufficiently powerful to do his own business without human aid, and that man should confine his care to the actions of his fellow-creatures, leaving to that Being to influence the thoughts as he may think proper.**

Notes on a Form of a Constitution for France, by Gouverneur Morris
1791[8]

That the citizens may discharge their duties and preserve their rights, it is proper that they be acquainted with both; therefore the State should provide for public education.

The education of young citizens ought to form them to good manners, to accustom them to labor, to inspire them with a love of order, and to impress them with respect for lawful authority.

Religion is the only solid basis of good morals; therefore education should teach the precepts of religion, and the duties of man towards God.

These duties are, internally, love and adoration; externally, devotion and obedience; therefore provision should be made for maintaining divine worship as well as education.

But each one has a right to entire liberty as to religious opinions, for religion is the relation between God and man; therefore it is not within the reach of human authority.

Letter from Gouverneur Morris to Lord George Gordon
June 28, 1792[9]

I believe that Religion is the only solid Base of Morals and that Morals are the only possible Support of free governments.

Letter from Gouverneur Morris to Thomas Jefferson August 22, 1792[10]

The different ambassadors are all taking flight, and if I stay I shall be alone. I mean, however, to stay, unless circumstances should summon me away; because, in the admitted case that my letters of credence are to the monarchy, and not to the Republic of France, it becomes a matter of indifference whether I remain in this country or go to England during the time which may be needful to obtain your orders or to produce a settlement of affairs here. Going hence, however, would look like taking part against the late Revolution, and I am not only unauthorized in this respect, but I am bound to suppose that, if the great majority of the nation adhere to the new form, the United States will approve thereof; because, in the first place, we have no right to prescribe to this country the government they shall adopt, and next, because the basis of our own Constitution is the indefeasible right of the people to establish it. It is true that the position is not without danger, but I presume that when the President did me the honor of naming me to this embassy it was not for my personal pleasure or safety, but to promote the interests of my country. **These, therefore, I shall continue to pursue to the best of my judgment, and as to consequences, they are in the hand of God.**

Letter from Gouverneur Morris to Thomas Pinckney December 3, 1792[11]

I have seen the worship of many idols, and but little of the true God; I have seen many of those idols broken, and some of them beaten to dust. I have seen the late Constitution, in one short year, admired as a stupendous monument of human wisdom and ridiculed as an egregious production of folly and vice. I wish much, very much, the happiness of this inconstant people. I love them. I feel grateful for their efforts in our cause, and I consider the establishment of a good constitution here as a principal means, **under Divine Providence**, of extending the blessings of freedom to the many millions of my fellow-men who groan in bondage on the Continent of Europe. But I do not greatly indulge the flattering illusions of hope, because **I do not yet perceive that reformation of morals without which liberty is but an empty sound**. My heart has many sinister bodings, and reason would strive in vain to dispel the gloom which always thickens where she exerts her sway.

Letter from Gouverneur Morris to President George Washington
February 14, 1793[12]

How all this will end **God only knows,** but I fear it will end badly. . . . **God bless you, my dear sir, and keep and preserve you.** Your cool and steady temper is now of infinite consequence to our country.

Letter from Gouverneur Morris to Alexander Hamilton
January 5, 1801[13]

Adieu, my dear Hamilton. **God bless you and send you many happy years**.

Letter from Gouverneur Morris to Lena Rutherford
January 4, 1804[14]

Religion offers higher and better Motives for Resignation to the Will of our Almighty Father. Infinite Wisdom can alone determine What is best to give What to leave and What to take away. . . .

Grief . . . turns our Affections from the World to
fix them more steadily and strongly on the proper
Objects and bends our Will to the Will of God.

**Letter from Gouverneur Morris to John Murray Jr.,
Chairman of the New York Committee on Schools
September 23, 1811**[15]

There are I think two distinct kinds of education. One,
of small comparative value is the education of the
head, or instruction. **The other, of great importance
both to individuals and to society, is the education
of the heart, or virtuous habits.** Instruction is, I
believe, considered as the special business of schools,
while the care of manners and morals is submitted to
parents and preachers. . . .

**How far instruction may promote religion and
virtue deserves serious consideration**, for more
value is attributed, perhaps, to reading and writing,
than they truly deserve. . . . **Those who can read
have, indeed, the means of meditating on the Holy
Writings; but do they improve the opportunity?
If we look around us, we shall, I fear, meet more
frequently with loose poems and idle novels, than
with Bibles and sermons. . . .**

**My object is merely to remind you of that knowledge,
which is more useful than learning.** As I write to
the wise, a word is sufficient. The gentlemen of your
board will pursue the subject I trust, to good effect,
while **I confine myself to the humble hope, that
they may introduce among the rising generation
those habits of virtuous industry, without which
earthly blessings are but the means of mischief.**

Letter from Gouverneur Morris to Charles Hare
June 30, 1812[16]

> I earnestly pray God that he will enable me to know and to do my duty; but I believe that little, if anything, will be left to my choice.

Letter from Gouverneur Morris to Robert Oliver
July 18,1813[17]

> **My humble and perfect reliance on God leads me to the belief**, and, I may say, conviction, that this impious war will not only destroy the vain hopes and expectations which led to the declaration of it, but, severely scourging the authors and abettors, rescue the nation from the despotism of democracy.

Diary Entry by Gouverneur Morris
January 1, 1816[18]

> Another year is buried in the abyss of a past eternity. **What the coming, or, rather, the arrived year may bring is known only to the Omniscient. But we know that, whatever may be its course and incidents, they will be what they ought to be.**

An Inaugural Discourse, Delivered before the New York Historical Society by the Honorable Gouverneur Morris, Its President
September 4, 1816[19]

> **The reflection and experience of many years have led me to consider the holy writings, not only as a most authentic and instructive in themselves, but as the clue to all other history. They tell us what man is, and they, alone, tell us why he is what he is: a contradictory creature that, seeing**

and approving what is good, pursues and performs what is evil. . . . But experience teaches that profligates may gain all the enticements of life, and criminals escape punishment, by the perpetration of new and more atrocious crimes. **Something more, then, is required to encourage virtue, suppress vice, preserve public peace, and secure national independence.** There must be something more to hope than pleasure, wealth, and power. Something more to fear than poverty and pain. Something after death more terrible than death. **There must be religion. When that ligament is torn, society is disjointed, and its members perish. . . . But the most important of all lessons is, the denunciation of ruin to every state that rejects the precepts of religion. Those nations are doomed to death who bury, in the corruption of criminal desire, the awful sense of an existing God, cast off the consoling hope of immortality, and seek refuge from despair in the dreariness of annihilation.** Let mankind enjoy at last the consolatory spectacle of thy throne, built by industry on the basis of peace and sheltered under the wings of justice. **May it be secured by a pious obedience to that divine will, which prescribes the moral orbit of empire with the same precision that his wisdom and power have displayed, in whirling millions of planets round millions of suns through the vastness of infinite space.**

Statement by Gouverneur Morris (on his deathbed) November 1816[20]

Sixty-five years ago it pleased the Almighty to call me into existence here, on this spot, in this very room; and how shall I complain that He is pleased to call me hence?

What follows is a
summary of an article
from contemporary American life . . .

nearly 250 years after
Gouverneur Morris
signed

the Articles of Confederation
and
the United States Constitution.

What Would Gouverneur Morris Think?

Mississippi school district fined $7500 for opening assembly with prayer

Brandon High School in Rankin, Mississippi held an assembly in honor of students who scored higher than a twenty-two on their ACT tests. Attendance was optional. The assembly opened with the offering of a prayer by a local Methodist pastor, Rev. Rob Gill.

United States District Judge Carlton Reeves imposed a $7,500 fine, holding that, even though attendance at the assembly was voluntary, the offering of a prayer violated his 2013 order requiring the school district to stop "proselytizing Christianity." He also threatened a $10,000 additional fine for any future infractions, and ordered the school district to pay attorney's fees. According to Judge Reeves, "The district's breach did not take very long and it occurred in a very bold way. Its conduct displays that the district did not make any effort to adhere to the agreed judgment."

https://www.foxnews.com/us/mississippi-school-district-fined-7500-for-opening-assembly-with-prayer.

Lewis Morris
(1726-1798)

Signer of the Declaration of Independence

Lewis Morris

Highest Office Attained:
Representative in Congress

Religious Affiliation:
Episcopalian

B orn into a wealthy New York family, Lewis Morris willingly relinquished much of his worldly possessions to British pillaging, all for the cause of freedom. He was descended from his Welsh great-grandfather, Richard Morris, who was a distinguished officer under Oliver Cromwell's command during the English civil war of 1648. Cromwell, a member of Parliament who had become commander of the Parliamentary army, was an outspoken critic of royal policies and, as a puritan convert, of the established Anglican church. Following the civil war, he established the Protectorate, effectively a monarchy by another name, with himself as Lord Protector. His reign was marked by strict religious and social laws, along radical Protestant lines. Following Cromwell's death in 1658, and the unsuccessful effort of his son to succeed him, Parliament offered the monarchy back to King Charles II, in return for promises of religious toleration and general amnesty. The restoration of the monarchy saw Cromwell's body exhumed in 1661, hung, decapitated, and his head displayed for the next twenty years outside Westminster Hall.

Following the Restoration, Richard Morris departed England for Barbados. There, he met Sarah Pole, and they were married in 1669 at St. Michael's (Episcopal) Church in Bridgetown, Barbados. In 1670, the couple emigrated to New York, where Richard and his brother, Colonel Lewis Morris, purchased from Jonas Broncks a large parcel of land in what is now the Bronx area of New York City. By 1673, both Richard and Sarah had died, leaving their infant son Lewis Morris—Morris's grandfather—in the care of his uncle, Colonel Morris.

Although orphaned at an early age, Lewis Morris—Morris's grandfather—was a man of great promise and accomplishment. Largely self-educated, having objected to his uncle's choice of a pious Quaker as his tutor, he learned to read Latin, Hebrew, Arabic, and German; he also demonstrated wide-ranging inter-ests in politics, law, history, science, and religion. But his home-life was difficult; at the age of seventeen, he left home, first for Bermuda and then for Jamaica. He soon returned and made amends with his uncle, who then facilitated young Lewis's mar-riage to Scottish-born Isabella Graham, the daughter of the New York attorney general, James Graham. When Colonel Morris died in 1691, the nephew found that he was not the sole exec-utor of his uncle's will; but after contesting the will, he ulti-mately prevailed to inherit the family estate, which by then numbered several thousand acres. In 1697, he acquired from Royal Governor Benjamin Fletcher of provincial New York a patent for the estate that then became known as the Manor of Morrisania. That nephew, grandfather Lewis, the first lord of the manor, went on to become the chief justice of New York and, having successfully advocated with the British crown for the separation of New Jersey from New York, the first gov-ernor of New Jersey. He was also a devout Christian and an active churchman; upon the granting of a charter for Trinity (Episcopal) Church in New York in 1697, and in order to fur-ther the Lord's work, he secured the largest and best logs that he could and donated the timber for the building of the church. So pleased were church leaders with the generous gift that they granted to the Morris family—which came to include eight chil-dren—the highest compliment that the social code of the day allowed—a square pew in the church. Grandfather Lewis also served from 1697 to 1700 as a vestryman of Trinity Church and encouraged the missionary efforts of the Society for the Propagation of the Gospel.

Upon grandfather Lewis's death in 1746, his son, Lewis—Morris's father—inherited the Manor of Morrisania. This Lewis served as a judge of the Vice-Admiralty Court of New York for many years, and married Tryntje (a/k/a Katrijntje or Catherine) Staats, the daughter of Dr. Samuel and Johanna Staats of Albany. Tryntje's grandfather, Dr. Major Abraham Staats, had emigrated with his wife, Tryntje Wessels Staats, from Amsterdam, Netherlands in 1642; he became a prominent member of Albany society and an officer and member of the Albany Dutch Church. Tryntje Staats Morris bore several children—including Lewis Morris, the signer—before her death in 1730. Morris's father later married his niece, Sarah Gouverneur (whose mother, Sarah, was Tryntje's sister); she bore him additional children, including Gouverneur Morris, later a drafter and signer of the United States Constitution, and a signer also of the Articles of Confederation.

Signer Lewis Morris was born to Lewis and Tryntje in 1726. Raised at Morrisania, he entered Yale College at the age of sixteen; he acquired, it has been said, a reputation of scholarship and strict morality. After college, he returned to Morrisania, devoting himself principally to agricultural pursuits. But he soon found himself also devoted to Mary Beekman Walton, whom he wed in 1749 at Trinity Church, and with whom he would have ten children.

The Walton family was an established and wealthy family of merchants. They traced their lineage to Captain Thomas Lawrence, who was born at St. Albans, Herfordshire, England. Captain Lawrence was raised and baptized, as was his family for generations, in the iconic Abbey Church at St. Albans. He emigrated to America in 1635, landing at Plymouth, Massachusetts with Governor John Winthrop; he made his way to New York, where he eventually became mayor of the city of New York and a justice of the New York Supreme Court.

Mary Walton's maternal lineage was equally consequential. Her grandfather, Dr. Gerardus Willemse Beekman, was a surgeon and a wealthy landowner in New York City; he served as the acting governor of the province of New York in 1710, as well as a deacon in the Dutch Reformed Church. His father, Wilhelmus Beekman, had emigrated from The Netherlands in 1647, accompanying Peter Stuyvesant; Stuyvesant was later the first governor of New York, and his son, Nicolas, would later marry Wilhelmus's daughter, Maria. Wilhelmus, who served as deputy mayor of New York City, was also deeply religious, having served as an officer in the Dutch Reformed Church in

Holland at the early age of twenty-one. Indeed, matters of religion were paramount in the Beekman family, as both of Wilhelmus's grandfathers were renowned ministers of the cloth. His paternal grandfather was Rev. Gerardus Beeekman, a distinguished Protestant theologian in Germany, whose services included translating the Bible for King James I. His maternal grandfather was Rev. William Baudertius, pastor of the Reformed Church at Zutphen, Gelderland, The Netherlands; he helped formulate the doctrines and forms of worship of the Dutch Reformed Church, was known as "one of Dutch Calvinism's most jealously orthodox protagonists," and was one of a handful of religious scholars selected to translate the Bible into the Dutch language. As the generations proceeded, others in the family similarly devoted themselves to the ministry; these included Wilhelmus's uncle, Rev. John Beekman; his brother, Rev. Gerhard Beckman; and, later, Rev. William Walton, the grandson of Mary Beekman Morris's brother, William Walton.

After his father died in 1762, Morris became the third lord of the manor. By then, he had been appointed judge of the Court of Admiralty, a position he held from 1760 to 1774. He was also elected to the colonial Assembly in 1769; he served there until it was disbanded by the royal governor, and he then was elected to the Provincial Assembly that he worked to re-form in 1775. Although he represented an area that was largely loyalist in its pre-revolutionary views, Morris became increasingly disenchanted with the British. He was elected to the Continental Congress in May, 1775, as a supporter of independence. But he was in New York at the time of the vote for independence — which occurred in Philadelphia — on July 2, 1776, working to persuade the New York Assembly to grant him the authority to sign the Declaration of Independence. Once that authority was secured on July 9, he returned to Philadelphia; in affixing his signature to the Declaration, he then declared, in the face of the near-certain personal destruction that awaited, "Damn the consequences, give me the pen!" He also served on committees for the defense of New York, attained the rank of brigadier general of the New York militia, and financed much of the war effort.

In the ensuing conflict, Morris indeed suffered greatly, as the British ransacked and destroyed his beloved Morrisania.

In 1777, Morris relinquished his seat in Congress to his younger half-brother, Gouverneur Morris. He returned to local duties by serving as a county judge and New York state senator. He returned also to the affairs of Morrisania, as he worked to rebuild the farmland and properties left ravaged by the British. As a delegate to the New York state convention in 1788, he worked with Alexander Hamilton to secure New York's ratification of the United States Constitution. He lived out his remaining days at his paternal estate at Morrisania, which at one point he offered as a possible site for the new nation's capital. He passed away there in 1798, and his body was interred in the family vault beneath St. Ann's (Episcopal) Church at Morrisania.

In His Own Words:

Petition to King George III, Signed by Lewis Morris and Certain Other Members of Congress
July 8, 1775[1]

> Knowing to what violent resentments and incurable animosities, civil discords are apt to exasperate and inflame the contending parties, **we think ourselves required by indispensable obligations to Almighty God**, to your Majesty, to our fellow subjects, and to ourselves, immediately to use all the means in our power, not incompatible with our safety, for stopping the further effusion of blood, and for averting the impending calamities that threaten the British Empire. . . .
>
> That your Majesty may enjoy a long and prosperous reign, and that your descendants may govern your dominions with honor to themselves and happiness to their subjects, **is our sincere and fervent prayer.**

Letter from Lewis Morris to Philip Schuyler
July 23, 1775[2]

> **God Send you Success**, all your Friends in this Place are well, and believe me Dr Sir Your Sincere friend and Most Hu Sert

Letter from Lewis Morris to John Jay
March 8, 1777[3]

> **I wish to God** we had more men in Jersey, you may be assured from the best authority Howe has not more than Seven Thousand Eight hundred Sick and well, shamefull to the Continent that they do not drive him out; however let us hope for the best.

Letter from Lewis Morris to the New York Convention
March 16, 1777[4]

> Tho' justice and impartiality should be the ruling principle in every publick Assembly, yet when Interest, ambition, or any such motives interfere, **such is the depravity of human Nature**, that they are apt to be biased, and when a majority is to determine a question, tho the Cause may be just, there is reason to dread the event; and this is the principal reason for my delaying the bringing on this Affair.

Will of Grandfather Lewis Morris
January 12, 1746[5]

> **In the name of God amen: God's will be done; but what I will or desire should be done after my decease, and how I would have what estate God has been pleased to bless me with**, disposed of, is contained in what follows:

But before I give any directions concerning the disposition of my body or estate, **I think it my duty to leave the following testimonial of my sense of the goodness of God to me, in protecting and wonderfully preserving of me, from my infancy to this present time, now in an advanced age.** . . .

Thus, by the sole goodness of Almighty God, my benign Creator, the designs against me were rendered ineffectual, without any contrivance or act of my own. . . .

Those who survive me, will commend or blame my conduct in life as they think fit, and I am not paying of any man for doing of either; but if any man, whether Churchman or Dissenter, in or not in priest's orders, is inclined to say any thing on that occasion, he may, if my executors think fit to admit him to do it.

I would not have any mourning worn for me by any of my descendants; for **I shall die in a good old age and when the Divine Providence calls me hence**; I die when I should die, and no relation of mine ought to mourn because I do so . . . .

I will (if it be not done before my death), that a vault of stone be built at or nigh the place at Morrisania, where my good uncle lies buried; and that the remains of my relations lying there, be collected and put into coffins in it; and my executors may get a tomb stone for me if they think fit.

I am now, and I doubt not I shall die, in the firme belief that there is one God, the Creator of all things, who governs the world, as he sees most suitable, to answer the purposes of his divine

providence. What the state of the dead is I know not, but believe it to be such as is most suitable for them, and that their condition and state of existence after death will be such as will fully show the wisdom, justice, and goodness of their great Creator to them. . . .

As to what estate it has pleased God to intrust and bless me with, I will and dispose of it as follows: . . .

And I recommend to my sons and children to be kind, tender and affectionate to their mother, she having been always so to them, and not to suffer the infirmities of old age to abate the respect and regard they ought to pay to her. I heartily recommend to them a love and affection to each other, and that they will avoid, as much as may be done, all occasions of difference and distrust amongst themselves. And **I humbly pray the good God may always protect, direct and influence them to act as becomes them.**

What follows is a
summary of an article
from contemporary American life . . .

nearly 250 years after
Lewis Morris
signed

the Declaration of Independence.

What Would Lewis Morris Think?

Bibles Banned! VA Removes Good Book from Clinic

admin
Oct 19, 2016

By Todd Starnes |

Shockingly, someone left a Bible in the waiting room of the Chillicothe Veteran Affairs Medical Center in Athens, Ohio. When the Military Religious Freedom Foundation learned of this, it intervened to warn the medical center that the presence of the Bible was "illicit and unconstitutional."

How did the center respond? First, by scouring the building to ensure that no other Bibles were present. And, second, by assuring the MRFF that VA staff members "routinely have environment of care rounding teams that look for such material." In other words, "don't worry; it will never happen again." Said the center's associate chief, Adam Jackson, "[t]he Athens CBOC is unsure how this came into the clinic but it has been removed."

The Chaplain Alliance for Religious Liberty described the banning of the Bible at the VA as "absolutely ridiculous." It said, "There is nothing wrong with a Bible being left in the waiting room along with other reading materials. If someone doesn't want to look at the Bible, they don't have to look at it. But it can be there for someone who may want to look at it and may find it helpful in a time of crisis." Apparently, not any more.

https://www.toddstarnes.com/uncategorized/ bibles-banned-va-removes-good-book-from-clinic/.

Epilogue

So, America, now that you know something about our
Founding Fathers . . .

and have seen *In Their Own Words* what they believed . . .

What Would Our Founding Fathers Think
of Today's God-less America?

And what do *YOU* think?

Do you prefer the *Godly* America of our Founding Fathers?
Or the *God-less* America of today?
America, it's time to decide.

God Bless America

Further Reading

Want to read more?

Each of the Signers of:
The Declaration of Independence,
The Articles of Confederation, and
The United States Constitution
has a unique and compelling story.

In Their Own Words
VOLUME 1
THE NEW ENGLAND COLONIES
(Massachusetts, New Hampshire, Connecticut,
Rhode Island, New York)

VOLUME 2
THE MIDDLE COLONIES
(Pennsylvania, New Jersey, Delaware, Maryland)

VOLUME 3
THE SOUTHERN COLONIES
(Virginia, North Carolina, South Carolina, Georgia)

Read them all.

And then *YOU* decide.

What Would Our Founding Fathers Think?

Acknowledgements

O ne cannot undertake an effort of this sort without the support and encouragement of one's family. In my case, that principally means one person—my wife, Martha. As my champion and cheerleader, she was forced to also endure the lonely evenings and weekends when I was cloistered from her, doing the research and writing that has now become this book. I will be forever grateful. She also consented to my sharing the history of her grandfather, Congressman Louis Rabaut, and of his authorship of the "Under God" amendment to the Pledge of Allegiance, a narrative that dovetails seamlessly with the under-lying message of this book—that this country was founded on our Founders' fervent belief in God. To Congressman Rabaut, thank you for your service to our country, for your authorship of the "Under God" amendment, and for your perseverance in our Founding Fathers' vision for America.

I must also thank my parents, who knew that the most important thing in life was to instill in their children the moral values that would guide them and their own children long after they were gone. To my dad, a self-taught accountant, and my mom, a homemaker and sometimes "Avon lady," the education of their children—both academically and religiously—was paramount. Unlike them, I was able to attend college (and even law school), but before that was raised in Christian schools, with a church family, and by Christian parents. Those were foundational years, years that molded the core of my being and that enabled me to appreciate the value of our Founders' vision and the dangers of losing it.

Thanks also to those who have encouraged me along the way. To our kids, Adam Boonstra, Logan Boonstra, Katherine Gutwald, and Chea Jackson (and their families and significant others), thanks for supporting me. Read especially the chapter on Thomas Stone (of Maryland), and take note of his letter to his son. He said it better than I ever could. To my sister and brother-in-law, Beth and Steve Hammond—you were among the very few to preview early chapters. Thank you for your encouragement. Dave Kuehnl, I know that you are reading this in Heaven. Sorry it took me so long. Erin Milligan, thanks your insights and encouragement, which helped me persevere.

Thanks to the fine folks at Liberty Hill Publishing for believing in my message, and for providing an avenue to share it.

Thank you to our Founding Fathers—who founded our great nation, who assured us that our rights were given to us by God, and who bequeathed to us a society better than the one we have today. I'm pretty sure I know what you would think of today's God-less America.

Most of all, I thank God for showing me the way.

Notes

Chapter Two–Massachusetts Signers

John Adams

1   http://www.wallbuilders.com/libissuesarticles.asp?id=8755, citing John Adams, *The Works of John Adams, Second President of the United States*, Charles Francis Adams (ed.) (Boston: Little, Brown and Company, 1856), Vol. II, 6-7.

2   John Adams, *The Works of John Adams, Second President of the United States*, Charles Francis Adams (ed.) (Boston: Charles C. Little and James Brown, 1865), Vol. III, 448-449, 456-457, https://books.google.com/books?id=2ps8AAAAIAAJ&printsec=frontcover&source=gbs_ge_summary_r&cad=0#v=onepage&q&f=false.

3   http://www.masshist.org/digitaladams/archive/doc?id=L17760415ja, John Adams to Abigail Adams, April 15, 1776.

4   "From John Adams to Mercy Otis Warren, 16 April 1776," *Founders Online*, National Archives, https://founders.archives.gov/documents/Adams/06-04-02-0044. [Original source: *The Adams Papers*, Papers of John Adams, vol. 4, *February–August 1776*, ed. Robert J. Taylor. Cambridge, MA: Harvard University Press, 1979, pp. 123–126.].

5   "John Adams to Zabdiel Adams, 21 June 1776," *Founders Online*, National Archives, https://founders.archives.gov/documents/Adams/04-02-02-0011. [Original source: *The Adams Papers*, Adams Family Correspondence, vol. 2, *June 1776–March 1778*, ed. L. H. Butterfield. Cambridge, MA: Harvard University Press, 1963, pp. 20–21.].

6   *Current Literature, A Magazine of Record and Review*, Vol. XVIII, No. 1 (New York: The Current Literature Publishing Company, July 1895), 1, https://books.google.com/books?id=AbUGAQAAIAAJ&pg=PA1#v=onepage&q&f=false.

7   *Adams Family Correspondence*, Vol. 2, https://www.masshist.org/publications/apde2/view?id=ADMS-04-02-02-0016, John Adams to Abigail Adams, July 3, 1776.

8   David McCullough, *John Adams* (New York: Simon & Schuster Paperbacks, 2001), 160.

9   http://www.mass.gov/courts/court-info/sjc/edu-res-center/jn-adams/mass-constitution-1-gen.html.

10 John Adams, *The Works of John Adams, Second President of the United States*, Vol. III, 421.

11 "From John Adams to Massachusetts Militia, 11 October 1798," *Founders Online*, National Archives, https://founders.archives.gov/documents/Adams/99-02-02-3102. [This is an Early Access document from The Adams Papers. It is not an authoritative final version.].

12 John Adams, *The Works of John Adams, Second President of the United States*, Charles Francis Adams (ed.) (Boston: Little, Brown and Company, 1854), Vol. IX, 172-174, https://books.google.com/books?id=-Wh3AAAAMAA-J&printsec=frontcover&source=gbs_ge_summary_r&cad=0#v=onepage&q&f=false.

13 "From John Adams to Benjamin Rush, 28 August 1811," *Founders Online*, National Archives, https://founders.archives.gov/documents/Adams/99-02-02-5678. [This is an Early Access document from The Adams Papers. It is not an authoritative final version.].

14 http://www.wallbuilders.com/libissuesarticles.asp?id=8755, citing Thomas Jefferson, *The Writings of Thomas Jefferson* (Washington D. C.: The Thomas Jefferson Memorial Association, 1904), Vol. XIII, 292-294.

15 "From John Adams to Thomas Jefferson, 14 September 1813," *Founders Online*, National Archives, https://founders.archives.gov/documents/Adams/99-02-02-6152. [This is an Early Access document from The Adams Papers. It is not an authoritative final version.].

16 http://www.wallbuilders.com/libissuesarticles.asp?id=8755, citing John Adams, *The Works of John Adams, Second President of the United States*, Charles Francis Adams (ed.) (Boston: Little, Brown and Company, 1856), Vol. X, 85.

17 www.wallbuilders.com/libissuesarticles.asp?id=8755, citing John Adams, *The Works of John Adams, Second President of the United States*,

Charles Francis Adams (ed.) (Boston: Little, Brown and Company, 1856), Vol. X, 254.

18   "From John Adams to Thomas Jefferson, 8 December 1818," *Founders Online,* National Archives, https://founders.archives.gov/documents/ Adams/99-02-02-7039. [This is an Early Access document from The Adams Papers. It is not an authoritative final version.].

Samuel Adams

1   Mark Puls, *Samuel Adams, Father of the American Revolution* (New York: St. Martin's Press, 2006), 32, https://books.google.com/books?id=1B-jVCQAAQBAJ&printsec=frontcover&source=gbs_ge_summary_r&-cad=0#v=onepage&q&f=false.

2   Harry Alonzo Cushing (ed.), *The Writings of Samuel Adams* (New York: G. P. Putnam's Sons, 1906), Vol. II, 262, https://archive.org/stream/ writitngssamadam02adamrich#.

3   Harry Alonzo Cushing (ed.), *The Writings of Samuel Adams*, Vol. II, 336.

4   Ibid., 352-355.

5   William V. Wells, *The Life and Public Services of Samuel Adams* (Boston: Little, Brown, and Company, 1865), Vol. III, 407-422, https://books. google.com/books?id=KF0sAAAAMAAJ&printsec=frontcover&-source=gbs_ge_summary_r&cad=0#v=onepage&q&f=false.

6   *Letters of Delegates to Congress*, Vol. 5 (August 16, 1776–December 31, 1776), 669-670, https://memory.loc.gov/ammem/amlaw/lwdglink.html, from Samuel Adams to Elizabeth Adams, December 26, 1776.

7   William V. Wells, *The Life and Public Services of Samuel Adams* (Boston: Little, Brown, and Company, 1865), Vol. II, 492, https://books.google. com/books?id=vQ53AAAAMAAJ&printsec=frontcover&source=gbs_ ge_summary_r&cad=0#v=onepage&q&f=false.

8   Harry Alonzo Cushing (ed.), *The Writings of Samuel Adams* (New York: G. P. Putnam's Sons, 1906), Vol. IV, 311, https://books.google.com/ books?id=6pILAAAAIAAJ&printsec=frontcover&source=gbs_ge_ summary_r&cad=0#v=onepage&q&f=false.

9   Harry Alonzo Cushing (ed.), *The Writings of Samuel Adams*, Vol. IV, 314.

10   William V. Wells, *The Life and Public Services of Samuel Adams*, Vol. III, 379.

11   Ibid., 324-325.

12   http://www.wallbuilders.com/libissuesarticles.asp?id=43.

13   http://www.wallbuilders.com/libissuesarticles.asp?id=148957.

14   Harry Alonzo Cushing (ed.), *The Writings of Samuel Adams*, Vol. IV, 401-402.

Francis Dana

1   H.W.L. Dana, *The Dana Saga,: Three Centuries of the Dana Family in Cambridge* (Cambridge: The Cambridge Historical Society, 1941, 22-23, https://archive.org/details/danasagathreecen00dana/page/n11/mode/2up.

2   W. P. Cresson, *Francis Dana, A Puritan Diplomat at the Court of Catherine the Great* (New York: Lincoln Mac Veagh, The Dial Press, 1930), 67, https://archive.org/details/francisdanapurit00cres/page/n9/mode/2up.

3   W. P. Cresson, *Francis Dana, A Puritan Diplomat at the Court of Catherine the Great*, 70.

4   Ibid., 81.

5   Ibid., 90.

6   Ibid., 115.

7   Ibid., 128.

8   Ibid., 132.

9   Ibid., 135-136.

10   Ibid., 289.

11   Ibid., 291.

12   *Papers of John Adams*, Vol. 15, https://www.masshist.org/publications/adams-papers/index.php/view/ADMS-06-15-02-0079, from Francis Dana to John Adams, July 29, 1783.

13   W. P. Cresson, *Francis Dana, A Puritan Diplomat at the Court of Catherine the Great*, 378.

14   Ibid., 385.

Elbridge Gerry

1   http://consource.org/document/elbridge-gerry-to-ann-gerry-1787-8-14/, Elbridge Gerry to Ann Gerry, August 14, 1787.

2   Elbridge Gerry, "Observations," E. H. Scott, (ed.), *The Federalist and Other Constitutional Papers by Hamilton, Jay, Madison, and Other Statesmen of Their Time* (Chicago: Scott, Foresman and Company, 1902, 715, https://books.google.com/books?id=n8c4AQAAMAAJ&printsec=frontcover&source=gbs_ge_summary_r&cad=0#v=onepage&q&f=false.

3   http://www.wallbuilders.com/libissuesarticles.asp?id=8755#R30.

4   Ibid.

5   http://www.wallbuilders.com/libissuesarticles.asp?id=18292.

6   http://www.wallbuilders.com/libissuesarticles.asp?id=8755#R30.

Nathaniel Gorham

1   Richard Frothingham. Jr., *The History of Charlestown, Massachusetts* (Boston: Charles C. Little and James Brown, 1845), 288, https://books.google.com/books?id=8bNIAQAAMAAJ&printsec=frontcover&source=gbs_ge_summary_r&cad=0#v=onepage&q&f=false.

2   Richard Frothingham. Jr., *The History of Charlestown, Massachusetts*, 300.

3   https://www.constitutionfacts.com/us-constitution-amendments/the-constitutional-convention/.

4   William V. Wells, *The Life and Public Services of Samuel Adams* (Boston: Little, Brown, and Company, 1865), Vol. III, 167-168, https://books.google.com/books?id=KF0sAAAAMAAJ&printsec=frontcover&source=gbs_ge_summary_r&cad=0#v=onepage&q&f=false.

John Hancock

1   *The Journals of Each Provincial Congress of Massachusetts in 1774 and 1775, and of the Committee of Safety*, (Boston: Dutton and Wentworth, Printers to the State, 1838), 91-93, https://archives.lib.state.ma.us/handle/2452/795664.

2   *The Journals of Each Provincial Congress of Massachusetts in 1774 and 1775, and of the Committee of Safety*, 144-145.

3   "Incidents in the Life of John Hancock, As Related by Dorothy Quincy
     Hancock Scott [From the Diary of General William H. Sumner]," Martha,
     J. Lamb (ed.), *Magazine of American History*, Vol. XIX (January–June,
     1888), 509-510, https://books.google.com/books?id=n882AQAAMAA-
     J&printsec=frontcover&source=gbs_ge_summary_r&cad=0#v=onep-
     age&q&f=false.

4   Peter Force, *American Archives: Containing a Documentary History of the
     English Colonies in North America* (Washington: M. St. Clair Clarke
     and Peter Force, 1851), Vol. II, 233, https://books.google.com/
     books?id=pLEzAQAAMAAJ&printsec=frontcover&source=gbs_ge_
     summary_r&cad=0#v=onepage&q&f=false.

5   http://www.wallbuilders.com/libissuesarticles.asp?id=121, citing
     Independent Chronicle (Boston), November 2, 1780, last page; and Abram
     English Brown, *John Hancock, His Book* (Boston: Lee and Shepard,
     1898), p. 269.

6   http://www.wallbuilders.com/libissuesarticles.asp?id=148952.

7   http://www.wallbuilders.com/libissuesarticles.asp?id=18294.

8   Sandi Bradley, *The Faith of the Founders*, The Federalist Papers
     Project, 47, http://www.thefederalistpapers.org/founders/
     the-faith-of-the-founding-fathers-by-sandi-bradley-free-ebook.

Samuel Holten

1   http://www.wallbuilders.com/libissuesarticles.asp?id=154173.

2   Abram English Brown, *Beside Old Hearth-Stones* (Boston: Lee and Shepard
     Publishers, 1897), 218, https://books.google.com/books?id=iyvSJ7dxq-
     isC&printsec=frontcover&source=gbs_ge_summary_r&cad=0#v=onep-
     age&q&f=false.

3   A.C. Goodell, "Additions and Corrections to: A Biographical Notice
     of the Officers of Probate for Essex County, from the Commencement
     of the Colony to the Present Time," *Historical Collections of the Essex
     Institute*, Vol. IV, No. 6 (Salem: G.M. Whipple & A.A. Smith, 1862),
     268-269, https://books.google.com/books?id=DSFEAQAAMAAJ&p-
     g=RA1-PA268&lpg#v=onepage&q&f=false.

4   *The Celebration of the One Hundred and Fiftieth Anniversary of the
     Establishment of the Town of Danvers, Massachusetts, as a Separate
     Municipality, June 15, 16, 17, 1902*, Printed by Vote of the Town (Boston:
     The Fort Hill Press, 1907), 188-189, https://books.google.com/

books?id=GWoWAAAAYAAJ&printsec=frontcover&source=gbs_ge_
summary_r&cad=0#v=onepage&q&f=false.

5   *Letters of Delegates to Congress*, Vol. 21 (October 1, 1783–October
     31, 1784), https://memory.loc.gov/cgi-bin/query/r?ammem/hlaw:@
     field(DOCID+@lit(dg0219)), Samuel Holten to Luke Webster, October
     2, 1783.

6   *Letters of Delegates to Congress*, Vol. 21, Samuel Holten to John Kettell,
     October 9, 1783.

Rufus King

1   Charles R. King (ed.), *The Life and Correspondence of Rufus King*, Vol.
     II (New York: G.P. Putnam's Sons, 1895), 33-34, https://archive.org/
     stream/rufuskingcorresp02kingrich#page/n9/mode/2up.

2   Charles R. King (ed.), *The Life and Correspondence of Rufus King*, Vol. III
     (New York: G.P. Putnam's Sons, 1896), 22, https://archive.org/stream/
     rufuskinglife03kingrich#page/n9/mode/2up.

3   Charles R. King (ed.), *The Life and Correspondence of Rufus King,* Vol. V
     (New York: G.P. Putnam's Sons, 1898), 103-104, https://archive.org/
     stream/lifecorresponden05king#page/n11/mode/2up.

4   Charles R. King (ed.), *The Life and Correspondence of Rufus King,* Vol. VI
     (New York: G.P. Putnam's Sons, 1900), 276, https://archive.org/stream/
     cu31924067113880#page/n11/mode/2up.

5   Charles R. King (ed.), *The Life and Correspondence of Rufus King*, Vol. VI,
     276-277.

6   Nathaniel H. Carter and William L. Stone, *Reports of the Proceedings and
     Debates of the Convention of 1821, Assembled for the Purpose of Amending The
     Constitution of the State of New York* (Albany: E. and E. Hosford, 1821), 575,
     https://archive.org/stream/reportsofproceed00newy#page/n9/mode/2up.

7   Charles R. King (ed.), *The Life and Correspondence of Rufus King*, Vol.
     VI, 677.

James Lovell

1   James Lovell, "An Oration, Delivered April 2d, 1771" (Boston: Edes
     and Gill, 1771), *The Annotated Newspapers of Harbottle Dorr, Jr.*, Vol. 3, 1009,
     1020, http://www.masshist.org/dorr/volume/3/sequence/1038.

2   *Some Papers Laid Before the Continental Congress, 1776: Taken from Volumes 4-6 of the Journals of the Continental Congress Issued by the Library of Congress* (Washington, Government Printing Office, 1906), 57, https://books.google.com/books?id=y1hYAAAcAAJ&pg=PA57&lpg#v=onepage&q&f=false.

3   Edmund C. Burnett (ed.), *Letters of Members of the Continental Congress*, Vol. II (Washington, DC: Carnegie Institute of Washington, 1923), 366-368, https://archive.org/stream/lettersofmembers02burn#page/n5/mode/2up

4   Edmund C. Burnett (ed.), *Letters of Members of the Continental Congress*, Vol. III (Washington, DC: Carnegie Institute of Washington, 1926), 470, https://archive.org/stream/lettersofmembers03burn#page/n5/mode/2up.

5   Edmund C. Burnett (ed.), *Letters of Members of the Continental Congress*, Vol. IV (Washington, DC: Carnegie Institute of Washington, 1928), 323, https://archive.org/stream/lettersofmember04burn#page.

6   Edmund C. Burnett (ed.), *Letters of Members of the Continental Congress*, Vol. V (Washington, DC: Carnegie Institute of Washington, 1931), 259, https://archive.org/stream/lettersofmember05burn#page/.

Robert Treat Paine

1   http://www.wallbuilders.com/libissuesarticles.asp?id=8755#R85, citing Robert Treat Paine, *The Papers of Robert Treat Paine*, Stephen T. Riley and Edward W. Hanson, editors (Boston: Massachusetts Historical Society, 1992), Vol. I, p. 49.

2   Paul H. Smith (ed.), *Letters of Delegates to Congress, 1774-1789*, May 16–August 15, 1776 (Washington: Library of Congress, 1979), 399, https://archive.org/stream/lettersofdelegat04smit#page/n3/mode/2up.

3   http://www.wallbuilders.com/libissuesarticles.asp?id=8755#R85, citing Last Will & Testament of Robert Treat Paine, attested May 11, 1814.

Chapter Three—New Hampshire Signers

Josiah Bartlett

1   Frank C. Mevers (ed.), *The Papers of Josiah Bartlett* (Hanover, New Hampshire: Published for the New Hampshire Historical Society by the University Press of New England, 1979), 75, https://books.google.

com/books?id=CmLRlCAB1OsC&printsec=frontcover&source=gbs_
ge_summary_r&cad=0#v=onepage&q&f=false.

2 Frank C. Mevers (ed.), *The Papers of Josiah Bartlett*, 77-78.

3 Ibid., 93-94.

4 Ibid., 137-138.

5 Ibid., 161.

6 Ibid., 199.

7 Ibid., 268-269.

8 Ibid., 324.

9 Ibid., 349.

10 Ibid., 355-356.

11 http://www.wallbuilders.com/LIBissuesArticles.asp?id=17865.

12 Frank C. Mevers (ed.), *The Papers of Josiah Bartlett*, 409.

Nicholas Gilman

1 *Letters of Delegates to Congress*, Vol. 24 (November 6, 1786-February 29, 1788), 531, https://memory.loc.gov/ammem/amlaw/lwdglink.html, Nicholas Gilman to John Langdon, October 30, 1787.

2 *Journal of the House of Representatives of the United States, 1789-1793*, Monday, April 6, 1789, https://memory.loc.gov/cgi-bin/query/r?ammem/hlaw:@field(DOCID+@lit(hj00130)):.

3 *Journal of the House of Representatives of the United States, 1793-1797*, Thursday, December 15, 1796, https://memory.loc.gov/cgi-bin/query/r?ammem/hlaw:@field(DOCID+@lit(hj002386)):.

4 *Journal of the Senate of the United States of America, 1789-1873*. Friday, July 16, 1813, https://memory.loc.gov/cgi-bin/query/r?ammem/hlaw:@field(DOCID+@lit(sj005337)):.

John Langdon

1 Charles R. Corning, *John Langdon* (Concord: Rumford Printing Company, 1903), 18, https://books.google.com/

books?id=cWvmHlUZUdEC&printsec=titlepage&source=gbs_sum-mary_r&hl=en#v=onepage&q&f=false.

2   Lawrence Shaw Mayo, *John Langdon of New Hampshire* (Concord, N.H.: The Rumford Press, 1937), 271, https://babel.hathitrust.org/cgi/pt?id=mdp.39015011257444&view=1up&seq=1.

3   http://www.wallbuilders.com/libissuesarticles.asp?id=133308.

4   Lawrence Shaw Mayo, *John Langdon of New Hampshire*, 264-265.

5   http://www.wallbuilders.com/libissuesarticles.asp?id=17936.

6   "John Langdon to Thomas Jefferson, 18 February 1810," *Founders Online,* National Archives, https://founders.archives.gov/documents/Jefferson/03-02-02-0191. [Original source: *The Papers of Thomas Jefferson*, Retirement Series, vol. 2, *16 November 1809 to 11 August 1810*, ed. J. Jefferson Looney. Princeton: Princeton University Press, 2005, pp. 230–232.].

7   Charles R. Corning, "John Langdon," *The New England Magazine*, New Series, Vol. XVI, No. 5 (Boston, Mass.: Warren F. Kellogg, Publisher, July, 1897), 630, https://books.google.com/books?id=zapJAQAAMAA-J&printsec=frontcover&source=gbs_ge_summary_r&cad=0#v=onepage&q&f=false.

8   http://www.wallbuilders.com/libissuesarticles.asp?id=78.

Matthew Thornton

1   Charles Thornton Adams, *Matthew Thornton of New Hampshire, A Patriot of the American Revolution* (Philadelphia, Penn.: Dando Printing and Publishing Co., 1903), 23-26, http://lcweb2.loc.gov/service/gdc/scd0001/2006/20061013008ma/20061013008ma.pdf.

2   Charles Thornton Adams, *Matthew Thornton of New Hampshire, A Patriot of the American Revolution*, 26-28.

3   Ibid., 55.

4   Ibid., 57.

5   Ibid., 58.

John Wentworth Jr.

1   "Sketch of Hon. John Wentworth, Jr." *Collections of the New-Hampshire Historical Society*, Vol. V (Concord: Printed by Asa McFarland for the Society, 1837), 243, https://books.google.com/books?id=V2QSAAAAYAAJ&printsec=frontcover&source=gbs_ge_summary_r&cad=0#v=onepage&q&f=false.

2   Ezra S. Stearns (ed.), *Genealogical and Family History of the State of New Hampshire*, Vol. III (New York and Chicago: Lewis Publishing Company, 1908), 1313, https://books.google.com/books?id=EthxO9RvKw-8C&printsec=frontcover&source=gbs_ge_summary_r&cad=0#v=onepage&q&f=false.

3   John Wentworth, *The Wentworth Genealogy: English and American*, Vol. I (Boston: Little, Brown and Company, 1878), 72-73, https://books.google.com/books?id=PypAAAAAYAAJ&printsec=frontcover&source=gbs_ge_summary_r&cad=0#v=onepage&q&f=false.

4   John Wentworth, *The Wentworth Genealogy: English and American*, Vol. I, 74-76.

5   Ibid., 77-78.

6   Ibid., 209-216.

7   Ibid., 374.

8   Ibid., 376-378.

9   Ibid., 379.

10 Henry G. Wheeler, *History of Congress: Biographical and Political*, Vol. II (New York: Harper & Brothers, Publishers, 1848), 534-535, https://books.google.com/books?id=vvw-AAAAYAAJ&printsec=frontcover&source=gbs_ge_summary_r&cad=0#v=onepage&q&f=false.

William Whipple

1   Massachusetts Historical Society, *Proceedings of the Massachusetts Historical Society*, April 1860 (Boston: John Wilson and Son, 1862), 3-4, https://books.google.com/books?id=9-J4gNnwibgC&printsec=frontcover&source=gbs_ge_summary_r&cad=0#v=onepage&q&f=false.

2   Paul H. Smith (ed.), *Letters of Delegates to Congress, 1774-1789*, May 16–August 15, 1776 (Washington: Library of Congress, 1979), 30-31, https://archive.org/stream/lettersofdelegat04smit#page/n3/mode/2up.

3   Paul H. Smith (ed.), *Letters of Delegates to Congress, 1774-1789*, 119.

4   Peter Force, *American Archives: Containing a Documentary History of the English Colonies in North America*, Vol. VI, (Washington: M. St. Clair Clarke and Peter Force, 1846), 708-709, https://books.google.com/books?id=yGlAAAAcAAJ&printsec=frontcover&source=gbs_ge_summary_r&cad=0#v=onepage&q&f=false.

5   Paul H. Smith (ed.), *Letters of Delegates to Congress, 1774-1789*, 300-301.

6   Paul H. Smith (ed.), *Letters of Delegates to Congress, 1774-1789*, 310.

7   Paul H. Smith (ed.), *Letters of Delegates to Congress, 1774-1789*, 413-414.

8   *Letters by Josiah Bartlett, William Whipple, and Others, Written Before and During the Revolution* (Philadelphia: Press of Henry B. Ashmead, 1889), 53, https://books.google.com/books?id=T4ZDAQAAMAAJ&printsec=-frontcover&source=gbs_ge_summary_r&cad=0#v=onepage&q&f=false.

9   William A. Sargent (ed.), *Maine Wills, 1640-1760* (Portland: Brown Thurston & Company, 1887), 41-42, https://archive.org/stream/cu31924081314852#page/n5/mode/2up.

Chapter Four–Connecticut Signers

Andrew Adams

1   http://www.jud.ct.gov/external/kids/cj/adams.htm.

2   *Letters of Delegates to Congress*, Vol. 10 (June 1, 1778–September 30, 1778), 574-575, https://memory.loc.gov/ammem/amlaw/lwdglink.html, from Andrew Adams to Andrew Adams Jr., undated.

3   Dwight C. Kilbourn, *Bench and Bar of Litchfield County, Connecticut, 1709-1909*, 217 (1909), https://www.cga.ct.gov/hco/books/The_Bench_and_Bar_of_Litchfield_County.pdf.

Titus Hosmer

1   "Silas Dean Papers," Box 1, Folder 15, *The Connecticut Digital Archive Collections*, http://collections.ctdigitalarchive.org/islandora/object/40002%3A2442#page/2/mode/2up.

2   "The Trumbull Papers," *Collections of the Massachusetts Historical Society*, Seventh Series–Vol. II (Boston: 1902), 256-257, https://books.google.com/books?id=vO9BAAAAYAAJ&printsec=frontcover&source=gbs_ge_summary_r&cad=0#v=onepage&q&f=false.

3   Joel Barlow, "An Elegy &c." (Ann Arbor: Text Creation Partnership, 2011), http://quod.lib.umich.edu/e/evans/N13211.0001.001/1:3?rgn=div1;view=fulltext.

4   David D. Field, DD, *Centennial Address* (Middletown, Conn.: William B. Casey, 1853), 98-99, https://quod.lib.umich.edu/m/moa/AAS0095.0001.001?rgn=main;view=fulltext.

Samuel Huntington

1   Sandi Bradley, *The Faith of the Founders,* The Federalist Papers Project, 53, http://www.thefederalistpapers.org/founders/the-faith-of-the-founding-fathers-by-sandi-bradley-free-ebook.

2   http://www.wallbuilders.com/libissuesarticles.asp?id=4084.

3   http://www.wallbuilders.com/libissuesarticles.asp?id=131292.

4   https://wallbuilders.com/founding-fathers-jesus-christianity-bible/.

William Samuel Johnson

1   E. Edwards Beardsley, *Life and Times of William Samuel Johnson, LL.D* (New York: Hurd and Houghton, 1876), 56, http://books.google.com/books?id=rdmfGCDg6YIC&printsec=titlepage#v=onepage&q&f=false.

2   E. Edwards Beardsley, *Life and Times of William Samuel Johnson, LL.D*, 66-68.

3   Ibid., 184, 200-201.

4   Ibid., 141-145.

Roger Sherman

1   Lewis Henry Boutell, *The Life of Roger Sherman* (Chicago: A. C. McClurg and Company, 1896), 46, https://archive.org/details/liferogersherma01boutgoog/page/n12/mode/2up.

2   Lewis Henry Boutell, *The Life of Roger Sherman*, 271-273.

3   Ibid., 269.

4   http://www.wallbuilders.com/libissuesarticles.asp?id=8755#R105, citing *Correspondence Between Roger Sherman and Samuel Hopkins* (Worcester, MA: Charles Hamilton, 1889), 9-10, from Roger Sherman to Samuel Hopkins, June 28, 1790.

5   http://www.wallbuilders.com/libissuesarticles.asp?id=8755#R105, citing *Correspondence Between Roger Sherman and Samuel Hopkins*, 26, from Roger Sherman to Samuel Hopkins, October 1790.

6   Boutell, 286-287.

7   http://www.wallbuilders.com/libissuesarticles.asp?id=8755#R105, *The Globe* (Washington DC newspaper), August 15, 1837, 1.

William Williams

1   *Letters of Delegates to Congress*, Vol. 5 (August 16, 1776–December 31, 1776), 156-157, https://memory.loc.gov/ammem/amlaw/lwdglink.html, from William Williams to Joseph Trumbull, September 13, 1776.

2   *Letters of Delegates to Congress*, Vol. 5, 208-212, from William Williams to Jonathan Trumbull Sr., September 20, 1776.

3   *Letters of Delegates to Congress*, Vol. 7 (May 1, 1777–September 18, 1777), 301-303, https://memory.loc.gov/ammem/amlaw/lwdglink.html, from William Williams to Jonathan Trumbull Sr., July 5, 1777.

4   *Letters of Delegates to Congress*, Vol. 7, 406-408, from William Williams to Jonathan Trumbull Sr., August 2, 1777.

5   Ibid., 558-559, from William Williams to Jonathan Trumbull Sr., August 26, 1777.

6   Ibid., 657-660, from William Williams to Jonathan Trumbull Sr., September 13, 1777.

7   *Letters of Delegates to Congress*, Vol. 8 (September 19, 1777–January 31, 1778), 34-36, https://memory.loc.gov/ammem/amlaw/lwdglink.html, from William Williams to Jonathan Trumbull Sr., September 30, 1777.

8   *Letters of Delegates to Congress*, Vol. 8, 44, from William Williams to Jonathan Trumbull Sr., October 2, 1777.

9   Ibid., 106-107, from William Williams to Jonathan Trumbull Sr., October 11, 1777.

10   Ibid., 197, from William Williams to Jonathan Trumbull Sr., October 26, 1777.

11   Paul Leicester Ford (ed.), *Essays on the Constitution of the United States, Published during Its Discussion by the People*, 1787-1788 (Brooklyn, N.Y.: Historical Printing Club, 1892), 207-209, https://archive.org/stream/EssaysOnTheConstitutionOfTheUnitedStates#page/n1/mode/2up, from William Williams to Mr. Babcock, February 11, 1788.

Oliver Wolcott

1   *Letters of Delegates to Congress*, Vol. 3 (January 1, 1776–May 15, 1776), 502-503, https://memory.loc.gov/ammem/amlaw/lwdglink.html, from Oliver Wolcott to Laura Wolcott, April 10, 1776.

2   *Letters of Delegates to Congress*, Vol. 5 (August 16, 1776–December 31, 1776), 605-607, https://memory.loc.gov/ammem/amlaw/lwdglink.html, from Oliver Wolcott to Laura Wolcott, December 13, 1776.

3   https://www.loc.gov/resource/rbpe.00400800/?sp=1.

4   http://www.litchfieldhistoricalsociety.org/library/families/wolcott_oliver.php.

5   Jonathan Elliot, *The Debates in the Several State Conventions on the Adoption of the Federal Constitution, as Recommended by the General Convention at Philadelphia in 1787,* Vol. II (Philadelphia: J. B. Lippincott Company, 1901), 201-202, https://books.google.com/books?id=WYxKAAAAYAA-J&printsec=frontcover&source=gbs_ge_summary_r&cad=0#v=onepage&q&f=false.

Chapter Five–Rhode Island Signers

John Collins

1   Irwin H. Polishook, "The Collins-Richardson Fracas of 1787," *Rhode Island History*, Vol. 22, No. 4, 117-121 (The Rhode Island Historical Society, October 1963), https://www.yumpu.com/en/document/read/34033565/untitled-rhode-island-historical-society, citing Collins to Ward, Newport, July 17, 1774, Gratz Collection, Mss., Historical Society of Pennsylvania, Case 1, Box 4 (A copy of this letter may be

found among the Ward Manuscripts, Rhode Island Historical Society, Box II, 1771-1775).

2   John Russell Bartlett (ed.), *Records of the State of Rhode Island and Providence Plantations in New England*, Vol. X (1784-1792) (Providence: Printed by the Providence Press Company 1865), 258-259, https://www.google.com/books/edition/Records_of_the_Colony_of_Rhode_Island_an/FVZOAQAAMAAJ?hl=en&gbpv=1.

3   John Russell Bartlett (ed.), *Records of the State of Rhode Island and Providence Plantations in New England*, Vol. X (1784-1792), 262.

William Ellery

1   *Letters of Delegates to Congress*, Vol. 4 (May 16, 1776–August 15, 1776), 429-430, https://memory.loc.gov/ammem/amlaw/lwdglink.html, from William Ellery Jr. to Benjamin Ellery, July 10, 1776.

2   *Letters of Delegates to Congress*, Vol. 5 (August 16, 1776–December 31, 1776), 653-656, https://memory.loc.gov/ammem/amlaw/lwdglink.html, from William Ellery Jr. to Nicholas Cooke, December 24, 1776.

3   *Letters of Delegates to Congress*, Vol. 9 (February 1, 1778–May 31, 1778), 300-302, https://memory.loc.gov/ammem/amlaw/lwdglink.html, from William Ellery Jr. to William Vernon, March 16, 1778.

4   *Letters of Delegates to Congress*, Vol. 10 (June 1, 1778–September 30, 1778), 199-200, https://memory.loc.gov/ammem/amlaw/lwdglink.html, from William Ellery Jr. to William Greene, June 27, 1778.

5   *Letters of Delegates to Congress*, Vol. 11 (October 1, 1778–January 31, 1779), 517-518, https://memory.loc.gov/ammem/amlaw/lwdglink.html, from William Ellery Jr. to Christoper Ellery, January 26, 1779.

6   *Letters of Delegates to Congress*, Vol. 12 (February 1, 1779–May 31, 1779), 441-442, https://memory.loc.gov/ammem/amlaw/lwdglink.html, from William Ellery Jr. to William Greene, May 8, 1779.

7   "To John Adams from the Second Congregational Church of Newport, Rhode Island, 26 May 1783," Founders Online, National Archives, https://founders.archives.gov/documents/Adams/06-14-02-0314. [Original source: The Adams Papers, Papers of John Adams, vol. 14, October 1782–May 1783, ed. Gregg L. Lint, C. James Taylor, Hobson Woodward, Margaret A. Hogan, Mary T. Claffey, Sara B. Sikes, and

Judith S. Graham. Cambridge, MA: Harvard University Press, 2008, pp. 498–501.].

8   *Letters of Delegates to Congress*, Vol. 22 (November 1, 1784–November 6, 1785), 145-146, https://memory.loc.gov/ammem/amlaw/lwdglink.html, from William Ellery Jr. to Christopher Ellery, January, 1785.

9   William Henry Channing (ed.), *Memoir of William Ellery Channing: With Extracts from His Correspondence and Manuscripts*, Vol. I (Boston: Wm. Crosby and H. P. Nichols, 1848), 8, https://books.google.com/books?id=L40EAAAAYAAJ&printsec=frontcover&source=gbs_ge_summary_r&cad=0#v=onepage&q&f=false.

10 https://www.god-and-country.info/WEllery.html, Letter from William Ellery Jr. to Rev. William Ellery Channing, June 10, 1806.

11 https://historyswomen.com/early-america/abigail-carey-ellery/.

Stephen Hopkins

1   Edward Field (ed.), *State of Rhode Island and Providence Plantations at the End of the Century: A History*, Volume One (Boston & Syracuse: The Mason Publishing Company, 1902), 434, https://books.google.com/books?id=hc5lSIofA3YC&printsec=frontcover&source=gbs_ge_summary_r&cad=0#v=onepage&q&f=false.

2   The Rhode Island Historical Society, https://www.rihs.org/collection_item/by-the-honorable-stephen-hopkins-esq-governor-of-rhode-island-a-proclamation-the-burthens-and-calamities-of-a-cruel-and-expensive-war-having-been-happily-terminated-by-a-just-and-gloriou/.

3   Stephen Hopkins, "*The Rights of the Colonies Examined*," https://teachingamericanhistory.org/library/document/the-rights-of-the-colonies-examined/.

4   https://www.sethkaller.com/item/807-Four-Years-Prior-to-Signing-the-Declaration,-R.I.'s-Stephen-Hopkins-Declares-His-Slave's-Independence.

5   http://www.gaspee.org/StephenHopkins.htm, Letter from Stephen Hopkins (and Others) to Samuel Adams, December 25, 1772.

6   *Letters of Delegates to Congress*, Vol. 2 (September 1775–December 1775), 351, https://memory.loc.gov/ammem/amlaw/lwdglink.html, from Stephen Hopkins to Ruth Hopkins, November 15, 1775.

7   *Letters of Delegates to Congress*, Vol. 2, 469, from Stephen Hopkins to Ruth Hopkins, December 9, 1775.

Henry Marchant

1   David S. Lovejoy, "Henry Marchant and the Mistress of the World," *The William and Mary Quarterly*, Vol. 12, No. 3 (July 1955) (Williamsburg, VA: Omohundro Institute of Early American History and Culture, July 1955), 398, https://www.jstor.org/stable/1917100.

2   John N. Cole, "Henry Marchant's Journal, 1771-1772," *Rhode Island History*, Vol. 57, No. 2 (Providence: The Rhode Island Historical Society, May 1999), 41, http://www.rihs.org/assetts/files/publications/1999_May.pdf.

3   John N. Cole, "Henry Marchant's Journal, 1771-1772," *Rhode Island History*, Vol. 57, No. 2, 42.

4   Ibid.

5   Ibid, 53.

6   *Letters of Delegates to Congress*, Vol. 7 (May 1, 1777–September 18, 1777), 601, https://memory.loc.gov/ammem/amlaw/lwdglink.html, from Henry Marchant to Nicholas Cooke, September 3, 1777.

7   *Letters of Delegates to Congress*, Vol. 7, 646, from Henry Marchant to Sarah Marchant, September 9, 1777.

8   *Letters of Delegates to Congress*, Vol. 10 (June 1, 1778–September 30, 1778), 324-325, https://memory.loc.gov/ammem/amlaw/lwdglink.html, from Henry Marchant to His Children (Sally, Betsy, and Billy Marchant), July 20, 1778.

9   *Letters of Delegates to Congress*, Vol. 10, 386, from Henry Marchant to William Green, August 3, 1778.

10 Ibid., 431, from Henry Marchant to the Rhode Island Assembly.

11 Ibid., 664-667, from Henry Marchant to Robert Treat Paine.

12 *Letters of Delegates to Congress*, Vol. 13 (June 1, 1779–September 30, 1779), 408, https://memory.loc.gov/ammem/amlaw/lwdglink.html, from Henry Marchant to General Horatio Gates, August 24, 1779.

13 "To John Adams from the Second Congregational Church of Newport, Rhode Island, 26 May 1783," Founders Online, National Archives, https://founders.archives.gov/documents/Adams/06-14-02-0314. [Original source: The Adams Papers, Papers of John Adams, vol. 14,

October 1782–May 1783, ed. Gregg L. Lint, C. James Taylor, Hobson Woodward, Margaret A. Hogan, Mary T. Claffey, Sara B. Sikes, and Judith S. Graham. Cambridge, MA: Harvard University Press, 2008, pp. 498–501.].

Chapter Six–New York Signers

James Duane

[1] *Letters of Delegates to Congress*, Vol. 1 (August 1774–August 1775), 392, https://memory.loc.gov/ammem/amlaw/lwdglink.html, James Duane's Notes for a Speech in Congress, May 23, 1775.

[2] *Letters of Delegates to Congress*, Vol. 1, 453, from James Duane to Robert Livingston, June 7, 1775.

[3] *Letters of Delegates to Congress*, Vol. 8 (September 19, 1777–January 31, 1778), 46, https://memory.loc.gov/ammem/amlaw/lwdglink.html, from James Duane to George Clinton, October 3, 1777.

[4] *Letters of Delegates to Congress*, Vol. 8, 303, from James Duane to John McKesson, November 22, 1777.

[5] *Letters of Delegates to Congress*, Vol. 11 (October 1, 1778–January 31, 1779), 462-463, https://memory.loc.gov/ammem/amlaw/lwdglink.html, from James Duane to Mary Duane, January 14, 1779.

[6] *Letters of Delegates to Congress*, Vol. 12 (February 1, 1779–May 31, 1779), 259, https://memory.loc.gov/ammem/amlaw/lwdglink.html, from James Duane to Mary Duane, March 29, 1779.

[7] *Letters of Delegates to Congress*, Vol. 13 (June 1, 1779–September 30, 1779), 276, https://memory.loc.gov/ammem/amlaw/lwdglink.html, from James Duane to Mary Duane, July 21, 1779.

[8] *Letters of Delegates to Congress*, Vol. 19 (August 1, 1782–March 11, 1783), 250, https://memory.loc.gov/ammem/amlaw/lwdglink.html, from James Duane to George Washington, October 12, 1782.

[9] *Letters of Delegates to Congress*, Vol. 21 (October 1, 1783–October 31, 1784), 22, https://memory.loc.gov/ammem/amlaw/lwdglink.html, from James Duane to Mary Duane, October 6, 1783.

[10] "To George Washington from James Duane, 8 April 1794," *Founders Online*, National Archives, https://founders.archives.gov/documents/Washington/05-15-02-0424. [Original source: *The Papers of George*

Notes

Washington, Presidential Series, vol. 15, *1 January–30 April 1794*, ed. Christine Sternberg Patrick. Charlottesville: University of Virginia Press, 2009, pp. 540–541.].

11 https://www.findagrave.com/memorial/7650682/james-duane.

William Duer

1 *Letters of Delegates to Congress*, Vol. 6 (January 1, 1777–April 30, 1777), 602, https://memory.loc.gov/ammem/amlaw/lwdglink.html, from William Duer to the New York Convention, April 17, 1777.

2 *Letters of Delegates to Congress*, Vol. 7 (May 1, 1777–September 18, 1777), 140, https://memory.loc.gov/ammem/amlaw/lwdglink.html, from William Duer to Robert R. Livingston, May 28, 1777.

3 *Letters of Delegates to Congress*, Vol. 7, 390, from William Duer to Philip Schuyler, July 29, 1777.

4 *Letters of Delegates to Congress* Vol. 9 (February 1, 1778–May 31, 1778), 102, https://memory.loc.gov/ammem/amlaw/lwdglink.html, from William Duer to Francis Lightfoot, February 14, 1778.

5 *Letters of Delegates to Congress*, Vol. 9, 224, from William Duer to Robert Morris, March 5, 1778.

6 Ibid., 254, from William Duer to Robert R. Livingston, March 10, 1778.

William Floyd

1 *Journals of the Continental Congress, 1774-1789*, Vol. 1, 106-113, https://memory.loc.gov/cgi-bin/query/r?ammem/hlaw:@field(DOCID+@lit(jc00142)).

2 *Journals of the Continental Congress, 1774-1789*, Vol. 1, 119-120.

3 *Letters of Delegates to Congress*, Vol. 14 (October 1, 1779–March 31, 1780), 290, https://memory.loc.gov/ammem/amlaw/lwdglink.html, from William Duer to George Clinton, December 21, 1779.

4 *Letters of Delegates to Congress*, Vol. 14, from William Duer to George Clinton, January 28, 1780.

5 *Journal of the House of Representatives of the United States, 1789-1793*, September 25, 1789, 123, https://memory.loc.gov/cgi-bin/query/r?ammem/hlaw:@field(DOCID+@lit(hj001169)).

Alexander Hamilton

1 "From Alexander Hamilton to The Royal Danish American Gazette, 6 September 1772," *Founders Online*, National Archives, https://founders. archives.gov/documents/Hamilton/01-01-02-0042. [Original source: *The Papers of Alexander Hamilton*, vol. 1, *1768–1778*, ed. Harold C. Syrett. New York: Columbia University Press, 1961, pp. 34–38.].

2 "The Soul ascending into Bliss, In humble imitation of Popes Dying Christian to his Soul, [17 October 1772]," *Founders Online*, National Archives, https://founders.archives.gov/documents/ Hamilton/01-01-02-0043. [Original source: *The Papers of Alexander Hamilton*, vol. 1, *1768–1778*, ed. Harold C. Syrett. New York: Columbia University Press, 1961, pp. 38–39.].

3 "*The Farmer Refuted*, &c., [23 February] 1775," *Founders Online*, National Archives, https://founders.archives.gov/documents/ Hamilton/01-01-02-0057. [Original source: *The Papers of Alexander Hamilton*, vol. 1, *1768–1778*, ed. Harold C. Syrett. New York: Columbia University Press, 1961, pp. 81–165.].

4 "From Alexander Hamilton to Elizabeth Schuyler, [8 August 1780]," *Founders Online*, National Archives, https://founders.archives.gov/docu-ments/Hamilton/01-02-02-0808. [Original source: *The Papers of Alexander Hamilton*, vol. 2, *1779–1781*, ed. Harold C. Syrett. New York: Columbia University Press, 1961, pp. 374–375.].

5 John C. Hamilton, The Life of Alexander Hamilton, Vol. I (London: Taylor, Printer, 1834), 378, https://books.google.com/books?id=O-V9iAAAAcAAJ&printsec=frontcover&source=gbs_ge_summary_r&-cad=0#v=onepage&q&f=false.

6 "From Alexander Hamilton to Elizabeth Hamilton, [15–18 September 1781]," *Founders Online*, National Archives, https://founders.archives. gov/documents/Hamilton/01-02-02-1196. [Original source: *The Papers of Alexander Hamilton*, vol. 2, *1779–1781*, ed. Harold C. Syrett. New York: Columbia University Press, 1961, pp. 675–676.].

7 E. H. Scott (ed.), *The Federalist and Other Constitutional Papers* (Chicago: Albert, Scott, and Company, 1894), 646, https://babel.hathitrust.org/cgi/ pt?id=pst.000012202621&view=1up&seq=1.

8 "The Vindication No. I, [May–August 1792]," *Founders Online*, National Archives, https://founders.archives.gov/documents/ Hamilton/01-11-02-0376. [Original source: *The Papers of Alexander*

Hamilton, vol. 11, *February 1792–June 1792*, ed. Harold C. Syrett. New York: Columbia University Press, 1966, pp. 461–465.].

9   "Views on the French Revolution, [1794]," *Founders Online*, National Archives, https://founders.archives.gov/documents/ Hamilton/01-26-02-0002-0442. [Original source: *The Papers of Alexander Hamilton*, vol. 26, *1 May 1802–23 October 1804, Additional Documents 1774–1799, Addenda and Errata*, ed. Harold C. Syrett. New York: Columbia University Press, 1979, pp. 738–741.].

10 "Enclosure: Draft of Washington's Farewell Address, [30 July 1796]," *Founders Online*, National Archives, https://founders.archives.gov/documents/Hamilton/01-20-02-0181-0002. [Original source: *The Papers of Alexander Hamilton*, vol. 20, *January 1796–March 1797*, ed. Harold C. Syrett. New York: Columbia University Press, 1974, pp. 265–288.].

11 "The Stand No. III, [7 April 1798]," *Founders Online*, National Archives, https://founders.archives.gov/documents/Hamilton/01-21-02-0233. [Original source: *The Papers of Alexander Hamilton*, vol. 21, *April 1797–July 1798*, ed. Harold C. Syrett. New York: Columbia University Press, 1974, pp. 402–408.].

12 "To George Washington from Alexander Hamilton, 21 October 1799," *Founders Online*, National Archives, https://founders.archives.gov/documents/Washington/06-04-02-0307. [Original source: *The Papers of George Washington*, Retirement Series, vol. 4, *20 April 1799–13 December 1799*, ed. W. W. Abbot. Charlottesville: University Press of Virginia, 1999, pp. 356–357.].

13 "An Address to the Electors of the State of New-York, [21 March 1801]," *Founders Online*, National Archives, https://founders.archives.gov/documents/Hamilton/01-25-02-0197. [Original source: *The Papers of Alexander Hamilton*, vol. 25, *July 1800–April 1802*, ed. Harold C. Syrett. New York: Columbia University Press, 1977, pp. 349–371.].

14 "From Alexander Hamilton to James A. Bayard, [16–21] April 1802," *Founders Online*, National Archives, https://founders.archives.gov/documents/Hamilton/01-25-02-0321. [Original source: *The Papers of Alexander Hamilton*, vol. 25, *July 1800–April 1802*, ed. Harold C. Syrett. New York: Columbia University Press, 1977, pp. 605–610.].

15 "From Alexander Hamilton to — — —, 13 April 1804," *Founders Online*, National Archives, https://founders.archives.gov/documents/Hamilton/01-26-02-0001-0179. [Original source: *The Papers of Alexander Hamilton*, vol. 26, *1 May 1802–23 October 1804, Additional Documents*

1774–1799, Addenda and Errata, ed. Harold C. Syrett. New York: Columbia University Press, 1979, pp. 219–220.].

[16] Ron Chernow, *Alexander Hamilton* (New York: Penguin Books, 2004), 660 (citing Columbia University, *John Church Hamilton Papers*, box 20), https://books.google.com/books?id=4z5eL5SGjEoC&printsec=front-cover&source=gbs_ge_summary_r&cad=0#v=onepage&q&f=false.

[17] Ron Chernow, *Alexander Hamilton*, 660 (citing Columbia University, *John Church Hamilton Papers*, box 20).

[18] "From Alexander Hamilton to Elizabeth Hamilton, [4 July 1804]," *Founders Online*, National Archives, https://founders.archives.gov/doc-uments/Hamilton/01-26-02-0001-0248. [Original source: *The Papers of Alexander Hamilton*, vol. 26, *1 May 1802–23 October 1804, Additional Documents 1774–1799, Addenda and Errata*, ed. Harold C. Syrett. New York: Columbia University Press, 1979, p. 293.].

[19] "From Alexander Hamilton to Elizabeth Hamilton, [10 July 1804]," *Founders Online*, National Archives, https://founders.archives.gov/doc-uments/Hamilton/01-26-02-0001-0262. [Original source: *The Papers of Alexander Hamilton*, vol. 26, *1 May 1802–23 October 1804, Additional Documents 1774–1799, Addenda and Errata*, ed. Harold C. Syrett. New York: Columbia University Press, 1979, pp. 307–308.].

[20] J. M. Mason, DD, *An Oration: Commemorative of the Late Major-General Alexander Hamilton* (London: Printed by R. Edwards, 1804), 34, https://babel.hathitrust.org/cgi/pt?id=njp.32101071961484;view=1up;seq=7.

Francis Lewis

[1] Morgan Dir, S.T.D., D.C.L., Ninth Rector (ed.,), *A History of the Parish of Trinity Church in the City of New York* (New York: G. P. Putnam's Sons, The Knickerbocker Press, 1901), 11-14, https://archive.org/details/historyofparisho02dixm_0/page/n3.

[2] Morgan Dir, S.T.D., D.C.L., Ninth Rector (ed.,), *A History of the Parish of Trinity Church in the City of New York*, 11-17.

Philip Livingston

[1] Philip Livingston, "Last Will and Testament, *The New York Public Library Digital Collections*, https://digitalcollections.nypl.org/items/e5017e50-f055-0133-3a23-00505686a51c.

2   L. Carroll Judson, "Philip Livingston," *The American Revolution Reference*, https://www.history1700s.com/index.php/18th-century-history-the-ba-sics/american-revolution-reference/175-sages-and-heroes-of-the-amer-ican-revolution/510-philip-livingston.html.

Gouverneur Morris

1   *Letters of Delegates to Congress*, Vol. 9 (February 1, 1778–May 31, 1778), 3-4, https://memory.loc.gov/ammem/amlaw/lwdglink.html, from Gouverneur Morris to John Jay, February 1, 1778.

2   *Letters of Delegates to Congress*, Vol. 9, 424-425, from Gouverneur Morris to Sarah Morris, April 16, 1778.

3   Jared Sparks, *The Life of Gouverneur Morris*, Vol. I (Boston: Published by Gray & Bowen, 1832), 167, https://books.google.com/books?id=-wYO-AAAAIAAJ&printsec=frontcover&source=gbs_ge_summary_r&cad=0#v=onepage&q&f=false.

4   *Letters of Delegates to Congress*, Vol. 9, 729-730, from Gouverneur Morris to Anthony Wayne, May 21, 1778.

5   *Letters of Delegates to Congress*, Vol. 10 (June 1, 1778–September 30, 1778), 590-591, https://memory.loc.gov/ammem/amlaw/lwdglink.html, from Gouverneur Morris to George Clinton, September 6, 1778.

6   Anne Cary Morris (ed.), *The Diary and Letters of Gouverneur Morris, Minister of the United States to France; Member of the Constitutional Convention*, Vol. I (New York: Charles Scribner's Sons, 1888), Chapter III, https://oll.liberty-fund.org/title/morris-the-diary-and-letters-of-gouverneur-morris-vol-1.

7   Anne Cary Morris (ed.), *The Diary and Letters of Gouverneur Morris, Minister of the United States to France; Member of the Constitutional Convention*, Vol. I, Chapter XIV.

8   Jared Sparks, *The Life of Gouverneur Morris*, Vol. III (Boston: Published by Gray & Bowen, 1832), 483, https://books.google.com/books?id=VgYOAAAAIAAJ&printsec=frontcover&source=gbs_ge_summary_r&cad=0#v=onepage&q&f=false.

9   Forrest McDonald, "The Political Thought of Gouverneur Morris," https://theimaginativeconservative.org/2013/05/political-thought-gou-verneur-morris.html, citing Beatrix Cary Davenport (ed.), *A Diary of the French Revolution by Gouverneur Morris 1752-1816 Minister to France during the Terror*, Vol. II, 452 (Boston, 1939).

10   Anne Cary Morris (ed.), *The Diary and Letters of Gouverneur Morris, Minister of the United States to France; Member of the Constitutional Convention*, Vol. I, Chapter XXV.

11   Anne Cary Morris (ed.), *The Diary and Letters of Gouverneur Morris, Minister of the United States to France; Member of the Constitutional Convention*, Vol. II (New York: Charles Scribner's Sons, 1888), Chapter LII, https://oll.liberty-fund.org/title/morris-the-diary-and-letters-of-gouverneur-morris-vol-2.

12   Anne Cary Morris (ed.), *The Diary and Letters of Gouverneur Morris, Minister of the United States to France; Member of the Constitutional Convention*, Vol. II, Chapter XXVII.

13   Anne Cary Morris (ed.), *The Diary and Letters of Gouverneur Morris, Minister of the United States to France; Member of the Constitutional Convention*, Vol. II, Chapter XLI.

14   Forrest McDonald, "The Political Thought of Gouverneur Morris," https://theimaginativeconservative.org/2013/05/political-thought-gouverneur-morris.html, citing Morris Papers, Library of Congress.

15   Jared Sparks, *The Life of Gouverneur Morris*, Vol. III (Boston: Published by Gray & Bowen, 1832), 269-271.

16   Anne Cary Morris (ed.), *The Diary and Letters of Gouverneur Morris, Minister of the United States to France; Member of the Constitutional Convention*, Vol. II, Chapter XLI.

17   Ibid.

18   Ibid., Chapter LII.

19   Gouverneur Morris, *An Inaugural Discourse, Delivered before the New York Historical Society by the Honorable Gouverneur Morris, (President,) 4th September, 1816* (New York: Printed and Published by T. & W. Mercein, 1816), 7-24, https://hdl.handle.net/2027/coo.31924093712572.

20   George S. Mann, "Gouverneur Morris," A Paper Read Before the Brookline Historical Society, November 25, 1908, http://brooklinehistoricalsociety.org/history/proceedings/1910/Morris.html.

Lewis Morris

1   *Letters of Delegates to Congress*, Vol. 1 (August, 1774–August, 1775), 159-160, https://memory.loc.gov/ammem/amlaw/lwdglink.html, Petition to the King, July 8, 1775.

2   *Letters of Delegates to Congress*, Vol. 25 (March 1, 1788–December 31, 1789), 555, https://memory.loc.gov/ammem/amlaw/lwdglink.html, from Lewis Morris to Philip Schuyler, July 23, 1775.

3   *Letters of Delegates to Congress*, Vol. 6 (January 1, 1777–April 30, 1777), 416, https://memory.loc.gov/ammem/amlaw/lwdglink.html, from Lewis Morris to John Jay, March 8, 1777.

4   *Letters of Delegates to Congress*, Vol. 6, 451, from Lewis Morris to the New York Convention, March 16, 1777.

5   Susan Clair Imbarrato (ed.), *Encyclopedia of American Literature*, Third Edition, 669 et seq., https://books.google.com/books?id=MKxbAgAAQ-BAJ&printsec=frontcover&source=gbs_ge_summary_r&cad=0#v=one-page&q&f=false; and http://www.iment.com/maida/familytree/morris/will.htm#uncle.